SRA Real Math

Stephen S. Willoughby

•

Carl Bereiter

•

Peter Hilton

•

Joseph H. Rubinstein

•

Joan Moss

•

Jean Pedersen

Columbus, OH

The McGraw·Hill Companies

Authors

Stephen S. Willoughby
Professor Emeritus of Mathematics
University of Arizona
Tucson, AZ

Carl Bereiter
Professor Emeritus
Centre for Applied Cognitive Science
Ontario Institute for Studies in Education
University of Toronto, Canada

Peter Hilton
Distinguished Professor of
Mathematics Emeritus
State University of New York
Binghamton, NY

Joseph H. Rubinstein
Professor of Education
Coker College
Hartsville, SC

Joan Moss
Associate Professor, Department of Human
Development and Applied Psychology
Ontario Institute for Studies in Education
University of Toronto, Canada

Jean Pedersen
Professor, Department of
Mathematics and Computer Science
Santa Clara University, Santa Clara, CA

PreKindergarten and Building Blocks Authors

Douglas H. Clements
Professor of Early Childhood and Mathematics Education
University at Buffalo
State University of New York, NY

Julie Sarama
Associate Professor of Mathematics Education
University at Buffalo
State University of New York, NY

Contributing Authors

Hortensia Soto-Johnson
Assistant Professor of Mathematics
University of Northern Colorado, CO

Erika Walker
Assistant Professor of Mathematics and Education
Teachers College, Columbia University, NY

Research Consultants

Jeremy Kilpatrick
Regents Professor of Mathematics Education
University of Georgia, GA

Alfinio Flores
Professor of Mathematics Education
Arizona State University, AZ

Gilbert J. Cuevas
Professor of Mathematics Education
University of Miami, Coral Gables, FL

Contributing Writers

Holly MacLean, Ed.D., Supervisor Principal, Treasure Valley
Mathematics and Science Center, Boise, ID
Edward Manfre, Mathematics Education Consultant, Albuquerque, NM
Elizabeth Jimenez, English Language Learner Consultant, Pomona, CA

Kim L. Pettig, Ed.D., Instructional Challenge Coordinator
Pittsford Central School District, Pittsford, NY
Rosemary Tolliver, M.Ed., Gifted Coordinator/Curriculum Director, Columbus, OH

National Advisory Board

Justin Anderson, Teacher, Robey Elementary School, Indianapolis, IN
David S. Bradley, Administrator, Granite, UT
Donna M. Bradley, Head of the Lower School, St. Marks Episcopal
Palm Beach Gardens, FL
Grace Dublin, Teacher, Laurelhurst Elementary, Seattle, WA
Leisha W. Fordham, Teacher, Bolton Academy, Atlanta, GA

Ebony Frierson, Teacher, Eastminister Day School, Columbia, SC
Flavia Gunter, Teacher, Morningside Elementary School, Atlanta, GA
Audrey Marie Jacobs, Teacher, Lewis & Clark Elementary, St. Louis, MO
Florencetine Jasmin, Elementary Math Curriculum Specialist, Baltimore, MD
Kim Leitzke, Teacher, Clara Barton Elementary School, Milwaukee, WI
Nick Restivo, Principal, Long Beach High School, Long Island, NY

SRAonline.com

Printed in the United States of America.

Send all inquiries to:
SRA/McGraw-Hill
4400 Easton Commons
Columbus, OH 43219

ISBN 0-07-603001-6

4 5 6 7 8 9 VHJ 12 11 10 09 08 07

Whole Numbers Refresher

Exploring 💡 Problem Solving Theme: Elections

Decimals

CHAPTER 3

Exploring 💡 Problem Solving   Theme: Metric Measurements

Function Rules

Exploring 💡Problem Solving Theme: Temperatures in Our Solar System

Exploring 💡Problem Solving Theme: Multicultural Museum

Mixed Numbers and Improper Fractions

CHAPTER 7

Exploring 💡 Problem Solving   Theme: Paul Revere

Exploring 💡 Problem Solving Theme: Codes

Geometry

CHAPTER 9

Exploring 💡 Problem Solving Theme: Native American Homes

Exploring 💡 Problem Solving   Theme: Old West

Rational Number and Percent Applications

CHAPTER 11

Exploring  **Theme: Search for a Sunken Ship**

Measurement and Graphing

Exploring 💡 Problem Solving Theme: Expedition

Violet
March

Dear Student,

You will find a lot of things in this *Real Math* book.

You will find games that will give you a chance to practice and put to use many of the skills you will be learning.

You will find stories and examples that will show you how mathematics can help you solve problems and cut down the amount of work you have to do.

You will be reading and talking about many of the pages with your classmates. That is because mathematics is something people often learn together and do together.

Of course, this book is not all fun and games. Learning should be enjoyable, but it also takes time and effort. Most of all, it takes thinking.

We hope you enjoy this book. We hope you learn a lot. And we hope you think a lot.

The Authors of *Real Math*

In This Chapter You Will Learn

- facts that are true of all whole numbers.
- how to add and subtract multidigit numbers.
- how to apply addition and subtraction to different situations.

Problem Solving

SOCIAL STUDIES

The students in Ms. Johnson's class vote each week to pick the class secretary. This week, Alicia, Paco, and Carol ran for the position. Each student voted by listing the three candidates in order.

| Carol Alicia Paco | Paco Carol Alicia | Alicia Carol Paco | **Alicia Carol Paco** |

Ms. Johnson's class counted all the ballots and wrote the results in a table. Unfortunately, they lost the number of first-place votes that Carol received.

Candidate	1st Place Votes	2nd Place Votes	3rd Place Votes
Alicia	11	4	13
Paco	9	16	3
Carol		8	12

Answer the following questions.

1. How can you figure out how many first-place votes Carol received?

2. If only Alicia and Paco had run, who do you think would have won? Explain. *they whould have same scores without win*

3. Based on the results, who do you think should be the class secretary this week? Why? *Paco he/she got the most votes*

4. If there are three candidates next week, how should Ms. Johnson's class decide the winner? *the most votes*

3

Estimating and Measuring

Key Ideas

Sometimes you can estimate, or make an educated guess, when you are measuring something.

Latoya is doing a measuring activity. First, she estimates how tall a person is and writes it on her table. Next, she measures and records the actual height of that person. She finds the difference between the estimate and the measurement. Then she repeats the procedure with the next person.

Name	Estimate (centimeters)	Measurement (centimeters)	Difference
Joan	133	140	7
Aretha	137	139	2
Florence	135	136	1
Carlos	140	141	1

Complete this measuring activity in a small group. Estimate and then measure each person. Record the results in a table like the one above. Find the differences between your estimates and measurements. Then answer the questions below on a separate sheet of paper.

① **Extended Response** Did Latoya's estimates get better after the first one? *yes they got closer*

② **Extended Response** Did your estimates get better after the first one? Why? *I Read the question carfuly*

③ Are any of the students you measured the same height? *NO*

Choose one student from your group to put your group's information into the table your teacher will create.

Writing + Math **Journal**

What strategy did you use when playing the **Order Game?**

e Textbook This lesson is available in the *eTextbook*.

Game

Addition and Strategies Practice

Order Game

Players: Two

Materials: Number Cubes (two 0–5 and two 5–10)

Object: To be the first to fill in all the boxes

Math Focus: Place value and mathematical reasoning

HOW TO PLAY

1. Make a game form like the one shown.

2. Roll all four cubes. If you roll a 10 on any cube, roll that cube again. You may choose to skip any turn after seeing the numbers that are rolled.

3. Combine any three numbers rolled to make a three-digit number. Write your first number on the top line on your game form.

4. Take turns rolling the cubes. On each turn, make a three-digit number greater than the last number you made, and write it on the next line.

5. If you cannot make a greater three-digit number, or if you choose not to, you lose your turn.

6. The first player to fill in all the lines on his or her game form is the winner.

7. If there is a tie, the player with the smaller final number wins.

8. Zero is allowed in any place. For example, 007 is allowed.

Start

Finish

Key Ideas

Tables and graphs are used to present information.

Everyone in Latoya's class did the measuring activity on page 4. Then they made a table of all the students and their heights. Here is part of that table.

Name	Height (cm)	Name	Height (cm)	Name	Height (cm)	Name	Height (cm)
Judy	133	Aretha	139	Latoya	142	Melba	146
Chen	134	Joan	140	Kareem	143	Donna	146
Tami	135	Marco	141	Frank	143	Herb	147
Myra	135	Carlos	141	Pedro	143	Gene	149
Florence	136	Steve	142	Melvin	143	Min-ja	150
José	137	Liz	142	Lance	143	Ana	151
Marie	139	Carmen	142	Tiwa	144		

Latoya decided to make a graph showing the number of students at each height. Her graph looked like this:

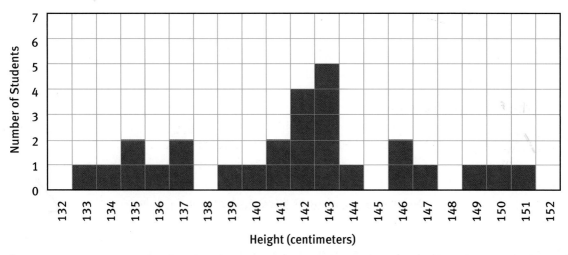

Answer these questions.

1 What grade do you think Latoya is in? 6th

2 **Extended Response** What can you predict about height measurements for a class one grade level before Latoya's? What about for a class that is one grade after Latoya's? Explain.

📱**Textbook** This lesson is available in the *eTextbook*.

③ **Extended Response** If you knew of a student in a different city who was in the same grade as Latoya, but you did not know what the student looked like, could you make a reasonable estimate about the height of that student? Would you be surprised if your estimate was wrong? Could you make a reasonable estimate about the distribution of heights of all the students in that person's class? Explain.

Complete the following activity. Then answer the question.

④ Using the information in the table from the measuring activity in Lesson 1.1, make your own bar graph like the one Latoya made.

⑤ Can you predict what the graph would look like if you made it at the end of the school year?

Save the graph you made. Toward the end of the school year, you will make another graph and compare it with this one.

Count on or back. Write the missing numbers.

⑥ 78, 79, 80, ▮, 88

⑦ 107, 106, 105, ▮, 98

⑧ 396, 397, 398, ▮, 406

⑨ 5,996; 5,997; 5,998; ▮; 6,004

⑩ 5,003; 5,002; 5,001; ▮; 4,997

⑪ 76,097; 76,098; 76,099; ▮; 76,103

⑫ 842,003; 842,002; 842,001; ▮; 841,997

Answer the following questions.

⑬ **Extended Response** Suki's parents are planning a neighborhood picnic. They bought 4 packs of 8 hotdogs and 3 bags of 10 hotdog buns. If Suki eats 2 of the hotdogs without buns before the picnic, which will her parents have more of—hotdogs or buns? How many more? Explain your answer.

 ⑭ Early Roman soldiers were paid with salt. One year, they were paid 3 rations of salt for their service. A year later, they were given 5 rations. The following year they received 8 rations. After another year, the soldiers got 12 rations. If this pattern continued, how many rations could the soldiers expect to get the next year? Describe the pattern.

Place Value

Key Ideas

The place value of each digit is ten times the place value of the digit to its right.

The place values in a whole number from right to left are ones, tens, hundreds, thousands, and so on.

Let's look at the number 403,897,652.

Millions			Thousands					
hundreds	tens	ones	hundreds	tens	ones	hundreds	tens	ones
4	0	3	8	9	7	6	5	2

Four hundred three million, eight hundred ninety-seven thousand, six hundred fifty-two

The 4 stands for 4 hundred millions.	400,000,000
The 0 stands for 0 ten millions.	0
The 3 stands for 3 millions.	3,000,000
The 8 stands for 8 hundred thousands.	800,000
The 9 stands for 9 ten thousands.	90,000
The 7 stands for 7 thousands.	7,000
The 6 stands for 6 hundreds.	600
The 5 stands for 5 tens.	50
The 2 stands for 2 ones.	2

Write these numbers in expanded form.

1   917,563 =

2   589,421 =

3   900,060,728 =

4   800,740,054 =

5   List the numbers above from greatest to least.

e Textbook This lesson is available in the *eTextbook*.

Write these numbers in standard form. Use the example as a guide.

Example: 7,000 + 20 + 6 = 7,026

6 40,000 + 2,000 + 50 + 9 = ▉ 42,059

7 800,000 + 60,000 + 7,000 + 600 + 40 + 2 = ▉ 867,642

8 70,000 + 5,000 + 20 + 7 = ▉ 75,027

9 8,000 + 600 + 40 + 1 = ▉ 8,641

10 List the numbers above in order from greatest to least.

 Answer the following questions.

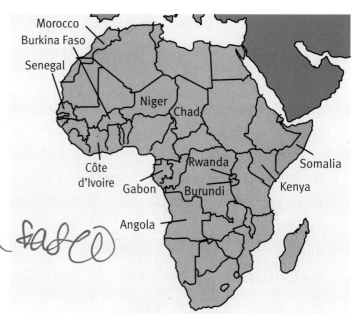

11 Which country has a greater area, Kenya or Somalia? _Somalia_

12 Which country has a greater area, Burundi or Rwanda? _Burundi_

13 Which country has a greater area, Niger or Côte d'Ivoire? _Niger_

14 Which country has a greater area, Gabon or Burkina Faso? _Burkina faso_

15 Which country has a greater area, Gabon or Burundi? _Gabon_

16 **Extended Response** Is Morocco's area more or less than 100,000 square miles? How can you tell?

17 List the countries in order from greatest to least area.

18 If the areas of the three largest countries listed in the chart are added together and the areas of the other five are added together, which total is greater? How much greater?

African Country	Area (sq. miles)
Burkina Faso	105,870
Burundi	10,747
Côte d'Ivoire	124,502
Gabon	103,346
Kenya	244,960
Niger	482,206
Rwanda	10,169
Somalia	246,199

Applying Math

Key Ideas

Arithmetic is often useful for solving real-world problems.

Answer each question.

$$\begin{array}{r} \times\ \ 0\ \ 9 \\ 5 \\ \hline 45 \end{array}$$

1. Anne earns $9 a day. How much money does she earn in 5 days?

2. Kele bought 8 comic books for $16. Each cost the same amount. How much did each book cost?

   4 5

   4 5

3. Lu has saved $6. His friend Charles has saved $3. If they combine their money, can they buy a set of checkers that costs $7?

4. The Tigers football team scored 3 touchdowns (6 points each), 2 extra points (1 point each), and 2 field goals (3 points each). How many total points did the Tigers score?

5. **Extended Response** Mike said, "My next birthday is in 13 months." Is that possible? Explain.

6. Lakeesha and 3 friends bought 2 pizzas. Each pizza was cut into 6 equal slices. If they share the pizzas equally, how many slices should each person get?

7. Soccer balls cost $8 each. Brad has $20. What is the greatest number of soccer balls that he can buy?

8. **Extended Response** Alma and her friends are working together to put on a show. They are setting up 45 chairs. Can they make 8 rows with the same number of chairs in each row, using all the chairs? Explain your answer.

9. Parking in Camargo's Garage costs $3 for the first hour and $2 for every hour after that. How much would it cost to park in Camargo's Garage for 5 hours?

10. Janice had $15. Then she earned $30 on her paper route this week. If used CDs cost $8 each, what is the greatest number she can buy?

e Textbook This lesson is available in the *eTextbook*.

By thinking about the situations, you should be able to answer the following questions.

11 Think about a stack of cubes that looks like the one in the figure, with three cubes along each edge. How many cubes are in the entire stack?

12 Suppose you painted the outside of this stack. How many of the little cubes would not be painted at all? How many would be painted on only one face? Two faces? Three faces? Four faces? Five faces? Six faces? Do the numbers add up to 27?

13 Think about a stack of cubes with only two cubes along each edge. How many cubes would there be in the entire stack? If you painted the outside of the stack, how many of the little cubes would not be painted at all? How many would be painted on only one face? How many would be painted on two faces? How many would be painted on three faces? How many would be painted on more than three faces?

14 Consider a stack of cubes with four cubes along each edge. If the outside of this stack were painted, how many of the little cubes would not be painted at all? How many would be painted on only one side? How many would be painted on just two sides? How many would be painted on three sides?

 **Journal**

Can you propose other ways to solve any of Problems 11–14? List the other ways and explain how you thought of them.

Exploring 💡 Problem Solving

Amy and Beth ran for student council president at Red Oak School. These slips of paper show the results for each grade in the school. Who won the election? By how many votes did she win?

Grade 1
Amy 57 Beth 54

Grade 3
Beth 63 Amy 48

Grade 5
Amy 55 Beth 51

Grade 2
Amy 61 Beth 59

Grade 4
Amy 56 Beth 53

Ken decided to solve the problem this way:

I Made a Plan and Made a Table.
I put all the results in a table.
I added up all the votes for Amy.
I added up all the votes for Beth
to see who had more votes. That
was the winner.
I subtracted the loser's votes
from the winner's votes to find
the difference.

Grade	Amy	Beth
1	57	54
2	▪	▪
3	▪	▪
4	▪	▪
5	▪	▪
Total	▪	▪

Think about Ken's strategy.
Answer the following questions.

❶ How is the table helpful for solving the problem?

❷ Will Ken's strategy work?

12

Carrie solved the problem this way:

I also Made a Plan and Made a Table.
I used the table to show who won for each grade and by how much.
I used the differences to figure out who got more votes in all and how many more.

Grade	Who won?	By how many votes?
1	Amy	3
2	▪	▪
3	▪	▪
4	▪	▪
5	▪	▪
Total		

Think about Carrie's strategy. Answer the following questions.

3 How could you use mental math to figure out that, for first grade, Amy won by 3 votes?

4 Amy received more votes in four of the five grades. Does that mean that Amy won? Why or why not?

5 Can you use Carrie's method to get the correct answer?

6 Solve the problem of who won the election and by how many votes. Use Ken's, Carrie's, or a strategy of your own. Why did you choose the strategy you did?

Cumulative Review

Missing Addends Grade 4 Lesson 1.7

Solve for *n*.

1. $n + 5 = 7$

2. $15 - n = 10$

3. $2 + n = 10$

4. $2 + n = 7$

5. $15 - n = 9$

6. $15 - n = 8$

7. $10 + n = 20$

8. $10 - n = 4$

9. $0 + n = 9$

10. $n + 6 = 14$

Using a Bar Graph Grade 4 Lesson 12.5

Interpret the graph. Answer the questions that follow.

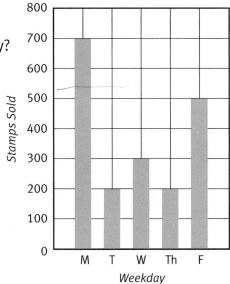

11. How many stamps were sold on Tuesday and Wednesday?

    a. 200   b. 400

    c. 500   d. 700

12. How many more stamps were sold on Friday than on Thursday?

    a. 200   b. 500

    c. 300   d. 100

13. On what day were the most stamps sold?

    a. Wednesday b. Thursday

    c. Friday   d. Monday

14. How many stamps were sold during that week?

    a. 2,200   b. 1,900

    c. 2,000   d. 1,500

15. On which two days were the same number of stamps sold?

    a. Monday and Friday   b. Wednesday and Friday

    c. Tuesday and Thursday   d. Tuesday and Wednesday

Textbook This lesson is available in the *eTextbook*.

Perimeter **Grade 4 Lesson 10.14**

Solve.

16. A square has a side length of 7 meters. What is its perimeter?

17. A rectangle has a length of 9 feet. What could its perimeter be?

   a. 15 feet   b. 18 feet

   c. 10 feet   d. 24 feet

18. A rectangle has a perimeter of 14 yards, and the lengths of the sides are whole numbers of yards. What could the length and width of the rectangle be?

19. Two squares have perimeters of 40 meters and 16 meters. What is the difference in the length of their sides?

Place Value **Lesson 1.3**

Write the following numbers in standard form.

20. $5,000 + 700 + 70 + 8 =$ ▮

21. $400,000 + 6,000 + 30 + 7 =$ ▮

22. $1,000,000 + 50,000 + 600 + 20 =$ ▮

Write the following numbers in expanded form.

23. $767,405 =$ ▮

24. $3,702,061 =$ ▮

25. $800,660 =$ ▮

Order and Parentheses

Key Ideas

Parentheses are used to avoid confusion with the value of expressions.

What does $3 \times 8 + 2$ mean? Does it mean to multiply 8 by 3 and add 2 to the product (26)? Or does it mean to add 8 and 2 and multiply the sum by 3 (30)? It could mean either.

The meaning of an expression may be clear if we know where the expression comes from. Conventions, such as doing whatever is in parentheses first, also enable you to decide what the other person meant. If you consider the original real-world situation that gave rise to the expression, you will not need to follow a convention. The situation will tell you how the expression should be evaluated.

Act out and discuss this story.

A Baking Problem

"May we help you bake?" the children asked.

"Yes," said Mrs. Evans. "But first help me figure out how many cookies to make. How much is $5 \times 3 + 2$?"

"It's 17," said Mindy, Ana, and Otis.

"It's 25," said Su-mi and José.

The children argued about the answer, but they couldn't decide. Finally Otis said, "Why don't you tell us the whole problem?"

"It doesn't seem like a hard problem," Mrs. Evans said. "I want to make 5 cookies for each child. There are 3 boys and 2 girls. That is $5 \times 3 + 2$ cookies."

"Now we know what the answer is because we understand the question," they all said. "We have to add $3 + 2$ and then multiply the sum by 5."

ⓔ Textbook This lesson is available in the *eTextbook*.

How could Mindy, Ana, and Otis have gotten the answer 17?

Here is a way to write the problem so that it means multiply 3 by 5 then add 2.

$(5 \times 3) + 2 = 15 + 2 = 17$

How could Su-mi and José get 25?

Here is a way to write the problem so that it means add 3 and 2 then multiply by 5.

$5 \times (3 + 2) = 5 \times 5 = 25$

The correct answer to Mrs. Evans's problem is 25. She wants to make 5 cookies for each child, so the total number of children should be found before multiplying by 5.

Can you think of a way to ask the question about 5, 3, and 2 so that people would know which way to answer it?

Here is an example: "How much is 5 times the sum of 3 and 2?"

If there is no doubt about the meaning of an expression, you do not have to use parentheses. For example:

$2 + 3 + 7 = 5 + 7$ or $2 + 10$ or $9 + 3 = 12$

Here the problem is clear because it only involves addition. A problem involving only multiplication $(3 \times 4 \times 7)$ would also be clear.

Here are some examples that use parentheses. When an expression can be calculated in more than one way, always do what is in parentheses first.

a. $24 \div (12 \div 3) = 24 \div 4 = 6$

b. $(4 + 3) \times (7 - 5) = 7 \times 2 = 14$

c. $28 \div (9 + 2 - 4) = 28 \div 7 = 4$

Solve for *n*.

1 $8 \times (3 + 1) = n$

2 $(8 \times 3) + 1 = n$

3 $12 \div (6 \div 2) = n$

4 $(12 \div 6) \div 2 = n$

5 $2 + (7 \times 2) = n$

6 $(6 + 1) \times (3 - 1) = n$

7 $12 \div (4 - 3 + 1) = n$

8 $(2 + 4) \div (10 - 7) = n$

9 $6 + (2 \times 3) = n$

10 $(6 + 2) \times 3 = n$

For each expression, see how many different answers you can get by putting parentheses in different places. The first two are done for you.

$3 + 5 + 7 = n$

$(3 + 5) + 7 = 15$

$3 + (5 + 7) = 15$

There is only one possible value.

$10 - 5 - 3 = n$

$(10 - 5) - 3 = 2$

$10 - (5 - 3) = 8$

There are two possible values.

11 $3 \times 4 \times 5 = n$

12 $24 \div 6 - 2 = n$

13 $24 \div 6 \div 2 = n$

14 $24 - 6 \div 2 = n$

15 $24 + 6 \times 2 = n$

16 $24 + 6 + 2 = n$

Solve the following problems.

17 **Extended Response** Sam can get his learning permit for his driver's license at the end of the calendar year. Today is April 30. How many days are there until the end of the year? Explain how you can find the answer without adding the number of days in each of the 8 months.

18 **Extended Response** How can you tell when an expression will have only one value? Explain your answer.

Writing + Math **Journal**

How do parentheses affect the meaning of an expression?

e Textbook This lesson is available in the *eTextbook.*

All Four Operations and Strategies Practice

Cubo Game

Players: Two or more

Materials: *Number Cubes* (two 0–5 and two 5–10)

Object: To score as close to 21 as possible

Math Focus: Mental arithmetic with all four operations

HOW TO PLAY

① Roll all four cubes on each turn.

② Use any combination of the four operations (addition, subtraction, multiplication, and division) on the numbers rolled. Use the number on each cube in any order once and only once. (If two cubes have the same number, you must use both.) Use parentheses if necessary.

If you rolled | 3 | 6 | 6 | 1 |

You could make these numbers	By doing these operations, for example:
19	$6 - 3 = 3$; $3 \times 6 = 18$; $18 + 1 = 19$
23	$3 \times 6 = 18$; $18 + 6 = 24$; $24 - 1 = 23$
21	$6 - 1 = 5$; $5 \times 3 = 15$; $15 + 6 = 21$
21	$6 - 3 = 3$; $6 + 1 = 7$; $3 \times 7 = 21$ or $(6 - 3) \times (6 + 1) = 21$

③ The player who scores 21 or closest to it is the winner of the round.

OTHER WAYS TO PLAY THIS GAME

① Make the goal a number other than 21; for example, 0.

② Choose a set of numbers, and try to make all the numbers in the set; for example, 0–10, 10–20, or the odd numbers from 1–15. It may not be possible to make every number in the chosen set of numbers.

Arithmetic Laws

Key Ideas

The more you know about how numbers work, the more you can save time and work when you do computation.

Commutative Laws	Examples	Short way to write laws
When you add or multiply two numbers, the order makes no difference in the answer.	$3 + 79 = 79 + 3$ $37 \times 10 = 10 \times 37$	$m + n = n + m$ $m \times n = n \times m$
Associative Laws	**Examples**	**Short way to write laws**
When you add or multiply 3 numbers, you can add or multiply the first and second number and then the third or you can add or multiply the second and third numbers and then the first.		$(n + m) + p = n + (m + p)$ $(n \times m) \times p = n \times (m \times p)$
Distributive Law	**Example**	**Short way to write law**
When you multiply two addends, you can multiply them separately and then add the products together without changing the result.	$6 \times 34 = (6 \times 30) + (6 \times 4)$	$n \times (m + p) = (n \times m) + (n \times p)$
Generalized Commutative Laws	**Examples**	**Short way to write law**
When you add a set of numbers, you can add them in any order. When you multiply a set of numbers, you can multiply them in any order.		$(a + b) + c = (a + c) + b$ $\qquad\qquad\quad = c + (a + b)$ $(a \times b) \times c = (a \times c) \times b$ $\qquad\qquad\quad = c \times (a \times b)$

ⓔ Textbook This lesson is available in the *eTextbook.*

Here are some other facts you know about our number system:

Multiplying by 0	Examples	Short way
If you multiply any number by zero, the product is 0	$0 \times 814 = 0$	$0 \times n = 0$
Identity Elements	**Examples**	**Short way**
If you add zero to a number the sum is that number. 0 is the identity element for addition.	$273 + 0 = 273$	$n + 0 = n$
If you multiply a number by 1, the product is that number. 1 is the identity element for multiplication.	$1 \times 2,386 = 2,386$	$1 \times n = n$
Closure	**Another way to say this**	
When you add two numbers, the result is always a number.	Our number system is *closed under addition*	
When you multiply two numbers, the result is always a number.	Our number system is *closed under multiplication*	

Use what you just learned to help you do these exercises quickly.

1. $73 + 64 = \rule{1cm}{0.4pt}$

2. $64 + 73 = \rule{1cm}{0.4pt}$

3. $3 \times 8 = \rule{1cm}{0.4pt}$

4. $8 \times 3 = \rule{1cm}{0.4pt}$

5. $8 + (92 + 47) = \rule{1cm}{0.4pt}$

6. $(92 + 47) + 8 = \rule{1cm}{0.4pt}$

7. $193 + 0 = \rule{1cm}{0.4pt}$

8. $2,538 \times 0 = \rule{1cm}{0.4pt}$

9. $100 \times 86 = \rule{1cm}{0.4pt}$

10. $(73 \times 86) + (27 \times 86) = \rule{1cm}{0.4pt}$

11. $3 \times 8 \times 94 \times 0 \times 504 = \rule{1cm}{0.4pt}$

12. $(57 \times 85) + (43 \times 85) = \rule{1cm}{0.4pt}$

13. $5 \times 4 \times 3 \times 2 \times 1 \times 0 = \rule{1cm}{0.4pt}$

14. $6 \times (200 + 8) = \rule{1cm}{0.4pt}$

15. $(18 \times 49) + (82 \times 49) = \rule{1cm}{0.4pt}$

16. $(65 \times 86) + (65 \times 14) = \rule{1cm}{0.4pt}$

17. $0 + 1 + 2 + 3 + 4 + 5 + 6 + 7 + 8 = \rule{1cm}{0.4pt}$

18. $8 + 7 + 6 + 5 + 4 + 3 + 2 + 1 + 0 = \rule{1cm}{0.4pt}$

Solve the following problems.

19. Abigail's thirteenth birthday is on August 26. Tomorrow will be March 1. How many days are there until she will be thirteen?

20. **Extended Response** Explain how you can get the answer to Problem 21 without adding the number of days in each of the 6 months.

 **Journal**

Write about two shortcuts you used in the exercises. Which of them would you like to use again in the future?

Key Ideas

Once you know how to add two numbers with two- or three-digit addends, you can add two numbers with any number of digits in each.

Think about the place value of each digit and its relation to the adjacent digits. Each place to the left is 10 times the value of the place to the right.

Alfinio has $4,517: 4 $1,000 bills, 5 $100 bills, 1 $10 bill, and 7 $1 bills. Hortensia gives him $625: 6 $100 bills, 2 $10 bills, and 5 $1 bills. How much money does Alfinio have now?

$$\begin{array}{r} 1 \\ 4517 \\ + \ 625 \\ \hline 2 \end{array}$$

Alfinio now has 12 $1 bills.

$$\begin{array}{r} 1 \\ 4517 \\ + \ 625 \\ \hline 42 \end{array}$$

He exchanged 10 $1 bills for 1 $10 bill. Now he has 4 $10 bills.

$$\begin{array}{r} 1\ 1 \\ 4517 \\ + \ 625 \\ \hline 142 \end{array}$$

Alfinio has 11 $100 bills. He exchanges 10 $100 bills for 1 $1,000 bill.

$$\begin{array}{r} 1 \\ 4517 \\ + \ 625 \\ \hline 5142 \end{array}$$

Alfinio has 5 $1,000 bills, 1 $100 bill, 4 $10 bills, and 2 $1 bills altogether.

e Textbook This lesson is available in the *eTextbook.*

Use the same method for addition to add three or more numbers. You don't have to write the numbers you regroup unless you need to.

Add the ones.	Add the tens.	Add the hundreds.
1	21	21
382	382	382
763	763	763
+ 479	+ 479	+ 479
4	24	1624

Find each sum. Use shortcuts when you can.

1
```
   24
 + 37
```

2
```
   42
 + 65
```

3
```
  123
 + 78
```

4
```
  327
+ 123
```

5
```
 7619
+ 835
```

6
```
 9723
+   64
```

7
```
  879
+ 1839
```

8
```
 2376
+ 6539
```

9
```
 5225
+ 2552
```

10
```
 1025
+ 1025
```

11
```
  673
+ 900
```

12
```
  598
+ 601
```

13
```
 1940
+   60
```

14
```
 2293
+ 4815
```

15
```
  562
+ 4015
```

16
```
  275347001
+ 125893178
```

17
```
  457091140
+ 230708729
```

18
```
   56
   78
 + 49
```

19
```
  247
  138
+ 787
```

20
```
  509
  746
+ 666
```

21
```
  500
   55
+ 500
```

22
```
  9000
   700
+ 2000
```

23
```
  879
  773
  254
+ 866
```

24
```
  300
  201
  370
+ 120
```

25
```
  200
  200
  200
+ 200
```

In each exercise, two of the answers don't make sense, and one answer is correct. Choose the correct answers.

26 694 + 426 = ▢
    a. 1,390
    b. 1,120
    c. 870

27 463 + 217 = ▢
    a. 1,290
    b. 770
    c. 680

28 7,200 + 320 = ▢
    a. 7,520
    b. 10,500
    c. 450

29 2,738 + 575 = ▢
    a. 2,023
    b. 3,313
    c. 7,215

30 5,525 + 5,735 = ▢
    a. 1,260
    b. 25,260
    c. 11,260

31 4,783 + 9,790 = ▢
    a. 14,573
    b. 10,573
    c. 14,570

32 9,762 + 1,003 = ▢
    a. 10,765
    b. 9,865
    c. 8,559

33 6,840 + 2,203 = ▢
    a. 9,043
    b. 28,843
    c. 2,883

34 6,123 + 1,098 = ▢
    a. 11,832
    b. 5,331
    c. 7,221

Solve the following problems.

35 An election was held to choose a mayor for Smallsville. There were 3 candidates in the election. The first candidate received 1,023 votes, the second received 2,017 votes, and the third received 1,477 votes. Smallsville has a voting-age population of nearly 5,000 people. About how many voters did *not* vote for one of the 3 candidates?

36 **Extended Response** It is 328 miles from Smallsville to the state capital. A bus takes 43 people from Smallsville to the state capital for a tour. How many miles will the bus have traveled after it returns from the capital? How did you get your answer? Explain.

> **Writing + Math** **Journal**
>
> Write three multidigit addition exercises whose sums can be found using an interesting shortcut. Describe the shortcuts.

    e Textbook This lesson is available in the *eTextbook*.

Multidigit Addition Strategies and Practice

Don't Go Over 1,000 Game

Players: Two or more

Materials: *Number Cubes* (two 0–5 and two 5–10)

Object: To get the sum closest to, but not over, 1,000

Math Focus: Place value, multidigit addition, and mathematical reasoning

HOW TO PLAY

❶ Roll all four cubes. If you roll a 10, roll that cube again.

❷ Combine three of the numbers rolled to make a three-digit number. You may use 0 in any place, including the hundreds place.

❸ Roll all four cubes again. Make a second three-digit number and add it to your first number.

❹ You may stop after your second roll, or you may roll once more and make another three-digit number and add it to your previous sum.

❺ The player whose sum is closest to, but not over, 1,000 is the winner.

SAMPLE GAME

Jon rolled

| 5 | 3 | 4 | 6 |

| 3 | 6 | 7 | 2 |

Jon wrote

```
  634
+ 362
-----
  996
```

Jon stopped.

Jon was the winner.

Fay rolled

| 0 | 5 | 9 | 1 |

| 3 | 7 | 7 | 1 |

| 8 | 2 | 3 | 9 |

Fay wrote

```
  519
+ 137
-----
  656
+ 329
-----
  985
```

The game also can be played with one person rolling the cubes and all players using the same numbers.

Subtracting Multidigit Numbers

Key Ideas

Subtraction is similar to addition in that, once you know how to subtract with two or three digits, you can subtract with any number of digits by thinking about the place value of each digit and its relation to the nearby digits.

Miguel had $637 (6 $100 bills, 3 $10 bills and 7 $1 bills). He wanted to give Aaliyah $248 (2 $100 bills, 4 $10 bills, and 8 $1 bills). How much money will he have left?

637
− 248

In order to give Aaliyah 8 $1 bills, Miguel has to exchange 1 of his $10 bills for 10 $1 bills.

2 17
6$3$7
− 248

He now has 6 $100 bills, 2 $10 bills, and 17 $1 bills.

2 17
6$3$7
− 248
    9

After giving Aaliyah 8 $1 bills, he has 6 $100 bills, 2 $10 bills, and 9 $1 bills.

5 12 17
$6$$3$7
− 248
  89

Now, to give her 4 $10 bills, he has to exchange a $100 bill for 10 $10 bills, so he has 5 $100 bills and 12 $10 bills.

5 12 17
$6$$3$7
− 248
389

After giving her 4 $10 bills, he had 8 $10 bills left.
After giving her 2 $100 bills, he has 3 $100 bills left.
So, Miguel has $389 left.

e Textbook This lesson is available in the *eTextbook.*

Sometimes it may appear there are no numbers to regroup.

```
  702
− 466
```
What do you do in a case like this? There are no tens to regroup.

. . . .

```
  6 9 12
  7̶0̶2̶
− 466
```
7 $100 bills are worth the same as 70 $10 bills, which can be thought of as 69 $10 bills and 10 $1 bills

. . . .

```
  6 9 12
  7̶0̶2̶
− 466
─────
  236
```
Now subtract.

Find the difference. Use shortcuts when you can.

1. $83 − 21 =$ ▨
2. $64 − 29 =$ ▨
3. $417 − 236 =$ ▨
4. $521 − 432 =$ ▨
5. $605 − 506 =$ ▨

6. $307 − 158 =$ ▨
7. $700 − 698 =$ ▨
8. $500 − 125 =$ ▨
9. $100 − 37 =$ ▨
10. $614 − 328 =$ ▨

Add or subtract. Watch the signs.

11. $655 + 345 =$ ▨
12. $1,000 − 345 =$ ▨
13. $1,000 − 655 =$ ▨
14. $2,001 − 1,980 =$ ▨

15. $247 + 68 =$ ▨
16. $921 + 79 =$ ▨
17. $1,000 − 6 =$ ▨
18. $5,005 + 1,234 =$ ▨

Add or subtract. Watch the signs.

⑲ 3,000 − 256 = ▢

⑳ 256 + 2,744 = ▢

㉑ 3,000 − 2,744 = ▢

㉒ 4,548 + 9,874 = ▢

㉓ 6,719 + 32 = ▢

㉔ 235 + 444 = ▢

㉕ 637 − 555 = ▢

㉖ 197 − 96 = ▢

㉗ 5,729 − 1,990 = ▢

㉘ 45 + 208 = ▢

㉙ 908,278,331 − 645,125,986 = ▢

㉚ 538,293,874 − 216,192,834 = ▢

Solve these problems.

㉛ **Extended Response** The Coldsborough Town Hall was dedicated on December 20, 1895. Because of a blizzard, its 100th anniversary (centennial) celebration was postponed for two weeks. This resulted in the celebration not taking place until the next year. Why did this happen? Explain.

㉜ Last year, 226 students were in the fourth grade at Karen's school. Over the summer, 17 of them moved away. If 6 new students joined the class, how many fifth graders are there this year?

 **Writing + Math** **Journal**

Write three multidigit subtraction exercises whose differences can be found using an interesting shortcut. Describe the shortcuts.

eTextbook This lesson is available in the *eTextbook*.

Multidigit Subtraction Strategies and Practice

Roll a Problem (Subtraction) Game

Players: Two or more

Materials: *Number Cubes* (one 5–10)

Object: To get the least difference that is 0 or greater

Math Focus: Place value, subtraction, and mathematical reasoning

HOW TO PLAY

1 Use blanks to outline a subtraction exercise on your paper, like this

2 The first player rolls the cube eight times.

3 Each time a cube is rolled, every player must write that number in one of the blanks on the outline. A 0 may be written in any space, including the first. If you roll a 10, roll that cube again.

4 When all the blanks have been filled, find the difference of the two four-digit numbers. If the bottom number is greater than the top number, the player is disqualified.

5 The player with the least difference is the winner.

Applying Addition and Subtraction

Add or subtract. Watch the signs.

1   470
     − 300

2   45
     − 29

3   243
     + 342

4   360
     − 180

5   2070
     − 199

6   847
     + 36

7   9000
     + 8927

8   1000
     + 525

9   5470
     + 129

10   601
     − 176

11   8010
     + 189

12   6006
     − 808

Choose the best approximation.

13 In one day, the United States Bureau of Engraving and Printing printed 12,450,000 $5 bills. What was the approximate value of the $5 bills printed that day?

    a. about $12,000,000

    b. about $6,200,000

    c. about $100,000,000

14 The words to "The Star-Spangled Banner" were written by Francis Scott Key in 1814. About how many years ago was that?

    a. about 120

    b. about 200

    c. about 350

    e Textbook This lesson is available in the *eTextbook.*

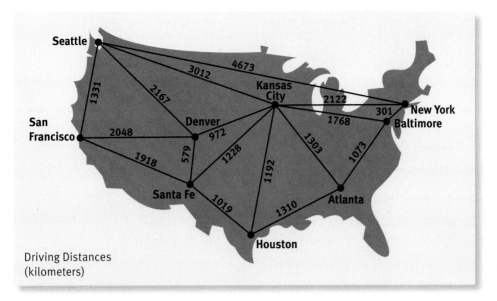

Seattle

3012   4673

1331   2167

Kansas
City

2122

301   New York

San
Francisco

2048   Denver   972

1768   Baltimore

1918   579   1228

1303   1073

1192

Santa Fe   1019

Atlanta

1310

Houston

Driving Distances
(kilometers)

Use the map to answer these questions.

15. How many kilometers is it from San Francisco to Denver?

16. How many kilometers is it from San Francisco to Kansas City if you go through Denver?

17. If you were going from Santa Fe to Kansas City, how much farther would it be to go through Denver?

18. Suppose you were going from San Francisco to Kansas City, and you wanted to visit Santa Fe and Denver on the way.

    a. Would it be shorter to visit Santa Fe or Denver first?

    b. How many kilometers shorter?

19. **Extended Response** Suppose you were in Kansas City and you wanted to visit Baltimore and New York City. Which round trip would be shorter? Why?

    a. Kansas City to Baltimore to New York City and back to Kansas City

    b. Kansas City to New York City to Baltimore and back to Kansas City

20. **Extended Response** Plan a trip that begins and ends in Seattle and goes through every city on the map. Try to make the trip as short as you can. How many kilometers is the trip you planned? Compare your answer with other students' answers.

Roman Numerals

Key Ideas

Roman numerals are formed using the letters C, D, I, L, M, V, and X.

Roman numerals have been in use for about 2,500 years. They were originally used for writing numerals in ancient Rome. They are not used as often today, but they are an important part of our culture. It is important to know what Roman numerals mean.

Try to figure out the value of each letter by examining the following list. Answer the questions below.

Arabic	Roman
25	XXV
35	XXXV
235	CCXXXV
137	CXXXVII
1237	MCCXXXVII
1737	MDCCXXXVII
1787	MDCCLXXXVII

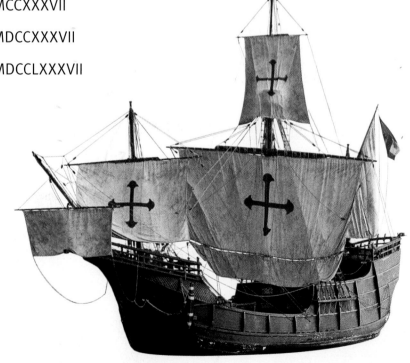

1. What is the value of M?

2. What is the value of D?

3. What is the value of C?

4. What is the value of I?

5. What is the value of V?

6. What is the value of X?

7. What is the value of L?

eTextbook This lesson is available in the *eTextbook*.

Roman numerals are formed from left to right. The letters having the greatest value are usually written first. You can use a rule to shorten the numeral. See if you can find the rule by studying the first few equations below.

VIII + I = IX   XII + II = XIV   MDCCXXX + X = MDCCXL

Complete the exercises below using the examples in the box above. Remember what you just learned about the values of the different numerals.

⑧ MCCC + C = ▢

⑨ XXX − I = ▢

⑩ MMCCXXX + X = ▢

⑪ CLXV + IIII = ▢

Look it up. When did the following events occur? Use Roman numerals to write the years.

⑫ The Declaration of Independence was signed.

⑬ The United States Civil War ended.

⑭ Dr. Martin Luther King Jr. was awarded the Nobel Prize for peace.

⑮ Christopher Columbus landed in America.

⑯ Pilgrims landed on Plymouth Rock.

Answer the following questions.

⑰ The pages of a book's preface are often numbered with Roman numerals. If there is information you need on page 13 of the preface, what Roman numeral would you look for?

⑱ **Extended Response** If you were watching a movie and saw the Roman numeral MMIV at the end of the credits, what number do you think it might represent? Explain.

 **Journal**

Compare arithmetic using Arabic numerals to arithmetic using Roman numerals. Why do you think we use Arabic numerals?

George W. Bush
Al Gore
Undecided

November 8, 2000

Too Close to Call

The morning after election day in 2000, United States citizens do not know who their next president will be.

Many people stayed up late into the night, watching the news to find out whether George W. Bush or Al Gore had won. By 11 P.M., television viewers knew a lot but not enough. The answer depended on the six states in yellow.

To understand what happened in the election of 2000, you need to know the method that is used to elect the president of the United States.

Each state has a certain number of electoral votes based on its population. The table shows how many of these electoral votes each state has. In general, if a majority of people in a state vote for a candidate, that candidate receives all the electoral votes for that state.

To win, a candidate needs at least 270 electoral votes, which is 1 more than half the total of 538.

Electoral Votes for Each State

State	Votes	State	Votes	State	Votes
Alabama	9	Kentucky	8	North Dakota	3
Alaska	3	Louisiana	9	Ohio	21
Arizona	8	Maine	4	Oklahoma	8
Arkansas	6	Maryland	10	Oregon	7
California	54	Massachusetts	12	Pennsylvania	23
Colorado	8	Michigan	18	Rhode Island	4
Connecticut	8	Minnesota	10	South Carolina	8
Delaware	3	Mississippi	7	South Dakota	3
D.C.	3	Missouri	11	Tennessee	11
Florida	25	Montana	3	Texas	32
Georgia	13	Nebraska	5	Utah	5
Hawaii	4	Nevada	4	Vermont	3
Idaho	4	New Hampshire	4	Virginia	13
Illinois	22	New Jersey	15	Washington	11
Indiana	12	New Mexico	5	West Virginia	5
Iowa	7	New York	33	Wisconsin	11
Kansas	6	North Carolina	14	Wyoming	3

By 11 P.M. on election night, George W. Bush had 242 electoral votes and Al Gore had 237.

Solve the following problems. Use the information on these pages to help you.

1 Suppose Al Gore had won all the states that were still undecided at 11 P.M. Would he have won the election? Explain.

2 At 11 P.M., was it still possible for this election to end in a tie? Explain.

Exploring Problem Solving

The after-school programs at the Oak School plan to work together to raise money. They are not sure whether to have a bake sale or a raffle, so they decide to vote. Because these students have just learned about how we elect the president of the United States, they decide to use an electoral system.

- Each group gets a certain number of electoral votes, depending on how many members it has.

- The members of each group will vote. If a majority of students in a group vote for the bake sale, then the bake sale gets *all* of the electoral votes for that club. If the majority votes for the raffle, then the raffle gets *all* of the electoral votes for that group.

- The winner is the fundraiser that gets more than half of the total electoral votes.

Club	Members	Electoral Votes
Computer Club	15	3
Music Club	33	6
Soccer Club	51	10
Student Council	11	2

Solve the following problems. Look for strategies that will make your work easier.

③ Is it possible for the same number of students to vote for the bake sale and the raffle? How can you tell?

④ Could the bake sale and the raffle get the same number of electoral votes? How do you know?

⑤ What rule do you think the students used to decide how many electoral votes each group would have?

⑥ An odd thing happened. Even though more students voted for the bake sale than for the raffle, the raffle won. How could that be?

Cumulative Review

Order and Parentheses Lesson 1.5

Solve for *n*.

① $6 \times (4 + 1) = n$

② $(5 \times 3) + 2 = n$

③ $12 \div (12 \div 2) = n$

④ $(36 \div 6) \div 2 = n$

⑤ $5 + (7 \times 8) = n$

⑥ $(6 + 4) \times (6 - 4) = n$

Arithmetic Properties Lesson 1.6

Use arithmetic properties to help complete these exercises quickly.

⑦ $18 + (82 + 35) = \boxed{}$

⑧ $94 + 46 + 6 = \boxed{}$

⑨ $3 \times 8 \times 54 \times 0 \times 123 = \boxed{}$

⑩ $(77 \times 35) + (23 \times 35) = \boxed{}$

⑪ $6 \times (100 + 7) = \boxed{}$

⑫ $8 + 7 + 6 + 5 + 4 + 3 + 2 + 1 + 0 = \boxed{}$

Space Figures Grade 4 Lesson 10.10

Identify the following shapes.

⑬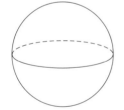

⑭

⑮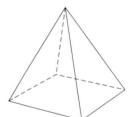

⑯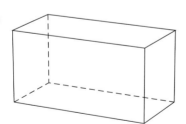

⑰

⑱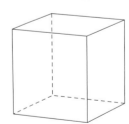

Adding and Subtracting Multidigit Numbers Lessons 1.7–1.8

Add or subtract. Use shortcuts when you can.

19. 123
    + 78
    ▨

20. 327
    + 123
    ▨

21. 7619
    + 835
    ▨

22. 4066
    + 3883
    ▨

23. 64 − 29 = ▨   24. 417 − 236 = ▨   25. 521 − 432 = ▨   26. 605 − 506 = ▨

Applying Addition and Subtraction Lesson 1.9

Solve.

27. The McDaniels drove 567 miles on Friday and 478 miles on Saturday. How far did they drive altogether?

28. Timmy counted his baseball cards and said he had 352. Rico said he had 125 more than Timmy. How many cards did Rico have?

29. Two bowling teams were competing for the league championship. The Strikers had scores of 156, 178, and 193, while the Alley Cats had scores of 144, 180, and 199. Which team had the greatest team score and by how many points did they win?

30. Stephanie is 9 years old. She is 5 years younger than her older brother and 2 years older than her younger brother. How old is Stephanie's younger brother?

Key Ideas Review

In this chapter, you reviewed computation strategies of multidigit addition and subtraction.

You learned conventions to shorten work.
You learned how to add and subtract multidigit numbers.

Write the following numbers in expanded form.

1. 6,259
2. 10,678
3. 6,205

Solve the following problems.

4. $3 \times (6 + 4) = n$

5. How can the Associative and Distributive Laws reduce work for a multiplication problem? Explain your answer and provide an example.

6. Why is the product not affected in the following expressions?

   $(3 \times 6) \times 2$ $3 \times (6 \times 2)$

7. How do parentheses affect a problem?

Add or subtract.

8. Trisha wants to buy some of the items in the table using $36 she received for her birthday. List two different sets of items she could purchase.

sleeping bag	$24
book	$16
poster	$8
DVD	$19
volleyball	$12

9. 15374
    + 2791
    ----

10. 10000
    − 6432

Lesson 1.3 **Write** the following numbers in expanded form.

1. $52,054 =$ ▨

2. $349,401 =$ ▨

3. $600,060,708 =$ ▨

4. $107,008,054 =$ ▨

Lesson 1.5 **Solve** for *n*.

5. $6 \times (2 + 3) = n$

6. $10 \div (7 - 2) = n$

7. $(36 \div 6) + 6 = n$

8. $15 \div (8 - 3) = n$

Lesson 1.7 **Add.**

9.
$$\begin{array}{r} 345 \\ + 587 \\ \hline \end{array}$$

10.
$$\begin{array}{r} 429 \\ 36 \\ + 141 \\ \hline \end{array}$$

11.
$$\begin{array}{r} 5683 \\ + 2842 \\ \hline \end{array}$$

12.
$$\begin{array}{r} 23845 \\ + 42658 \\ \hline \end{array}$$

Lesson 1.8 **Subtract.**

13.
$$\begin{array}{r} 517 \\ - 234 \\ \hline \end{array}$$

14.
$$\begin{array}{r} 700 \\ - 318 \\ \hline \end{array}$$

15.
$$\begin{array}{r} 4526 \\ - 1837 \\ \hline \end{array}$$

16.
$$\begin{array}{r} 63400 \\ - 31734 \\ \hline \end{array}$$

ⓔ **Textbook** This lesson is available in the *eTextbook*.

Lesson 1.9 **This** table shows the lengths of the ten longest rivers in the world. Use the table to answer the following questions.

River	Length (in miles)
Amazon	3,912
Huang He (Yellow)	2,900
Irtish	2,758
Mississippi-Missouri-Red Rock	3,880
Nile	4,180
Ob	3,459
Paraná	2,795
Yangtze Kiang	3,602
Yenisei	2,800
Zaire (Congo)	2,716

17 Which river is the longest?

18 Which river is longer than the Zaire but not as long as the Paraná?

19 How much longer than the Ob is the Nile?

20 Suppose a person traveled from the source of the Amazon to the mouth and back again to the source. How many miles would he or she travel in all?

21 Which is longer—the Nile or the combined lengths of the two shortest rivers listed? By how much?

22 What is the difference between the length of the Nile and the length of the next longest river?

Practice Test

Count on or back. Write the missing numbers.

1. 8,097; 8,098; 8,099; ▢; ▢; ▢; ▢; 8,104   **8,100**

2. 51,013; 51,012; 51,011; ▢; ▢; ▢; ▢; 51,006

Write the following numbers in standard form.

3. 400,000 + 50,000 + 2,000 + 3

4. 10,000 + 400 + 20

Write the following numbers in expanded form.

5. 700,802

6. 53,002,710

Solve for n.

7. $6 \times (8 + 1) = n$

8. $(6 \times 8) + 1 = n$

Answer the following questions.

9. According to a recent census, Arkansas has a population of 2,673,400, Iowa has a population of 2,926,324, and Mississippi has a population of 2,844,658. Which state has a greater population, Iowa or Mississippi?

10. Jorge drinks 8 ounces of water 2 times a day. How many ounces does he drink in 4 days?

11. A baseball stadium can seat 32,780 people. If 31,455 people attended last night's baseball game, how many seats were empty?

Textbook This lesson is available in the *eTextbook*.

Choose the correct answer.

12. Which number has the greatest value?

Ⓐ 22,200   Ⓑ 22,002

Ⓒ 22,202   Ⓓ 22,022

13. Kevin invited 44 people to his birthday party. If he can fit 6 people to a table, how many tables will he need for his party?

Ⓐ 6   Ⓑ 7

Ⓒ 8   Ⓓ 9

14. 24058
   + 2580
   ▧

Ⓐ 26,638   Ⓑ 26,538

Ⓒ 22,538   Ⓓ 21,478

15. 26057
   − 967
   ▧

Ⓐ 25,010   Ⓑ 25,090

Ⓒ 26,910   Ⓓ 27,014

16. Dylan has saved $16. His brother has saved $12. If they combine their money to buy a game that costs $25, how much money will they have left?

Ⓐ $28   Ⓑ $13

Ⓒ $4   Ⓓ $3

17. Which unit of measurement should be used to measure the length of a room?

Ⓐ liters   Ⓑ miles

Ⓒ ounces   Ⓓ feet

18. Solve for n.

$20 - (4 \times 3) = n$

Ⓐ n = 8   Ⓑ n = 13

Ⓒ n = 32   Ⓓ n = 48

19. 199500079
   + 1890341
   ▧

Ⓐ 197,609,739 Ⓑ 200,390,310

Ⓒ 201,390,420 Ⓓ 201,400,320

20. 500999
   − 45126
   ▧

Ⓐ 546,125   Ⓑ 455,873

Ⓒ 445,873   Ⓓ 50,873

Practice Test

Choose the correct answer.

21. Which equation is an example of the identity element for addition?

    Ⓐ $3 \times 2 = 2 \times 3$

    Ⓑ $4 \times 1 = 4$

    Ⓒ $(4 + 5) + 9 = 4 + (5 + 9)$

    Ⓓ $5 + 0 = 5$

22. Which line is a line of symmetry?

    Ⓐ line *A*   Ⓑ line *B*

    Ⓒ line *C*   Ⓓ line *D*

23. Round 2.07 to the nearest tenth.

    Ⓐ 2.0   Ⓑ 2

    Ⓒ 2.17   Ⓓ 2.1

24. Which of the following sets has the numbers in order from least to greatest?

    Ⓐ 4.44, 4.08, 4.115, 4.002

    Ⓑ 4.08, 4.115, 4.002, 4.44

    Ⓒ 4.002, 4.08, 4.115, 4.44

    Ⓓ 4.002, 4.08, 4.44, 4.115

25. What is 2,415.468 rounded to the nearest hundred?

    Ⓐ 2,420   Ⓑ 2,415.5

    Ⓒ 2,415.47   Ⓓ 2,400

26. $4\overline{)428}$

    Ⓐ 107   Ⓑ 108

    Ⓒ 112   Ⓓ 114

27. What is the measure of an obtuse angle?

    Ⓐ less than 90°

    Ⓑ 90°

    Ⓒ greater than 90°

    Ⓓ greater than 180°

28. How many inches are in 14 yards?

    Ⓐ 36   Ⓑ 42

    Ⓒ 140   Ⓓ 504

e Textbook This lesson is available in the *eTextbook*.

Extended Response **Solve** the following problems.

29. There are 12,058 people who take the bus to and from work each day in Ranthem. About 4,500 more people take the train to work than take the bus. If there are 45,000 people who commute to work each day, how many do not take the bus or train to work? Explain.

30. The fifth-grade class had a car wash to raise money for a field trip. They asked for donations of $3 per car. They collected $270 on Saturday and $180 on Sunday. If 20 people did not make a donation for their car, how many cars did the fifth graders wash in all? Explain.

In This Chapter You Will Learn

- how to multiply any two whole numbers.
- how to divide by a one-digit divisor.
- how to interpret remainders.
- how to write and evaluate exponents.

Problem Solving

Imagine you read and hear three different estimates of how many people were at the basketball game.

REAL WORLD

Wow, was it loud! I bet there were 50,000 people there.

Tonight's attendance is 19,374

About 10,000 fans watched as...

Use the seating charts and the photo on page 46 to answer the following questions.

1. Which of the three estimates do you think is closest to the actual number of people at the game?

2. How did you decide which figure is closest? Explain your answer.

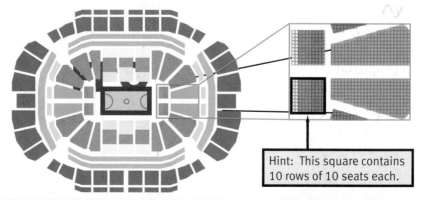

Hint: This square contains 10 rows of 10 seats each.

Multiplying Multiples and Powers of 10

Key Ideas

Because we use a base-ten number system, each place in a number is worth ten times the place to its right.

So, to multiply by 10, we can move each digit one place to the left. This can be done by writing zero after a whole number.

- To multiply a whole number by 10, write one zero to the right of the number.

  $3 \times 10 = 30$, and $10 \times 3 = 30$

  Remember, 3 and 10 are factors, and 30 is their product. When we multiply a number of 10s together, we call the product a power of 10. The number 10 itself is a power of 10, as are 100; 1,000; 10,000; 100,000 and so on.

- To multiply a whole number by 100, write two zeros to the right of the number.

  $100 \times 5 = 500$, and $5 \times 100 = 500$

- To multiply a whole number by 1,000, write three zeros to the right of the number.

  $1,000 \times 40 = 40,000$, and $40 \times 1,000 = 40,000$

Find each product.

1. $6 \times 10 =$ 60
2. $60 \times 10 =$ 600
3. $85 \times 10 =$ 850
4. $85 \times 100 =$ 850
5. $100 \times 64 =$ 6400
6. $10 \times 64 =$ 640
7. $1,000 \times 6 =$ 6,000
8. $62 \times 100 =$ 6,200
9. $100 \times 92 =$ 9200
10. $1,000 \times 4 =$ 4,000
11. $170 \times 100 =$ 17000
12. $10 \times 200 =$ 2,000
13. $1,000 \times 5 =$ 5,000
14. $10 \times 10 =$ 100
15. $100 \times 10 =$ 1,000
16. $10 \times 1,000 =$ 10,000
17. $100 \times 100 =$ 10,000
18. $1,000 \times 1,000 =$ 1,000,000

- To multiply a whole number by a multiple of 10, such as 40, multiply by 4 and write one zero to the right of the product to represent tens.

  $40 \times 6 = 240$, and $6 \times 40 = 240$.
  (Think $6 \times 4 = 4 \times 6 = 24$.)

- To multiply a whole number by a multiple of 100, such as 600, multiply by 6 and write two zeros to the right of the product to represent hundreds.

  $600 \times 3 = 1{,}800$, and $3 \times 600 = 1{,}800$.
  (Think $3 \times 6 = 6 \times 3 = 18$.)

- To multiply a whole number by a multiple of 1,000, such as 8,000, multiply by 8 and write three zeros to the right of the product to represent thousands.

  $8{,}000 \times 5 = 40{,}000$, and $5 \times 8{,}000 = 40{,}000$.
  (Think $5 \times 8 = 8 \times 5 = 40$, and notice the fourth 0 in the product.)

Find each product.

19 $7 \times 3 =$ 21

20 $7 \times 30 =$ 210

21 $7 \times 300 =$ 2100

22 $4 \times 9 =$ 36

23 $40 \times 9 =$ 360

24 $400 \times 9 =$ 3,600

25 $6{,}000 \times 90 =$ 540000

26 $200 \times 70 =$ 14000

27 $4{,}000 \times 600 =$ 2400000

28 $60 \times 5{,}000 =$ 300000

29 $5{,}000 \times 500 =$ 2500000

30 $8{,}000 \times 700 =$ 7600000

31 How many minutes are in

   a. one hour?

   b. one day?

   c. one week?

32 How many seconds are in

   a. one minute?

   b. one hour?

   c. one day?

33 Seth and his sister worked together on a project for health class. They kept track of the amount of time Seth spends watching TV. They found that on weekdays, he watches an average of 4 hours of TV. On weekends, he watches about 6 hours each day. About how many *minutes* of TV per week does Seth watch altogether?

34 **Extended Response** At the flea market, Sylvia wants to buy 20 stamps at 10 cents each, 3 drinking glasses at 50 cents each, and 8 packs of batteries at 70 cents a pack. She has $10. Does she have enough money to buy everything? How can she be sure? Explain.

Multiplying by a One-Digit Number

Key Ideas

Multiplying a two- or three-digit number by a one-digit number can be done by breaking the task into smaller parts.

A long hallway was neatly tiled with square tiles, each 1 foot by 1 foot. Melissa wanted to know how many tiles there were altogether. She counted the tiles along the edge of the hall from one end to the other. There were 37 tiles along that edge. She thought, "There must be the same number of tiles in each row."

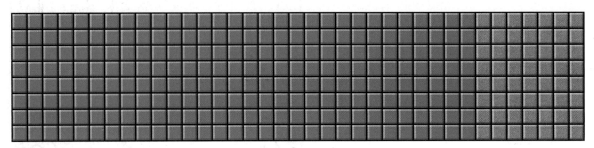

There were 8 rows. She decided she could get the answer by just adding 37 to itself 8 times: 37 + 37 + 37 + 37 + 37 + 37 + 37 + 37.

She decided she did not have to add all those 7s. She said, "I know that 8 × 7 is 56. I'll write that down."

"If I only knew how much eight 30s is, I'd have the answer. But 30 is just 3 tens, so eight 30s must be the same as 8 × 3 tens. I know what that is. It's 24 tens." So, she wrote 24 tens (or 240) under 56. Finally she added 240 and 56 to get an answer of 296.

$$
\begin{array}{r}
37 \\
\times\ 8 \\
\hline
56 \\
+\ 240 \\
\hline
296
\end{array}
$$

56 ←—— (8 × 7)
+ 240 ←—— (8 × 30)

"That was easier than counting all those tiles. That was even easier than adding 37 to itself 8 times," said Melissa.

Find the number of tiles in a hallway, using the given information. Solve the problems in whatever way you wish.

1. 5 tiles wide and 9 tiles long

2. 7 tiles wide and 8 tiles long

3. 5 tiles wide and 50 tiles long

4. 8 tiles wide and 25 tiles long

5. 5 tiles wide and 59 tiles long

6. 8 tiles wide and 80 tiles long

e Textbook This lesson is available in the *eTextbook*.

Later, Melissa wanted to find out how many tiles there were in a hallway 437 tiles long and 8 tiles wide. "I don't want to count another row of those," she thought. "I don't even want to add 437 to itself 8 times. If I add 7 to itself 8 times, I'll get 56, so I can write that down. I also know that 8 × 3 tens is 24 tens. So, I can write 24 tens, or 240.

$$
\begin{array}{r}
437 \\
\times\ \ 8 \\
\hline
56 \\
240 \\
+\ 3200 \\
\hline
3,496
\end{array}
$$

"Now if I can only figure out what I'd get if I add 400 to itself 8 times, I'll be able to finish the problem. I know! 8 × 4 hundreds must be 32 hundreds, or 3,200." She wrote that down and added all three numbers together to get 3,496. "That was certainly easier than counting all those tiles, or even adding 437 to itself 8 times."

Melissa discovered she did not have to write all the numbers on her paper. After she multiplied 8 × 7, she could write the 6 and remember that she still had 5 tens to add. Then, when she got 24 tens, she simply added the 5 tens, for a total of 29 tens. She wrote 9 tens on her paper and remembered she still had 2 hundreds to add. Finally, she added the 2 hundreds to 32 hundreds and was able to write the answer with even less work.

$$
\begin{array}{r}
437 \\
\times\ \ 8 \\
\hline
3,496
\end{array}
$$

Let's check to see that the answer makes sense.

- The answer should be less than 500 × 8, which is 4,000.

- The answer should be greater than 400 × 8, which is 3,200.

- The answer, 3,496, is less than 4,000 and greater than 3,200; therefore, 3,496 makes sense.

Solve the following problems. Find the number of tiles in a hallway in each case, using the given information.

7 6 tiles wide and 90 tiles long

8 8 tiles wide and 53 tiles long

9 5 tiles wide and 359 tiles long

10 5 tiles wide and 124 tiles long

11 9 tiles wide and 578 tiles long

12 9 tiles wide and 636 tiles long

Find each product. Check to see whether your answers make sense.

⑬	247 × 3	⑭	29 × 4	⑮	856 × 7	⑯	41 × 9	⑰	700 × 6
⑱	800 × 6	⑲	809 × 6	⑳	80 × 9	㉑	79 × 9	㉒	444 × 2

㉓ A storekeeper needs to know how much it costs to run her store for a 7-day week. Each day, for 5 days each week, she pays each of her 2 employees $12 per hour for 8 hours of work. She also pays $30 per day, 7 days a week, for rent and an extra $25 per week for other expenses.

- What are her expenses for the week?

- If sales for the week were $1,700, did she make a profit or did she lose money for the week? How much?

㉔ **Extended Response** Chuck and Marcus were playing checkers. They had half of the 24 checkers cleared from the board when the bell rang, signaling that recess was over. They had to figure out who won. Marcus claimed he had captured 2 more checker pieces than Chuck had captured. Chuck disagreed, so they decided to count. They found Marcus was correct.

- How many checker pieces did Chuck have?

- How many did Marcus have?

- How can you know for sure? Explain.

Writing + Math **Journal**

Answer the following questions after you have played the **Cube 100 Game.**

- Which **Number Cube** do you think you should roll first in the **Cube 100 Game?** Why?

- Which **Number Cube** would you roll second?

- Does the second decision depend on what happened on the first roll? How?

e Textbook This lesson is available in the *eTextbook.*

Game

Addition and Strategies Practice

Cube 100 Game

Players: Two individuals or teams

Materials: *Number Cubes* (two 0–5, two 5–10)

Object: To score as close to 100 as possible without going over

Math Focus: Adding and multiplying one- and two-digit numbers by one-digit numbers, mathematical reasoning, probability

HOW TO PLAY

1. Roll the cubes one at a time, adding the numbers as you roll.

2. After any roll, instead of adding that number, you may multiply it by the sum of the previous numbers. However, when you multiply, your turn is over.

3. The player or team with the score closer to, but not greater than, 100 wins the round.

SAMPLE GAME

Maria rolled 6, then 3.

$6 + 3 = 9$

Then she rolled 9.

$9 \times 9 = 81$

She stopped after three rolls.

Maria's score was 81.

Abdul rolled 5, then 5.

$5 + 5 = 10$

Then he rolled 6.

$10 + 6 = 16$

He rolled another 6.

$16 \times 6 = 96$

Abdul's score was 96.

Abdul won the round.

Multiplying Any Two Whole Numbers

Key Ideas

If you can multiply a single-digit number by a multidigit number, you can multiply any two whole numbers.

At work, Melissa was given a project to determine how many 1-foot square tiles would be needed to cover an outdoor eating area that was 43 feet by 687 feet. She drew a picture of the area using the measurements.

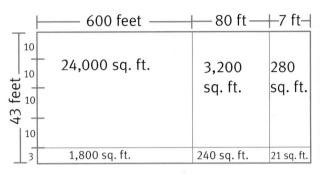

She could easily calculate the area of each little rectangle. She added the six numbers together.

```
  24000
   3200
    280
   1800
    240
+    21
 29,541
```

She decided that the total area was 29,541 square feet. Then she thought about what she had done and decided there was an easier way to solve the problem. She noticed that each of the digits 6, 8, and 7 had been multiplied by 4 and by 3. She thought that if she could figure out where to put each product, she could do this without the picture.

```
    687
  × 43
   2061
  27480
 29,541
```

Then she thought, "I saved work before by starting with the ones then the tens, so suppose I start by multiplying each of the digits in 687 by 3."

- She started by multiplying 7 by 3. Instead of writing 21, she wrote the 1 and saved the 2 tens until she multiplied 3 × 80, and got 24 tens. She added the 2 tens she saved, getting 26 tens, or 2 hundreds and 6 tens.

- She wrote 6 in the tens column. Then she added the 2 hundreds to the 18 hundreds she got by multiplying 3 × 6 hundreds (to get 20 hundreds or 2 thousands).

- She followed the same procedure when she multiplied 4 × 687. She got 27,480 because the 4 is really 4 tens, or 40. Since 687 × 4 = 2,748, she got 687 × 40 = 27,480. She then added 2,061 and 27,480 to get 29,541 square feet.

eTextbook This lesson is available in the *eTextbook*.

Find each product. Use shortcuts when you can.

1. $25 \times 25 =$ ▢
2. $38 \times 10 =$ ▢
3. $11 \times 11 =$ ▢
4. $13 \times 9 =$ ▢
5. $213 \times 344 =$ ▢
6. $216 \times 10 =$ ▢
7. $216 \times 100 =$ ▢
8. $216 \times 101 =$ ▢
9. $216 \times 111 =$ ▢
10. $406 \times 23 =$ ▢
11. $769 \times 10 =$ ▢
12. $514 \times 306 =$ ▢
13. $400 \times 100 =$ ▢
14. $473 \times 100 =$ ▢
15. $100 \times 473 =$ ▢
16. $624 \times 1,000 =$ ▢
17. $1,000 \times 624 =$ ▢
18. $1,001 \times 624 =$ ▢
19. $100 \times 76 =$ ▢
20. $1,000 \times 541 =$ ▢
21. $2,000 \times 2,000 =$ ▢
22. $6,242 \times 1,964 =$ ▢

23. The Hillside School drama club and the glee club are working together to put on a play. The auditorium has 10 rows of 24 seats and 20 rows of 30 seats.

    a. How many people can be seated at one time?

    b. Two rows of 30 seats were empty during the play, but all the other seats were taken. How many people attended the play?

    c. **Extended Response** If Tara claimed there were 720 people at the play when 2 rows of 30 seats were empty, is she wrong? If so, what error do you think Tara made in her computation? Explain.

24. **Extended Response** The drama club and the glee club decided to perform their next play in the gymnasium. The gymnasium has 50 rows of 15 chairs and 20 rows of 25 bleacher seats. If all 50 rows of 15 chairs and the first 8 rows of 25 bleacher seats have been sold, how many people were in the audience? How much money will be made? How can you tell? Explain.

25. If there are 6 students in the glee club, twice as many students in the drama club, and 1 teacher advisor needed for every 6 students working on the play, how many teacher advisors are needed?

 **Journal**

How would you rephrase the directions for multiplying any two whole numbers? Write a clear explanation in your math notebook.

Key Ideas

Tables often contain important information in an easy-to-read format.

Here is a hint to help you read the table below.

Locate the information you need by looking at the words on the left and running your finger across the row until you stop under the appropriate column heading.

For example, if you want to know how many grams of fat an apple has, point to the word *apple* and move your finger across the row, stopping in the *fat* column. You will see that an apple has 0 grams of fat.

Use this table to answer Problems 1–10 on the next page.

Food (serving size)	Calories	Fat (g)	Calcium (mg)	Vitamin A (IU) *
Whole milk (8 oz.)	146	8	291	249
2% milk (8 oz.)	137	5	297	184
Apple (1)	72	0	8	75
Orange (1)	65	0	61	317
Banana (1)	105	0	6	76
Carrots (1 cup)	52	0	42	15,406
White bread (1 slice)	66	1	38	0
Sandwich cookie (1)	82	5	6	1
Apple pie (1 slice)	411	20	11	90

*IU is the symbol for International Unit—a measure of the amount of a vitamin.

A fifth grader's diet should provide about 2,400 calories, 1,000 milligrams of calcium, and 5,000 IU of vitamin A each day, with no more than 60 grams of fat.

1. Every day for one week, Raulito ate 1 apple for dessert. For the same week, his sister Juanita ate 1 slice of apple pie instead.

    At the end of the week,
    a. about how many calories did Juanita consume for dessert?

    b. about how many calories did Raulito consume for dessert?

2. Typically, every 4,000 calories that the body does not use for daily activities or during exercise are stored as a pound of fat.

    a. Compared with her brother, how many more calories did Juanita consume during the week?

    b. If Juanita and Raulito continue eating these desserts for 10 weeks, about how many more calories will Juanita have consumed than Raulito?

    c. If Juanita doesn't use the calories through exercise, about how many extra pounds will she likely have gained?

3. How many sandwich cookies would it take to provide more than a full day's allowance of fat?

4. Do 6 sandwich cookies have more calories or fewer calories than a slice of apple pie?

5. Would 4 servings of whole milk provide the daily requirement for calcium? If not, how many more servings are needed?

6. **Extended Response** Renée estimated that 20 apples would have more calcium than 3 servings of 2% milk. Is she correct? Why or why not?

7. Do 2 cups of carrots have more calories or fewer calories than 1 banana?

8. Which would provide more calcium: 2 slices of white bread or 4 bananas? How much more?

9. Would 3 servings of whole milk and 1 slice of apple pie provide more than the daily allowance of fat?

10. Morgan calculated that 1 slice of apple pie has more calories than 2 sandwich cookies. Is he correct? What is the difference between the calories in 1 slice of apple pie and the calories in 2 sandwich cookies?

Key Ideas

Two important parts of problem solving are understanding what you already know and understanding what you want to find out in each problem.

Read the problems and answer the questions.

1 For the school picnic, Amy bought 15 bags of potato chips. They cost 87¢ a bag. She also bought 26 containers of juice. They cost 97¢ each.

   a. How much did she pay for all the potato chips?

   b. How much did she pay for the juice?

   c. How much did she pay for both?

2 Miguel sleeps about 8 hours a night.

   a. About how many hours does Miguel sleep in 1 week?

   b. About how many hours does he sleep in 1 year (365 days)?

   c. About how many hours a week is Miguel awake?

   d. **Extended Response** Explain two ways you can calculate the answer to Problem 2c.

   e. About how many hours a year is he awake?

   f. **Extended Response** Give two ways you can calculate how many hours are in 1 year, using some of the information in this set of problems.

e Textbook This lesson is available in the *eTextbook*.

3 Triangle Park measures about 240 meters on each of its 3 sides.

    a. What is the perimeter of Triangle Park?

    b. Emiko runs around the park twice every morning. About how far does she run?

    c. Victor runs around the park 8 times a day. About how far does he run?

    d. One day, Lisa ran around the park 29 times. About how far did she run?

4 The new bakery puts 12 muffins in each long box. It puts 6 muffins in each short box. Will 11 full long boxes and 4 full short boxes be enough for 80 people to have 2 muffins each? If not, how many more muffins are needed?

5 At work, Carlos is writing and illustrating a narrative based on something funny that happened at a family reunion. He usually works on the story for 2.5 hours each day. If it takes him 10 days to finish the story, how many hours of work should he be paid for?

6 Mr. McDonald takes 27 papers to the copying service. He needs to make 29 copies of each paper.

    a. How many copies will he make in all?

    b. How much will the copying cost if he pays 5¢ for each copy?

7 Canned tuna is on sale. The sale price is 6 cans for $6.25. How much will a half dozen cans cost?

8 There are about 25 desks in each classroom in Fort Meadow School. There are 14 classrooms in the school. About how many desks are there altogether?

Oh, no! Paint has been spilled on this page. In each problem, two of the possible answers are clearly wrong, and one is correct. Choose the correct answer.

9
$$\begin{array}{r} 52 \\ + 5 \end{array}$$

a. 10

b. 105

c. 150

10
$$\begin{array}{r} 7 \\ + 30 \end{array}$$

a. 700

b. 400

c. 1,090

11
$$\begin{array}{r} 3 \\ \times 1 \end{array}$$

a. 3,663

b. 2,336

c. 9,999

12
$$\begin{array}{r} 2 \\ - 64 \end{array}$$

a. 412

b. 1,412

c. 2,412

13
$$\begin{array}{r} 76 \\ - 3 \end{array}$$

a. 4,1 7

b. 1,4 7

c. 4

14
$$\begin{array}{r} 73 \\ \times 60 \end{array}$$

a. 7

b. 43

c. 4,38

15
$$\begin{array}{r} 29 \\ 39 \\ + 11 \end{array}$$

a. 885

b. 18 5

c. 3 5

16
$$\begin{array}{r} 58 \\ - 1234 \end{array}$$

a. 4,444

b. 444

c. 44

17
$$\begin{array}{r} 8 \\ \times 49 \end{array}$$

a. 5,0 7

b. 4,21

c. 3,21

eTextbook This lesson is available in the *eTextbook*.

18
```
    3
 × 17
```
a. 26
b. 54
c. 91

19
```
   46
  × 6
```

a. 2,8 6
b. 2,3 6
c. 2,0 6

20
```
    1
 + 8 4
```
a. 65
b. 26
c. 445

21
```
 × 4
```
a. 745
b. 748
c. 751

22
```
 × 7
```
a. 4,249
b. 4,252
c. 4,255

23
```
 × 3
```
a. 2,852
b. 2,854
c. 2,856

24
```
  111
 ×
```
a. 754
b. 777
c. 802

25
```
  123
 ×
```
a. 738
b. 798
c. 858

26
```
  207
 ×
```
a. 2,077
b. 2,177
c. 2,277

Writing + Math **Journal**

Think about your favorite activity. Suppose you could make a schedule that would allow you to spend as much time as you wish doing that activity. How many hours a day would you spend on it? How many hours a week is that? How many hours a month? A year? Include the name of the activity and the answers to these questions in your math notebook.

Exploring Problem Solving

There are three ways to score points in basketball.

Three-point field goal
a shot from more than 20 feet away, outside the three-point line

Two-point field goal
a shot from less than 20 feet away, inside the three-point line

Free throw (one point)
an unguarded shot from the foul line by a player whose opponent committed a personal or technical foul

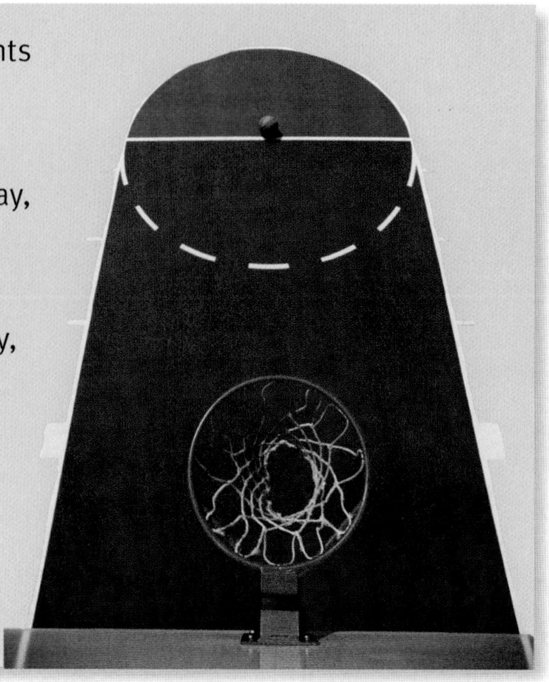

This table shows how four players scored their points in the playoffs one year. But some of the numbers are smudged.

Player	Shots Made			Total Points
	3-Point Field Goals	2-Point Field Goals	Free Throws	
Joreen Smith	16	37	35	[redacted]
Nikki Fields	15	29	[redacted]	118
Cheryl Hall	10	[redacted]	8	58
Keesha Phillips	[redacted]	12	25	82

Find the numbers and explain how you found them.

1. How many points did Smith score in the playoffs?
2. How many free throws did Fields make in the playoffs?
3. How many two-point field goals did Hall make?
4. How many three-point field goals did Phillips make?

Rodriguez made 65 baskets in all. How many 3-point field goals did she make? How many 2-point field goals did she make?

| Player | Baskets Made | | | Total Points |
	3-Point Field Goals	2-Point Field Goals	Free Throws	
Bea Rodriguez	▓▓▓	▓▓▓	21	117

James solved the problem this way:

I used the Guess, Check, and Adjust and Make a Table Strategies.
Rodriguez made a total of 44 field goals.
These 44 shots counted for 96 points.
For my first guess, I'll try 20 three-point field goals and 24 two-point field goals.

	3-pt. FGs	2-pt. FGs	Points from Field Goals	Result
1st Guess	20	24	$(20 \times 3) + (24 \times 2) =$ $60 + 48 = 108$	too high
2nd Guess				

Answer the following questions.

⑤ How does James know Rodriguez made 44 field goals altogether?

⑥ How does James know that those 2- and 3-point field goals add up to 96 points?

⑦ Will James's strategy work? Why or why not?

⑧ What numbers do you think James should try next? Why?

⑨ Solve the problem. Use James's strategy or a strategy of your own.

⑩ Why did you choose the strategy you did?

Cumulative Review

Rounding and Approximating Grade 4 Lesson 5.5

Solve.

1 A backyard is about 42 meters long and 58 meters wide. Approximate the area by finding two numbers that the area must be between. Which of these could be the actual area?

   a. 1,856 square meters

   b. 3,056 square meters

   c. 2,436 square meters

In Problems 2–5, two of the answers are clearly wrong and one is correct. Choose the correct answer.

2 32 × 17 = ▢

   a. 264

   b. 544

   c. 914

3 46 × 61 = ▢

   a. 2,806

   b. 2,316

   c. 2,026

4 28 × 195 = ▢

   a. 5,460

   b. 6,140

   c. 7,440

5 206 × 38 = ▢

   a. 5,828

   b. 7,828

   c. 4,828

Multiplying by a One-Digit Number Lesson 2.2

Multiply.

6   74
  × 7

7   385
  × 8

8   77
  × 8

9   976
  × 4

10   888
  × 7

11   528
  × 6

Applying Math Lesson 1.4

Solve.

⑫ Chung's bedroom is 13 feet long and 9 feet wide. What is the area of his room?

⑬ Carpet is sold in rolls measuring 10 feet by 5 feet. How many rolls of carpet will Chung need to cover his bedroom floor?

⑭ What is the perimeter of Chung's room?

⑮ What is the area of a square with a perimeter of 40 inches?

⑯ A rectangle with a perimeter of 62 feet could have which of the following dimensions?

    a. 50 feet by 12 feet

    b. 30 feet by 2 feet

    c. 28 feet by 3 feet

    d. 20 feet by 21 feet

Converting Customary Units Grade 4 Lesson 6.6

Solve.

⑰ How many fluid ounces are in 7 cups?

⑱ How many fluid ounces are in 1 pint?

⑲ How many fluid ounces are in 1 quart?

⑳ How many inches are in 8 feet?

㉑ How many feet are in 15 yards?

㉒ In math class, Angie sits 42 inches from Mrs. Packard's computer. Jenny sits 3 feet from Mrs. Packard's computer. Who sits closer to the computer, Angie or Jenny?

Applying Multiplication Lesson 2.4

Solve.

Eduardo and Ming each do odd jobs after school. Eduardo earns $15 for each lawn mowed and $10 for each car washed. Ming earns $17 per lawn and $8 per car.

㉓ Eduardo mowed 7 lawns and washed 4 cars. How much did he earn?

㉔ Ming mowed 6 lawns and washed 5 cars. How much did he earn?

㉕ Ming's goal is to earn $200. How can he do it?

Key Ideas

The answers to computations that involve division require careful interpretation.

When we do a division problem, such as $9\overline{)74}$, we often write the remainder with an *R* next to the quotient: 8 *R*2.

Read each problem. Discuss your answers in your small group.

Example 1

Steve, Charla, Alicia, and Jorge found a box of old comic books in Steve's grandparents' basement. After getting permission, they decided to share the books so that each of the friends got the same number. Steve said, "If there are any left over, let's give them to Jorge's little brother." They counted 29 comic books in the box.

Steve said, "There are 4 of us. I know that $4 \times 7 = 28$, and $4 \times 8 = 32$. If we each get 7 comic books, there will be 1 left over for Carlos."

Jorge said, "Carlos is getting 1 comic book. That's 2 fewer than 3—the most he could get no matter how many were in the box."

Why is Jorge right?

Example 2

Sara's class was planning a field trip. Her teacher said, "We will be traveling by car. There are 29 students in the class, and we can have only 4 students in each car. That means we need 8 cars."

Sara said, "But there are only seven 4s in 29, not eight."

Her teacher replied, "That's right, Sara. But you're forgetting the remainder. What about the 1 student who wouldn't have a ride?"

Why does the class need 8 cars?

Example 3

Aponi is stacking boxes of paper on the shelves in the storeroom. Each box of paper is 4 centimeters high. The space between the shelves is 29 centimeters. Aponi thought she could put 8 boxes on each shelf.

Is Aponi right? Why or why not?

ⓔ **Textbook** This lesson is available in the *eTextbook*.

Divide.

1. $9\overline{)83}$

2. $8\overline{)49}$

3. $7\overline{)19}$

4. $6\overline{)35}$

5. $6\overline{)52}$

6. $8\overline{)29}$

7. $6\overline{)24}$

8. $8\overline{)72}$

9. $5\overline{)46}$

10. $7\overline{)32}$

11. $9\overline{)60}$

12. $3\overline{)18}$

13. $13 \div 4 = $ ☐

14. $56 \div 7 = $ ☐

15. $62 \div 8 = $ ☐

16. **Extended Response** Parents of Fairfield Elementary School students decided to carpool in order to take the greatest number of students to the high school basketball game. If each car can hold 6 students, how many cars are needed to take 26 students to the basketball game? Explain your answer.

17. The cook in a restaurant wants to make omelets. He uses 3 eggs to make an omelet, and he has 23 eggs.

    a. How many omelets can he make?

    b. **Extended Response** How many eggs will be left over? Explain.

18. A parcel service has 5,600 kilograms worth of packages that need to be sorted. One pallet will hold 750 kilograms. How many pallets are needed?

 **Journal**

Write two problems solved using the same division fact, one in which the answer is rounded up and one in which the answer is rounded down. How did you know whether to round up or down? Explain.

Key Ideas

Division involves dividing one number, the dividend, by another number, called the divisor.

You can use division to solve problems such as this one: 7 people want to divide $2,053 equally among themselves. They have two $1,000 bills, zero $100 bills, five $10 bills, and three $1 bills. How much money will each person get?

$$7\overline{)2053}$$

If they go to the bank and exchange the two $1,000 bills for twenty $100 bills, how many will each person get? Will there be any money left over?

Each person takes two $100 bills, leaving six.

$$\begin{array}{r} 2 \\ 7\overline{)20^6 53} \end{array}$$

They exchange the six leftover $100 bills for sixty $10 bills. How many $10 bills do they have altogether?

$$\begin{array}{r} 2 \\ 7\overline{)20^6 53} \end{array}$$

There are sixty-five $10 bills. If we split these up, what happens?

$$\begin{array}{r} 2\,9 \\ 7\overline{)20^6 5^2 3} \end{array}$$

Each person takes nine $10 bills, leaving two.

$$\begin{array}{r} 2\,9 \\ 7\overline{)20^6 5^2 3} \end{array}$$

They exchange two $10 bills for twenty $1 bills. How many $1 bills do they have left?

$$\begin{array}{r} 2\,9\,3\ R2 \\ 7\overline{)20^6 5^2 3} \end{array}$$

Each person takes three of the twenty-three $1 bills, leaving two $1 bills.

So, each person gets $293, and there are two $1 bills remaining.

e *Textbook* This lesson is available in the eTextbook

Divide.

1. ◻ 3)52

2. ◻ 2)21

3. ◻ 5)43

4. ◻ 8)187

5. ◻ 6)342

6. ◻ 6)345

7. ◻ 4)575

8. ◻ 7)8145

9. ◻ 9)648

10. ◻ 9)649

11. ◻ 9)650

12. ◻ 9)651

13. ◻ 8)804

14. ◻ 5)6798

15. ◻ 6)3798

16. ◻ 3)999

17. ◻ 3)131

18. ◻ 4)1466

19. 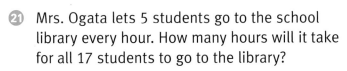 Mrs. Ogata has 17 students. She must order a computer disk for each student. The disks come 5 to a box. How many boxes should she order? Explain.

 20. The science class is studying rocks and minerals. The students need to work in groups to do an experiment, but their teacher says that each group may not have more than 3 people. There are 17 students in the class. What is one way to organize the groups? How many students would there be in each group? (Hint: There is more than one possibility.)

21. Mrs. Ogata lets 5 students go to the school library every hour. How many hours will it take for all 17 students to go to the library?

22. To raise money for a trip to the science museum, Mrs. Ogata's class held a car wash and a bake sale. They need $100 to rent a charter bus. The class also needs $45 for food and beverages. Admission to the museum is $4 per student for 17 students. The class raised $220. Is that enough? If so, will they have any money left over? If not, how much more do they need?

Find the missing digit.

23 40 ☐ ÷ 4 = 100 R2

24 4,☐07 ÷ 7 = 701

25 220 ÷ ☐ = 44

26 670 ÷ 4 = 1☐7 R2

27 71 ÷ 8 = 8 R ☐

28 360 ÷ ☐ = 120

29 ☐,403 ÷ 8 = 800 R3

30 32 ÷ 9 = 3 R ☐

31 64 ÷ 7 = ☐ R1

32 700 ÷ ☐0 = 70

33 2,505 ÷ ☐ = 501

34 6,613 ÷ 6 = ☐,102 R1

35 A basketball league has 475 students to assign to 9-person teams. If all spots must be filled, how many students will not have a team?

36 Pictures of all the students will be printed in the school yearbook. Only 9 pictures will fit on each page. If there are 475 students, how many pages will be needed to print pictures of all the students?

37 Suppose 475 students buy yearbooks for $9 each. How much money will be collected?

38 **Extended Response** Did you notice any similarities among Problems 35–37? Explain what you observed.

39 **Extended Response** Did you get the same answers for any of these three problems? Explain why or why not.

40 All of the fourth- and fifth-grade students at City School are going to watch a movie in the auditorium. There are 9 seats in each row, and there are 124 students. How many rows of seats can be completely filled?

Writing + Math **Journal**

What strategy did you use while playing the **Roll a Problem (Division) Game** in order to get the greatest quotient? What strategy did you use to get the least quotient?

🄴 **Textbook** This lesson is available in the *eTextbook.*

Game

Division Strategies and Practice

Roll a Problem (Division) Game (One-Digit Divisor)

Players: Two or more

Materials: *Number Cube* (One 0–5)

Object: To get the greatest quotient

Math Focus: Place value and mathematical reasoning

HOW TO PLAY

❶ Use blanks to outline a division problem on your paper like this:

❷ The first player rolls the **Number Cube** five times.

❸ After each roll, write the number in one of the blanks in your outline before taking the next roll. Zero may be in any place except the divisor. Since division by 0 is impossible, a player is disqualified if his or her divisor is 0.

❹ After all the blanks have been filled, find the quotient of the two numbers.

❺ The player with the greatest quotient is the winner.

OTHER WAY TO PLAY THIS GAME

Try to get the least quotient.

Exponents

Key Ideas

We use exponents to show how many times a given factor is repeated in a multiplication expression. The factor is called the base.

$5^3 = 5 \times 5 \times 5 = 125$

5 is the base. 3 is the exponent. 5^3 is read "five to the third," "five to the third power," or "five cubed."

$5^2 = 5 \times 5 = 25$

5 is the base. 2 is the exponent. 5^2 is read "five to the second," or "five to the second power," or "five squared."

Evaluate each expression by multiplying.

1. $3^8 = 3 \times 3 \times 3 \times 3 \times 3 \times 3 \times 3 \times 3 = \ \Box$

2. $8^3 = 8 \times 8 \times 8 = \ \Box$

3. $2^{10} = 2 \times 2 \times 2 \times 2 \times 2 \times 2 \times 2 \times 2 \times 2 \times 2 = \ \Box$

4. $5^6 = 5 \times 5 \times 5 \times 5 \times 5 \times 5 = \ \Box$

Write each product using exponents.

5. $7 \times 7 \times 7 \times 7 = \ \Box$

6. $4 \times 4 \times 4 = \ \Box$

7. $5 \times 5 \times 5 \times 5 \times 5 = \ \Box$

8. $3 \times 3 \times 3 \times 3 \times 3 \times 3 = \ \Box$

Many calculators have an exponent key $\boxed{y^x}$. To find the value of 3^6 on a calculator, press $\boxed{3}$, $\boxed{y^x}$, $\boxed{6}$, $\boxed{=}$. The display will read 729.

Evaluate the following by using multiplication or your calculator if you have one.

9. $9^4 =$

10. $2^9 =$

11. $4^5 =$

12. $6^3 =$

13. $3^4 =$

14. $3^8 \times 3^4 =$

Use the facts in the following table to do the exercises below. Do *not* use your calculator. Write your answers in standard form (without exponents).

$7^1 =$	7	$7^2 =$	49	$7^3 =$	343
$7^4 =$	2,401	$7^5 =$	16,807	$7^6 =$	117,649
$7^7 =$	823,543	$7^8 =$	5,764,801	$7^9 =$	40,353,607
$7^{10} =$	282,475,249	$7^{11} =$	1,977,326,743	$7^{12} =$	13,841,287,201

15 $7^2 \times 7^3 =$

16 $7^7 \times 7^4 =$

17 $7^6 \times 7^6 =$

18 $7^5 \times 7^4 =$

19 $7^1 \times 7^1 =$

20 $7^{10} \times 7^2 =$

21 $7^3 \times 7^4 =$

22 $7^4 \times 7^4 =$

23 $16,807 \times 823,543 =$

24 $2,401 \times 823,543 =$

25 $343 \times 823,543 =$

26 $49 \times 117,649 =$

27 $117,649 \times 343 =$

28 $2,401 \times 2,401 =$

29 $7 \times 5,764,801 =$

30 $343 \times 49 =$

A calculator with an eight- or ten-digit display cannot show a number such as 13,841,287,201 in standard form.

Check to see what your calculator does with large numbers.

31 Use your calculator to find 8^2, 8^3, 8^4, and so on.

a. Extended Response When does the calculator stop displaying numbers in standard form? What does it show instead?

b. What is the greatest exponent of 6 that will allow an answer to be displayed in standard form on your calculator?

32 For a food drive, two fifth-grade classrooms collected cans of food for four weeks. Here are Classroom A's results: Week 1: 38, Week 2: 31, Week 3: 33, Week 4: 18. Here are Classroom B's results: Week 1: 40, Week 2: 35, Week 3: 30, Week 4: 27. What is each classroom's average number of cans collected for a week?

 **Writing + Math** **Journal**

Write two rules for using exponents you have learned in this lesson.

Key Ideas

There are ways to decide whether a number has certain factors.

A factor is a whole number (1, 2, 3, and so on) that divides exactly into another whole number.

$1 \times 12 = 12$ $3 \times 4 = 12$ $6 \times 2 = 12$

So 1, 12, 3, 4, 6, and 2 are all factors of 12.

$12 \div 3 = 4$ $12 \div 4 = 3$ $12 \div 1 = 12$

$12 \div 6 = 2$ $12 \div 2 = 6$ $12 \div 12 = 1$

We can say, "12 is divisible by 1, 2, 3, 4, 6, and 12."

A prime number is greater than 0 and has exactly two factors, 1 and the number itself. For example, the number 5 is a prime number whose factors are 1 and 5.

A composite number is greater than 0 and has more than two factors. For example, the number 6 is a composite number whose factors are 1, 2, 3, and 6.

How many distinct factors does the number 1 have?

The number 1 is the only whole number greater than 0 that is neither prime nor composite because it has only one factor.

- Because our number system is based on 10, every number divisible by 10 ends with 0. Because $10 = 2 \times 5$, all multiples of 10 are also divisible by 2 and 5.

- If 5 is added to a number divisible by 10, the number will end in 5. It also will be divisible by 5 because the original number was divisible by 10 (and therefore by 5), and 5 is divisible by 5. So, any number ending in 0 or 5 is divisible by 5.

- For a similar reason, if a number ends in 2, 4, 6, 8, or 0, it is divisible by 2. As you know, these are called *even numbers*.

ⓔ **Textbook** This lesson is available in the *eTextbook*.

Write all the factors for the following numbers.

1. 32
2. 15
3. 29
4. 80
5. 100
6. 295

7. How can you decide whether a number has a factor of 5?

8. How can you decide whether a number has a factor of 2?

9. How can you decide whether a number is divisible by 6? (Hint: Think about other factors.)

Decide whether each of the following numbers is a prime number or a composite number. If it is prime, write *P* on your paper. If it is composite, write the number in factored form, using exponents when there are two or more factors of a prime number.

For example, $35 = 5 \times 7$. No exponents are needed.

$36 = (2 \times 2 \times 3 \times 3) = 2^2 \times 3^2$. You must use exponents. $37 = P$

10. 2
11. 8
12. 24
13. 51
14. 12
15. 9
16. 29
17. 111
18. 11
19. 387
20. 1,000
21. 7,000
22. 800
23. 10,000
24. 7,000,000

25. On your paper, write every number from 1 to 100. After each number, write *prime* if the number is prime. If the number is composite, write the number as a product of prime factors, using exponents to show multiples of a factor (for example, $24 = 2 \times 2 \times 2 \times 3 = 2^3 \times 3$).

26. Using the rules you have learned about identifying numbers that have factors of 2, 3, 5, 9, and 10, every whole number less than 100 (besides 1) is either a prime number or can easily be shown to be a composite number except for one number. Which number is the exception? What are its factors? What is the next composite number that is not obviously composite? What are its factors?

Writing + Math **Journal**

How many prime numbers do you think there are? Why?

LESSON 2.10

Applications Using Customary Measurement

Key Ideas

In the United States and a few other countries, the measurement system that is commonly used is often referred to as the customary system of measurement.

The following table shows measures of length commonly used in the United States and their relationships to one another.

Unit	Symbol	Relationships
inch	in. or "	This line is 1 inch long: ——
foot	ft or '	There are 12 inches in 1 foot.
yard	yd	There are 36 inches or 3 feet in 1 yard.
mile	mi	There are 5,280 feet or 1,760 yards in a mile.

Ounces (oz), pounds (lb), and tons (tn) are commonly used measures of weight in the United States.

Unit	Symbol	Relationships
ounce	oz	A slice of bread weighs about 1 ounce.
pound	lb	There are 16 ounces in one pound.
ton	tn	There are 2,000 pounds in one ton.

This table shows the relationships among many common units of time.

Unit	Symbol	Relationships
second	s	It takes about 1 second to say "one Mississippi."
minute	min	There are 60 seconds in 1 minute.
hour	hr	There are 60 minutes in 1 hour.
day	day	There are 24 hours in 1 day.
week	wk	There are 7 days in 1 week.
month	mo*	There are about 4 weeks in 1 month.
year	yr	There are 12 months in 1 year. There are 365 days in 1 common year and 366 days in a leap year.
century		There are 100 years in 1 century.
millennium		There are 10 centuries or 1,000 years in 1 millennium.

*Some months have 31 days, and some have 30 days. February has only 28 days. In leap years, February has 29 days.

In some of the following situations, an incorrect measurement has been given. If the unit is appropriate, write "yes." If the unit is inappropriate, write an appropriate unit.

1. The envelope is 7 feet long.

2. The envelope and letter together weigh a little less than 1 ton.

3. The dog weighs 16 pounds.

4. Kevin ran 7 inches today.

5. That person is 62 centuries old.

6. The basketball hoop is 10 miles high.

7. A basket of apples weighs about 5 ounces.

8. The front door is 1 yard wide.

9. My dad's truck weighs 2 pounds.

10. The United States is more than 2 millennia old.

11. Mr. Ramirez rode his bike 4 miles yesterday.

12. The bike path is 10 inches long.

Answer the following questions.

13. Professional baseball fields have 90 feet between bases. How many feet does a player run if he hits a home run?

14. Monica said that her birthday will be in 20 days. If she said that on June 14, what is her birthday? Is there another famous birthday on that day?

15. Jong-Hyun said that he was strong enough to carry 10,000 pencils. Could he be right? Explain.

16. Juanita said that her birthday will be in 14 months. Could she be right? Explain.

17. How many ounces are in 16 pounds?

18. Is it possible to have 53 Mondays and 53 Tuesdays in the same year? Explain.

19. Is it possible to have 53 Mondays, 53 Tuesdays, and 53 Wednesdays all in the same year?

20. Is it possible to have 53 Mondays, 53 Tuesdays, 53 Wednesdays, and 53 Thursdays in the same year?

Use a calculator and any other necessary tools (such as a ruler or tape measure), and work with another student to answer these questions.

21. How many days old are you? Do not forget leap years.

22. About how many minutes old are you?

23. Without measuring, estimate the length of your classroom in feet.

24. Measure the length of the classroom in feet. How close was your estimate in Problem 23?

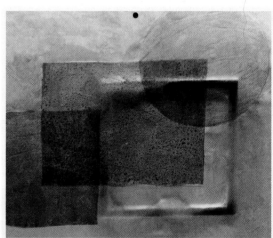

e Textbook This lesson is available in the *eTextbook.*

Extended Response **Use** a calendar to answer the following questions.

25. Why do April 1 and July 1 fall on the same day of the week? Do they always?

26. Why do September 1 and December 1 fall on the same day of the week? Do they always?

27. Why do January 1 and October 1 fall on the same day of the week? Do they always?

28. Why do February 1 and March 1 fall on the same day of the week? Do they always?

29. For which three months does the first day of the month fall on the same day of the week? Why? Will they always?

30. Carrie and Sophia went to a movie. The movie was 97 minutes long and started at 5:30. If Carrie's mom arrived to pick them up at 7:15, was she on time, early, or late? Is there a way to tell without doing any arithmetic? Explain.

31. Sabina had 210 minutes on her calling card. She used 42 minutes talking to her friend Casey. Then she talked to her cousin for 1 hour and 13 minutes. Her mom then added 2 hours to the card. How many minutes can she use so she will have exactly 1 hour of talking time left?

SOCIAL STUDIES 32. **Extended Response** A holiday that is important to many people of Mexican heritage is the Day of the Dead. It is celebrated during the first two days of November. Luis is going to Mexico on November 1st to celebrate the Day of the Dead. He will be in Mexico for 42 days. After Luis leaves Mexico, he will go on two business trips that will last a total of 11 days. Will he be back home in time to celebrate his birthday on December 29th? Explain.

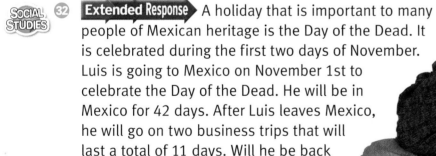

 **Journal**

When converting from a number of large units to a number of small units, will the number of small units be less than or greater than the number of large units? Explain.

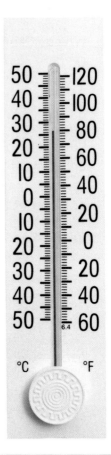

LESSON 2.11 Temperature

Key Ideas

There are three different scales for measuring temperature that are commonly used today. The Fahrenheit scale is most commonly used in the United States and a few other countries.

- **Fahrenheit** The first scale for measuring temperature was invented by Gabriel Daniel Fahrenheit (1686–1736). Fahrenheit chose 100° on his scale to be human body temperature. He chose 0° to be the coldest temperature he could create by mixing salt and ice. These choices mean water freezes at about 32° F and boils at about 212° F.

- **Celsius** The second measure of temperature was invented by Anders Celsius (1701–1744). Celsius chose 0° as the temperature at which water freezes, and 100° as the temperature at which water boils. He actually had these two reversed, but it was later changed so temperature would become greater with greater warmth. The Celsius scale is sometimes called the *centigrade scale* and is the most commonly used temperature scale in the world outside of the United States.

- **Kelvin** The third temperature scale was invented by William Thompson Kelvin (1824–1907). He used the same size for the unit of measure as Celsius, but he chose his 0 mark (0 K) as the coldest possible temperature, called *absolute zero,* which is about −459° F (Fahrenheit) or −273° C (Celsius). Units on the Kelvin scale are called *Kelvins,* and we report them using only a K, not the ° symbol.

Use the table below, which shows mean (or average) temperatures (in degrees Fahrenheit) for three United States cities, to answer the questions on the following page.

	JAN	FEB	MAR	APR	MAY	JUN	JUL	AUG	SEP	OCT	NOV	DEC
A	22	25	35	47	56	66	71	69	61	49	39	28
B	−14	−16	−14	−1	20	35	40	39	31	15	−1	−11
C	54	58	63	70	79	89	93	91	86	75	62	54

80

Textbook This lesson is available in the *eTextbook.*

1. What is the coldest month in City A? In City B? In City C?

2. What is the warmest month in each city?

3. **Extended Response** Where do you think City B is? Explain.

4. **Extended Response** Where do you think City C is? Explain.

5. **Extended Response** Where do you think City A is? Explain.

6. Which city has the greatest difference between its highest and lowest mean monthly temperature?

7. Which city has the least difference between its highest and lowest mean monthly temperature?

8. For the other city, what is the difference between its highest and lowest mean monthly temperature?

9. Which city do you think would be most comfortable in June? Which would be most comfortable in January?

10. Which city has the greatest difference in mean temperatures between two consecutive months? What is that difference?

Exploring Problem Solving

Defenders Reign in Overtime

As the ball floated toward the basket, the buzzer sounded. An instant later, the hushed silence of thousands of fans erupted in celebration as the ball from Katie Freeman's jump shot slid through the hoop. The New York Defenders had taken the opening game of the best-of-three Eastern Conference finals by the slim margin of 80 to 78.

Fifteen seconds earlier, the North Carolina Flyers had been in control with a chance to win the game. But Maria Payne stripped the ball from a Flyers player, and Freeman's buzzer-beating running jumper sealed the victory for the Defenders.

Twelve days later, the playoffs ended. The Sacramento Stars, a team from the Western Conference, won the championship. The post-season action was marked by a string of outstanding performances from individuals on all eight playoff teams.

The table below shows the scoring records of eight players during these playoffs.

Player	Team	Games Played	Shots Made			Total Points
			3-pt. FGs	2-pt. FGs	FTs	
Krystal Moore	Los Angeles Lightning	3	1	17	13	50
Mai Li	North Carolina Flyers	8	6	17	16	68
Tameeka Wright	Arizona Roadrunners	3	7	10	15	56
Joy Engle	Cleveland Rocks	3	4	14	14	54
Emily Young	Atlanta Thunderbirds	5	13	29	4	101
Angela Perez	New York Defenders	6	2	26	17	75
Roberta Collins	Sacramento Stars	8	4	26	43	107
Char DeLaura	Nevada Nighthawks	2	0	10	4	24

Solve the following problems. Use the information in the table to help you.

① How many shots did Roberta Collins make during the playoffs?

② How does that add up to 107 points?

③ On average, how many points did Char DeLaura score in each playoff game?

④ If you wanted players on your team who scored a lot of points, which two of these players would you choose first? Why?

⑤ The abbreviation *ppg* stands for *points per game*. This is the average number of points a player scores in a game. What formula could you write to show how to calculate the *ppg* for a player? Explain what each abbreviation in your formula means.

⑥ What other data might help you decide if a player is a good scorer?

⑦ What other data might help you decide how good a player is overall?

Exploring Problem Solving

In basketball and other sports, teams keep records of how every player performs. This table shows more information about the playoff shooting of the players listed on page 82. How do coaches and fans make sense of all these statistics?

Player	3-pt. FGs		2-pt. FGs		Free Throws	
	Made (A)	Tried (B)	Made (C)	Tried (D)	Made (E)	Tried (F)
Moore	1	4	17	37	13	13
Li	6	20	17	41	16	21
Wright	7	20	10	26	15	16
Engle	4	13	14	32	14	15
Young	13	33	29	45	4	5
Perez	2	9	26	77	17	22
Collins	4	11	26	54	43	53
DeLaura	0	2	10	14	4	4

Some people use formulas to combine different statistics into one number. Then they use that number to compare players.

Imagine you are a coach and want to compare the shooting ability of your players. You create a formula to calculate a number that will help you compare. Call this number "S" to stand for *Shooting Index*.

Shooting Index: $S = (A + C) \div E \qquad S = A + C + E$

Solve the following problems.

8. Which formula do you think does a better job of describing a player's shooting ability? Why?

9. Which scoring statistics are most important to you? Which are least important?

10. Create your own formula for the shooting index. Use your formula to calculate the shooting index for the eight players in the chart above.

11. Record the shooting index you calculate for each player. Use the shooting indexes to rank the players from 1 to 8; the player with the highest index is 1, the next highest is 2, and so on.

12. Compare your formula and your results. Did all groups agree?

Cumulative Review

Interpreting Remainders Lesson 2.6

Solve.

1. For his family reunion, Chet needs enough buns for 50 hamburgers and 75 hot dogs. Hamburger rolls come in 8-packs; hot dog rolls come in 10-packs. How many packages of each type of bun does Chet need?

There are 32 fans who need to be transported to a football game.

2. If 5-person cars are available, how many cars are needed?

3. If 7-person vans are available, how many vans are needed?

There are 43 students interested in playing basketball.

4. How many 5-person teams can be selected?

5. How many more students are needed so that an equal number of 5-person teams can be selected?

- -

Dividing by a One-Digit Divisor Lesson 2.7

Divide.

6. $8\overline{)66}$

7. $7\overline{)89}$

8. $9\overline{)775}$

9. $6\overline{)125}$

- -

Exponents Lesson 2.8

Write each answer in standard form.

10. $5 \times 10^2 =$

11. 10^3

12. $22 \times 10^1 =$

13. $7 \times 10^5 =$

14. $9 \times 10^6 =$

15. $8 \times 10^2 =$

Write each in exponential form.

16. 5,000

17. 3,000,000

18. 1,300

19. 10,000

20. 45,000,000

21. 600

Prime and Composite Numbers Lesson 2.9

For each of the following numbers, write P if the number is prime. If it is composite, write the number in factored form using exponents when there are two or more factors of a prime number.

㉒ 47 ㉓ 17 ㉔ 87 ㉕ 143

㉖ 1,500 ㉗ 79 ㉘ 370 ㉙ 315

Applying Math Lesson 1.4

Solve.

㉚ Alayna's 30th birthday was in 2005. In what year was her 10th birthday?

㉛ Ron bought 11 pencils. Each pencil cost 7¢. He gave the storekeeper 80¢. How much change should he get?

㉜ David paid 63¢ for 7 pears. How much did each pear cost?

㉝ Five pounds of beans cost $2.00. If Terri buys 20 pounds, how much does she spend?

㉞ A theater has 50 rows of seats. Each row has 33 seats. Can 1,700 people sit in the theater?

㉟ How can you make 74¢ using 9 coins?

Adding and Subtracting Multidigit Numbers Lessons 1.7–1.8

Add or subtract.

㊱ $556 + 444 =$ ▢

㊲ $3,000 - 1,645 =$ ▢

㊳ $2,000 - 857 =$ ▢

㊴ $4,001 - 1,960 =$ ▢

㊵ $567 + 123 =$ ▢

CHAPTER 2

Key Ideas Review

In this chapter, you reviewed methods to help solve multiplication and division problems.

You learned conventions to shorten work.
You learned how to multiply and divide multidigit numbers.

Select the appropriate answer.

1 $25 \times 12 =$ ⬜

   a. 301

   b. 300

   c. 325

2 $19 \times 7 =$ ⬜

   a. 133

   b. 140

   c. 126

3 $395 \div 8 =$ ⬜

   a. 4 R93

   b. 49

   c. 49 R3

4 $1,396 \div 3 =$ ⬜

   a. 456 R1

   b. 465 R1

   c. 46 R51

Answer the following questions.

5 What is a shortcut you can use when computing 36×7?

6 How are multiplication and division used to convert between customary units? Provide an example in your answer.

7 What does 9^3 mean? What does 9^3 equal?

8 Is 91 a prime or composite number? Explain how you came to your conclusion.

9 How can you check quotients that have remainders?

10 How does knowing how to multiply by powers of 10 help when multiplying numbers such as 22×17?

Chapter Review

Lessons 2.1–2.3 **Multiply.**

①
$$\begin{array}{r} 7 \\ \times\ 8 \\ \hline \end{array}$$

②
$$\begin{array}{r} 8 \\ \times\ 9 \\ \hline \end{array}$$

③
$$\begin{array}{r} 24 \\ \times\ 16 \\ \hline \end{array}$$

④
$$\begin{array}{r} 100 \\ \times\ 65 \\ \hline \end{array}$$

⑤
$$\begin{array}{r} 30 \\ \times\ 40 \\ \hline \end{array}$$

⑥
$$\begin{array}{r} 243 \\ \times\ 378 \\ \hline \end{array}$$

⑦
$$\begin{array}{r} 66 \\ \times\ 77 \\ \hline \end{array}$$

⑧
$$\begin{array}{r} 170 \\ \times\ 98 \\ \hline \end{array}$$

⑨
$$\begin{array}{r} 345 \\ \times\ 534 \\ \hline \end{array}$$

Lesson 2.4 **Solve.**

⑩ Pencils cost 18¢ and erasers cost 12¢.

    a. How much do 4 pencils and 3 erasers cost?

    b. How much do 6 pencils and 5 erasers cost?

    c. Is $2 enough money to buy one dozen pencils?

⑪ Mark wants to buy 4 books at $15 each. He has $70. Does he have enough money to buy all 4 books if the total tax is about $4?

Lessons 2.6–2.7 **Divide.**

⑫ $4\overline{)36}$ **⑬** $4\overline{)37}$ **⑭** $8\overline{)560}$ **⑮** $2\overline{)324}$

⑯ $9\overline{)2133}$ **⑰** $6\overline{)1656}$ **⑱** $7\overline{)9024}$ **⑲** $8\overline{)7540}$

Lessons 2.8–2.9 For each of the following numbers, write *P* if the number is prime. If it is composite, write the number in factored form using exponents when there are two or more factors of a prime number.

20. 37

21. 71

22. 57

23. 187

24. 500

25. 97

26. 270

27. 784

Lesson 2.10 Answer the following questions.

28. Melinda placed her baseball bat next to a yardstick. The bottom end of the bat was at the 3-inch mark. The top of the bat was aligned with the other end of the yardstick. How long was the bat?

29. **Extended Response** Diego's birthday is June 15, which is a Wednesday in 2005. On what day of the week will his birthday fall in 2010? Explain your answer.

30. How many seconds are in $4\frac{1}{2}$ hours?

31. If the average class lasts 45 minutes, how many classes will fit in 6 hours?

32. Jerome cut a 7-ounce piece from a $2\frac{1}{2}$ pound chunk of cheese. How many ounces of cheese are left?

Practice Test

Solve the following problems.

1. Evaluate 6^4 by using multiplication.

2. Write all the factors for 36.

3. How many minutes are in 2 weeks?

4. How many yards are in 3 miles?

5. A restaurant orders 2 aprons for each waiter. There are 37 waiters in the restaurant. Aprons come 6 to a package. How many packages does the restaurant need to order?

6. An average of 240 people go to the grocery store every day. How many people go to the store over 10 days?

7. For the movie night at school, Mr. Davies bought 16 liters of juice. Each liter cost 99¢. How much did Mr. Davies pay for all the juice?

8. The auditorium at school can fit 22 rows of 18 seats each. How many people can be seated at one time?

Choose the correct answer.

9. 675
   $\times$ 7
   ___

   Ⓐ 4,225

   Ⓑ 4,295

   Ⓒ 4,695

   Ⓓ 4,725

10. $120 \times 100 =$

    Ⓐ 120

    Ⓑ 1,200

    Ⓒ 12,000

    Ⓓ 120,000

11. Milk spilled on Kevin's paper. Which answer could be the correct product?

    4 ⬤ $\times$ 26 =

    Ⓐ 1,300

    Ⓑ 1,275

    Ⓒ 1,092

    Ⓓ 1,000

12. 325
    $\times$ 74
    ___

    Ⓐ 24,050

    Ⓑ 23,030

    Ⓒ 3,575

    Ⓓ 1,300

Ⓔ **Textbook** This lesson is available in the *eTextbook.*

Choose the correct answer.

13. 6)‾434‾

    Ⓐ 82 R4

    Ⓑ 72 R2

    Ⓒ 70 R4

    Ⓓ 62 R2

14. About 48 people enter the subway station in 1 hour. At that rate, about how many people enter the subway station in 4 hours?

    Ⓐ 192

    Ⓑ 182

    Ⓒ 162

    Ⓓ 122

15. Felicity invited 28 people to her birthday party and gave each person 2 balloons. Balloons come in packages of 5. How many packages of balloons did Felicity buy?

    Ⓐ 28

    Ⓑ 12

    Ⓒ 6

    Ⓓ 5

16. Which answer shows the prime factors of 30?

    Ⓐ $2^2 \times 3^2$

    Ⓑ $2 \times 3 \times 5$

    Ⓒ 5×6

    Ⓓ 1×10^3

17. $4^3 = $

    Ⓐ 64

    Ⓑ 32

    Ⓒ 12

    Ⓓ 8

18. Melody bought a 6-pound bag of sugar. How many ounces did she buy?

    Ⓐ 36

    Ⓑ 60

    Ⓒ 72

    Ⓓ 96

19. Which number is the greatest?

    Ⓐ 55,500

    Ⓑ 55,005

    Ⓒ 55,505

    Ⓓ 55,055

Choose the correct answer.

20. Samantha and her 2 friends bought 2 bags of pretzels. Each bag has about 18 pretzels. If they share the bags equally, how many pretzels will each person get?

    Ⓐ 6

    Ⓑ 8

    Ⓒ 12

    Ⓓ 18

21. $\begin{array}{r} 573 \\ + 532 \\ \hline \blacksquare \end{array}$

    Ⓐ 1,105

    Ⓑ 1,106

    Ⓒ 1,006

    Ⓓ 1,005

22. $\begin{array}{r} 854 \\ - 765 \\ \hline \blacksquare \end{array}$

    Ⓐ 81

    Ⓑ 89

    Ⓒ 111

    Ⓓ 199

23. Giorgio saved all his allowance for 6 weeks to buy a pair of jeans that cost $36. How much does he get for an allowance each week?

    Ⓐ $216

    Ⓑ $18

    Ⓒ $7

    Ⓓ $6

24. Which answer shows 100,000 + 6,000 + 4 in standard form?

    Ⓐ 160,004

    Ⓑ 106,004

    Ⓒ 100,604

    Ⓓ 1,604

25. Solve for n: $16 - (3 \times 2) = n$

    Ⓐ $n = 26$

    Ⓑ $n = 11$

    Ⓒ $n = 10$

    Ⓓ $n = 8$

Ⓔ **Textbook** This lesson is available in the *eTextbook*.

Use the provided information to solve the following problems. Show your work.

26. **Extended Response** Kerwick Elementary School is having a picnic. About 350 students and 180 adults are expected to attend. Hamburger buns come 8 to a package, and hot dog buns come 6 to a package.

   a. About how many people are expected to attend the picnic altogether?

   b. If each adult eats 2 hamburgers, how many hamburgers will the adults eat altogether?

   c. If each person at the picnic eats 1 hot dog, how many packages of hot dog buns will be opened? Explain how you found your answer.

   d. If each student eats 1 hamburger, how many packages of hamburger buns will be opened for the students? Explain how you found your answer.

Decimals

In This Chapter You Will Learn

- how to add and subtract decimals.
- how to multiply and divide decimals.
- how decimals apply to measurement and money.

Problem Solving

In the early 1980s, astronomers discovered that a window in the Temple of the Sun at Machu Picchu directly faced sunrise on the first day of winter. Many other buildings in the city also appeared to line up with special positions of objects in the sky.

SOCIAL STUDIES

Look at these two satellite photos of Machu Picchu and its surroundings.

 (A)   (B)

Answer the following questions.

1. A distance in Photo A appears many times greater than the same distance in Photo B. How many times greater? Choose the best estimate.

   a. 2   **b.** 10   **c.** 100   **d.** 1,000,000

2. How did you decide which estimate is best?

3. If a wall is 10 centimeters long in Photo A, how long would it be in Photo B?

4. Could you measure that distance with a standard centimeter ruler?

Key Ideas

Working with money is a good example of using decimals.

You can write amounts of money using the cents sign (75¢). You can also use a dollar sign and decimal point ($0.75).

Write the amount of money using a dollar sign and a decimal point.

1

2

3

4    ,

5

6

Use <, >, or = to complete each statement.

7 5.04 ▢ 4.05

8 6.40 ▢ 0.64

9 643.00 ▢ 643

10 101.01 ▢ 110.11

11 0.51 ▢ 51

12 16.05 ▢ 16.50

13 69.77 ▢ 697.70

14 3,015.13 ▢ 3,105.31

15 0.07 ▢ 0.70

16 505.05 ▢ 505.50

17 140.00 ▢ 140

18 1.10 ▢ 110

ⓔ **Textbook** This lesson is available in the *eTextbook*.

When you add numbers, such as 386 and 248, you line them up as follows:

386   You add ones to ones, tens to tens, and hundreds to hundreds.
+ 248

When you add amounts of money, such as $3.86 and $2.48, you line up the decimal points.

$3.86   You add pennies to pennies, dimes to dimes, and dollars to
+ 2.48   dollars.

When you subtract numbers, such as 289 from 453, you line them up as follows:

453
− 289

When you subtract amounts of money, such as $2.89 from $4.53, you line up the decimal points.

$4.53
− 2.89

Add or subtract. Watch the signs.

19.
```
  $14.53
+  27.99
```

20.
```
  $216.22
+  132.80
```

21.
```
  $0.96
+  1.04
```

22.
```
  $275.70
−   65.60
```

23.
```
  $40.61
+  61.22
```

24.
```
  $52.25
−  35.10
```

25.
```
  $76.70
−  16.45
```

26.
```
  $705.25
+  861.88
```

Solve for *n*.

27 $622.17 − $446.18 = *n*

28 $48.12 + $19.12 = *n*

29 $146.64 + $24.46 = *n*

30 $4.40 − $1.50 = *n*

31 $67.26 − $13.14 = *n*

32 $37.25 − $12.15 = *n*

33 $0.23 + $66.79 = *n*

34 $94.20 + $0.76 = *n*

35 $77.63 − $18.13 = *n*

36 $19.90 + $12.56 = *n*

37 $312.20 + $22.13 = *n*

Solve the following problems.

38 Raymond bought three packages of hamburger at the store. They cost $3.01, $3.25, and $2.49. How much did the hamburger cost altogether?

39 **Extended Response** A basketball costs $7.16, including tax. Brooke gave the clerk some money and got $2.84 in change. How much money did Brooke give the clerk? Explain some different ways to show that amount.

40 Enrique's father gives Enrique the money he saves from using coupons when he shops. During October, he gave Enrique $1.25, $0.75, $1.00, and $0.73. How much money did Enrique get altogether?

e Textbook This lesson is available in the *eTextbook.*

Game

Decimal and Strategies Practice

Roll a Problem (Decimals) Game

Players: Two or more

Materials: *Number Cube* (one 5–10)

Object: To get the sum that is closest to 100

Math Focus:
Addition, place value, approximation

HOW TO PLAY

1 Use blanks to outline an addition problem on your paper as follows:

____ ____ ____ + ____ ____ ____ =

2 One player rolls the *Number Cube* six times.

3 Each time the *Number Cube* is rolled, write that number in one of the blanks in your outline. If a ten is rolled, don't count it, and roll again. After a number is placed, it cannot be moved.

4 When all the blanks have been filled, place a decimal point in each number so that the sum is as close as possible to 100. The sum can be under or over 100.

5 Determine the greatest sum. The player whose sum is closer to 100 wins.

SAMPLE GAME:

Numbers Rolled 8 6 7 8 8 7

Liam   8 7.6 + 8.7 8 = 96.38

Rosa   8 8.7 + 8.6 7 = 97.37

Rosa is the winner.

Her sum is closer to 100.

Place Value and Decimals

Key Ideas

The decimal number system is based on powers of 10.

In our number system, called the *decimal system*, digits have place values based on powers of 10 (such as 1s, 10s, and 100s). We can write numbers less than 1 by using tenths, hundredths, thousandths, and so on. Look at the number 777.7777 below.

The red 7 stands for 7 ones, or 7.

The brown 7 stands for 7 tens, or 70.

The green 7 stands for 7 hundreds, or 700.

The blue 7 stands for 7 tenths, or 0.7.

The orange 7 stands for 7 hundredths, or 0.07.

The purple 7 stands for 7 thousandths, or 0.007.

The yellow 7 stands for 7 ten-thousandths, or 0.0007.

hundreds	tens	ones	.	tenths	hundredths	thousandths	ten thousandths
7	7	7	.	7	7	7	7

- As you move to the left, each place is worth ten times as much as the previous place.

For example, the 7 in the tens place (70) is worth ten times the value of the 7 in the ones place (7), and the 7 in the hundreds place (700) is worth ten times the value of the 7 in the tens place (70).

- If you move to the right, it is just the opposite. Each place is worth one-tenth as much as the previous place.

For example, the 7 in the tens (70) place is worth one-tenth as much as the 7 in the hundreds place (700), and the 7 in the ones place (7) is worth one-tenth as much as the 7 in the tens place (70).

eTextbook This lesson is available in the *eTextbook.*

Each time we add a 0 to the right of a decimal number, we are referring to a whole that has been divided into smaller parts—first a whole divided into tenths, then tenths divided by ten into hundredths, and hundredths divided by ten into thousandths. This means the decimal number is increasing in precision. For instance, in this first number line, we can represent only tenths of numbers; for example, 0.2 or 0.3.

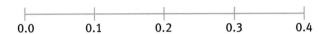

In this second number line, we can represent ten times as many numbers; for example, from 0.20 to 0.30.

With this third number line, we can represent ten times as many numbers.

Use $<$, $>$ and $=$ to complete the following.

1. 5.2 ▢ 5.4

2. 17.63 ▢ 17.64

3. 8.12 ▢ 8.120

4. 8.09 ▢ 8.12

5. 8.9 ▢ 8.12

6. 4.34 ▢ 4.7

7. 6 ▢ 6.000

8. 410 ▢ 4.03

9. 4.1 ▢ 4.03

10. 12.79 ▢ 16.79

Order the following numbers from least to greatest.

11. 0.7, 1.3, 0.09

12. 3.49, 3.2, 3.109

13. 6.12, 6.8, 6.18

14. 1.01, 1.1, 1.11

15. 0.4, 1.4, 0.01

16. 0.9, 1.0, 0.09

17. 3.5, 3.03, 3.1

18. 7.007, 7.7, 7.07

19. 1.81, 1.80, 1.08

20. 0.5, 5.0, 0.0005

Comparing and Ordering Decimals

Key Ideas

Writing a 0 to the right of a decimal number is a helpful way to compare decimals without changing the value of the decimal.

Which is greater, 4.1 or 4.09?

To help you compare 4.1 and 4.09, you may write a 0 after 4.1 (to make it 4.10), so that both numbers are expressed in hundredths. This does not change the value of the number, but it makes it easier to see that 4.10 > 4.09.

Replace ▨ with <, >, or = to make each statement true.

1. 5.2 ▨ 5.4
2. 17.63 ▨ 17.64
3. 8.12 ▨ 8.120
4. 8.09 ▨ 8.12
5. 8.9 ▨ 8.12
6. 4.34 ▨ 4.7
7. 6 ▨ 6.000

8. 410 ▨ 4.03
9. 4.1 ▨ 4.03
10. 12.79 ▨ 16.79
11. 12.79 ▨ 12.8
12. 1.0001 ▨ 1.001
13. 3.04 ▨ 3.0068
14. 2.1 ▨ 3.1

Write the following sets of numbers in order from least to greatest.

15. 8.7, 8.65, 8.9
16. 2.16, 2.3, 2.19
17. 1.005, 1.05, 1.0052
18. 4.1, 4.2, 4.03
19. 0.7, 1.3, 0.09

20. 3.49, 3.2, 3.109
21. 6.12, 6.8, 6.18
22. 1.01, 1.1, 1.11
23. 0.4, 1.4, 0.01
24. 0.9, 1.0, 0.09

Writing + Math ⮞ Journal

Write two or three sentences about what you think is most important to remember when comparing and ordering decimals.

ⓔ **Textbook** This lesson is available in the *eTextbook.*

Game

Roll a Decimal Game

Players: Two or more

Materials: *Number Cubes* (one 0–5, one 5–10)

Object: To make the greater decimal less than 1

Math Focus: Place value, comparing decimal numbers, and mathematical reasoning

HOW TO PLAY

1. Roll the 0–5 *Number Cube.* If a 0 is rolled, roll that cube again.

2. Write a 0 and a decimal point followed by as many blanks as the number rolled. For example, if you roll a 3, you would write: 0. ____ ____ ____

3. Roll the 5–10 cube as many times as there are blanks in your decimal. If you roll a 10, roll that cube again.

4. Each time you roll the 5–10 cube, write the number rolled in one of your blanks.

5. The player with the greater decimal is the winner.

SAMPLE GAME

Sara rolled:	Sara wrote:	David rolled:	David wrote:
0	rolled again	3	0. ____ ____ ____
2	0. ____ ____	6	0. ____ 6 ____
6	0. ____ 6	9	0.96 ____
7	0.76	6	0.966

David was the winner.

ANOTHER WAY TO PLAY THIS GAME

Roll two 0–5 cubes. Choose either number rolled to determine how many decimal places you will write.

Key Ideas

When adding or subtracting decimals, line up the decimal points.

Two women, Svetlana and Camila, were involved in a gymnastics competition.

SOCIAL STUDIES

Camila's scores were 9.437 on the uneven bars and 8.525 on the balance beam.

Svetlana's scores were 9.725 on the uneven bars and 8.287 on the balance beam.

What were the total points scored by these gymnasts?

- When you add or subtract decimals, line up the decimal points. Lining up the decimal points will make the other place values line up.

Camila:

$$\begin{array}{r} 9.437 \\ + \ 8.525 \\ \hline 17.962 \end{array}$$

Svetlana:

$$\begin{array}{r} 9.725 \\ + \ 8.287 \\ \hline 18.012 \end{array}$$

At the end of the first three events, Camila's team earned 26.24 points, and Svetlana's team earned 25.726 points. By how many points is Camila's team ahead of Svetlana's?

- It is possible that a problem may not have the same number of decimal places. Line up the decimals; if it helps, write a 0 to fill the place value. Then subtract.

$$\begin{array}{r} 26.240 \\ - \ 25.726 \\ \hline 0.514 \end{array}$$

e Textbook This lesson is available in the *eTextbook*.

Choose the correct answer.

1 $38.17 + $1.65 = ▢

   a. $54.67

   b. $38.33

   c. $39.82

2 $426.13 + $7.21 = ▢

   a. $498.23

   b. $433.34

   c. $1,147.13

3 $652.17 − $2.81 = ▢

   a. $649.36

   b. $654.98

   c. $624.06

4 0.63 + 0.56 = ▢

   a. 11.9

   b. 1.19

   c. 0.07

5 27.3 + 4.6 = ▢

   a. 63.3

   b. 31.9

   c. 319

6 47.1 − 23.4 = ▢

   a. 70.5

   b. 2.37

   c. 23.7

Solve for n. Watch the signs.

7 $34.2 + 16.7 = n$ **8** $34.2 − 16.7 = n$ **9** $107.82 − 69.7 = n$ **10** $107.82 + 69.7 = n$

11 $1.02 − 0.56 = n$ **12** $0.1 + 1.2 = n$ **13** $0.005 + 0.005 = n$ **14** $0.1 − 0.05 = n$

Solve the following problems.

15 Mr. Stein's yard is in the shape of a rectangle. It is 11.75 meters long and 9.25 meters wide. How long a fence does Mr. Stein need if he wants it to go completely around the yard?

16 Sharon is 148.3 centimeters tall. Last year she was 140.2 centimeters tall. How much has she grown since last year?

17 At 6:00 last night, Eliza had a fever of 100.1°F. Three hours later, her temperature was up by 1.1°F. This morning her temperature was 98.9°F. By how much did her temperature go down overnight?

18 **Extended Response** Simon wants to build a frame for a picture he made on his computer. He has 91.44 centimeters of wood he can use to make the frame. What are some possible dimensions the finished frame could have if Simon uses all the wood?

Applying Math

Key Ideas

You can apply what you know about decimals to solve different problems.

Solve the following problems.

1 A local caterer is advertising a special on trays of lasagna. The first tray ordered costs $14.00, but each additional tray costs only $8.50. Raphael has $40 to spend on the party he is planning and would like to get 4 trays of lasagna.

    a. Can Raphael afford 4 trays of lasagna?

    b. How much change will he have left, if any?

2 Norman owns a hot dog stand. He sells only hot dogs and soft drinks. He sells about 500 hot dogs and 700 soft drinks each day. His profit is 60¢ for each hot dog and 50¢ for each soft drink. About how much profit does Norman make each day?

3 Kishi bought 12 stickers for 25¢ each. She sold one sticker to Brenda for 25¢, 3 stickers to Andre for 78¢, and 8 stickers to Jeff for $1.60. How much profit did Kishi make?

4 Joe was born in 1966. He was 24 years old when he graduated from college and 32 years old when he got married.

    a. In what year did Joe graduate from college?

    b. In what year did he get married?

5 Mr. Tyler's bank account has a balance of $123.46. How much does he need to deposit in order to have a balance of $250?

6 **Extended Response** The Deluxe Supermarket advertised a liter of milk for $2.65. The Best Prices grocery store advertised half a liter of milk for $1.30. Which is the better buy? Explain.

    e Textbook This lesson is available in the *eTextbook*.

Solve the following problems.

7 LizAnne cut a string into 3 equal parts. If 1 piece was 48 centimeters long, how long was the string before LizAnne cut it?

8 Miss Farr owns a fruit stand. Her sales for one week were $136.75, $143.00, $164.25, $140.10, and $131.27. Her expenses were $366.80. How much profit did she make that week?

9 Mr. Chang owns a music store. Last Wednesday he sold 15 CDs for $12 each and 4 CDs for $15 each. He makes a profit of $6 each on the $12 CDs and a profit of $7.50 each on the $15 CDs. How much profit did Mr. Chang make on CDs last Wednesday?

10 José and Dave need to make banners for the school election. They have 15.5 feet of paper to use. José would like to make banners that are 4.5 feet long.

   a. How many 4.5-feet-long banners could José make?

   b. How much paper will be left?

   c. If Dave wants to make 5 banners all the same length, how long can each banner be?

11 The Rogers Elementary School principal has 144 packages of construction paper. If he plans to give each of the 9 teachers the same amount of paper, how many packages will each teacher receive?

12 The Clark Middle School principal wants to have a conference with each of the 277 students during the early part of the school year. If she can meet with 9 students each day, how many days will it take her to meet with all the students?

Multiplying and Dividing Decimals

Key Ideas

You can multiply or divide a decimal number by a power of 10 by moving the decimal point to the right or left, which moves the digits to the right or left.

The value of a digit's place is ten times as much as the value of the place to its right. You can multiply by 10 by moving the decimal point one place to the right because the digit moves one place to the left. Sometimes you may need to write a 0.

$75.9 \times 10 = ?$ $75.9.$ $75.9 \times 10 = 759$

To multiply by 100, move the decimal point two places to the right. You may need to write one or two 0s.

$6.7 \times 100 = ?$ $6.70.$ $6.7 \times 100 = 670$

To multiply by any power of 10, count the number of 0s in the power of 10, then move the decimal point that many places to the right. You may need to write more 0s.

Find each product.

1. $10 \times 75 =$ ▢
2. $10 \times 62.97 =$ ▢
3. $10 \times 89 =$ ▢
4. $10 \times 9.28 =$ ▢
5. $10 \times 0.06 =$ ▢
6. $10 \times 58.39 =$ ▢
7. $10 \times 95.17 =$ ▢
8. $10 \times 0.975 =$ ▢
9. $100 \times 8 =$ ▢
10. $82.45 \times 100 =$ ▢
11. $100 \times 0.47 =$ ▢
12. $100 \times 9.27 =$ ▢
13. $20.1 \times 100 =$ ▢
14. $67.29 \times 100 =$ ▢
15. $12.3 \times 100 =$ ▢
16. $100 \times 97.31 =$ ▢
17. $10,000 \times 0.978 =$ ▢
18. $0.792 \times 100 =$ ▢
19. $0.97653 \times 10,000 =$ ▢
20. $1,000 \times 63.576 =$ ▢
21. $15.1 \times 1,000 =$ ▢
22. $10,000 \times 1.17149 =$ ▢
23. $0.36781 \times 1,000,000 =$ ▢
24. $10 \times 627 =$ ▢

ⓔ **Textbook** This lesson is available in the *eTextbook.*

The value of a digit's place is one-tenth the value of the digit to its left. You can divide by 10 by moving the decimal point one place to the left because the digit moves one place to the right. Sometimes you need to write a 0.

36.9 ÷ 10 = ?   3.6.9   36.9 ÷ 10 = 3.69

To divide by 100, move the decimal point two places to the left. You may need to write extra 0s.

65.7 ÷ 100 = ?   .65.7   65.7 ÷ 100 = 0.657

To divide by any power of 10, first count the number of 0s in the power of 10. Then move the decimal point that many places to the left. You may need to write more 0s.

Find each quotient.

25. 27 ÷ 10 =

26. 0.09 ÷ 10 =

27. 18,390 ÷ 100 =

28. 2.7 ÷ 10 =

29. 0.76 ÷ 10 =

30. 1,839 ÷ 100 =

31. 89.261 ÷ 10 =

32. 36.143 ÷ 1,000 =

33. 42.9 ÷ 100 =

34. 0.9267 ÷ 1,000 =

35. 39 ÷ 1,000 =

36. 6.814 ÷ 100 =

Multiply or divide.

37. 347.26 ÷ 1,000 =

38. 0.07 ÷ 10 =

39. 100 × 47.3 =

40. 1,000 × 0.01 =

41. 66.41 × 1,000 =

42. 280.03 ÷ 100 =

Metric Units

Key Ideas

The metric system, like decimals, is based on powers of 10.

Most countries in the world use the metric system to measure length, weight, and volume. In the metric system of measurement, it is easy to convert from one unit to another.

The basic unit of length in the metric system is the *meter*. The meter is divided or multiplied by powers of 10 to produce the other units of length. The following table shows some metric units of length, weight, and volume. Notice that each unit in the table is ten times greater than the one above it.

In the table below, the underlined part of each word is called a *prefix*. The words with prefixes underlined with dotted lines are commonly used, but not as common as the words with prefixes underlined with an unbroken line. The prefixes and their part of the symbols are the same for metric units of length, weight, and volume.

Units of Length	Units of Weight	Units of Volume	U.S. Currency	Amount of Units in **Basic Unit**
millimeter (mm)	milligram (mg)	milliliter (mL)	mill	1,000
centimeter (cm)	centigram (cg)	centiliter (cL)	cent	100
decimeter (dm)	decigram (dg)	deciliter (dL)	dime	10
meter (m)	**gram (g)**	**liter (L)**	**$1 bill**	1
dekameter (dam)	dekagram (dag)	dekaliter (daL)	$10 bill	0.1
hectometer (hm)	hectogram (hg)	hectoliter (hL)	$100 bill	0.01
kilometer (km)	kilogram (kg)	kiloliter (kL)	$1,000 bill	0.001

Use a dictionary and the table to help answer the following questions.

1. What does the prefix *milli-* mean?

2. How many millimeters are in a meter?

3. How many milliliters are in a liter?

4. What does the prefix *centi-* mean?

5. How many centimeters are in a meter?

6. How many cents are in a dollar?

7. What does the prefix *kilo-* mean?

8. How many grams are in a kilogram?

Find the missing measure.

9. 14 m = ▯ cm

10. 0.001 L = ▯ mL

11. 200 mL = ▯ L

12. 3 dm = ▯ m

13. 16.2 mm = ▯ cm

14. 17.241 km = ▯ m

15. 4,000 g = ▯ kg

16. 1,796 m = ▯ km

17. 17.241 dm = ▯ m

18. 3.02 m = ▯ cm

19. 17.1 kg = ▯ g

20. 17.241 cm = ▯ mm

21. A meter has 1,000 millimeters, and 100 centimeters are in a meter.

   a. Which is longer, a millimeter or a centimeter?

   b. How many times longer?

Solve for *n*. **Algebra**

22. $n + 3.006 = 5.126$

23. $5.72 - 2.65 = n$

24. $72.6 - n = 52.9$

25. $7.421 + n = 10$

Key Ideas

Common sense can help you decide what is the most appropriate unit for a measurement.

Common benchmarks are helpful when thinking about metric measurements. Possible examples include the following:

- You can walk one *kilometer* in about 12 minutes.
- Most classroom doors are about 1 *meter* wide.
- Four average-size glasses together hold about 1 *liter* of liquid.
- A United States nickel weighs about 5 *grams*.
- This book is about 3 *centimeters* thick.
- This book weighs a little less than 1 *kilogram*.

Choose the measure that makes the most sense for each sentence.

1. Chad is ___ tall.
   a. 14 cm   **b.** 140 cm   **c.** 140 m

2. Nick's cat weighs ___.
   a. 2 kg   **b.** 20 g   **c.** 200 mg

3. I drank ___ of water during the soccer game.
   a. 500 mL   **b.** 5 mL   **c.** 50 L

4. Courtney's fifth-grade classroom is ___ long.
   a. 15 cm   **b.** 15 km   **c.** 15 m

5. Ms. Teal weighs ___.
   a. 5.2 g   **b.** 52 g   **c.** 52 kg

6. A basketball weighs about ___.
   a. 600 g   **b.** 60 kg   **c.** 600 kg

7. John ran ___ this morning.
   a. 2 cm   **b.** 2 m   **c.** 2 km

Textbook This lesson is available in the *eTextbook.*

Choose an appropriate measure.

8 The basket on a basketball court is about ___ above the ground.

   a. 30 cm   **b.** 3 m   **c.** 30 m

9 The glasses are about ___ wide.

   a. 12 m   **b.** 120 cm   **c.** 12 cm

10 A baseball weighs about ___.

   a. 14.5 g   **b.** 145 g   **c.** 14.5 kg

11 The new swimming pool is ___ deep.

   a. 1.5 m   **b.** 15 m   **c.** 5 m

12 A baseball bat is about ___ long.

   a. 100 cm   **b.** 10 m   **c.** 100 m

13 A box of textbooks weighs about ___.

   a. 10 kg   **b.** 10 g   **c.** 1 kg

14 Brian lives ___ from the school.

   a. 5 km   **b.** 5 m   **c.** 5 cm

15 **Extended Response** Explain whether the measurement in the following sentence is appropriate or inappropriate: Suppose your friend says, "The pitcher holds 2 milliliters of water." Does this make sense? If not, what would make more sense?

Writing + Math **Journal**

Most countries in the world use only the metric system. Write a letter to an imaginary pen pal in a foreign country. Describe your school and classroom using only metric units.

Exploring Problem Solving

If you travel about 4,500 kilometers north from Machu Picchu, you will find the third largest pyramid of the ancient world. The Pyramid of the Sun is part of a sprawling metropolis built by people who lived in this part of Mexico before the Aztecs.

You are going to build a scale model of this city for a museum of ancient astronomy. Each length in the model will be 0.01 as long as the actual length. The area of the square base of the Pyramid of the Sun is 46,440 square meters. What area will be covered by the pyramid on your scale model?

Paul solved the problem this way:

I started to Guess, Check, and Adjust.
First I figured out the length of the actual pyramid.

Guess	Check	Result
100	100 × 100 = 10,000	too low
500	500 × 500 = 250,000	too...

Think about Paul's strategy. Answer the following questions.

1. How will knowing the length of the actual pyramid help Paul solve the problem?

2. What would your next guess be if you were using Paul's strategy?

3. Would you use Paul's strategy? Why or why not?

Gina solved the problem another way:

I decided to Use Simpler Numbers, Make a Table, and Look for a Pattern.

First, I will see how length and area are related.

I'll start with a small square and see what happens as it grows.

Enlarged figure	Length compared to original length	Area compared to original area
	2 times the original	4 times the original
	3 times the original	

Think about Gina's strategy, and answer these questions.

④ What will Gina write about the area of the 3 × 3 square?

⑤ What do you think Gina will draw and write in the next row?

⑥ How would finding a pattern help Gina solve the problem?

⑦ Use any strategy you like to solve the problem. Why did you choose the strategy you did?

Cumulative Review

Place Value **Lesson 1.3**

Count on or back. Write the missing numbers.

1. 53, 54, 55, ☐, 63

2. 507, 506, 505, ☐, 498

3. 996; 997; 998; ☐; 1,004

4. 9,996; 9,997; 9,998; ☐; 10,002

Adding and Subtracting Decimals **Lesson 3.4**

Solve.

5. Jen has $25 to spend on books. The books cost $5.95 each.

   A. How many books can she buy?

   B. How much change will she get?

6. Steve rides his bicycle to and from school each day. The school is 2.2 miles from his house.

   A. How many miles does he ride in 1 day?

   B. How many miles does he ride in 5 days?

   C. How many miles does he ride in 10 days?

Arithmetic Laws **Lesson 1.6**

Use arithmetic laws to make computation easier.

7. $(45 \times 8) + (5 \times 8) = $ ☐

8. $(5 \times 17 \times 4) = $ ☐

9. $(16 \times 9) + (9 \times 4) = $ ☐

10. $(100 \times 22 \times 0.01) = $ ☐

Adding Multidigit Numbers **Lesson 1.7**

Add.

11.
```
   27652
+ 384986
```
☐

12.
```
   37373
+ 98989
```
☐

13.
```
  896
  432
+ 175
```
☐

ⓔ **Textbook** This lesson is available in the *eTextbook*.

Multiplying by a One-Digit Number Lesson 2.2
Multiply.

⑭ 659
   × 9

⑮ 747
   × 8

⑯ 694
   × 7

⑰ 876
   × 4

Interpreting Remainders Lesson 2.6
Solve.

⑱ There are 3 pizzas with 8 slices each that need to be divided equally among 7 friends. How many whole slices will each person get? If the remaining slices are divided equally, how much more would each person get?

⑲ There are 30 fans who need a ride to the football game. They have 7-passenger minivans and 5-passenger cars available to use. What is the minimum number of vehicles needed to transport everyone?

Applications Using Customary Measurement Lesson 2.10
Solve.

⑳ Seth has 4 wooden boards at home. Their measurements are 38 inches, 26 inches, 3 feet, and 8 inches. If he needs 24 feet of wood, how much more wood does Seth need to buy?

㉑ On June 10, 2007, Abe says he will be 10 years old in 15 months. What month and year will that be? In what year will he be 15?

Exponents Lesson 2.8
Evaluate.

㉒ $4^3 =$

㉓ $8^2 =$

㉔ $3^4 =$

㉕ $2^5 =$

Write in exponential form.

㉖ $7 \times 7 \times 7 \times 7 =$

㉗ $9 \times 9 \times 9 =$

㉘ $8 \times 8 =$

Key Ideas

Multiplying with decimals is like multiplying with whole numbers. The difference is that you have to decide where to put the decimal point in the product.

A box of blueberry muffins costs $2.35. Abby needs 6 boxes for a brunch she is planning. How much will they cost altogether?

- To find out, you would multiply $2.35 by 6. If you do not know how to multiply a decimal by a whole number, you could add $2.35 six times.

2.35 + 2.35 + 2.35 + 2.35 + 2.35 + 2.35 = 14.10

- Another way would be to find the answer in cents.

Multiply 235¢ by 6.

```
  235
×   6
 1410
```

1,410¢ is $14.10.

Abby will pay 1,410¢, or $14.10. So $2.35 × 6 must be $14.10.

Look at the two multiplications side by side.

```
  235          2.35
×   6         ×   6
 1410         14.10
```

The problems and the answers are the same, except for the decimal point.

Multiplication is commutative—meaning that we can multiply two whole numbers in either order and get the same result.

For example, 4 × 5 = 5 × 4 = 20.

The same is true for multiplication with decimals.

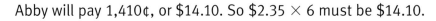 **Textbook** This lesson is available in the *eTextbook*.

To multiply a decimal and a whole number:

Multiply the same way you would multiply two whole numbers. Write the decimal point in the answer as many places from the right as it is in the decimal factor.

Example: 514 × 2.3

Begin by estimating the product: 514 × 2 = 1,028 and 514 × 3 = 1,542. Therefore, the product must be between these numbers.

$$
\begin{array}{r}
514 \\
\times\ 2.3 \\
\hline
1542 \\
+\ 1028 \\
\hline
11822
\end{array}
$$

Multiply as you would with two whole numbers.

Remember that we get the same answer whether we multiply 514 × 2.3 or 2.3 × 514.

$$
\begin{array}{r}
514 \\
\times\ 2.3 \\
\hline
1542 \\
+\ 1028 \\
\hline
1,182.2
\end{array}
$$

Place the decimal point in the answer so that the answer is between the upper and lower bounds of the approximations (1,028 and 1,542). Notice that one factor is a whole number and the other involves a whole number and tenths. So the answer should involve a whole number and tenths. The decimal point is between the second to the last and the last digit (1,182.2).

Because 1,182.2 is slightly more than 1,000 and less than 1,500, the answer makes sense.

$$
\begin{array}{r}
5.03 \\
\times\ 19 \\
\hline
4527 \\
+\ 503 \\
\hline
95.57
\end{array}
$$

If one factor is written to the hundredths place and the other is a whole number, the product is written to the hundredths place. So the number of digits to the right of the point should be the same in the product as it is in the only factor that is not a whole number.

$$
\begin{array}{r}
256 \\
\times\ .036 \\
\hline
1536 \\
+\ 768 \\
\hline
9.216
\end{array}
$$

→ The decimal point is **three** places from the right.

→ Write the decimal point **three** places from the right.

Multiply. Check your answers to see whether they make sense.

1. $2.4 \times 5 = $
2. $5 \times 2.4 = $
3. $0.02 \times 173 = $
4. $1.02 \times 173 = $
5. $1.2 \times 173 = $
6. $0.12 \times 173 = $
7. $4 \times 0.25 = $
8. $4 \times 2.5 = $
9. $7 \times 0.25 = $
10. $5 \times 0.2 = $
11. $0.75 \times 8 = $
12. $8 \times 7.5 = $
13. $6 \times 54 = $
14. $6 \times 5.4 = $
15. $0.6 \times 54 = $
16. $26 \times 4.2 = $
17. $0.05 \times 20 = $
18. $0.005 \times 20 = $
19. $1.05 \times 10 = $
20. $10 \times 1.5 = $
21. $9 \times 6.08 = $
22. $6.8 \times 9 = $
23. $4.23 \times 2 = $
24. $0.2 \times 423 = $

Solve the following problems.

25. Mrs. Lundquist is making shelves from a board that is 5 meters long. Each shelf must be 1.45 meters long. Can she cut 4 shelves from the board?

26. Suppose you must pay $0.05 in sales tax for each dollar that something costs. How much sales tax would you have to pay for something that costs $52?

27. The Last Federal Trust Company pays $0.06 in interest for each dollar that you keep in a savings account for a year. If you keep $250 in a savings account for one year, how much interest will they pay you?

28. **Extended Response** Mandy's father wants to cut 4 pieces of rope to make 2 tree swings in the backyard. Each piece of rope must be 6.5 feet long. He has a piece of rope that is 28 feet long. Does he have enough rope to make the 2 swings? Explain.

This lesson is available in the *eTextbook*.

Men's Outdoor Track and Field World Records

Distance	Time	Year	Runner(s)
100 m	9.78 sec	2002	Tim Montgomery, United States
200 m	19.32 sec	1996	Michael Johnson, United States
400 m	43.18 sec	1999	Michael Johnson, United States
800 m	1 min, 41.11 sec	1997	Wilson Kipketer, Denmark
1,000 m	2 min, 12.00 sec	1999	Noah Ngeny, Kenya
10,000 m	26 min, 20.31 sec	1996	Kenenisa Bekele, Ethiopia
4 × 100 m relay	37.40 sec	1992	United States Team
4 × 200 m relay	1 min, 18.68 sec	1994	United States Team

Use the chart above to answer the following questions.

29 Look at the world record for 100 meters.

   a. How long would 200 meters take at this pace?

   b. How long would 400 meters take at this pace?

30 **Extended Response** How do the records for 200 meters and 400 meters compare to your answers to Problem 29? What are some possible explanations for the differences?

31 In the 4 × 100 meter relay, 4 sprinters run 100 meters each. If members of the team ran their relay legs in 9.9 seconds, would they beat the world record?

32 **Extended Response** If all the members of the 4 × 100 meter relay team ran at a pace equal to the world record speed for 100 meters, would they beat the record? Why do you think that is?

33 **Extended Response** In the 4 × 200 meter relay, four sprinters run 200 meters each. If all members of a relay team ran at a pace equal to the world record speed for 200 meters, would they beat the record? Why do you think that is?

34 How much longer is the world record time for 10,000 meters than 10 times the record for 1,000 meters?

Rounding and Approximating Numbers

Key Ideas

How much we round a number, and whether we round it up or down, depends on the situation.

In many cases, an approximated figure is all you need. For example, when you go to the store, you can often approximate the total cost of your purchase to make sure you have enough money.

- Round 48 to the nearest ten.

48 is between 40 and 50, but it is closer to **50**.

- Round 4.8 to the nearest whole number.

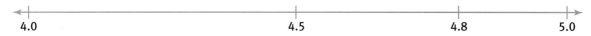

4.8 is between 4 and 5, but it is closer to **5**.

- Round 432 to the nearest hundred.

432 is between 400 and 500, but it is closer to **400**.

- Round 0.43 to the nearest tenth.

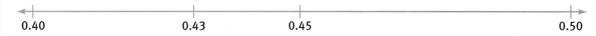

0.43 is between 0.4 and 0.5, but it is closer to **0.4**.

- Round 7,298 to the nearest thousand.

7,298 is between 7,000 and 8,000, but it is closer to **7,000.**

- Round 7.298 to the nearest hundredth.

7.298 is between 7.20 and 7.30, but it is closer to **7.30.**

- Round 7.2985 to the nearest thousandth.

7.2985 is between 7.298 and 7.299, but it is equally close to 7.298 and 7.299. What should we do?

Sometimes we would round up to 7.299. Sometimes we would round down to 7.298. So to round 7.2985 to the nearest thousandth, we can round up to 7.299 or down to 7.298. Most people round up. However, sometimes how we round depends more on the situation than on following a rule.

ⓔ Textbook This lesson is available in the *eTextbook*.

How much we round and whether we round up or down depends on the problem we are trying to solve. Possible examples include the following:

- Mrs. Ramirez has $40. She wants to know if she has enough money to buy 4 cans of paint for $8.48 each.

Mrs. Ramirez rounds $8.48 up to $9.00. She knows that $9 \times 4 = 36$. The paint will cost less than $36, so she knows she has enough money.

Suppose Mrs. Ramirez rounds $8.48 down to the nearest dollar, or $8.00. She knows that $8 \times 4 = 32$, so she knows that the paint costs more than $32, but does not know whether $40 is enough money.

Of course, Mrs. Ramirez could have multiplied $8.48 by 4 to find the exact cost of the paint. By rounding up, she avoided a longer calculation and was still able to answer the question.

Round each number.

1. 67 to the nearest 10
2. 209 to the nearest 10
3. 1,255 to the nearest 100
4. 1,500 to the nearest 1,000
5. 745 to the nearest 100
6. 2,561 to the nearest 10
7. 39,417 to the nearest 1,000
8. 25 to the nearest 10
9. 488,965 to the nearest 1,000
10. 6.8 to the nearest 1

11. 5.529 to the nearest 0.1
12. 0.0295 to the nearest 0.01
13. 7.5602 to the nearest 0.001
14. 900.77 to the nearest 0.1
15. 14.3843 to the nearest 0.01
16. 14.5 to the nearest 1
17. 0.3329 to the nearest 0.001
18. 17.76 to the nearest 1
19. 212.425 to the nearest 0.01
20. 52.0373 to the nearest 0.001

Discuss solutions to the following questions. Try to find solutions without doing calculations on paper.

21 The Johnson family will vacation in a city that is 1,578 kilometers from where they live. They plan to spend 2 days driving and would like to drive about the same distance each day. How far should they drive the first day?

22 Mrs. Kamata has 29 test papers to correct. She knows that each paper will take about 20 minutes. About how long will it take her to correct all the papers? If she can work on the papers for 3 hours each day, how many days will it take her to finish?

23 **Extended Response** If Mark saves $1 a week, can he save $100 a year? If he saves $2 a week, can he save $100 a year? Explain why or why not.

24 **Extended Response** Holly gets an allowance of $4.50 each week. If she saves half her allowance each week, can she save $100 a year? $200 a year? Explain why or why not.

25 David wants to buy 15 small bags of candy for $1.98 each and a mask for $7.98. He has $35.07 with him.

a. Will he have enough money?

b. How many bags of candy can he buy after he buys the mask?

e Textbook This lesson is available in the *eTextbook*.

Solve the following problems without using a calculator or paper and pencil. Discuss your methods with others.

26 Grant measured a filing cabinet that was 91.5 centimeters wide. He wants to put as many filing cabinets as possible along the wall of a room that is 5 meters long. How many cabinets can fit along the wall?

27 Ms. Smith has measured the distance from home to work on her car's odometer. The distance is 7.9 miles.

    a. About how long is the round trip to work and back? About how far will she travel in a week if she drives to and from work 5 days a week and does not drive anywhere else?

    b. Ms. Smith estimates that she gets about 25 miles to a gallon of gasoline, and her car's manual says the tank holds 16 gallons of gas. About how many miles can she drive on a full tank of gas?

    c. If Ms. Smith fills her tank just before going to work on Monday, about how many weeks can she drive before she needs gas again?

28 Audrey needs to buy 5 tomatoes for $0.79 each, a bag of flour for $1.49, and 3 gallons of milk for $2.29 each. If she has $15.00 in her wallet, does Audrey have enough money to buy everything she needs?

29 Kevin earns $23.50 a week delivering newspapers. About how much money does he earn in 15 weeks?

30 Max wants to buy a portable stereo that costs $137.99. If he earns $5 an hour, about how many hours will he have to work to earn enough money to buy the stereo?

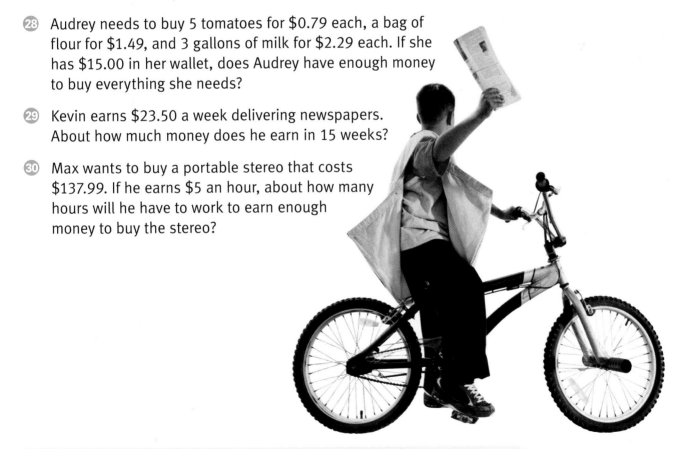

 **Journal**

Write two or three sentences that explain how to round and approximate numbers.

Approximation Applications

Key Ideas

Approximating an answer before finding an exact solution can help you notice if you make a mistake.

In each exercise, two of the answers are clearly wrong and one is correct. Approximate to select the correct answers.

1 $47.968 + 4.952 =$ ▢

   a. 25.920

   b. 52.920

   c. 95.220

2 $63.313 - 36.392 =$ ▢

   a. 26.921

   b. 62.921

   c. 92.621

3 $51.6 \times 284 =$ ▢

   a. 41,654.4

   b. 14,654.4

   c. 61,454.4

4 $55.55 - 19.99 =$ ▢

   a. 65.53

   b. 35.56

   c. 53.56

5 $5.280 + 6.820 =$ ▢

   a. 11.100

   b. 10.120

   c. 12.100

6 $965 \times 1.01 =$ ▢

   a. 1,974.65

   b. 9,074.65

   c. 974.65

7 $255 \times 2.13 =$ ▢

   a. 345.15

   b. 543.15

   c. 453.15

8 $56.301 - 19.654 =$ ▢

   a. 36.647

   b. 46.647

   c. 16.647

9 $1,019.09 + 9,091.01 =$ ▢

   a. 10,110.10

   b. 1,101.10

   c. 101,010.10

10 $5.2768 + 2.5022 =$ ▢

   a. 9.7770

   b. 7.7790

   c. 8.3770

11 $2.85 \times 29 =$ ▢

   a. 682.50

   b. 32.85

   c. 82.65

12 $7,654.3 - 1,234.5 =$ ▢

   a. 5,419.8

   b. 6,419.8

   c. 7,419.8

ⓔ Textbook This lesson is available in the *eTextbook*.

Solve each of the following problems by approximating.

13. The Green Thumb Nursery has 6 greenhouses. Each greenhouse has 5 benches. Each bench can hold 495 flowerpots. About how many flowerpots can be held in the Green Thumb's greenhouses?

14. The Green Thumb Nursery sells about 1,500 plants each day. At the end of each day, new plants are brought in to replace the ones that were sold. About how many new plants are put in the greenhouses each day?

15. **Extended Response** Pedro had 497 football cards. Melissa said she had about 100 cards. Pedro bought all her cards for $3.50. About how many does Pedro have now? Explain how you arrived at your answer.

16. The Riverview Library has a total of 87,989 books. The librarian says that about 5,000 books are out on loan at any time. About how many books are in the library at any time?

17. **Extended Response** If a family of 2 adults and 3 children goes to the movies, how much does the family spend on tickets if adult tickets cost $5.75 each and child tickets cost $3.25 each?

18. The length of a garden is 34 feet, 3 inches, and the width is 29 feet, 9 inches. What is the total length of fence needed to go around the garden?

Understanding Decimal Division Problems

Key Ideas

Division problems with remainders may be carried out to have a decimal quotient instead of a remainder.

Tamala does a lot of work at the library. One day, she rode her bicycle there in the morning and then home for lunch. She rode back to the library after lunch, and she rode home again in the afternoon.

"That's 4 trips I've made today between my house and the library," said Tamala. The odometer on her bicycle showed that she had ridden a total of 6.0 kilometers that day. "I'm going to figure out how far it is from my house to the library," she said. Tamala did the problem this way:

$$\frac{1 \text{ R}2}{4 \overline{)6}}$$

"So it's more than 1 kilometer from my house to the library, but less than 2 kilometers," said Tamala. "But I'd like to get a more exact answer."

Here's how Tamala can get a decimal answer.

$4\overline{)6}$ There is one 4 in 6.

$4\overline{)6.0}$ Write a decimal point and a 0. We can write 6.0 for 6 if the original measurement is precise enough to say 6.0.

$\dfrac{1.}{4\overline{)6.^20}}$ There is one 4 in 6 (write 1. in the answer). The remainder is 2 (write a small 2 in front of 0).

$\dfrac{1.5}{4\overline{)6.^20}}$ There are five 4s in 20 (write 5 in the answer). The remainder is 0.

The decimal point in the quotient is placed directly above the decimal point in the dividend, so 1.5 is the answer.

The distance from Tamala's house to the library is 1.5 kilometers.

Check the answer. Does 4×1.5 equal 6.0?

 **eTextbook** This lesson is available in the **eTextbook**.

$$\begin{array}{r} 1.39 \\ 3\overline{)4.17} \end{array} \longrightarrow \begin{array}{r} 1.39 \\ 3\overline{)4.^{1}1^{2}7} \end{array}$$

The answer is 1.39. Check the answer by multiplying (or adding if it is easier). You will see that 3×1.39 equals 4.17.

Divide. Do not use remainders. All the exercises have exact decimal answers. Check your answers by multiplying (or adding if it is easier).

1. $5\overline{)6}$ 2. $2\overline{)1}$ 3. $4\overline{)2}$ 4. $5\overline{)3}$ 5. $4\overline{)5}$

6. $2\overline{)4.7}$ 7. $4\overline{)5.16}$ 8. $5\overline{)4}$ 9. $8\overline{)9}$ 10. $5\overline{)46}$

11. $8 \div 5 = \square$

12. $8.4 \div 6 = \square$

13. $10 \div 8 = \square$

14. $9.9 \div 9 = \square$

15. $7.3 \div 2 = \square$

16. $35.8 \div 2 = \square$

17. $56 \div 5 = \square$

18. $15 \div 8 = \square$

19. $2.4 \div 4 = \square$

20. $24.1 \div 4 = \square$

Solve the following problems. Write 0s in the dividend when you need to.

21. $1 \div 8 = \square$

22. $3 \div 8 = \square$

23. $1 \div 3 = \square$

24. $2 \div 6 = \square$

25. Answer the following questions about Problems 23 and 24.

   a. Were the answers exact after you wrote more 0s to the right of the dividend?

   b. Do you think the answers would ever be exact if you continued to write more 0s?

Mr. Kwan had 10 pens he wanted to divide equally among his 4 children. He divided this way: ⟶

$$4\overline{)10.{}^2 0} \qquad 2.5$$

He said, "I'll give each of my children 2.5 pens."

- Why doesn't Mr. Kwan's solution make sense?

Mr. Kwan realized his mistake. "I know," he said. "I'll round 2.5 up to 3 and give each child 3 pens."

- What is wrong with that idea?

Mrs. Kwan did not think her husband's answers made sense. She did the problem this way: ⟶

$$4\overline{)10} \qquad 2\ R2$$

She said, "Let's give each child 2 pens, and we'll have 2 left over to save."

In some situations, you need to carry division out to decimal places. In other situations, it makes more sense to use remainders or to round the answer to a whole number.

Solve the following problems. Check your answers by multiplying.

26. Josh needs to buy 20 cupcakes for a party. The cupcakes he wants come in packages of 8. How many packages does he need to buy?

27. Lydia, Inéz, and Latisha earned $17.50 altogether for shoveling snow. If they want to divide the money equally, how much should each person get?

28. Ricardo is cutting short wooden dowels from a long dowel that is 40 centimeters long. How many 6-centimeter dowels can he cut from the long dowel?

29. If a stack of 100 cards is 3 centimeters thick, how thick is each card?

30. Suppose Yoshi divides 18 paintbrushes equally among 5 friends. How many paintbrushes will he have left?

31. Mark needs 14 folders for school. The folders come in packages of 3. How many packages does he need to buy?

For each of the following problems, you must divide 34 by 5. Read each problem, and then match the problem with its answer.

32 If 5 people can ride in a car, how many cars will be needed to take 34 people to a picnic?

33 Mr. Jones can make 1 suit from 5 yards of material. How many suits can he make with 34 yards of material?

34 Suppose 5 people went to lunch together. They agreed to split the bill among them equally. If the bill was exactly $34, how much should each person pay?

35 The Robinson family uses 5 frozen dinners each day. If they have 34 frozen dinners in the freezer, how many days will the dinners last?

36 Suppose 5 people agree to share 34 small rolls of candy equally. The rolls of candy have been cut so that they are easily divided into 5 equal parts. How much candy should each person get?

| **a.** 6.80 | **b.** 6 R4 | **c.** 6 | **d.** 7 | **e.** $6\frac{4}{5}$ |

Notice that the situation in Problem 36 affects what you do with the remainder.

37 **Extended Response** Can you think of any question for which the answer 6.8 might be a reasonable response to "What is 34 ÷ 5"?

Extended Response **Create** your own division word problems for each of the following situations.

38 The answer must be rounded down to the next whole number.

39 The answer should be divided to the hundredths place.

40 The answer should be given as a mixed number.

 **Journal**

Have you discovered any shortcuts for dividing by decimals? If so, explain them.

Interpreting Quotients and Remainders

Key Ideas

The way we write the quotient of a division problem often depends on the situation of the problem it comes from.

Divide. Do not use remainders. Round answers to the nearest hundredth when needed.

1. $2\overline{)1}$

2. $4\overline{)3}$

3. $7\overline{)6.44}$

4. $5\overline{)11.35}$

5. $3\overline{)46}$

6. $3\overline{)8.25}$

7. $2\overline{)6.28}$

8. $8\overline{)8.8}$

9. $8\overline{)74}$

10. $3\overline{)17}$

11. $4\overline{)37.6}$

12. $7\overline{)2.87}$

13. $9\overline{)21.33}$

14. $5\overline{)92.4}$

15. $7\overline{)43}$

16. $3\overline{)27.9}$

17. $3\overline{)28}$

18. $4\overline{)64.8}$

19. $4\overline{)63}$

20. $6\overline{)8.9}$

Solve the following problems using division. Make sure your answers make sense.

21 Kenji needs 50 buns for the class picnic. Buns come in packages of 8. How many packages does Kenji need to buy?

22 Jeremy wants to bring oranges to share at the picnic. He decides that 100 oranges will be enough for everyone. If the oranges are sold in packages of 30, how many packages does he need to bring to the picnic? How many oranges will be left over?

23 After the picnic, the class decided to play basketball. If 34 students are in the class, how many teams of 5 can play?

24 Luis bought fruit for 9 students in his class. He spent $4.59 for the fruit. If each student shares the cost of the fruit equally, how much should each student pay?

25 Miss Chang needs 57 bags of concrete for some work on the foundation of her house. The warehouse sells concrete in batches of 6 bags. How many batches must she buy?

26 Brian and his 3 sisters want to divide the $487 they earned doing yard work over the summer. They did the same amount of work, so the money should be divided equally. How much should each person receive?

27 Janis plans to set up a row of square tables placed end to end. Each table is 2 meters on a side. How many tables can fit across a room that is 11 meters long?

28 Karen is cleaning her room and packing away some books to store in the closet. She fills square boxes that measure 3 feet on a side. How many boxes can fit along the back wall of a closet that is 8 feet long?

29 Doug bought a birthday gift for his mother. His brother and sister told him they would help pay for the gift, which cost $26.25. If the 3 siblings share the cost of the gift equally, how much should each of them pay?

30 Olivia has 9 DVDs and 14 CDs. She wants to divide them equally among herself and 4 friends. How many DVDs or CDs will each of Olivia's friends receive?

Decimals and Multiples of 10

Key Ideas

You can often simplify a division problem by dividing both the divisor and dividend by the same power of 10.

To multiply or divide by a power of 10, first count the number of 0s in the power of 10. To multiply, move the decimal point that many places to the right, which moves the digits two places to the left. To divide, move the decimal that many places to the left, which moves the digits that many places to the right. You may need to write more 0s.

- Example: 4.3×100

Move the decimal point two places to the right.

$4.3 \times 100 = 4.30$ Write a 0 so you can move the decimal point two places.

- Example: $12.5 \div 1,000$

Move the decimal point three places to the left.

$12.5 \div 1,000 = 0.012.5$ Write a 0 so you can move the decimal point three places.

Multiply or divide.

1. $79.6 \div 10 =$ ☐

2. $79.6 \div 100 =$ ☐

3. $0.796 \times 10,000 =$ ☐

4. $8.35 \div 100 =$ ☐

5. $0.835 \times 1,000 =$ ☐

6. $83.5 \div 10 =$ ☐

7. $10 \times 1.0540 =$ ☐

8. $1.0540 \times 1,000 =$ ☐

9. $105.40 \div 100 =$ ☐

Solve the following problems.

10. **Extended Response** A 10-pound smoked ham sells for $29.84 at the deli. At this price, how much does 1 pound of smoked ham cost? Explain how you could solve the problem without doing any arithmetic.

11. Jasper, a truck driver, added 100 gallons of diesel fuel to his truck's gas tank. If the total cost of the diesel fuel was $225.70, how much does 1 gallon of diesel fuel cost?

ⓔ Textbook This lesson is available in the **eTextbook.**

Bob and Inez were helping set up a career fair in a classroom. They wanted to place tables end to end across the room. They measured the room with a tape measure and found it to be 12 meters wide. They wanted to know how many tables would fit. Their teacher had told them each table was 200 centimeters long.

"I remember that 12 meters is 1,200 centimeters, so we can divide to find out," said Inez. She wrote: $200\overline{)1200}$

"But we don't know how to divide by 200," said Bob. "I wish the numbers were smaller."

"We can make them smaller," said Inez, "and we can do it without changing the answer!"

"How?" asked Bob.

"The room is 12 meters wide," said Inez. "But we could also say that because each table is 200 centimeters long, the length is 2 meters."

"Oh, okay. So the problem is how many 2-meter tables fit into a 12-meter space," said Bob. He thought: $2\overline{)12}$

"Now it's easy," said Bob. "The answer is 6. That's how many tables will fit across the room."

Look at these two drawings:

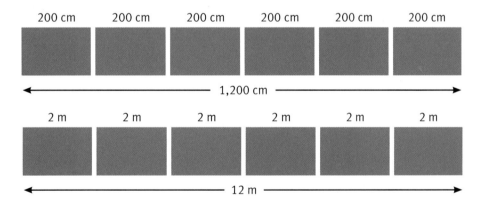

- How many 200-centimeter tables will fit across the 1,200-centimeter room?

- How many 2-meter tables will fit across the 12-meter room?

- Do you see why 1,200 ÷ 200 produces the same answer as 12 ÷ 2?

Before doing a division problem that requires an exact answer, you can divide the divisor and the dividend by the same amount. It is usually helpful to make the divisor a one-digit number, if possible.

Examples:

$400)\overline{2400}$ ⟶ Divide both numbers by 100. ⟶ $4)\overline{24}$ ⟶ $4)\overline{24}^{\,6}$

You can check to see whether your answers make sense by multiplying: $6 \times 400 = 2,400$.

$70)\overline{210}$ ⟶ Divide both numbers by 10. ⟶ $7)\overline{21}$ ⟶ $7)\overline{21}^{\,3}$

Check: $3 \times 70 = 210$

$600)\overline{900}$ ⟶ Divide both numbers by 100. ⟶ $6)\overline{9}$ ⟶ $6)\overline{9.0}^{\,1.5}$

Check: $1.5 \times 600 = 900$

$40)\overline{816}$ ⟶ Divide both numbers by 10. ⟶ $4)\overline{81.6}$ ⟶ $4)\overline{81.6}^{\,20.4}$

Check: 20.4×40 is about 800. So the answer makes sense.

Try to make the divisor a one-digit number. Remember that you must divide both the divisor and the dividend by the same amount.

Divide. Give exact answers. Check your answers to see whether they make sense.

12. $9)\overline{63}$　　　　13. $90)\overline{630}$　　　　14. $900)\overline{6300}$

15. $6)\overline{54}$　　　　16. $6)\overline{540}$　　　　17. $40)\overline{124}$

18. $70)\overline{3752}$　　　19. $6)\overline{300}$　　　　20. $800)\overline{5600}$

21. $60)\overline{480}$　　　　22. $10)\overline{1600}$　　　23. $8)\overline{500}$

24. $70)\overline{3500}$　　　25. $20)\overline{8005}$　　　26. $40)\overline{156}$

Solve the following problems. Check to see that your answers make sense.

27. Mr. Ebert must pack 600 books in boxes. He can fit 30 books in each box. How many boxes will he need?

28. **Extended Response** After making 10 equal deposits into her savings account, Cathy saved $555.00. If she made 10 equal deposits and recorded each of those deposits as $5.550, is she correct? Explain.

29. Suppose 30 players on the soccer team want to charter a bus to take them to see a championship game. The bus will cost $600.00.

   a. How much should each player pay to cover the cost of the bus?

   b. Suppose the bus costs $630.00. How much would each player pay?

30. The 42 members of the Healthful Health Club are planning to march from Chicago, Illinois, to Washington, D.C. They want people to know that exercise is important. They know the distance is about 700 miles, and they have 60 days in which to complete the trip.

   a. About how many miles must they walk each day?

   b. Can healthy adults walk that much in one day?

31. Ms. Jones is part of a team that is putting up fences along a highway. The fencing comes in pieces that are 30 feet long.

   a. How many pieces are needed for each mile?

   b. Ms. Jones and her work team can put up 4 pieces an hour. How many hours will it take to put up 1 mile of fence?

   c. Ms. Jones' team works 8 hours each day, but it takes about 30 minutes in the morning to set up and 30 minutes in the late afternoon to put things away. How many days will it take to put up 1 mile of fence?

32. Samuel needs to read a book that has about 600 pages for a class project. He has 10 days to read the book, and he can read about 30 pages in an hour. How many hours per day will Samuel need to read to finish the book?

Applying Decimals

Key Ideas

You can apply what you now know about decimals to many different situations.

Solve the following problems using your addition, subtraction, multiplication, and division skills. You may want to draw pictures to help you solve some of the problems.

① Miss Echohawk wants to fence her yard on 3 sides. Her lot is square and measures 31.5 meters per side. How many meters of fencing does she need?

② Miss Flores buys items in large quantities for a department store. She buys T-shirts in boxes of 50 shirts per box. A box costs $62.50. How much does each shirt cost the store?

③ Kate runs a restaurant. She can buy a 50-kilogram bag of potatoes for $10.54 from the Farmer's Outlet. She can buy a 20-kilogram bag of potatoes from the Restaurant Supply Company for $5.21. Kate wants to buy 100 kilograms of potatoes. Which supplier gives her the better buy?

④ Isaac bought 3 packages of pens at $1.35 a package and 2 packs of pencils at 63¢ a pack. How much did he pay altogether?

⑤ Mr. Chu's class is going on a field trip to a museum. It will cost a total of $94.50 to charter a bus. The people going on the trip will equally share the cost.

　a. If 30 people are going, how much should each person pay?

　b. If 20 people are going, how much should each person pay?

Solve the following problems.

Darryl and his classmates plan to sell hot dogs, peanuts, and soft drinks at their school's big baseball game. They plan to donate the money they earn to the local hospital. They know that last year 400 people came to the game and bought 190 cans of soda for $0.50 each and 110 hot dogs at $1.25 each.

6 How many dollars worth of soda and hot dogs were sold last year?

They have to decide how many hot dogs and cans of soda to buy this year and how much to charge. The cost of 1 hot dog and a bun is $0.80. If they buy at least 125 hot dogs, they can get free mustard, relish, and napkins. They can buy cans of cola or lemon-lime soda for $0.25 each. They can return any unsold soda, but unsold hot dogs cannot be returned.

7 How many cans of soda should they buy? What other information would be useful for making a decision?

8 How many hot dogs should they buy? What other information would be useful for making a decision?

9 **Extended Response** Make a plan for how much of each item you would buy. Explain your reasons in the plan.

Darryl and his friends will buy 125 hot dogs and buns, 150 cans of cola, and 100 cans of lemon-lime soda.

10 How much will they spend?

They will charge $0.75 for each can of soda and $1.00 for each hot dog.

11 **Extended Response** Why do you think they plan to charge these amounts?

At the end of the game, they sold all 125 hot dogs and 78 cans of soda.

12 How much money did they collect?

13 After cleaning up and returning the unsold soda, what was their profit?

14 **Extended Response** Do you think they should have bought more hot dogs? Charged more for the hot dogs? Why or why not?

15 **Extended Response** Do you think they charged the right amount for the soda? Could they have made more money by charging less? Why or why not?

Exploring Problem Solving

"Welcome to *Oldies but Goodies,* the show that turns the tables on time. Today we travel to Chaco Canyon, New Mexico, where 700 years ago a tribe called the Anasazi mysteriously disappeared. An advanced knowledge of astronomy can be seen in the structures the Anasazi left behind."

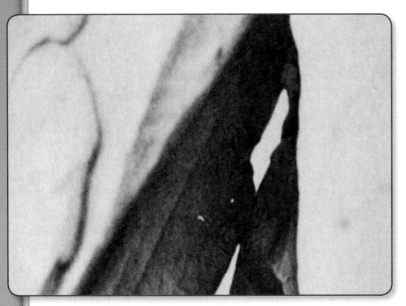

"One such structure is on Fajada Butte, which rises 135 meters above the valley floor. From this rocky pillar you can see far and wide; it's a perfect spot for observing the sun, moon, and stars."

"At certain times of the day, the sun shines through these giant stone slabs, casting daggers of light on the cliff behind them. The Anasazi may have used this observatory to predict the beginning of each season."

e Textbook This lesson is available in the *eTextbook.*

> "Behind the leaning slabs of stone, two spirals are carved in the rock face. The larger spiral has $9\frac{1}{2}$ turns in the shape of an ellipse that measures 34 centimeters by 41 centimeters."

> "On June 21, the first day of summer, a single dagger of sunlight pierces the center of the carved spiral. With each passing day, the light spear moves farther and farther to the right of center. On December 21, the first day of winter, two light daggers touch the outer edges of the carving."

Summer Solstice

Winter Solstice

Solve these problems.

1. What is the shape and size of the larger of the two spirals carved onto the cliff?

2. About how far is it between two consecutive loops on the large spiral? How did you estimate?

3. Estimate a different way by drawing a scale diagram.

4. Did your two estimates match?

Imagine you are part of an archaeological team studying the sun dagger site. You are analyzing this sequence of photos from the site.

(a) 11:10:45 A.M.

(b) 11:13:00 A.M.

(c) 11:16:45 A.M.

(d) 11:20:45 A.M.

Solve these problems.

⑤ On what date were these photos taken? How do you know?

⑥ At what average speed did the top of the dagger move from the time of photo b to the time of photo d?

⑦ At what speed did it move from the time of photo c to the time of photo d?

⑧ Four days before the first day of summer, the light dagger is 0.2 cm from the center of the spiral. Would that difference be noticeable?

⑨ Could you use the information from Problem 8 to predict how long it would be until the first day of summer?

ⓔ Textbook This lesson is available in the *eTextbook*.

Cumulative Review

Subtracting Multidigit Numbers **Lesson 1.8**

Subtract.

1
```
  632417
−  28691
```
■

3
```
  75213
− 69789
```
■

2
```
  3998743
−  216043
```
■

4
```
  12035
−  9648
```
■

· ·

Multiplying by Two Whole Numbers **Lesson 2.3**

Multiply.

5
```
  654
× 74
```
■

7
```
  9876
× 789
```
■

6
```
  781
× 44
```
■

8
```
  7342
× 89
```
■

· ·

Dividing by a One-Digit Divisor **Lesson 2.7**

Find the missing digit.

9 20■ ÷ 4 = 51

12 350 ÷ 4 = ■7 R2

10 2,■17 ÷ 5 = 563 R2

13 65 ÷ 9 = 7 R■

11 440 ÷ ■ = 88

14 160 ÷ ■ = 40

Prime and Composite Numbers Lesson 2.9
Find the prime number.

15 Which of the following numbers is prime?

Ⓐ 49   Ⓑ 399   Ⓒ 29   Ⓓ 99

16 Which of the following numbers is not prime?

Ⓐ 91   Ⓑ 79   Ⓒ 89   Ⓓ 107

Factor.

17 120   18 105

....

Comparing and Ordering Decimals Lesson 3.3
Write <, >, or = in place of ▨ to make a true statement.

19 5.43 ▨ 5.34   20 4.23 ▨ 4.023   21 4.09 ▨ 4.12

22 1.9 ▨ 1.89   23 9.34 ▨ 9.340   24 6.010 ▨ 6.1001

....

Applying Addition, Subtraction, and Multiplication Lessons 1.9 and 2.4

Driving Distances		
From	To	Miles
home	store	5
home	gym	7
home	work	25
gym	store	10
gym	work	20
store	work	22

How many miles does Alex drive if he goes from

25 home to gym to work to home?

26 home to work to store to home?

27 home to gym to work to store to home?

28 home to work and back 5 times in a week?

29 work to the gym then home 3 times in a week?

30 If Alex pays $2 for a gallon of gas and buys 13 gallons how much did he spend altogether?

CHAPTER 3

Key Ideas Review

In this chapter you reviewed decimals as numbers and how to compute decimals.

You learned how decimal numbers are based on powers of ten.

You learned how to compute with decimal numbers.

Solve for *n*.

1 $32.04 + n = 48.54$

2 $12.025 - 3 = n$

3 $7.95 \times 4 = n$

4 $9.27 \div 6 = n$

Fill the ▨ with an appropriate metric unit.

kilometers	meters

5 Cory ran 100 ▨ in 20.2 seconds.

6 Cory's mom drove 100 ▨ in 3.5 hours.

Solve.

7 When converting within the metric system, we multiply and divide by powers of ten. What operation is being used when a decimal point moves one place value to the right?

8 What does it mean to round a number? Why do we round numbers?

9 Why is it important to align decimal points when adding or subtracting decimal numbers?

10 How does knowing that 36 divided by 4 equals 9 help to find the quotient to 3,600 ÷ 400?

Chapter Review

Lesson 3.1 **Add** or subtract.

① $\begin{array}{r} \$35.37 \\ +\ 1.99 \\ \hline \end{array}$ **③** $\begin{array}{r} 21.67 \\ -\ 19.98 \\ \hline \end{array}$

② $\begin{array}{r} \$30.02 \\ -\ 17.11 \\ \hline \end{array}$ **④** $\begin{array}{r} 14.79 \\ 3.57 \\ +\ 1.98 \\ \hline \end{array}$

Lesson 3.2 **Order** these numbers from least to greatest.

⑤   0.5, 0.566, 0.56

⑥   5.2, 4.99, 5.01

Lesson 3.6 **Multiply** or divide. Watch the signs.

⑦ $199.77 \div 1{,}000 =$ **⑩** $1{,}000 \times 0.04 =$

⑧ $0.8 \div 10 =$ **⑪** $8.58 \times 1{,}000 =$

⑨ $100 \times 3.45 =$ **⑫** $0.0678 \div 100 =$

Lesson 3.7 **Find** the missing measure.

⑬ $0.005\ \text{L} =$ mL   **⑯** $5{,}500\ \text{g} =$ kg

⑭ $200\ \text{mL} =$ L   **⑰** $52.34\ \text{cm} =$ mm

⑮ $6.34\ \text{km} =$ m   **⑱** $26\ \text{m} =$ cm

Lesson 3.9 **Solve.**

⑲   Luz bought 2 hand weights for $9.98 each. She must pay $1.25 in tax. What is the total cost of the 2 weights?

⑳   Timmy bought 7 pears that cost 28¢ each. If he gives the clerk a $5 bill, how much change should he get?

Lesson 3.12 Divide.

(21) $8\overline{)18}$ (24) $6\overline{)1083}$

(22) $5\overline{)17}$ (25) $4\overline{)25}$

(23) $9\overline{)8.19}$ (26) $8\overline{)21}$

Lesson 3.13 Divide.

Round quotients with remainders to the nearest tenth.

(27) $9\overline{)56.4}$ (29) $8\overline{)4804}$

(28) $7\overline{)81.33}$ (30) $3\overline{)5.26}$

Lesson 3.14 Multiply or divide.

(31) $9{,}876 \times 100 = $ ▪   (33) $362.18 \times 10{,}000 = $ ▪

(32) $0.24 \times 1{,}000 = $ ▪   (34) $6{,}789 \div 100 = $ ▪

Lesson 3.15 Solve.

(35) Chin bought books at the fair. One book was $3.99, two were $4.59 each, and three were $4.79 each. How much did the books cost altogether?

(36) Which is the better buy, 5 pounds of flour for $2.59 or 2 pounds for $1.10?

Practice Test

Replace ▧ with <, >, or =.

1. $42.30 ▧ $42.03

2. 0.478 ▧ 0.48

3. $802.00 ▧ $802

4. 31.14 ▧ 31.104

Find the answer.

5. 3.15
   × 502
   ▧

6. 740.28
   + 32.62
   ▧

   ▧
7. 9)877.5

8. 4210
   × 0.8
   ▧

9. 42.09
   − 7.99
   ▧

Find the missing measure.

10. 5,050 mg = ▧ g

11. 2.5 kL = ▧ L

Solve.

12. About 34,500 people can fit into the baseball stadium. If 32,598 people are at the game, how many seats are empty?

Choose the correct answer.

13. Which measure makes the most sense to complete this statement? The table is ▢ long.

    Ⓐ 150 km   Ⓑ 15 cm

    Ⓒ 1.5 m   Ⓓ 0.5 dm

14. Karen spent $12.50 on 5 candles. How much did each candle cost?

    Ⓐ $2.08   Ⓑ $2.50

    Ⓒ $3.13   Ⓓ $4.17

15. Which is 612.068 rounded to the nearest tenth?

    Ⓐ 610   Ⓑ 612.0

    Ⓒ 612.06   Ⓓ 612.1

16. Which has the numbers in order from least to greatest?

    Ⓐ 1.11, 1.01, 1.111, 1.001

    Ⓑ 1.01, 1.111, 1.001, 1.11

    Ⓒ 1.001, 1.01, 1.111, 1.11

    Ⓓ 1.001, 1.01, 1.11, 1.111

17. Dante has saved $216.68. He deposits $15.75 every week. How much money does he have in his savings account after 2 weeks of deposits?

    Ⓐ $248.18   Ⓑ $232.43

    Ⓒ $200.93   Ⓓ $185.18

18. It takes Betsy about 3.2 seconds to walk from her desk to the copy machine at work. If she goes to the copy machine 100 times in one day, how many seconds does she spend walking to the copy machine?

    Ⓐ 3.2   Ⓑ 32

    Ⓒ 320   Ⓓ 3,200

19. Divide.

$$4\overline{)5.4}$$

    Ⓐ 1.3   Ⓑ 1.35

    Ⓒ 1.4   Ⓓ 1.45

20. In a game where players try to make the greatest sum, Galen made the sum of 152.15. Isaac made the sum of 138.2. How much greater was Galen's sum?

(A) 26.15   (B) 24.95

(C) 13.95   (D) 13.33

21.   9.99
       $\times$ 26

(A) 259.74   (B) 2,597.4

(C) 25,974   (D) 259,740

22. Which is the following amount written in dollars and cents?

(A) $2.04   (B) $2.14

(C) $2.24   (D) $2.54

23.   384
       $\times$ 78

(A) 29,952   (B) 24,122

(C) 5,760   (D) 3,072

24. Which of the following is a prime number?

(A) 4   (B) 3

(C) 9   (D) 27

25. Which number is the greatest?

(A) 55,500   (B) 55,005

(C) 55,505   (D) 55,055

26. Divide.

$$7\overline{)828}$$

(A) 118 R2   (B) 118

(C) 108 R2   (D) 104

27. Solve for n.

$$(25 - 13) \times 4 = n$$

(A) $n = 8$ (B) $n = 27$

(C) $n = 36$ (D) $n = 48$

28. $5^3 = $ ▮

(A) 15   (B) 25

(C) 125   (D) 625

Use the following information to answer Problem 29. Show your work.

29. The Fun Center Amusement Park charges $12.95 for an adult ticket and $7.95 for children under age 12.

   a. How much would a family of 4 spend on tickets if 2 are adults, one child is 10, and the other child is 15?

   b. Each summer about 10,000 people go to the Fun Center. What is the maximum amount of money spent on tickets for 10,000 people?

   c. A group of 20 or more people receives a discount on ticket prices. If 20 children under age 12 pay $130 total, what is the price for one ticket?

30. At the same amusement park, vendors sell club sandwiches and smoothies to the customers. If every person buys a smoothie for $0.75 and a club sandwich for $1.50, how much money is spent if 896 people go to the park in one week?

Function Rules

In This Chapter You Will Learn

- how your calculator works.
- how to operate a function machine.
- how to add, subtract, multiply, and divide integers.

Problem Solving

On January 4, 2004, a remote-controlled robot named Spirit landed on Mars, ready to explore the rocky surface with an array of mechanical tools and electronic eyes and ears.

Imagine you are in the command center on Earth, sending signals 200 million miles through space to control a rover on Mars. But the vehicle has malfunctioned and can no longer move on its own. And worse yet, it can only process two motion commands: *Go forward 50 meters* and *Go backward 30 meters*.

Straight ahead of the rover, 260 meters away, is a light-toned rock that you need to analyze. Your mission is to maneuver the rover to this rock.

Solve the following problems.

1 How can you command the rover to accomplish the mission?

2 What is the fewest number of commands you can give to accomplish the mission? Explain.

Using Your Calculator

Key Ideas

Calculators may produce different responses because of how they are programmed.

To use your calculator correctly, you need to understand how it works. You also need to know how to tell it what to do and how to interpret the results within the original context.

Use your calculator to answer the following questions.

1. Where does your calculator get the energy it needs to run?

2. How can you get an error message on your calculator?

3. Suppose you are adding 589, 793, and 864. You enter 589 + 793, but instead of 864, you see that you have entered 886. What is the quickest way to correct your mistake and find the correct answer?

4. What is the least number greater than 0 that your calculator can display?

5. What is the greatest number that your calculator can display?

6. If your calculator has a key marked y^x, what does that key do?

7. How can you store a number in your calculator's memory? How can you delete a number from the memory?

8. **Extended Response** A theater group sells 315 tickets to the Friday night performance and 287 tickets to the Saturday performance. Tickets cost $15 each. How much money did the group collect? How would you solve this problem using your calculator? Explain your answer.

 Textbook This lesson is available in the *eTextbook*.

Race the Calculator

Complete the following exercises as a race between a group of your classmates with calculators and a group without them to see which is quicker. Those using the calculator must push every key.

9 $10 \times 73 = n$

10 $100 \times 73 = n$

11 $1{,}000 \times 73 = n$

12 $10{,}000 \times 73 = n$

13 $100{,}000 \times 73 = n$

14 $10 + 73 = n$

15 $100 + 73 = n$

16 $1{,}000 + 73 = n$

17 $10{,}000 + 73 = n$

18 $100{,}000 + 73 = n$

19 $800 + 500 = n$

20 $800 - 500 = n$

21 $8 \times 5 = n$

22 $7{,}568 \times 0 = n$

23 $84{,}595 \times 0 = n$

24 $730 \div 10 = n$

25 $7{,}300 \div 100 = n$

26 $73{,}000 \div 1{,}000 = n$

Different calculators can give different values for an expression, such as $2 + 3 \times 4$. Some are programmed to do operations in the order in which they are presented: $2 + 3 = 5$ and $5 \times 4 = 20$. Other calculators are programmed to do multiplication and division before addition and subtraction, so they find $3 \times 4 = 12$ and then add 2 to get 14.

Evaluate the following expressions using each of these rules:

A. Perform the operations in order from left to right.

B. Do multiplications and divisions first, then additions and subtractions.

C. Do additions and subtractions first, then multiplications and divisions.

27 $7 + 8 - 3 = $ ▨

28 $2 \times 3 \times 4 = $ ▨

29 $24 - 4 \div 4 = $ ▨

30 $24 \div 4 - 4 = $ ▨

31 $3 + 3 \times 3 = $ ▨

32 $1 + 1 \times 1 = $ ▨

Journal

Discuss how the use of parentheses in the above exercises can be used to clarify which answer you want.

LESSON 4.2

Using Number Patterns to Predict

Key Ideas

Most calculators have a **constant** function. Some will repeat the last operation if you just keep pressing "=."

- For example, if you press `C·CE` , `+` , `5` , `=` `=` `=` , the display will show 5, then 10, then 15 .

- Other calculators require you to press some other key or to do something else to use the constant function.

Figure out how to use the constant function on your calculator. The following instructions assume your calculator's constant function involves the use of "=."

Answer each of the following questions.

1 Turn on your calculator. Press `C·CE` , then `+` , then `2` , then `=` , and `=` again.

    a. What does the display show?

    b. Press `=` again. What does the display show?

    c. What will the display show if you press `=` again?

    d. Keep pressing `=` . Each time, predict what the display will show before you press it.

2 Start with 100. Now press `−` , `7` , `=` `=` .

    a. What do you get?

    b. Press `=` two times. What do you get each time?

    c. Keep pressing `=` . Before you press it each time, predict the number you will get. Eventually you will get down to the number 2. What happens next?

ⓔ Textbook This lesson is available in the *eTextbook*.

Answer the following questions.

③ **Extended Response** ➤ **a.** If you start at 0 and add 3 each time, will you hit 10 exactly, or will you pass it?

b. How do you know? Explain.

c. Do you have to do the addition to be sure?

d. Which of these numbers will you hit? 12, 15, 16, 30

④ **a.** If you start at 0 and add 2 each time, will you hit 20?

b. How do you know?

c. Do you have to do the addition to be sure?

d. Which of these numbers will you hit? 100; 101; 200; 1,000

⑤ **a.** Suppose you start at 5 and add 2 each time. Will you hit 15?

b. How do you know? Explain.

c. Will you hit 20?

d. How do you know? Explain.

⑥ **a.** If you start at 24 and subtract 3 each time, will you hit 0?

b. How do you know?

c. Do you have to do the subtraction to be sure?

Read the table below and predict which numbers you will hit.

If you start at this number	and you keep doing this	will you hit these numbers?		
⑦ 0	add 4	a. 20	b. 100	c. 105
⑧ 0	add 3	a. 90	b. 100	c. 1,000
⑨ 8	add 5	a. 58	b. 143	c. 200
⑩ 1,000	subtract 2	a. 0	b. 500	c. 470
⑪ 1,000	subtract 3	a. 0	b. 1	c. 2
⑫ 2,000	subtract 4	a. 1,000	b. 500	c. 10

Repeated Operations: Savings Plans

Key Ideas

Thinking can help you predict the results of repeated operations.

Elena and Kevin use different plans for spending and saving money. Look for patterns as you fill in the tables.

Savings Plan A

Elena earns $4.00 each week. Every week she puts half of the money in her savings account and spends the other half.

Elena made a table to keep a record of her money.

Copy and complete this table on a separate sheet of paper.

1

Week	Amount Earned	Amount to Spend	Amount to Save	Amount in Savings
1	$4.00	$2.00	$2.00	$2.00
2	$4.00	$2.00	$2.00	$4.00
3	$4.00	$2.00	$2.00	$6.00
4	$4.00	$2.00	$2.00	
5	$4.00	$2.00	$2.00	
6	$4.00	$2.00	$2.00	
7				
8				
9				
10				

2 How much money will Elena have saved at the end of 20 weeks?

3 How much money will she have saved at the end of 52 weeks?

Textbook This lesson is available in the *eTextbook*.

Savings Plan B

Kevin also earns $4.00 a week; however, he uses a different savings plan. Every week he adds the $4.00 to the money he already has in his savings. He spends half of the total and leaves the other half in his savings. Whenever the division is not exact, he saves the extra cent.

Kevin made a table to keep a record of his money.

Copy and complete this table on a separate sheet of paper.

4

Week	Amount at Beginning of Week	Amount Earned	Amount Before Spending	Amount to Spend	Amount Left in Savings
1	$0.00	$4.00	$4.00	$2.00	$2.00
2	$2.00	$4.00	$6.00	$3.00	$3.00
3	$3.00	$4.00	$7.00	$3.50	$3.50
4	$3.50	$4.00	$7.50	$3.75	▨
5	$3.75	$4.00	$7.75	$3.87	▨
6	$3.88	$4.00	$7.88	$3.94	▨
7	$3.94	$4.00	$7.94	$3.97	▨
8	$3.97	$4.00	$7.97	$3.98	▨
9	▨	$4.00	▨	▨	▨
10	▨	$4.00	▨	▨	▨

5 How much money will Kevin have saved at the end of 20 weeks?

6 How much money will Kevin have saved at the end of 52 weeks?

7 Suppose Kevin spent the extra cent when the division was not exact. Create a new table that shows what his record would look like for the first 10 weeks.

8 **Extended Response** Think about Elena's and Kevin's savings plans, and answer the following questions.

  a. How different are Kevin's original table and the second table you made? Explain.

  b. If Elena and Kevin were to compete to see who could save the most money during a year, who would win? Explain your answer.

Function Machines

Key Ideas

You can put numbers into a **function machine** and get out other numbers, according to an arithmetic rule.

in → +8 → out

The rule for this function machine is +8. This machine adds 8 to every number you put in. If you put in 10, what will come out?

Here are some ways we can write that, using an arrow.

10 ———(+8)——→ 18   18 ←——(+8)——— 10

The arrow can go in any direction, but it should always point from the number that goes in to the number that comes out.

These tables show some numbers that went into a +8 machine. In each case, write the number that came out.

1

x → +8 → y

In	Out
10	18
2	
5	

2

x → +8 → y

In	Out
0	
100	
1,000	

e Textbook This lesson is available in the *eTextbook*.

Sometimes you can figure out what number went into a function machine if you know what number came out.

On the +8 machine, if 16 comes out, what number went in? (Hint: Think about what number added to 8 gives you 16.) The answer is 8.

We often use *x* to stand for the number going into a function machine and *y* to stand for the number coming out.

These tables show some numbers that went in and came out of a +8 machine. Copy and complete the tables on a sheet of paper. **Algebra**

3 *x* +8 *y*

x	*y*
8	16
▢	9
4	▢
▢	28

4 *x* +8 *y*

x	*y*
22	▢
▢	31
▢	19
5	▢

Find the number that went in (*x*), the number that came out (*y*), or an addition rule that each function machine could be using.

5 *x* +6 13

7 10 ? 100

6 5 +8 *y*

8 *y* +18 5

9 **Extended Response** A sculptor requests an additional 200 pounds of sand to complete his sand sculpture. The next day, he receives 12 buckets, each containing 28 pounds of sand. How can you tell that the sculptor has too much sand without working the problem? Explain.

Exploring Problem Solving

Even though radio signals zoom through space at the speed of light, there is a significant delay when we communicate across our solar system.

Imagine you are controlling a rover on the surface of one of Saturn's moons. At 4:17 P.M., you send a signal that commands the rover to start moving toward its target 38 meters away. At 7:53 P.M., you receive a signal from the craft telling you that it has reached its target. You know it takes 67 minutes for a signal to travel one way between the rover and Earth. You want to know how long the rover took to travel those 38 meters.

Juana decided to solve the problem this way:

I Drew a Diagram and Worked Backward.

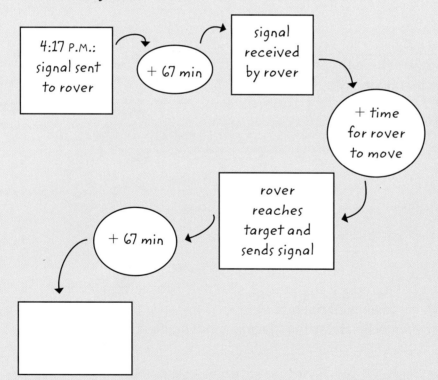

e Textbook This lesson is available in the *eTextbook*.

Think about Juana's strategy. Answer the following questions.

① What do you think Juana will write in the last box?

② What time was it at the command center when the rover received your signal to start moving?

③ How can Juana work backward to find how long it took the rover to move to the target?

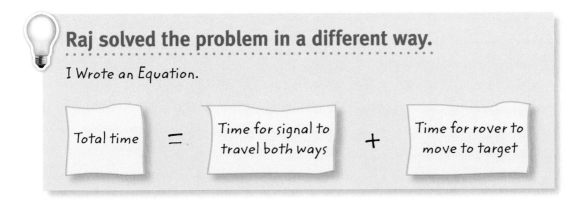

Raj solved the problem in a different way.

I Wrote an Equation.

| Total time | = | Time for signal to travel both ways | + | Time for rover to move to target |

Think about Raj's strategy. Answer the following questions.

④ Does Raj's equation make sense? Why or why not?

⑤ How can Raj figure out the total time?

⑥ How can Raj figure out the time for the signal to travel both ways?

⑦ Finish solving the problem. Use Juana's strategy, Raj's strategy, or a strategy of your own.

⑧ What strategy did you use? Why?

⑨ Was the rover's average speed greater than or less than 0.1 kilometer per hour? Explain.

Cumulative Review

Multiplying Any Two Whole Numbers Lesson 2.3

Multiply.

1 265
$\times$ 3
◻

2 84
$\times$ 35
◻

3 300
$\times$ 52
◻

4 175
$\times$ 25
◻

5 896
$\times$ 7
◻

6 42
$\times$ 53
◻

7 375
$\times$ 120
◻

8 798
$\times$ 114
◻

· ·

Dividing by a One-Digit Divisor Lesson 2.7

Divide.

9 ◻ $7\overline{)56}$

10 ◻ $9\overline{)108}$

11 ◻ $8\overline{)560}$

12 ◻ $8\overline{)384}$

13 ◻ $6\overline{)6565}$

14 ◻ $5\overline{)4500}$

15 ◻ $3\overline{)7024}$

16 ◻ $8\overline{)5496}$

· ·

Prime and Composite Numbers Lesson 2.9

For each of the following numbers, write P if the number is prime. If it is composite, write the number in factored form.

17 41

18 79

19 87

20 209

21 300

22 101

23 195

24 238

Applications Using Customary Measurement Lesson 2.10

Solve.

25 A rectangular table has dimensions of $5\frac{1}{2}$ feet by 18 inches. What is the perimeter?

26 A quart container of water is used to fill a pint bottle and an 8-ounce measuring cup. How much water is left in the container?

27 A fast runner can run a 1-mile race in about 4 minutes. About how long should it take that runner to run a 440-yard race? (Hint: there are 5,280 feet in 1 mile)

  a. 75 seconds

  b. 2 minutes

  c. 55 seconds

  d. 20 seconds

28 How many 10-ounce glasses can a half-gallon bottle of milk fill?

  a. 6

  b. 7

  c. 8

  d. 9

29 What is the area of a rectangular tray that is 1 foot 5 inches long and 6 inches wide?

30 How many ounces are in 3 pounds of steak?

  a. 27

  b. 36

  c. 54

  d. 48

LESSON 4.5

Multiplication Function Rules

Key Ideas

A calculator can be used as a multiplication function machine.

Minuwa's class is doing the Multiplication Rule Activity. Miss Swensen has made the calculator a multiplication function machine. The students are trying to find a multiplication rule. Minuwa asked, "What happens when you put in 5?" Miss Swensen pushed **5** , **=** , and 30 came out.

The calculator is using the rule $\times 6$ because $6 \times 5 = 30$.

Find a multiplication rule in each case.

Miss Swensen pushed: **The display showed:**

1. **3** , **=**   →   18.

2. **1** , **5** , **=**   →   30.

3. **1** , **=**   →   75.

4. **1** , **0** , **0** , **=**   →   1,100.

5. **5** , **=**   →   25.

6. **1** , **7** , **=**   →   51.

7. **2** , **5** , **=**   →   75.

8. **2** , **=**   →   100.

9. **2** , **=**   →   102.

Draw and complete each table on a sheet of paper.

10 $x \to \times 7 \to y$

in	out
5	
9	
8	
6	

11 $x \to \times 8 \to y$

in	out
4	
	80
	56
	72

12 $x \to \times 9 \to y$

in	out
	81
6	
	45
	36

13 $x \to \times 5 \to y$

in	out
4	
	30
	40
10	

14 $x \to \times 3 \to y$

in	out
0	
	9
6	
	27

15 $x \to \bigcirc \to y$

in	out
0	0
3	18
6	36
9	54

The rule is ▢.

16 **Extended Response** Irial put 3 into a function machine, which then produced 12. She said the rule has to be ×4 because 4 × 3 = 12. Paul disagreed and said there is another rule that could result in the machine giving 12 when 3 is put into it. What function could Paul be thinking of? Could Irial and Paul both be correct? How could they find out? Explain.

Finding Function Rules

Key Ideas

Often there is more than one rule that can relate two numbers.

When using a function machine, you can start with 2 and add 6 to get 8, but you can also start with 2 and multiply by 4 to get 8. These machines either add or multiply, and whether they add or multiply does not depend on the number put in. This means you may need to examine more than one pair of numbers to see which rule is correct.

Find an addition or multiplication function rule that works for both pairs of numbers.

1
10 → ? → 30

20 → ? → 40

2
10 → ? → 30

20 → ? → 60

3
0 → ? → 0

7 → ? → 56

4
0 → ? → 0

7 → ? → 7

Find the addition or multiplication rule the calculator is using.

5
2 , = ⟶ 10.
1 , = ⟶ 5.

6
1 , 0 , = ⟶ 30.
2 , 0 , = ⟶ 40.

7
1 , 0 , = ⟶ 37.
0 , = ⟶ 27.

8 **Extended Response** For which of Problems 5–7 could you have determined the function rule from only one of the pairs of numbers given? Why?

ⓔ Textbook This lesson is available in the *eTextbook*.

Function Rules Strategies and Practice

Find the Function Rule

Players: Two or more

Materials: One calculator

Object: To find the function rule put into the calculator

Math Focus: Mental arithmetic, finding simple function rules, and mathematical reasoning

HOW TO PLAY

❶ The lead player chooses an addition or multiplication rule and makes the calculator a function machine that uses this rule.

❷ The second player puts a number into the calculator to see what comes out.

❸ The second player tries to figure out the function rule. If the player does not get it, he or she tries again. The player puts in another number, sees what comes out, and tries again to figure out the rule.

❹ After the second player has found the rule, he or she becomes the lead player.

SAMPLE GAME

Luis was the first player. He entered the function rule ×4.

He pushed **4** , **×** , **4** , **=** , **0** , **=** .

Ellen took the calculator. She pushed **1** , **=** and read the display,

which showed 4.

Ellen thought: "1 ——(?)—→ 4." Ellen said that the rule was +3.

Luis said that was not the correct rule, so Ellen tried again.

She pushed **1** , **0** , **=** and the display read 40.

| 40. |

. Ellen figured out that the function rule was ×4.

It was now Ellen's turn to be lead player.

Subtraction Rules and Negative Numbers

Key Ideas

Sometimes subtraction results in a number that is negative, that is, less than 0.

Minuwa's class is doing the Subtraction Rule Activity. Miss Swensen has made the calculator into a subtraction function machine. The students are trying to find a subtraction rule. Minuwa asked, "What happens if you put in 21?" Miss Swensen pushed **2**, **1**, **=**, and 17 came out.

The calculator is using the rule −4 because 21 − 4 = 17.

Find the subtraction rule in each case.

Miss Swenson pushed:		The display showed:
❶ **3**, **7**, **=**	→	31.
❷ **1**, **2**, **=**	→	0.
❸ **1**, **0**, **7**, **=**	→	50.
❹ **5**, **8**, **=**	→	57.
❺ **4**, **9**, **=**	→	28.
❻ **2**, **4**, **=**	→	3.
❼ **1**, **0**, **=**	→	2.
❽ **1**, **0**, **=**	→	1.
❾ **1**, **0**, **=**	→	0.
❿ **1**, **0**, **=**	→	−1.

Brian and Armando were doing the Subtraction Rule Activity. Brian was the lead player. He chose the rule −70. He entered this by pushing

Armando took the calculator, pushed 5 , 0 , = , and the

display showed ‎ −20. ‎ "What does that mean?" he asked,

pointing to the display.

"That's a negative 20," said Brian. "When you entered 50, the machine subtracted 70 from 50. Negative 20 is the answer it gave. That's 20 less than 0."

"But you can't take 70 away from 50," said Armando. "If I have 50 books, how can someone take 70 of them away?"

In some situations, like Armando's example, you cannot subtract 70 from 50.

As you use your calculator, you may see a negative number on the display. Negative numbers are less than zero. Sometimes it is realistic to have a negative number as an answer to a problem, but sometimes it is not realistic. It depends on the situation.

If the temperature is 15°C and it goes down 20°, what will the temperature be?

This is the way we write this problem: $15 - 20 = -5$

This is read "negative 5" or "5 below zero."

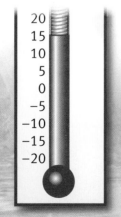

15°C   Goes Down   5° Below 0°C
         20°   (or −5°C)

Copy and complete the following tables on a sheet of paper.

⑪

Temperature Before Change	Temperature Change	Temperature After Change
10°C	up 5°	
−5°C (5° below 0°C)	down 10°	
−15°C (15° below 0°C)	up 15°	
5°C	down 10°	

Ahmed is scuba diving 20 feet below sea level. He goes down another 15 feet. He is now swimming 35 feet below sea level.

This is how we write this problem:

$(-20) - 15 = -35$

⑫

Ahmed's Depth	Movement	Ahmed's New Depth
−20 feet	down 5 feet	
−10 feet	up 5 feet	
−15 feet	down 10 feet	
−25 feet	up 20 feet	

ⓔ Textbook This lesson is available in the *eTextbook.*

Add or subtract. Do not use a calculator. Watch for negative numbers.

⑬ 50 + 10 = ▨

⑭ (−25) + 25 = ▨

⑮ 0 − 15 = ▨

⑯ 15 + 15 = ▨

⑰ 60 − 50 = ▨

⑱ 0 + 10 = ▨

⑲ (−3) + 4 = ▨

⑳ (−6) + 5 = ▨

㉑ 10 + 5 = ▨

㉒ 0 − 10 = ▨

㉓ (−2) + 1 = ▨

㉔ 9 − 12 = ▨

㉕ 15 − 20 = ▨

㉖ 2 − 4 = ▨

㉗ 4 − 6 = ▨

Here is how to work with negative numbers on your calculator: Use the key to enter negative numbers.

If your calculator does not have a key like this, try using the

▨ key to enter negative numbers like this: start with 0 and

then subtract whichever number you want to be negative.

For example, if you want −20, key , , ,

▨ , ▨ .

Add or subtract. Watch for negative numbers.

㉘ 10 − 20 = ▨

㉙ (−5) + 10 = ▨

㉚ (−5) − 20 = ▨

㉛ Now use your calculator to do Exercises 28–30 again. See if the calculator gives the correct answers.

㉜ **Extended Response** Mr. Marks had $375 in his checking account. He wrote two checks, one for $250 and the other for $320. Then he deposited $120 in his account. What is his account balance now? Explain.

 **Journal**

Write one word problem, using at least two operations and two negative numbers in the question, the answer, or both. Trade with a classmate and solve each other's problem.

LESSON 4.8 Adding and Subtracting Integers

Key Ideas

Integers are positive and negative whole numbers or zero. You can use a number line to help you add and subtract integers.

- The numbers 1, 2, 3, and so on are sometimes called *positive integers* because they are greater than 0. It is common to write them in the same way you write the whole numbers: 1, 2, 3. They may also be written with a "+" sign: +1, +2, +3.

- *Negative integers* are less than 0 and are shown to the left of 0 on the number line. They may be written as (−1), (−2), (−3), and so on.

- The **absolute value** of an integer is the number's distance from 0 on the number line. It is written, for example, as |−5| = 5, and is read as, "The absolute value of negative 5 is 5." Another example is |5| = 5, which is read as "The absolute value of positive 5 is 5."

Answer the following questions using a number line.

1. If you start at 2 and subtract 3 (move 3 places to the left), where will you be? 2 − 3 = ☐ If you start at −1 and add 3, where will you be? −1 + 3 = ☐

2. If you start at 0 and move left 3 places, and then move left 2 more places, where will you be? You have added negative 3 and negative 2. (−3) + (−2) = ☐

3. You know that subtraction is the inverse of addition; subtraction "undoes" addition. So, if 4 + 5 = 9, then 9 − 5 = 4.
Therefore, if −5 + 2 = −3, what is −3 − (+2)?

4. What is (−5) − (−2); what can you add to −2 to get −5? Would you have gotten the same answer by adding 2 to −5?

5. What is −6 + 9?

174

Textbook This lesson is available in the *eTextbook*.

Complete the following sentences by indicating whether the answer is *positive* or *negative*. These completed sentences may help you when doing arithmetic with integers. Notice the relation of the absolute values in each exercise and answer.

6 If you subtract a positive number from a smaller positive number, the answer is ▢ .

For example, $2 - 10 = -8$. Notice that the distance on the number line from -8 to 2 is 10.

7 If you add a negative number to another negative number, the answer is ▢ .

8 If you subtract a negative number from a negative number with a smaller absolute value, the answer is ▢ .

9 If you subtract a negative number from a negative number with a greater absolute value, the answer is ▢ .

10 If you subtract a negative number from a positive number, the answer is ▢ .

11 If you add a negative number to a positive number with a smaller absolute value, the answer is ▢ .

12 If you add a negative number to a positive number with a greater absolute value, the answer is ▢ .

Complete each exercise.

13 $(-7) + (-8) = $ ▢

14 $(-7) - (-8) = $ ▢

15 $7 + 8 = $ ▢

16 $7 - 8 = $ ▢

17 $|-5| = $ ▢

18 $|-3| - |-5| = $ ▢

19 $|3| - |-5| = $ ▢

20 $|-3| + |-5| = $ ▢

21 $|-3| + |5| = $ ▢

22 $(8) + 0 = $ ▢

23 $(-8) - 0 = $ ▢

24 $0 + 8 = $ ▢

25 $0 - (-8) = $ ▢

26 $(-473) - (-473) = $ ▢

27 $(-473) + (-473) = $ ▢

28 **Extended Response** Ana's family has 9 pairs of shoes that they no longer wear. Her father donated 11 of them to a homeless shelter. How many pairs of shoes do they have left? Explain.

Key Ideas

The product of two numbers with the same signs (both positive or both negative) is positive. If the numbers have different signs, the product is negative. The same is true for division.

For example, if you multiply 10 by 3, you get 30. What happens if you multiply by a negative number? The activity below should answer the question.

When you look at an object through a magnifying glass, the size of the object seems to change, but something else happens. The object seems to be upside down. If you hold a small magnifying glass about a foot from your eye and look at a picture that is five or six feet away, the picture will appear upside down. If the picture seems to be twice as big, the magnifying glass can be said to have multiplied the heights in the picture by −2 (twice as big, but upside down). (See Figure 1).

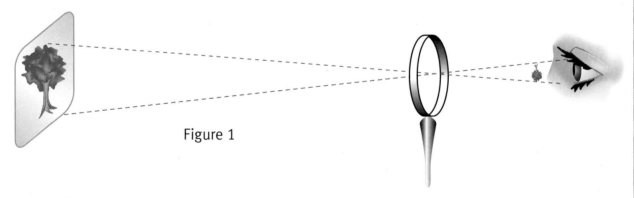

Figure 1

If you hold another magnifying glass about a foot farther from your eye between the first glass and the picture and focus both glasses so you can see the picture, you will discover the picture now seems to be right-side up. (See Figure 2).

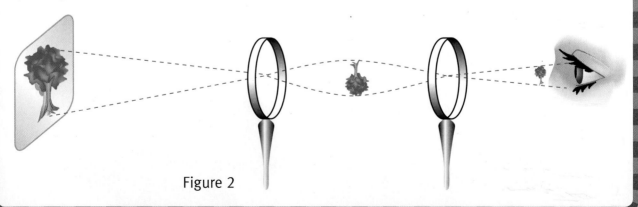

Figure 2

ⓔ **Textbook** This lesson is available in the *eTextbook.*

If we think of one magnifying glass as multiplying by -2 and the other as multiplying by -3, then $(-2) \times (-3) = 6$. So, a negative number times a negative number is a positive number.

Complete the following exercises on your own. Watch the signs.

1. $-7 \times 4 = $ ▢

2. $-7 \times (-4) = $ ▢

3. $4 \times (-7) = $ ▢

4. $8 \div (-2) = $ ▢

5. $-8 \div (-2) = $ ▢

6. $-8 \div 2 = $ ▢

7. $5 + (-12) = $ ▢

8. $-5 + 12 = $ ▢

9. $-17 + (-8) = $ ▢

10. $-17 - 8 = $ ▢

11. $9 \times (-9) = $ ▢

12. $-81 \div 9 = $ ▢

13. In golf, players count the number of strokes they take to get the ball in the hole. "Par" is a number of strokes that seems reasonable to officials. If a player has a score below par, it is a good score. At the end of the third day of a tournament, Tiger Woods had a three-day total of 11 under par (-11). His score on the third day was 3 under par (-3). What was his score at the beginning of the third day?

14. Early one winter morning, the thermometer read $-16°$ F. By late afternoon, the temperature had risen by $12°$. What was the temperature then? What did you have to do to find the answer?

15. Cecilia has a new cell phone plan that allows 60 minutes of free long distance time. She talks on Wednesday for 11 minutes, on Friday for 7 minutes, and on Sunday for 23 minutes. Does she have enough minutes left for a 10-minute phone conversation, or will she exceed her time limit? If she has enough minutes, how many will she have left after the conversation?

16. **Extended Response** A group of friends set up a lemonade stand one hot summer day. They spent $7 on lemonade mix, $3 on paper cups, $4 on a pitcher, and $2 on ice. Over the first weekend, they had sales of $14. Did they make a profit, or did they lose money? Explain.

 **Journal**

Write any rules you learned in this lesson that will help you remember how to multiply and divide integers.

LESSON 4.10 Patterns

Key Ideas

A **pattern** is something that repeats or follows a particular process in an orderly way. You can use what you know about a pattern to help you predict what will come next in a sequence.

Here are some examples of patterns:

2, 5, 8, 11, 14, 17, 20

A rhythm in a song may also follow a pattern in the form of accented and unaccented beats. Are there any patterns in your favorite song?

Describe each pattern in your own words.

1   36   28   20   12   4   −4   −12   −20

2   18   54   162   486   1,458   4,374

3

4

5

178

Replace the ▨ with missing shapes or numbers of the pattern. Then tell what the pattern is.

6

7

8 −19, −14, −9, ▨, ▨, ▨, ▨, 16

9

10 −72, −24, ▨, −2.7, −0.9, ▨, ▨ −0.03

11 Yenfen put the number 5 into a function machine and got 9. Cory took the 9 and put it into a second function machine, and 7 came out. Yenfen put −2 into her function machine and got 2, and when Cory put 2 into his machine, he got 0. What pattern was being used?

12 **Extended Response** Write or draw a sequence that uses a particular pattern. Then find a partner. Describe your pattern but do not let your partner see it; have him or her draw, write, or act out that pattern. Then have your partner describe his or her pattern so you can draw it, write it, or act it out.

 **Journal**

What patterns do you see in your everyday life? How can they help predict what will come next?

Where No Spacecraft Has Gone Before

The space probe *Huygens* made history as it survived its landing on Saturn's largest moon. After a seven-year voyage in space, piggybacked on the *Cassini* spacecraft, the cone-shaped *Huygens* ejected from its mother ship, smashed into Titan's dense atmosphere, and parachuted safely to the surface. Sixty-seven minutes later, its faint signals reached Earth, setting off a long-awaited celebration in mission control.

Artist conception of *Cassini* spacecraft at Saturn

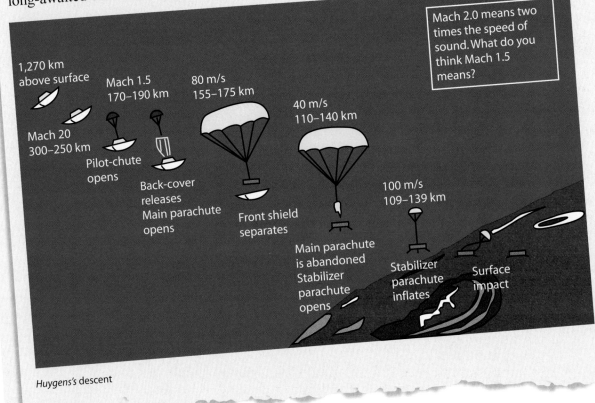

1,270 km above surface

Mach 1.5
170–190 km

80 m/s
155–175 km

Mach 20
300–250 km

Pilot-chute opens

Back-cover releases
Main parachute opens

Front shield separates

40 m/s
110–140 km

Main parachute is abandoned
Stabilizer parachute opens

100 m/s
109–139 km

Stabilizer parachute inflates

Surface impact

Mach 2.0 means two times the speed of sound. What do you think Mach 1.5 means?

Huygens's descent

As it sped through the upper atmosphere of Titan, the *Huygens* craft had to withstand extreme temperatures. When its main parachute opened, the probe had slowed down enough to safely discard its heat shield, enabling its electronic sensors to work.

Each detail of the descent was carefully planned. This timeline shows just a few of the hundreds of steps necessary for a successful landing.

Scheduled Timeline of Events for Huygens's Descent

Time (compared to time of entry)	Event
−20d 07h	*Huygens* probe separates from Orbiter
−07d 00h	Probe relay critical sequence begins
−02h 40m	Set Solid State Recorder pointers for probe recording
−02h 28m	Transition to thruster control for relay
−02h 16m	Turn on probe receivers
−00h 22m	Probe turns transmitters on; Low power mode
00h 00m	Probe reaches entry altitude (1,270 km)
+00h 03m	Pilot chute deployed at 170–190 km altitude
+00h 04m	Probe begins transmission to Orbiter; Release front shield
+00h 19m	Main parachute separation; Deploy stabilizer chute; 110–140 km altitude
+00h 36m	Surface proximity sensor activated at 60 km altitude
+02h 21m	Surface impact; End descent phase

Solve the following problems. Use the information in the timetable and the descent diagram.

1. How long were the probe's transmitters turned on before they began transmitting to the Orbiter?

2. How long after *Huygens* separated from the Orbiter were its receivers turned on?

3. How long had the probe been separated from the Orbiter when it hit the surface of Titan?

4. How long did it take the probe to slow down from $1\frac{1}{2}$ times the speed of sound (about 331 meters per second) to about 80 meters per second?

Exploring Problem Solving

Imagine you are planning a mission that will send a spacecraft past Saturn and beyond Pluto. You have to be sure the probe can withstand the extremely low temperatures since it will be so far from the sun.

Scientists often use a temperature scale that has no numbers below zero. It is called the *Kelvin scale.* Zero Kelvin (0 K) is the coldest temperature imaginable, called *absolute zero.*

You can convert from Celsius to Kelvin simply by adding 273.

For example,

Temperature in degrees Celsius	$100°C \longrightarrow\ + 273 \longrightarrow\ 373\ K$	Temperature in Kelvin

So, 373 Kelvin is the same temperature as 100 degrees Celsius.

The table shows what the temperature of your spacecraft will be at different distances from the sun. You need to predict what will happen even farther out in space.

Distance from Sun (millions of miles)	Temperature (K)
100	300
200	212
400	150
800	106
1,600	

Work in groups. Give your spacecraft a name. Then discuss and solve the following problems.

5. If you add 273 to convert from degrees Celsius to Kelvin, what should you do to convert from Kelvin to degrees Celsius?

6. What will be the temperature of your craft in degrees Celsius when it is 200 million miles from the sun?

7. What will be the temperature of your craft in Kelvin when it is 1,600,000,000 miles from the sun? (Hint: You might look for a pattern.)

8. What is your answer to Problem 7 in degrees Celsius?

Cumulative Review

Adding and Subtracting Decimals Lesson 3.4
Solve.

Lunch Menu		
Sandwich	**Side**	**Drink**
Hamburger $1.99	Fries $.89	Milk $.59
Chicken $2.69	Beans $.79	Lemonade $1.09
Fish $2.99	Cole slaw $.59	Juice $.79

1. Colleen has $5 for lunch. Can she afford to buy chicken, beans, and lemonade?

2. Shenita has $4. She wants fish, fries, and juice. Can she afford those? If not, does Colleen have enough change to loan her?

3. Shenita really wants the fish but can she buy a side and drink too?

4. How much is the cheapest combo of sandwich, side, and drink?

5. How much is the most expensive combo of sandwich, side, and drink?

Comparing and Ordering Decimals Lesson 3.3
Write these numbers in order from least to greatest.

6. 9.16, 9.3, 9.19

7. 3.027, 3.27, 3.0272

8. 3.888, 3.88, 3.088

9. 0.5, 2.1, 0.07

10. 3.23, 3.3, 3.33

Multiplying and Dividing Decimals by Powers of 10 Lesson 3.6
Multiply or divide. Watch the signs.

11. $88.41 \times 1,000 = $ ▢

12. $244.03 \div 100 = $ ▢

13. $357.76 \div 1,000 = $ ▢

14. $0.07 \div 10 = $ ▢

15. $0.7 \div 100 = $ ▢

16. $3,000 \times 0.01 = $ ▢

Order and Parentheses Lesson 1.5

Solve for *n*.

17 $6 \times (5 + 2) = n$

18 $(6 \times 5) + 2 = n$

19 $5 + (8 \times 7) = n$

20 $(9 + 1) \times (5 - 3) = n$

21 $24 \div (4 + 3 + 1) = n$

22 $(2 + 4) \div (13 - 7) = n$

Interpreting Quotients and Remainders Lesson 3.13

Solve.

23 A camp counselor plans to have 2 hot dog buns and 2 hot dogs for each of the 25 campers attending a cookout. If hot dogs come in packages of 10 and buns come in packages of 8, how many packages of hot dogs and buns are needed?

24 Which is the better buy, 8 pounds of dog food for $14.40 or 9 pounds for $15.40?

25 25 students want to divide into 6-person dodgeball teams. How many more students are needed to form an even number of teams?

26 Four boys want to share 14 cookies. How many should each one get?

Repeated Operations: Savings Plans Lesson 4.3

Carlos began the year with $40 and saves $9 each week toward his goal of $500. Lilla began the year with $65 and saves $4 each week toward her goal of $300.

27 About how many months will it take for Carlos to reach his goal?

28 About how many months will it take for Lilla to reach her goal?

29 If Carlos continues saving at the same rate, will he have $900 in 24 months?

30 If Lilla continues saving at the same rate, will she have $500 in 24 months?

Key Ideas Review

In this chapter you learned about the patterns created by computing numbers with function machines.

You learned how to repeat mathematical operations to predict outcomes. You learned how to compute with integers.

Use the calendar to answer the questions.

Shane's mom labels his calendar so he knows what is taking place each day.

☼ = Shane has a football game.

■ = Shane helps with dinner.

▲ = Shane cleans his room.

SUN	MON	TUE	WED	THU	FRI	SAT
	1 ■	2	3 ■	4 ▲	5 ■	6 ☼
7 ■	8 ▲	9 ■	10	11 ■	12 ▲	13 ■ ☼
14	15 ■	16 ▲	17 ■	18	19 ■	20 ☼ ▲

Describe a pattern for the following symbols.

1 ☼

2 ■

3 ▲

4 If this month has 31 days, what symbol will appear on the 28th day?

5 Which event occurs most frequently throughout the month?

Solve the following problems.

6 Using the constant function on a calculator, start with −3 and add 2. At what point will you reach the first multiple of 3?

7 Takara entered 3 + 6 × 4 on a calculator and got an answer of 27. How is this possible?

8 Explain how to multiply and divide integers.

Chapter Review

CHAPTER 4

Lesson 4.2

If you start at this number	and you keep doing this	will you hit these numbers?
① 5	add 2	**a.** 100 **b.** 105 **c.** 150
② 3	add 3	**a.** 10 **b.** 45 **c.** 75
③ 1,000	subtract 4	**a.** 500 **b.** 100 **c.** 10

Lesson 4.3 ④ Maddie is saving her allowance to buy a jacket that costs $60. She normally receives $3 per week, but if she does additional chores she can earn an extra $2 per week. How much sooner can she purchase the jacket if she does extra chores every week? Explain.

⑤ Maddie decides to do the extra chores each week, but wants to spend $1 per week on snacks. How long will it be before she will have enough to buy the jacket?

Lessons 4.4 In each problem find the number that went in (x), the number that came out (y), or an addition rule that the function machine could be using.

⑥ 7 ⟶ (+11) ⟶ y

⑦ x ⟶ (+9) ⟶ 13

⑧ 5 ⟶ (?) ⟶ 17

⑨ 5 ⟶ (+7) ⟶ y

⑩ 11 ⟶ (+12) ⟶ y

⑪ 5 ⟶ (+14) ⟶ y

e Textbook This lesson is available in the *eTextbook.*

Lessons 4.5–4.6 **Find** a function rule that works for both pairs of numbers for each function.

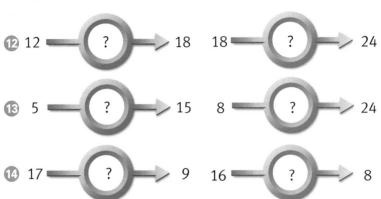

12 12 ⟶ ? ⟶ 18 18 ⟶ ? ⟶ 24

13 5 ⟶ ? ⟶ 15 8 ⟶ ? ⟶ 24

14 17 ⟶ ? ⟶ 9 16 ⟶ ? ⟶ 8

Lessons 4.7–4.9 **Solve.**

15 $10 - 15 =$

16 $-8 \times 9 =$

17 $|7| - |-9| =$

18 $-8 + 8 =$

19 $6 - (-7) =$

20 $-7 \times (-5) =$

21 $-10 \div 5 =$

22 $-10 \div |-5| =$

23 $-56 \div -8 =$

24 Alexis received $50 for her birthday. She bought 3 pairs of socks for $3 each and 1 hat. She had $21 left. How much did the hat cost?

25 If the temperature is −9° C and goes up 5°, what will the new temperature be?

26 If the temperature is −6° C and goes up 10°, what will the new temperature be?

Lesson 4.10 **Find** the pattern and fill in the missing numbers.

27 5, 8, 11, ▢, 17, 20, ▢, ▢, 29

28 20, ▢, 8, 2, ▢, −10, ▢, −22, −28

Practice Test

Find the unknown for each problem. It may be the number that went in (*x*), the number that came out (*y*), or the addition rule that the function machine is using.

1.

$8 \longrightarrow (+5) \longrightarrow y$

2.

$x \longrightarrow (+9) \longrightarrow 21$

3.

$7 \longrightarrow (\blacksquare) \longrightarrow 17$

4.

$22 \longrightarrow (+6) \longrightarrow y$

Complete each table using the given function rule.

5.

$x \longrightarrow (\times 7) \longrightarrow y$

x	*y*
2	■
4	■
6	■
8	■

6.

$x \longrightarrow (\times 5) \longrightarrow y$

x	*y*
■	5
■	30
8	■
■	100

7.

$x \longrightarrow (\times 9) \longrightarrow y$

x	*y*
2	■
■	36
9	■
■	99

Solve.

8. $3 - 7 = \blacksquare$

9. $(-4) + 6 = \blacksquare$

10. $-3 \times -4 = \blacksquare$

11. $12 \div -4 = \blacksquare$

Choose the correct answer.

12. If you start at 0 and keep adding 7 on a calculator, which number will you reach?

    (A) 12   (B) 22

    (C) 32   (D) 42

13. Becca earns $4.00 a week. Each week she saves $1.50. How much will she have saved after 5 weeks?

    (A) $7.50   (B) $5.50

    (C) $3.50   (D) $1.50

14. The temperature at noon is 12°F. The temperature at midnight is −2°F. By how many degrees did the temperature fall?

    (A) 10°   (B) 12°

    (C) 14°   (D) 16°

15. Which function rule works for both pairs of numbers?

    (A) ×2   (B) ×3

    (C) +10   (D) +15

16. What is the next number in the following pattern?

    $-10, -6, -2$

    (A) −1   (B) 2

    (C) 4   (D) 6

17. The rule for a function machine is −8. If 2 comes out of the function machine, which number went in?

    (A) −6   (B) 6

    (C) 10   (D) 16

18. If you start at 100 and keep subtracting 3 on a calculator, which number will you hit?

    (A) 90   (B) 80

    (C) 70   (D) 60

19. Solve for n.
    $7 - (-5) = n$

    (A) $n = 12$ (B) $n = 2$

    (C) $n = -2$ (D) $n = -12$

20. The rule for a function machine is +5. If 2 went into the function machine, what number will come out?

    (A) 7   (B) 8

    (C) 9   (D) 10

Choose the correct answer.

21. Solve for *n*.
$6 \times (-3) = n$

Ⓐ $n = -24$ Ⓑ $n = -18$
Ⓒ $n = -2$ Ⓓ $n = 18$

22. Miguel pushed 〔 **5** 〕, 〔 **=** 〕 on his calculator, and the display showed 35. What is the multiplication rule for this function?

Ⓐ ×10   Ⓑ ×9
Ⓒ ×8   Ⓓ ×7

23. About 2,100 students take the bus to school. Only 410 students walk. How many more students take the bus than walk to school?

Ⓐ 2,510   Ⓑ 2,390
Ⓒ 1,690   Ⓓ 1,600

24. Greta is 128.15 centimeters tall. Her brother Nate is 124.2 centimeters tall. How much taller is Greta than her brother?

Ⓐ 4.15 cm   Ⓑ 3.95 cm
Ⓒ 15.73 cm   Ⓓ 23.95 cm

25. Which number is the greatest?

Ⓐ 800,500   Ⓑ 808,005
Ⓒ 880,500   Ⓓ 808,055

26. Ricky spent $20.50 on 5 books. How much did each book cost if they cost the same amount?

Ⓐ $4.01   Ⓑ $4.10
Ⓒ $5.10   Ⓓ $5.13

27. Write the number 3,002,202 in expanded form.

Ⓐ 3,000,000 + 2,000 + 200 + 2

Ⓑ 3,000,000 + 20,000 + 200 + 2

Ⓒ 300,000 + 2,000 + 200 + 2

Ⓓ 300,000 + 20,000 + 200 + 2

28. Which of the following sets of numbers is in order from least to greatest?

Ⓐ 2.52, 2.05, 2.205, 2.002

Ⓑ 2.05, 2.205, 2.002, 2.52

Ⓒ 2.002, 2.05, 2.52, 2.205

Ⓓ 2.002, 2.05, 2.205, 2.52

Solve.

29. **Extended Response** Rachel drew the following pattern:

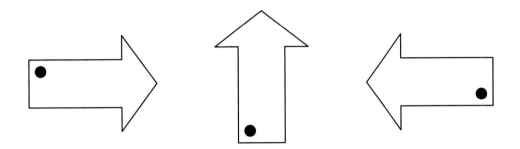

    a. Describe the next two shapes in the pattern.

    b. Describe the pattern in your own words.

30. **Extended Response** Find an addition or multiplication function rule that works for both pairs of numbers in each problem.

    a.

        1 ⟶ ▢ ⟶ 10   10 ⟶ ▢ ⟶ 100

    b.

        0 ⟶ ▢ ⟶ 25   10 ⟶ ▢ ⟶ 35

    c.

        4 ⟶ ▢ ⟶ 16   8 ⟶ ▢ ⟶ 20

    d. For which pair could you have determined the function rule by looking at only the first pair of numbers given? Why?

Graphing Functions

In This Chapter You Will Learn

- how to graph in one or four quadrants.
- how to get an ordered pair from a function and then graph the ordered pair.
- how to evaluate linear functions in standard notation.

Problem Solving

The National Museum of African Art is in this bird's eye illustration between the Washington Monument and the United States Capitol building.

SOCIAL STUDIES

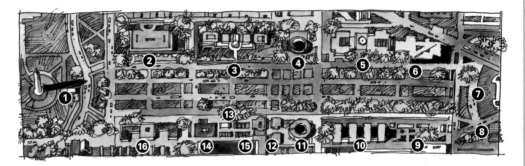

Complete the following questions. Compare the aerial illustration with the map below to help you.

1. The address of the National Museum of African Art is 950 Independence Avenue. Which of the buildings in the illustration could it be?

2. Examine the four addresses on the map. What pattern do you think is used for addresses in this part of Washington, D.C.?

3. According to that system, which of the buildings in the illustration is most likely the National Museum of African Art?

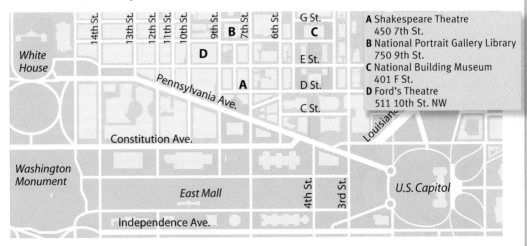

A Shakespeare Theatre
  450 7th St.
B National Portrait Gallery Library
  750 9th St.
C National Building Museum
  401 F St.
D Ford's Theatre
  511 10th St. NW

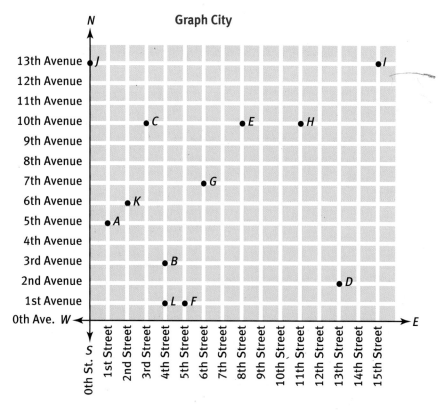

LESSON 5.1 Coordinates

Key Ideas

Coordinates are numbers that tell where a point lies on a graph.

To find a point, such as (4, 6), find the first number (4) on the horizontal axis (goes left to right). Then find the second number (6) on the vertical axis (goes up and down). Point to each number and move your fingers together on the graph until they meet. The place where your fingers meet is (4, 6), which is read "the point four six."

Graph City was planned with numbered streets running east and west and numbered avenues running north and south.

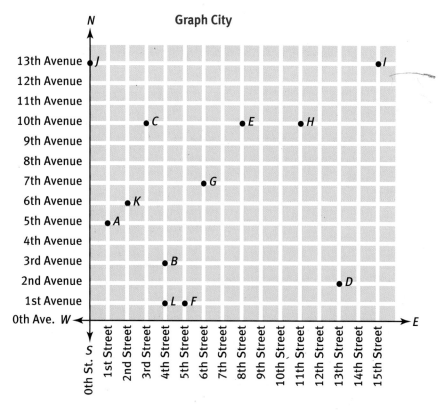

Graph City

Look at the map of Graph City. Answer the following questions.

① The corner of 1st Street and 5th Avenue is at point *A*. Where is point *B*?

② Suppose José asked you to meet him at the corner of 1st and 5th in Graph City. Where would you go?

3 If José was not where you went, where do you think he might be?

4 **Extended Response** How would you find José? Explain your answer.

When describing a location, the people of Graph City have agreed to always give the street name first and the avenue name second. Answer the following questions.

5 Where is the corner of 1st and 5th?

6 Where is the corner of 5th and 1st?

7 How many blocks would you have to walk to get from 1st and 5th to 5th and 1st? (You must walk along streets or avenues.)

8 **Extended Response** Is there more than one way to get from 1st and 5th to 5th and 1st by walking only 8 blocks? See how many ways you can find.

9 Suppose you walk only along streets or avenues, and you do not walk in a wrong direction on purpose.

   a. Do all ways of getting from 1st and 5th to 5th and 1st require walking exactly 8 blocks?

   b. Is there a shorter way?

   c. What must you do to make the path longer?

10 How many blocks would you have to walk to get from 7th and 7th to 7th and 7th?

11 How many blocks would you have to walk to get from 5th and 8th to 9th and 3rd?

   a. In what direction would you walk to get from 5th Street to 9th Street?

   b. In what direction would you walk to get from 8th Avenue to 3rd Avenue?

12 How many blocks would you have to walk to get from 2nd and 3rd to 12th and 4th?

13 How many blocks would you have to walk to get from 15th and 13th to 11th and 6th?

14 Give the location of all the points (A–L) on the map of Graph City. Always give the street name first and the avenue name second.

The people in Graph City say "1st and 5th" as a shorter way to say "the corner of 1st Street and 5th Avenue."

Here is an even shorter way: (1, 5).

You can use this way for the graph on page 197. For example, to tell where point *B* is, you can write (3, 8).

The two numbers that tell the location of a point on a graph are called the coordinates of that point. Because they are given in order, we call them *ordered pairs*. The horizontal coordinate is given first. The vertical coordinate is given second.

The coordinates of point *B* are (3, 8). The coordinates of point *E* are (13, 2).

Answer the following questions using the graph on page 197.

15 What are the coordinates of point *Q*?

16 What are the coordinates of point *U*?

17 What are the coordinates of point *A*?

18 What are the coordinates of point *R*?

19 What are the coordinates of point *K*?

20 What are the coordinates of point *G*?

21 What are the coordinates of point *P*?

22 What are the coordinates of point *N*?

23 What are the coordinates of point *T*?

24 What are the coordinates of point *Z*?

25 What are the coordinates of point *V*?

This lesson is available in the *eTextbook*.

Answer these questions by writing the correct letter for each of the coordinates.

26 What bird can spot a rabbit three kilometers away?
(0, 5); (1, 2); (11, 12); (14, 10); (13, 2); (2, 13)
(13, 2); (6, 6); (0, 5); (11, 12); (13, 2)

27 What is the largest bird alive today?
(1, 2); (3, 10); (0, 12); (10, 7); (7, 10); (5, 13); (1, 11)

28 What bird beats its wings up to 90 times per second?
(1, 11); (12, 11); (8, 3); (8, 3); (7, 10); (2, 13); (0, 5); (3, 8); (7, 10);
(10, 7); (14, 10)

29 Which bird has the most feathers (more than 25,000)?
(3, 10); (5, 2); (6, 6); (2, 13)

30 What bird gets its pink color from the brine shrimp that it eats?
(2, 1); (11, 12); (6, 6); (8, 3); (7, 10); (2, 13); (0, 5); (1, 2)

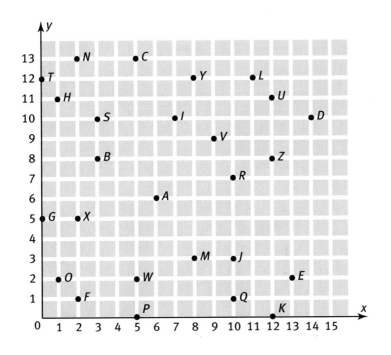

Make up more questions. Share them with a friend.

Functions and Ordered Pairs

Key Ideas

The input and output of a function machine can be thought of as an ~~ordered pair,~~ **which can be graphed.**

Look at the function machine below. In this case, *x* is the input and *y* is the output.

In the function rule, if you put in 2 for *x*, you get 7 for *y* because 2 + 5 = 7. We can think of the pair of numbers (2, 7) as an ordered pair of numbers produced by the function rule *x* ──(+5)──▶ *y*. Notice that we write the *x* first and the *y* second.

Copy each list of ordered pairs, but replace the *x* or *y* with the correct number. The first one is done for you. **Algebra**

① *x* ──(+5)──▶ *y*

    (7, 12); (12, *y*); (15, *y*); (0, *y*); (*x*, 7)

② *x* ──(−9)──▶ *y*

    (11, *y*); (20, *y*); (25, *y*); (*x*, 0); (*x*, 8); (*x*, 9)

③ *x* ──(×0)──▶ *y*

    (7, *y*); (12, *y*); (50, *y*); (2,589, *y*); (*x*, 0)

Draw and complete these function-machine tables on a sheet of paper.

④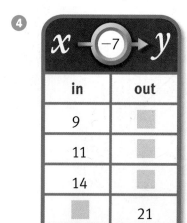

in	out
9	▢
11	▢
14	▢
▢	21

⑤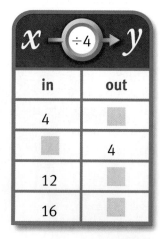

in	out
4	▢
▢	4
12	▢
16	▢

⑥

in	out
▢	▢
▢	▢
▢	▢
▢	▢

ⓔ **Textbook** This lesson is available in the *eTextbook*.

If you use the function rule $x \longrightarrow (+3) \longrightarrow y$, you get an ordered pair of (2, 5) when you substitute 2 for x.

To graph the point for that pair, you would move right 2 steps from the (0, 0) point on the graph and up 5 steps.

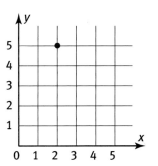

- The horizontal line at the bottom of the graph is called the x-axis. The number of steps sideways is the x-coordinate of the point.

- The first number of the ordered pair (the value of x) tells how far to go to the right.

- The vertical line is called the y-axis. The number of steps up is called the y-coordinate.

- The second number of the ordered pair (the value of y) tells how far to go up.

Find three ordered pairs for each function rule and graph them.

7 $x \longrightarrow (\times 2) \longrightarrow y$

9 $x \longrightarrow (\div 2) \longrightarrow y$

8 $x \longrightarrow (\times 1) \longrightarrow y$

10 $x \longrightarrow (\times 0) \longrightarrow y$

11 Jorge got a $500 paycheck on Friday. By the following Monday, he had spent $56 from his checking account. On Tuesday, Jorge wrote checks to pay bills, which totaled $147. On Wednesday he wrote a $225 check for a new stereo. By that time, Jorge had $1,378 in his checking account. How much money did he have before he got paid?

12 **Extended Response** Sarah put 6 into a ×7 function machine. She claimed that the ordered pair she got was (7, 42). Juan disagreed. Sarah said that $6 \times 7 = 42$, and that there could be no other ordered pair. Who is correct and why? Explain.

Composite Functions

Key Ideas

Some functions use more than one step. The output from the first step becomes the input for the second step.

Star Bank offers a special checking account service. The bank charges $7.50 each month plus $0.25 for each check cashed. The table shows the cost of writing different numbers of checks each month.

The monthly charge can be calculated this way:

Step 1: Multiply the number of checks by 0.25. Use this function rule: $x \xrightarrow{\times 0.25} n$.

Step 2: Add $7.50 to the value. Use this function rule: $n \xrightarrow{+7.50} y$.

We can write these two functions together: $x \xrightarrow{\times 0.25} n \xrightarrow{+7.50} y$

The values of x and y can then be entered on the table.

Draw and complete this table on a sheet of paper. Then graph the ordered pairs.

1

Number of checks cashed during the month (x)	0	1	2	3	4	5	6	7	8	9	10	15	20	30	40
Charge for the month in dollars (y)															

eTextbook This lesson is available in the eTextbook.

We can describe the cost for each number of checks using two functions. When two functions are put together in this way, it is called a **composite** function because the function has more than one part.

Suppose we put 8 into this composite function machine.

8 ——$\times 0.25$—→ n ——$+7.50$—→ y

Then 2 would come out of the first machine and go into the second

machine. 8 ——$\times 0.25$—→ 2 ——$+7.50$—→ y

And 9.50 would come out of the second machine.

8 ——$\times 0.25$—→ 2 ——$+7.50$—→ 9.50

So (8, 9.50) is one ordered pair of this composite function because 9.50 comes out when we put in 8. Writing 8 checks in one month costs $9.50.

Work individually or in small groups. For each composite function, draw and complete the table. Then graph the ordered pairs.

❷ x —— $\times 2$ —→ n —— $+1$ —→ y

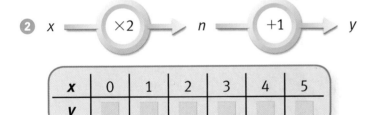

x	0	1	2	3	4	5
y						

❸ x —— $\times 4$ —→ n —— $+2$ —→ y

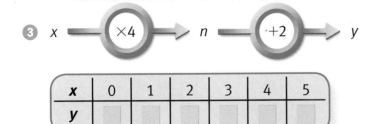

x	0	1	2	3	4	5
y						

❹ **Extended Response** Does the order of the steps in a composite function make a difference? For example, is x ——$\times 8$—→ n ——$+3$—→ y the same as

x ——$+3$—→ n ——$\times 8$—→ y? Explain how to check your answer.

Key Ideas

Points can be graphed with negative, as well as positive, coordinates.

You saw Graph City in Lesson 5.1. Since then, the city has grown.

The people of Graph City wanted all their roads—even the new ones—to have numbers and to be in order. E. 1st St. stands for East 1st Street, W. stands for West, N. for North, and S. for South.

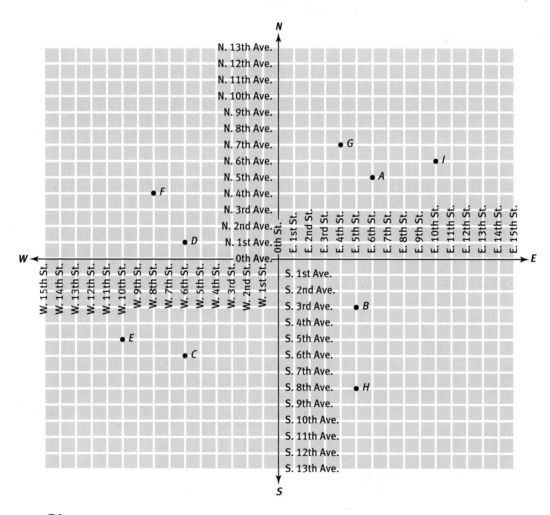

Give the locations of these points.

1 A   **2** B   **3** C   **4** E

There is a shorter way to describe where points on a graph are. Look at this graph. Notice the negative numbers. Each of the four sections is called a quadrant.

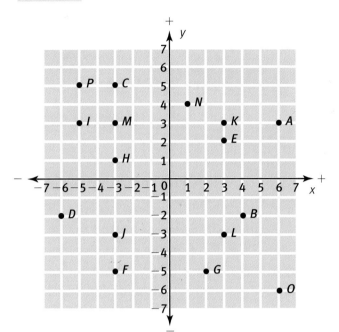

The coordinates of point *A* are (6, 3).

The coordinates of point *B* are (4, −2).

The coordinates of point *C* are (−3, 5).

The coordinates of point *D* are (−6, −2).

Find the coordinates of the following points.

5 *E*　　　　**6** *F*　　　　**7** *G*　　　　**8** *H*　　　　**9** *I*　　　　**10** *J*

Find the points with the following coordinates.

11 (3, −3)　　**12** (−3, 3)　　**13** (1, 4)　　**14** (3, 3)　　**15** (6, −6)　　**16** (−5, 5)

Copy and complete these tables on a sheet of paper. Then graph the ordered pairs.

17

x	0	2	5	6	−2
y	−5				

18

x	1	2	3	4	5
y	6				

Writing + Math ▶ **Journal**

How would you compare and contrast graphing in four quadrants with graphing in one quadrant? Explain.

Graphing Strategies and Practice

Get the Point Game

Players: Two

Materials: Graph paper, crayons or markers (four colors), a black pen or pencil

Object: To find the coordinates of the secret point

Math Focus: Locating and plotting coordinates on a graph, intuitive geometry, and mathematical reasoning

HOW TO PLAY

1 Decide what size "playing field" will be used. Then make a playing field by drawing coordinate axes on a sheet of graph paper.

2 The first player chooses a secret point and draws two diagonal straight lines through the point. Draw the lines at 45° angles to the axes as shown in the example below. This separates the playing field into four parts. Then the first player colors each of the four parts a different color.

3 Without seeing what the first player has done, the second player guesses a point by calling out its coordinates. Then the first player tells the color of that point. A point on one of the two dividing lines is described as black.

4 The second player keeps guessing until he or she gets the secret point.

SAMPLE GAME

Erin and Billy decided on a playing field that goes from −5 to 5 on each axis. Erin was the first player. She chose (3, −2) as the secret point, drew two lines, and colored the sections as shown.

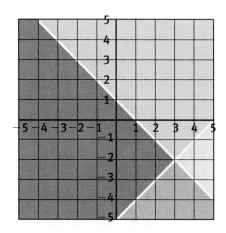

SAMPLE GAME, continued

Billy made a playing field just like Erin's but without the lines and colors. On his field, Billy kept a record of each move.

1 Billy guessed, "(0, 0)." Erin said, "Red." Billy circled the point (0, 0) in red.

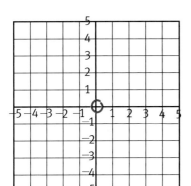

2 Billy guessed, "(1, 1)." Erin said, "Green." Billy circled the point (1, 1) in green. He knew there was a line between (0, 0) and (1, 1) so he drew it.

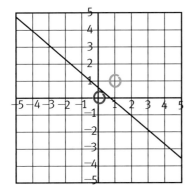

3 Billy guessed, "(4, −2)." Erin said, "Yellow." Billy circled the point (4, −2) in yellow.

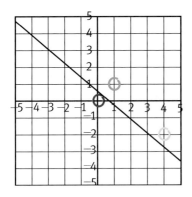

4 Billy guessed, "(2, 0)." Erin said, "Green." Billy circled the point (2, 0) in green.

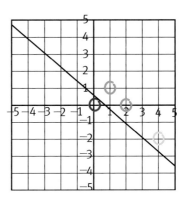

5 Billy guessed, "(4, −1)." Erin said, "Black." Billy circled the point (4, −1) in black.

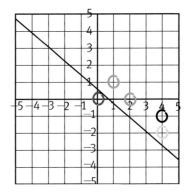

6 Billy said, "(3, −2)." Erin said, "That's the point I chose. You got it in six moves."

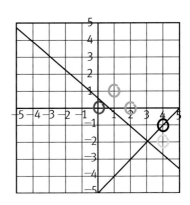

Making and Using Graphs

Graphing functions can help you solve problems.

Mr. Schultz owns a barbershop. He charges $9.50 for each haircut, but it costs him $0.50 for lotions and other materials needed for each haircut. So he makes $9.00 on each haircut.

To find out how much money he makes during a week, Mr. Schultz uses this function rule:

If Mr. Schultz gives 30 haircuts in a week, he makes $270. Not all that money is profit though. He has to pay for rent, heat, electricity, and insurance for his shop. All these add up to about $240 a week.

To figure out his profit for the week, Mr. Schultz subtracts $240 from the money he makes on the haircuts. The function rule for his profit looks like this:

x ⟶ ×9 ⟶ n ⟶ −240 ⟶ y

If Mr. Schultz gives only 10 haircuts during a week, does he have a profit or a loss for that week? He takes in $90, and it costs him $240 to stay in business. Because $90 - 240 = -150$, he has a loss of $150 for the week. Remember, a negative profit means a loss of money.

Copy and complete this table using the function rule above.

1

Number of haircuts during the week	0	1	2	5	10	15	20	30	50	70
Profit for the week (dollars)										

2 Copy and complete the graph on page 207. Graph the ordered pairs from the table you just completed. The first few points are plotted to help you check your answers.

 Textbook This lesson is available in the *eTextbook*.

3 **Extended Response** How many haircuts must Mr. Schultz give to break even for the week? To break even means to make exactly enough money to pay all expenses and have a profit of $0. Explain your answer.

4 About how much profit will Mr. Schultz make if he gives 40 haircuts during one week?

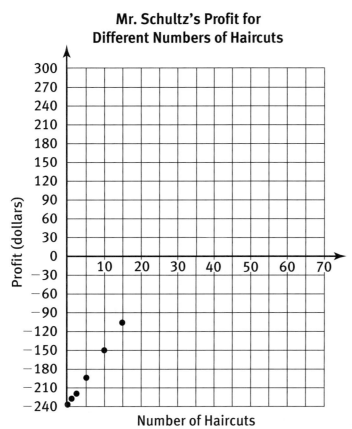

Mr. Schultz's Profit for Different Numbers of Haircuts

Profit (dollars)

Number of Haircuts

Writing + Math **Journal**

Describe a situation for which you could write a function rule that would work for some numbers but which would make no sense for other numbers. Think about the haircut problem in this lesson and the checking-account problem in Lesson 5.3.

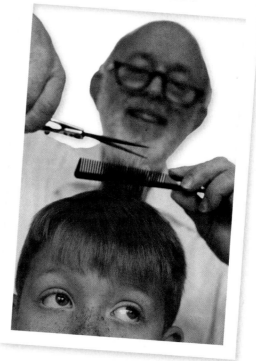

Exploring Problem Solving

Imagine you are in charge of a remote-control robot that guards a museum at night. All is well until the robot malfunctions. It can no longer move any way you want it to. It can follow only these eight commands:

Command	Meaning	Example
$x + 7$	Add 7 to x-coordinate.	If the robot is at $(-3, 5)$, it will go to $(4, 5)$.
$x - 7$	Subtract 7 from x-coordinate.	If the robot is at $(7, -4)$, it will go to $(0, -4)$.
$y + 7$	Add 7 to y-coordinate.	If the robot is at $(-1, -1)$, it will go to $(-1, 6)$.
$y - 7$	Subtract 7 from y-coordinate.	If the robot is at $(3, 0)$, it will go to $(3, -7)$.

The other four commands are $x + 13$, $x - 13$, $y + 13$, and $y - 13$.

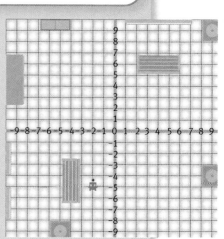

Suddenly something at coordinate $(3, 6)$ triggers an alarm. You need to maneuver the robot from its current position at $(-2, -5)$ to the trouble point.

What series of commands will move the robot to where it needs to go?

Rachel solved the problem this way:

I Made a Physical Model.

Command	Location
$x + 7$	$(5, -5)$
$y + 13$	

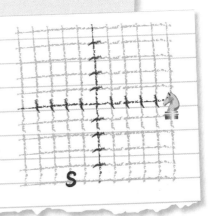

e Textbook This lesson is available in the *eTextbook*.

Think about Rachel's strategy, and answer the
following questions.

1 What is Rachel doing to try to solve the problem?

2 What do you think Rachel will write next?

3 Will Rachel's strategy work?

Ernesto solved the problem another way.

I Thought of a Related Problem I had already solved.

This reminds me of a problem I solved in the Chapter 4
Introduction.

First I'll move the
robot back and forth
until it's at point A.

Then I'll move the
robot up and down to
get to the target.

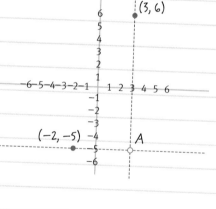

Think about Ernesto's strategy and answer the following questions.

4 How is this problem like the one Ernesto is thinking of? How is it
different?

5 How far from point A does the robot start?

6 Do you think Ernesto's strategy will work? Why or why not?

7 Finish solving the problem. Use Rachel's strategy, Ernesto's strategy, or
a strategy of your own. What strategy did you use? Why?

Cumulative Review

Solve.

Abdul and Caitlin are both saving money to buy bicycles for $100 each.
Each week, Abdul gets $5 but spends $2 of that, and Caitlin gets $4
and spends $2 of that.

1 How many weeks will it take for each person to save enough money to
buy a bicycle?

2 How much sooner will they have enough money if they each spend only
$1 each week?

3 How many weeks will it take for each person to save enough money
if they do not spend any?

Function Rules **Lesson 4.6**

Find a function rule that works for both pairs of numbers.

4
$$20 \longrightarrow \boxed{?} \longrightarrow 50$$
$$15 \longrightarrow \boxed{?} \longrightarrow 45$$

6

$$50 \longrightarrow \boxed{?} \longrightarrow 30$$
$$40 \longrightarrow \boxed{?} \longrightarrow 20$$

5

$$7 \longrightarrow \boxed{?} \longrightarrow 21$$
$$8 \longrightarrow \boxed{?} \longrightarrow 24$$

7
$$20 \longrightarrow \boxed{?} \longrightarrow 4$$
$$100 \longrightarrow \boxed{?} \longrightarrow 20$$

e Textbook This lesson is available in the *eTextbook*.

Decimals and Money Lesson 3.1

Solve.

⑧ Jimmy was at the ballpark and wanted a hot dog ($2.50), chips ($1.50), and a drink ($1.75). His mother had only a $5 bill and a $10 bill.

    A. Was the $5 bill enough or did Jimmy need the $10 bill?

    B. How much change did he get?

⑨ Renee's lunch at school this week will cost between $2.25 and $3.00 each day. How much money does she need to be sure to have enough to pay for all her lunches this week?

⑩ Fara had $10. She loaned her friends Jay and Peggy $2.75 each to buy snacks. How much did Fara have left?

Metric Units Lesson 3.7

Find the missing measure.

⑪ 350 mL = ☐ L

⑫ 50 dm = ☐ m

⑬ 16.2 mm = ☐ cm

⑭ 17.241 km = ☐ m

⑮ 4,000 g = ☐ kg

⑯ 1,796 m = ☐ km

⑰ 17.241 dm = ☐ m

⑱ 25 m = ☐ cm

⑲ 0.050 L = ☐ mL

Adding and Subtracting Integers Lesson 4.8

Complete each exercise.

⑳ $(-4) - (-5) =$ ☐　㉑ $9 + 8 =$ ☐　㉒ $3 - 8 =$ ☐

㉓ $|-7| =$ ☐　　　㉔ $-|-5| =$ ☐　　㉕ $|-8| - |-5| =$ ☐

Inverse Functions

Key Ideas

Some pairs of function machines have opposite operations. One machine undoes the operation of the other machine. These are called **inverse** operations, an important idea in algebra.

If you put 6 in this machine, you get 24. $6 \longrightarrow (\times 4) \longrightarrow 24$

This machine does the opposite. If you put in 24, you get 6. $24 \longrightarrow (\div 4) \longrightarrow 6$

Because these machines do opposite things, we say that $\times 4$ is the inverse of $\div 4$ and $\div 4$ is the inverse of $\times 4$. Remember, we can draw these arrows in any direction. You can also use the inverse function rule to find what number went into the function machine $x \longrightarrow (\times 6) \longrightarrow 21$

Because $21 \div 6 = 3.5$, x must be 3.5; therefore, $3.5 \longleftarrow (\div 6) \longleftarrow 21$.

Write the inverse of each of these functions. **Algebra**

1.

2.

3.

Find the value of x in each case. If it helps you, use the inverse function.

4. $x \longrightarrow (+7) \longrightarrow 8$

5. $0 \longleftarrow (-20) \longrightarrow x$

6. $x \longrightarrow (\times 4) \longrightarrow 32$

e Textbook This lesson is available in the *eTextbook*.

Answer the following questions.

Tickets to the Apple County Fair cost $4 each.

7 How would you find the cost of 4 tickets?

8 How would you find the cost of *x* tickets?

9 The Gartner family spent $20 on tickets. Write the function rule to find the cost of *x* tickets. How many did they buy?

Groups can make advance reservations for fair tickets by calling the ticket office. There is a $3 service charge added to the total cost for orders taken over the phone.

10 The Ramirez family's ticket order cost $31.

    a. Write the function rule to find the cost of *x* tickets with the service charge.

    b. What was the cost before the service charge?

    c. How many tickets did the Ramirez family order?

11 The Hilltown softball team's ticket order cost $51.

    a. What was the cost before the service charge?

    b. How many tickets did the team order?

12 The Girl Scout troop's ticket order was $83. At the last minute, the troop had to order 5 more tickets, which included another service charge.

    a. What was the cost of the first order before the service charge?

    b. How many tickets did the troop order the first time?

    c. What was the cost of the second order, including the service charge?

    d. What was the total amount spent on tickets for the Girl Scout troop?

 **Journal**

Write a definition of *inverse operation*. Then write an example of an inverse function.

Inverse of a Composite Function

Key Ideas

The inverse of a composite function undoes what the original function did.

Remember, the inverse is the opposite function and undoes what the first function does. The inverse of a ×4 function is ÷4, and the inverse of a −7 function is +7. But what is the inverse of this composite

function? x —(×4)→ n —(−7)→ y

It is y —(+7)→ n —(÷4)→ x.

Notice that the operations must be performed in the opposite order.

In this case, first add 7, and then divide by 4.

The arrows can go in any direction. Another way to write the inverse is

x ←(÷4)— n ←(+7)— y.

Write the inverse function of each of these functions.

1 x —(+2)→ n —(×3)→ y **2** y ←(×4)— n ←(+8)— x

Put each of the numbers below into the function rule x —(×2)→ n —(+4)→ y.

Put that result into the inverse function y —(−4)→ n —(÷2)→ x.

3 0   **4** 2   **5** 22.7   **6** 10

The function that always gives back the same number you put in is called the *identity function*.

Think of a number. Add 6 to it, and then multiply by 2.

- Here is what these steps would look like in function-machine notation:

  x —$(+6)$→ n —$(\times 2)$→ y.

- How would you undo these steps? Divide by 2, and then subtract 6.

  y —$(\div 2)$→ n —(-6)→ x

Think of a number. Multiply it by 6, and then divide by 2.

- Here is what these steps would look like in function-machine notation:

  x —$(\times 6)$→ n —$(\div 2)$→ y.

- Is there a function with fewer steps that would always give the same output as this function? Yes, if you multiply by 3 like this:

  x —$(\times 3)$→ y.

- How would you undo this function using as few steps as possible?

  By dividing by 3: y —$(\div 3)$→ x.

Rewrite each composite function rule as a one-step function that does the same thing, if possible. Give the inverse of each function.

7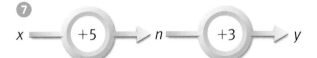

11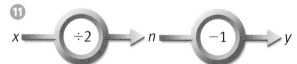

8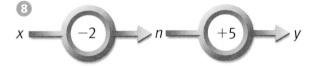

12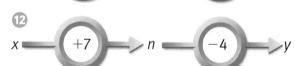

9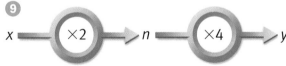

13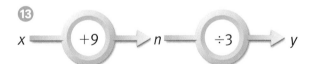

10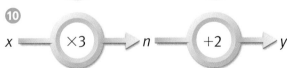

14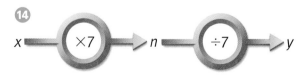

The identity function always gives back the same number you put in.

There are many different rules for the identity function. For example:

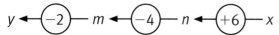

$x \longrightarrow (+5) \longrightarrow n \longrightarrow (-5) \longrightarrow y.$

Here is a function rule that uses three operations for the identity function:

$y \longleftarrow (-2) \longleftarrow m \longleftarrow (-4) \longleftarrow n \longleftarrow (+6) \longleftarrow x$

15 What is a rule for the identity function that uses only one operation?

16 Give as many rules as you can think of for an identity function that uses exactly two operations. For example:

$x \longrightarrow (+5) \longrightarrow n \longrightarrow (-5) \longrightarrow y$

17 Give three rules for an identity function that uses three different operations. For example:

$x \longrightarrow (+3) \longrightarrow n \longrightarrow (-3) \longrightarrow m \longrightarrow (\times 1) \longrightarrow y$

18 **Extended Response** Is this a rule for the identity function? Explain why or why not.

$x \longrightarrow (+3) \longrightarrow n \longrightarrow (\div 2) \longrightarrow y$

19 If you put a number into the function machine in Problem 18, do you get the same number back? Try some numbers.

   a. If you put in 1, what number comes out of the function machine?

   b. If you put in 2, what number comes out of the function machine?

   c. If you put in 3, what number comes out of the function machine?

   d. When you put 3 into the function machine, do you get the same number back?

Look at this function:

$x \longrightarrow \boxed{\times 2} \longrightarrow n \longrightarrow \boxed{-6} \longrightarrow y$

20 Is there a number that you can put into this function machine and get out the same number? Is there another number?

For each function, find a number that you can put in and get out the same number.

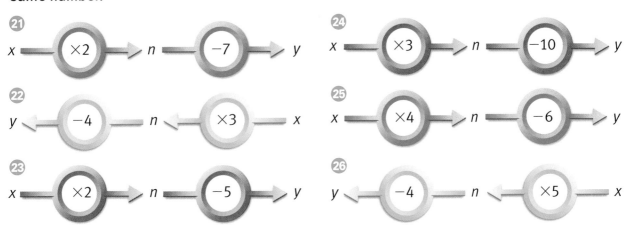

21 $x \longrightarrow \boxed{\times 2} \longrightarrow n \longrightarrow \boxed{-7} \longrightarrow y$

24 $x \longrightarrow \boxed{\times 3} \longrightarrow n \longrightarrow \boxed{-10} \longrightarrow y$

22 $y \longleftarrow \boxed{-4} \longleftarrow n \longleftarrow \boxed{\times 3} \longleftarrow x$

25 $x \longrightarrow \boxed{\times 4} \longrightarrow n \longrightarrow \boxed{-6} \longrightarrow y$

23 $x \longrightarrow \boxed{\times 2} \longrightarrow n \longrightarrow \boxed{-5} \longrightarrow y$

26 $y \longleftarrow \boxed{-4} \longleftarrow n \longleftarrow \boxed{\times 5} \longleftarrow x$

 **Journal**

What are inverse functions? What is the identity function?

Using Composite Functions

Key Ideas

Composite functions may be useful in many situations.

Odessa has started a bracelet business. She makes and sells bracelets to order. She charges $3.00 for each bracelet plus a $0.50 handling charge. If you ordered 3 bracelets, she would charge you $9.00 for the bracelets plus a $0.50 handling charge—a total of $9.50.

Odessa wants to make a table that will tell her the total charge for different numbers of bracelets ordered.

Answer the following questions. $x \longrightarrow \boxed{\times 3} \longrightarrow n \longrightarrow \boxed{+0.50} \longrightarrow y$

Number of bracelets ordered							7
Total charge	$3.50		$9.50				

1. Help Odessa. Copy the table and fill in the correct amounts.

2. **Extended Response** Shiro ordered some bracelets, and then told Odessa he should be charged $5.00. Could that be right? Explain.

3. Odessa found a bill she was supposed to send to Celia. The bill was for $12.50. How many bracelets had Celia ordered?

4. Odessa received an order for bracelets. The order form listed the total for the order as $27.50, but the number of bracelets was not listed. How many bracelets were ordered?

5. **Extended Response** Tom and Elise each wanted a bracelet. Elise had an idea. "Tom," she said, "let me order both bracelets." Why did Elise think this was a good idea? Explain.

6. **Extended Response** During one month, Odessa sold 26 bracelets. During that same month her expenses were $23.64. Without knowing anything else, can you figure out the most profit she might have made? Can you figure out the least profit she might have made? Explain how you found your answer.

eTextbook This lesson is available in the *eTextbook*.

Odessa keeps records of her bracelet business. This table shows her records for the first year she was in business.

Month	Number of Bracelets Sold	Total Income (Sales)	Total Expenses	Total Profit
January	0	0	0	0
February	0	0	0	0
March	1	$3.50	$37.50	−$34.00
April	7	$24.00	0	$24.00
May	12	$37.00	$18.23	$18.77
June	5	$17.00	$8.04	$8.96
July	6	$21.00	0	$21.00
August	10	$34.50	0	$34.50
September	8	$26.50	$10.13	$16.37
October	3	$10.00	$7.88	$2.12
November	7	$22.00	$6.38	$15.62
December	9	$29.00	$14.21	$14.79

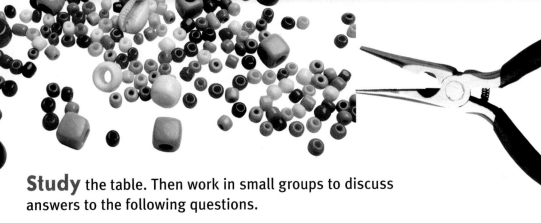

Study the table. Then work in small groups to discuss answers to the following questions.

7. In what month do you think Odessa started her business?

8. Do you think she started near the beginning of the month or near the end of the month?

9. In which month were Odessa's expenses the highest?

10. Why do you think Odessa had the most expenses that month?

11. **a.** In which two-month period did Odessa have the most profit?

   b. **Extended Response** What might have happened during those two months to account for this?

12. **Extended Response** In which month did Odessa have the most customers? (This need not be the month in which the most bracelets were sold.) Explain how you found your answer.

Temperature Conversions

Key Ideas

You can use a composite function to convert between the Fahrenheit and Celsius temperature scales. You can also use a simpler composite function to estimate how close one temperature is to another.

There are two commonly used temperature scales in the world. The United States and some other countries use the Fahrenheit scale. On that scale, 32° is the freezing point for water, and 212° is the boiling point. In most of the rest of the world, the Celsius scale is used. On that scale, 0° is the freezing point of water, and 100° is the boiling point.

The relationship between degrees Fahrenheit and degrees Celsius can be written as a function rule:

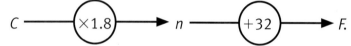

This composite function converts Celsius temperatures to Fahrenheit temperatures.

Answer the following questions.

SCIENCE

1. Normal body temperature for most people is said to be about 37° C. What is the same temperature on the Fahrenheit scale?

2. **Extended Response** What is the inverse function of the composite function that converts Celsius temperatures to Fahrenheit temperatures? What would this new composite function do? Explain.

3. Instead of 1.8, which we used in the composite function for converting from Celsius to Fahrenheit, some people use $\frac{9}{5}$. What would the function rule be in that case?

4. Using the fraction rather than the decimal, what would the inverse function rule be?

5. Use either form of the function rule and its inverse to complete the following table:

Celsius temp.	−10		10		30		40	50	100
Fahrenheit temp.		32		68		98.6			212

ⓔTextbook This lesson is available in the *eTextbook*.

Some people like to use a different function to estimate conversions between Fahrenheit and Celsius temperatures. That function rule is

C —($\times 2$)→ n —($+30$)→ F.

Suppose the temperature is 15° Celsius. You can use this function rule to find the approximate temperature on the Fahrenheit scale.

$15 \times 2 = 30$, and $30 + 30 = 60$

So 15° Celsius is about 60° Fahrenheit. Using the exact function, you would get 59°.

Note that the inverse of the composite function shown above looks

like this: F —(-30)→ n —($\div 2$)→ C

Use the estimating function and its inverse to answer the following questions.

6 If C is 0, about what is F?   **8** If C is 10, about what is F?

7 If C is 100, about what is F?   **9** If C is 37, about what is F?

10 Using the estimating rule and its inverse, complete the following table:

Celsius temp.	−10	0			30	37	40	50	100
Fahrenheit temp.		30	50	68		104		130	

11 **a.** For what Celsius temperature do the exact function and the "estimating" function give the same Fahrenheit temperature?

b. **Extended Response** For which values of C are the estimates reasonably close? For which are they pretty far apart? Explain.

12 Using the horizontal axis for C and the vertical axis for F, with C ranging from −10° to 100° and F ranging from 0° to 230°, graph the table of the function on page 220 and the table of the estimating function above.

Writing + Math **Journal**

Explain why the "estimating" function gives results close to the actual temperatures.

Key Ideas

Function rules can be written in a shorter form than with arrow notation.

Look at this function machine. We can use an arrow to show what this machine does: $x \longrightarrow (+5) \longrightarrow y$.

There is a shorter way to write this: $x + 5 = y$
When we use this short way, we often write the y at the left:
$y = x + 5$. (We say, "y equals x plus 5.") This shorter form is the standard notation or *standard form*.

This is a shorter way to say that any number (y) that comes out of the machine is 5 more than the number (x) that went into the machine. If x is 7, then y is $7 + 5 = 12$.

We can also use this short form for function machines that subtract.

Any number (y) that comes out of this machine is 3 less than the number (x) that went into it. So we can write the function this way: $y = x - 3$ and say it "y equals x minus 3." If x is 5, then y is $5 - 3 = 2$.

Copy and complete each table. Algebra

1 $y = x + 3$

x	0		4	
y	3	5		2

2 $y = x - 6$

x	10	8		4
y	4		0	

3 $y = x + 10$

x	1	4		20
y	11		19	

The short form works for multiplication and division rules, too.

Look at this function machine. We can write the rule for this machine

in this way: $x \longrightarrow \boxed{\times 6} \longrightarrow y$.

We could, however, use the new short form and write it in this way:
$y = x \times 6$ or $y = 6 \times x$.

But $6 \times x$ can be confusing because $\times$ and x look so much alike.
Instead, we write $6x$, and the function becomes $y = 6x$. Remember,
$6x$ means "6 times x," or "6 multiplied by x." We say that "y equals
6 times x" or "$y = 6x$." If x is 4, y is $6 \times 4 = 24$.

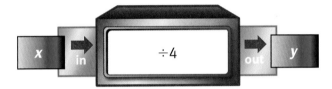

This function machine divides every number that goes into it by 4.

We can write that in this way: $x \longrightarrow \boxed{\div 4} \longrightarrow y$.

We could, however, use the new short form and write the function this
way: $y = x \div 4$.

Or we can use an even shorter form and write it like this: $y = \frac{x}{4}$

We say, "y equals x over 4" or "y equals x divided by 4."
If x is 8, then y is $\frac{8}{4}$, which is $8 \div 4 = 2$.

Copy and complete each table.

4 $y = 9x$

x	2			8	
y	18	36	54		90

5 $y = \frac{x}{3}$

x	3	6	11	15	
y	1				6

6 $y = \frac{x}{5}$

x	0	5		40	
y			4		9

Composite Functions in Standard Notation

Key Ideas

Composite function rules are usually written using the shorter form.

Remember, two function machines can be put together to make a composite function machine, which has more than one step.

What happens to a number that goes into this machine?

First it is multiplied by 3. Then 5 is added to the result.

We can use the short form to write it like this: $y = 3x + 5$.

We say, "y equals 3 x plus 5."

If x is 2, then what is y?

The "$3x$" means to multiply x by 3: $3 \times 2 = 6$.

The "$+5$" means to add 5 to the result: $6 + 5 = 11$.

So if x is 2, then y is $(3 \times 2) + 5 = 11$.

Copy and complete each table. **Algebra**

1 $y = 4x - 7$

x	8		2	1	
y		13			-7

3 $y = 6x + 9$

x		3	8		
y	39			33	21

2 $y = 7x + 3$

x		2	7		5
y	66			31	

4 $y = 5x - 6$

x	8	2		6	
y			9		19

e Textbook This lesson is available in the *eTextbook*.

| x | in | $\div 2$ | out | n | in | -4 | out | y |

Here is another composite function machine. When a number (x) goes in, it is divided by 2, and then 4 is subtracted.

$y = \frac{x}{2} - 4$

We say, "y equals x over 2, minus 4," "y equals x divided by 2, minus 4," or "y equals one-half x, minus 4."

If x is 10, then what is y?

The $\frac{x}{2}$ means divide x by 2: $\frac{10}{2} = 5$. The "-4" means subtract 4 from the result: $5 - 4 = 1$.

So if x is 10, y is $\frac{10}{2} - 4 = 1$.

Copy and complete these tables.

5 $y = \frac{x}{2} + 7$

x	0			8	4
y		15	8		

6 $y = \frac{x}{3} + 4$

x				3	6
y	9	7	4		

7 $y = 4x + 5$

x	0	6			7
y			17	9	

8 $y = \frac{x}{5} - 3$

x	20		10	15	
y		3			4

9 $y = 2x - 1$

x		5		4	1
y	5		3		

10 $y = 6x + 3$

x	4	0			5
y			15	39	

11 **Extended Response** Doug put 3 into a composite function machine and out came 24. Write two possible composite functions in standard notation that make Doug's output true.

12 **Extended Response** Give an example of a real-life situation in which you would use the function rule $y = 6x - 5$.

Solve the following problems.

13. Ms. Chee runs a computer repair service. She charges $50 to make a service call plus $60 for each hour she spends working on a computer.

    a. If she works on a computer for 3 hours, how much will Ms. Chee charge?

    b. What is a function rule for her charges? Make a table showing how much she charges (y) for any number of hours (x) from 1–10.

    c. Graph the data from your table. Be careful to choose your scale so that the graph will fit on your paper.

14. Mr. Alexander also runs a computer repair service. He charges only $30 per hour while he is working on a computer, but he charges $100 to make a service call.

    a. If he works on a computer for 3 hours, how much will he charge?

    b. Make a function rule for Mr. Alexander's charges. Make a table showing how much he charges for any number of hours from 1–10.

    c. Graph the data from this table on the same graph that you used for Ms. Chee's charges.

15. **Extended Response** Which of the two computer services costs less? Explain your answer.

Complete each function table and graph the ordered pairs for each.

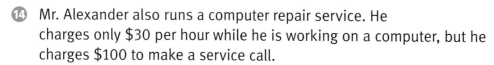

16. $y = 4x - 2$

x	y
2	
1	
	10

17. $y = \frac{x}{4} + 1$

x	y
8	
	4
4	

18. $y = \left(\frac{2}{3}\right)x + 3$

x	y
3	
0	
	7

Choose three x-values to put into the following functions rules. Then graph the ordered pairs.

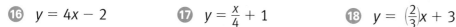

19. $y = 2x - 4$

20. $y = 3x + 1$

21. $y = \frac{x}{2} + 5$

Textbook This lesson is available in the *eTextbook*.

Complete the following exercises.

22 $7 \times 3 = $ ▨

23 $7 - 3 = $ ▨

24 $7 \div 3 = $ ▨

25 $9 \times 6 = $ ▨

26 $9 + 6 = $ ▨

27 $9 \div 6 = $ ▨

28 $7 \times 8 = $ ▨

29 $7 + 8 = $ ▨

Solve for *n*. **Algebra**

30 $10 \times 5 = n$ ▨

31 $10 - n = 5$ ▨

32 $10 + 5 = n$ ▨

33 $10 \div n = 2$ ▨

34 $10 \times 2 = n$ ▨

35 $n \div 2 = 10$ ▨

36 $8 \times 4 = n$ ▨

37 $8 \div n = 2$ ▨

38 $8 + 4 = n$ ▨

Divide. Round answers to the nearest hundredth. Look for patterns that will help you.

39 $7\overline{)1.54}$

40 $6\overline{)34.2}$

41 $3\overline{)1}$

42 $3\overline{)2}$

43 $10\overline{)43.21}$

44 $4\overline{)36}$

45 $400\overline{)3600}$

46 $40\overline{)3600}$

47 $40\overline{)36}$

48 $39\overline{)3600}$

49 $39\overline{)360}$

50 $39\overline{)36}$

51 **Extended Response** Give an example of a real-life situation for which you would use the function rule $y = 4x$.

52 Darla and Hong are playing a game in which they get 6 points for every time one of them kicks a ball past a certain line. Which rule fits this situation if *x* is the number of times they kick the ball past the line?

a. $y = x + 6$

b. $y = 6x$

c. $y = x - 6$

Key Ideas

If you know the output of a function in standard form, you can find the input.

Suppose you want to know what went into the function machine below. To find out, you can do the inverse operation for each step.

$x \longrightarrow \boxed{\times 3} \longrightarrow n \longrightarrow \boxed{+5} \longrightarrow 23$ *Subtract 5.* $23 - 5 = 18$

$x \longrightarrow \boxed{\times 3} \longrightarrow 18$ *Divide by 3.* $18 \div 3 = 6$

$x = 6$ $x = 6$

Evaluate each equation by solving for either *x* or *y*. Algebra

1 $5x - 7 = 33$

2 $4x + 12 = 52$

3 $12(3) - 34 = y$

4 $\frac{x}{9} \times 6 = 48$

5 $x + 6(7) = 63$

6 $\frac{12}{4} - 56 = y$

7 $12x + 6 = 78$

8 $32 - 8(4) = y$

9 $17x - 26 = -77$

10 $25(8) + 31 = y$

11 $7x - 63 = 21$

12 $\frac{x}{3} + 25 = 67$

13 $24.5x + 39 = 186$

14 $7x - 46 = -67$

15 $36(9) - 176.8 = y$

16 $-16.4x + 51 = 51$

17 $45(5) - 69 = y$

18 $\frac{x}{8} - 56 = -36.5$

19 $4x + 1,245 = 1,577$

20 $-6x + (-19) = -49$

21 $32(3) - 32 = y$

22 $12.6x + 43 = -20$

Solve the following problems.

23 Jason took a cab home from the airport. The sign on the side of the cab said that the charge would be $2.00 to start the trip plus 35¢ for each $\frac{1}{5}$ of a mile. The trip cost $18.45. Jason noticed that the meter said $2.35 as soon as the cab started. Jason wanted to know how far it is from the airport to his home. What is the answer? He was pretty sure the distance was less than 10 miles. Is he right? Is your answer exactly right? If not, what is the range of possible distances?

24 **Extended Response** In small groups, choose one equation from this lesson and graph the x- and y-values. Then, put three different x-values into the equation and graph those ordered pairs, too. What are your observations of the graph you made?

25 Look at the following equations. Would you expect them to have the same answer? Why?

a. $3(x + 5) = 18$ b. $3x + 15 = 18$

Exploring Problem Solving

How Many Museums in a Mile?

I'm here in New York City at El Museo del Barrio, a museum that showcases Latino culture. Across the street is Central Park. Behind me you can see some of the 50,000 people enjoying music, artwork, and free admission to El Museo and eight other museums—all within a twenty-three block stretch of Fifth Avenue. No wonder they call this the "Museum Mile."

If you are nearby, there is still time to join in the fun at this year's festival. During the festival, children make chalk murals and Guatemalan Sawdust Carpets at El Museo del Barrio.

If your schedule is booked, maybe next June you can come to help celebrate the cultural diversity of this city and the entire country.

Do you see why this section of Fifth Avenue is called the "Museum Mile"?

e Textbook This lesson is available in the *eTextbook*.

You can get to El Museo del Barrio and the rest of the Museum Mile Festival in several ways, including by bus or by train. This map shows only a part of the extensive subway network that weaves under the streets of New York City.

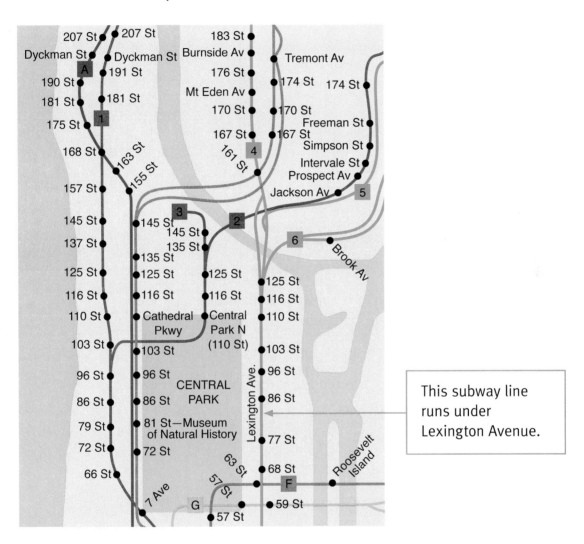

This subway line runs under Lexington Avenue.

Answer the following questions.

1. How is the layout of the streets near Museum Mile similar to the layout of Graph City on page 202? How is it different?

2. Which subway station is closest to El Museo del Barrio?

3. Suppose you walked at an average speed of 3 miles per hour. About how long would it take to walk to El Museo del Barrio from the nearest subway station? Explain how you made your estimate.

Exploring 💡 Problem Solving

Imagine you work for the Graph City Rapid Transit Department. The Historical Society is erecting a new multicultural museum, and you are going to help plan a subway line from the airport to the museum entrance.

- The museum entrance will be at $(-4, -5)$, which is the corner of West 4th Avenue and South 5th Street.

- The subway will go in a straight line.

- The subway will pass directly under $(3, 9)$.

Work in groups to graph your subway line, and then discuss and solve the following problems.

4. List three other intersections the subway will pass directly under. Write each pair of coordinates in a table.

5. Will the subway pass directly under $(0, 0)$? How do you know?

6. What equation could be used to represent the path of the subway?

7. Take the first pair of x- and y-values from your table. What happens if you use them in place of x and y in your equation?

8. List an intersection the subway will not pass under.

9. What happens if you use those values for x and y in your equation?

10. What happens if you use other pairs of x- and y-values from your table and use them in your equation?

11. Explain why you agree or disagree with each of the following statements:

- If an intersection is along the subway line, then its coordinates make the equation true.

- If an intersection is not along the subway line, then its coordinates make the equation false.

🄴 **Textbook** This lesson is available in the *eTextbook*.

Cumulative Review

Multiplying and Dividing Integers Lesson 4.9

Solve.

1 $-6 \times 4 =$ ▨   2 $-4 \times (-8) =$ ▨   3 $4 \times (-9) =$ ▨   4 $25 \div (-5) =$ ▨

5 $63 \div (-9) =$ ▨   6 $-27 \div 3 =$ ▨   7 $9 + (-15) =$ ▨   8 $-10 + 17 =$ ▨

Functions and Ordered Pairs Lesson 5.2

Find three ordered pairs for each function rule, and graph them.

9

11

10

12

Patterns Lesson 4.10

Use the pattern to find the missing numbers.

13 7, 10, 13, ▨, ▨, 22, ▨, ▨

14 1, 3, 9, ▨, ▨, 243

15 100, 85, 70, ▨, ▨, 25, ▨

16 40, 50, 45, 55, 50, ▨, ▨, 65, ▨, ▨

Multiplying Decimals by Whole Numbers Lesson 3.9

Multiply.

17   542
   $\times\ 2.6$
   ▨

18   74.62
   $\times\ 68$
   ▨

19   3.176
   $\times\ 24$
   ▨

20   25.24
   $\times\ 9$
   ▨

Interpreting Quotients and Remainders Lesson 3.13

Divide. Do not use remainders. Round answers to the nearest hundredth when needed.

㉑ 10)5

㉒ 8)6

㉓ 7)8.24

㉔ 3)38.25

Solve.

㉕ Aaron, Eric, and Iris shoveled their neighbor's driveway and were given $20 to share. How much should each person get?

㉖ The Lima School seventh- and eighth-grade classes were going together on a field trip. Each bus has 40 seats. If there are 56 seventh graders and 68 eighth graders, how many buses are needed?

Rounding and Approximating Lesson 3.10

Round to the nearest hundredth.

㉗ 102.548

㉘ 99.966

㉙ 107.589

㉚ 89,348.272

Solve.

㉛ A bottle of juice costs $2.19. If Jerry has $10, how many bottles can he purchase?

㉜ Don's van holds 18 gallons of gas and gets about 20 miles per gallon. He plans to travel about 400 miles. Can he make the trip without stopping for gas? If not, about how far would he get?

Customary Measurements Lesson 2.10

Solve.

㉝ Beth says she is 7 years and 3 months old. Josh says he was born 80 months ago. Who is older?

㉞ 4 feet = ▢ inches

㉟ 3 tons = ▢ pounds

Key Ideas Review

In this chapter, you learned how function machines can help to compute equations.

You learned how to use functions to compute ordered pairs and how to graph them.
You learned how to solve equations using various functions.

Use the graph below to answer the following questions.

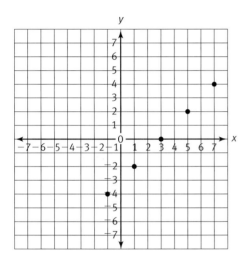

1. Name two points on the graph.

2. Use the points on the graph to describe the function represented.

Use the following composite function to answer the questions below.

$$x \longrightarrow \boxed{\times 3} \longrightarrow n \longrightarrow \boxed{-6} \longrightarrow y$$

3. What number can be put into the function to get the same number out?

4. Write the inverse of the composite function above.

Solve the following problems.

5. If a Celsius thermometer reads 24°, what is the temperature in Fahrenheit degrees?

6. $6x - 7 = 53$

7. $\dfrac{36}{4} - 15 = y$

8. $12(x) + 12 = 72$

Chapter Review

Lessons 5.1 and 5.4 **Give** the coordinates of these points.

1. A
2. B
3. C
4. D

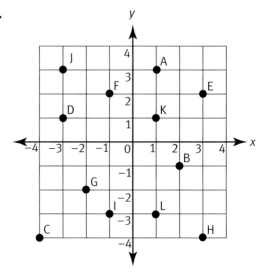

Give the correct letter for each of these coordinates.

5. $(1, -3)$
6. $(-3, 3)$
7. $(-2, -2)$
8. $(3, 2)$

Lessons 5.2 and 5.3 **Complete** each chart. Make a graph of each set of ordered pairs.

9.

$x \xrightarrow{\times 3} y$

x	y
−1	
	0
1	
2	
	9

10.

$x \xrightarrow{+3} n \xrightarrow{\times 2} y$

x	y
−2	
−1	
	6
2	
	14

Lesson 5.6 **Write** the inverse of each of these.

11.

12.

Lesson 5.7 **Write** the inverse of each of these.

⑬

x —— (+1) ➔ n —— (÷9) ➔ y

⑭

x —— (−6) ➔ n —— (×3) ➔ y

For each function, find a number that you can put in to get out the same number.

⑮

x —— (×2) ➔ n —— (−5) ➔ y

⑯

x —— (+14) ➔ n —— (÷3) ➔ y

Lesson 5.12 **Solve.**

⑰ $x - 8 = 15$

⑱ $4x + 6 = 30$

⑲ $3x - 20 = 100$

⑳ $\frac{x}{4} - 10 = 4$

㉑ $\frac{x}{2} + 8 = 40$

㉒ $x + 10 = 8$

Practice Test

Use the graph to find the coordinates of each point or to find the letters that match the given coordinates.

1. *B*

2. *G*

3. (−5, 2)

4. (0, −2)

5. (−5, −3)

Complete the table for each composite function. Then graph the ordered pairs.

6.

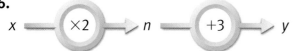

x → ×2 → n → +3 → y

x	0	1	2	3	4
y	▨	▨	▨	▨	▨

7.

x → ÷2 → n → −1 → y

x	2	4	6	8	10
y	▨	▨	▨	▨	▨

Use the inverse function rule to find the value of *x*.

8.

x → ÷4 → 20

9.

x → +14 → 11

e Textbook This lesson is available in the *eTextbook*.

Choose the correct answer.

10. What is the inverse function of the following composite function?

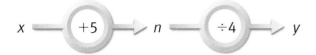

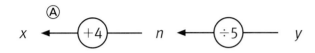

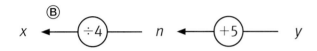

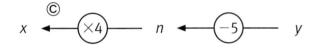

11. In $5x + 6 = y$, if y is 21, what is x?

- Ⓐ $x = 3$
- Ⓑ $x = 4$
- Ⓒ $x = 5.4$
- Ⓓ $x = 7$

12. What does $3x$ mean?

- Ⓐ $3 + x$
- Ⓑ $3 - x$
- Ⓒ $3 \times x$
- Ⓓ $3 \div x$

13. If the temperature is $18°$ C, what is a good estimate of the temperature in Fahrenheit?

- Ⓐ $76°F$
- Ⓑ $68°F$
- Ⓒ $48°F$
- Ⓓ $36°F$

14. Using the function

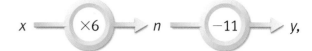

if x is 4, what is y?

- Ⓐ $y = 12$
- Ⓑ $y = 13$
- Ⓒ $y = 19$
- Ⓓ $y = 21$

15. Which ordered pair does *not* satisfy this function rule?

- Ⓐ $(10, 5)$
- Ⓑ $(14, 7)$
- Ⓒ $(18, 10)$
- Ⓓ $(22, 11)$

16. Janis sells boxes of cookies for $2 each. If she sells $140 worth of cookies in one day, how many boxes of cookies does she sell?

- Ⓐ 90
- Ⓑ 80
- Ⓒ 70
- Ⓓ 60

17. Which equation matches this composite function?

- Ⓐ $y = \frac{x}{5} + 8$
- Ⓑ $y = 5x + 8$
- Ⓒ $y = \frac{x}{8} + 5$
- Ⓓ $y = 8x + 5$

18. Which of the following is an identity function?

Ⓐ
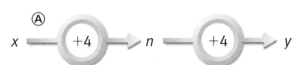

Ⓑ
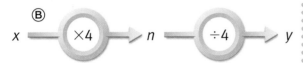

Ⓒ
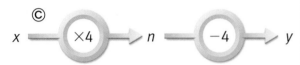

Ⓓ
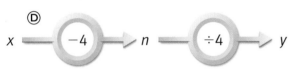

Choose the correct answer.

19. In the equation $\frac{x}{6} - 2 = y$, if x is 36, what is y?

   Ⓐ $y = 34$ Ⓑ $y = 6$
   Ⓒ $y = 4$ Ⓓ $y = 2$

20. The temperature at midnight is −6°F. If the temperature at noon is 12°F, by how many degrees did the temperature rise?

   Ⓐ 20°   Ⓑ 18°
   Ⓒ 12°   Ⓓ 6°

21. Solve for n.

$$3 \times (58 + 15) = n$$

   Ⓐ $n = 45$ Ⓑ $n = 129$
   Ⓒ $n = 189$ Ⓓ $n = 219$

22. Choose the measure that makes the most sense for this sentence: The book is ▢ long.

   Ⓐ 3,000 m   Ⓑ 300 km
   Ⓒ 30 cm   Ⓓ 3 m

23. Each section of the auditorium has 44 chairs. If there are 12 sections, how many chairs are in the auditorium?

   Ⓐ 528   Ⓑ 428
   Ⓒ 132   Ⓓ 88

24. What is 1,264.029 rounded to the nearest hundredth?

   Ⓐ 1,264   Ⓑ 1,300
   Ⓒ 1,264.1   Ⓓ 1,264.03

25. What is the next number in the pattern 18, 12, 6, 0?

   Ⓐ 6   Ⓑ −6
   Ⓒ 8   Ⓓ 12

26. $5^4 = $ ▢

   Ⓐ 20   Ⓑ 125
   Ⓒ 625   Ⓓ 3,125

e Textbook This lesson is available in the *eTextbook*.

Answer the following questions using the given information.

27. Jasmine makes and sells cakes. She spends about $20 a month on ingredients. She charges $12 for each cake. To figure her profit, she uses the following function rule:

   a. Complete the table using the given function rule.

Number of Cakes Sold	Profit for the Month (dollars)
0	⬜
1	⬜
5	⬜
10	⬜
20	⬜

   b. Make a graph and plot the ordered pairs from the table above.

   c. How many individual cakes must Jasmine sell in order to break even for the month?

   d. How much profit will Jasmine make if she sells 30 cakes?

28. Jasmine charges an additional $10 for orders of 5 cakes or more. To determine how much to charge for each order, she uses the following function rule:

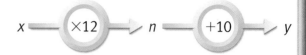

   a. Jasmine received an order for 5 cakes. How much money did she charge?

   b. A bakery received a bill from Jasmine for $310. How many cakes did the bakery order?

CHAPTER 6 Fractions

In This Chapter You Will Learn

- about comparing fractions.
- decimal equivalents of fractions.
- about adding and subtracting fractions.

These circle graphs show the nutritional breakdown for the dishes below.

Recipe	Type of Food	Fat	Carbohydrates	Protein
arroz con pollo	Puerto Rican	22 g	85 g	39 g
gumbo	Creole	3 g	7 g	16 g
lentil curry	Indian	9 g	26 g	5 g
hot pot (sin-su-lo)	Korean	24 g	126 g	44 g

A.
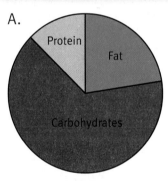

B.
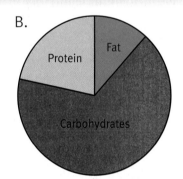

C.
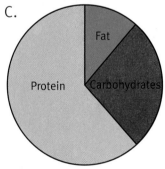

D.
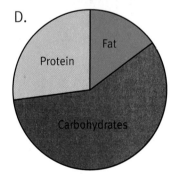

Work in groups to answer the following questions.

1 Which graph represents which dish?

2 How did you decide which foods go with Graphs A and C?

3 Graphs B and D look alike. How did you match each of these graphs with the correct dish?

Fractions of a Whole

Key Ideas

Fractions can be used to describe specific parts of a whole.

The denominator, or bottom number, of a fraction tells how many equal parts of a whole thing there are. The numerator, or top number, tells how many of those parts to consider.

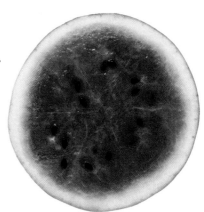

$\dfrac{1}{6}$ ←——— numerator
←——— denominator

When a fraction has a top number (numerator) that is *less than* its bottom number (denominator), the fraction describes a *portion of a whole.*

$\dfrac{4}{6}$ of a whole:

When a fraction has a top number (numerator) that is *equal to* its bottom number (denominator), the fraction describes the *entire whole.*

$\dfrac{6}{6}$ of a whole:

When a fraction has a top number (numerator) that is *greater than* its bottom number (denominator), the fraction describes a *portion greater than the whole.*

$\dfrac{8}{6}$ of a whole:

We will discuss this last case in the next chapter. In this chapter, we will focus on fractions as a portion of a whole.

eTextbook This lesson is available in the *eTextbook*.

Solve the following problems.

1. Mr. Estrada just made a raspberry pie. He cut it into 8 equal pieces. He gave a piece to Miss Wu and ate a piece himself.

   a. What fraction of the pie is left?

   b. What fraction of the pie did Miss Wu eat?

   c. What fraction of the pie did Mr. Estrada and Miss Wu eat altogether? Draw a picture that shows your answer.

2. Ramon bought 12 bagels. He ordered 6 sesame bagels, 4 garlic bagels, and 2 onion bagels.

   a. What fraction of Ramon's bagels are sesame bagels?

   b. What fraction of the bagels are garlic?

   c. What fraction are onion?

3. Rob had $14.00. He bought a puzzle for $4.50 and a pen for $3.00. Did he spend more than $\frac{1}{2}$ of his money?

4. Lydia and her parents went out for pizza last week. They ordered a large pizza with pepperoni and cheese. The cook cut the pizza into 12 equal slices. Lydia ate 3 slices, her father ate 4, and her mother ate 3.

   a. What fraction of the pizza did Lydia eat?

   b. What fraction of the pizza did her father eat?

   c. What fraction of the pizza did her mother eat?

   d. What fraction of the pizza was eaten altogether?

   e. What fraction of the pizza was left over?

You can think of finding a fraction of a whole number in the same way you would use a fraction to describe a portion of a set of objects:

- What is $\frac{1}{4}$ of 24?

Divide 24 into 4 equal portions.

$24 \div 4 = 6$

There are 6 eggs in each $\frac{1}{4}$-portion of the 24 eggs. So, $\frac{1}{4}$ of 24 is 6.

- What is $\frac{3}{7}$ of 14?

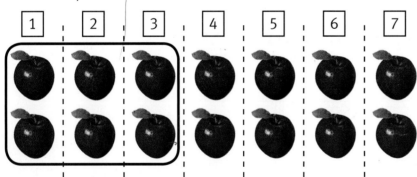

Divide 14 into 7 equal portions.

$14 \div 7 = 2$

There are 2 apples in each $\frac{1}{7}$-portion of the 14 apples. So, $\frac{1}{7}$ of 14 is 2.

We need 3 of those $\frac{1}{7}$ portions to have $\frac{3}{7}$ of 14.

Take 3 of those portions: $3 \times 2 = 6$. So, $\frac{3}{7}$ of 14 is 6.

The denominator of a fraction tells how many equal portions there are altogether. The numerator tells how many of those equal portions to consider.

ⓔ **Textbook** This lesson is available in the *eTextbook*.

Solve for *n*. Algebra

5. $\frac{1}{3}$ of 15 = *n*

6. $\frac{2}{3}$ of 15 = *n*

7. $\frac{3}{3}$ of 15 = *n*

8. $\frac{1}{5}$ of 15 = *n*

9. $\frac{1}{5}$ of 30 = *n*

10. $\frac{1}{5}$ of 60 = *n*

11. $\frac{2}{5}$ of 30 = *n*

12. $\frac{2}{5}$ of 60 = *n*

13. $n = \frac{2}{6}$ of 90

14. $n = \frac{1}{6}$ of 90

15. $n = \frac{0}{6}$ of 90

16. $n = \frac{4}{6}$ of 90

17. $n = \frac{4}{6}$ of 60

18. $n = \frac{2}{3}$ of 60

19. $n = \frac{2}{5}$ of 120

20. $n = \frac{4}{10}$ of 120

21. $n = \frac{4}{8}$ of 64

22. $n = \frac{2}{4}$ of 64

23. $n = \frac{1}{4}$ of 36

24. $n = \frac{2}{4}$ of 36

25. $n = \frac{4}{5}$ of 30

26. $n = \frac{2}{5}$ of 45

27. $n = \frac{1}{8}$ of 24

28. $n = \frac{6}{8}$ of 36

Answer the following questions. You may wish to draw a picture of each answer choice to help you decide on the correct fraction.

29. Chen asked the 30 people in his class to name their favorite flower. If 9 people said they liked roses best, then what fraction of the class chose roses?

   a. $\frac{2}{5}$

   b. $\frac{1}{2}$

   c. $\frac{3}{10}$

30. Holly has read 6 pages of a 24-page research paper. What fraction of the research paper has Holly read?

   a. $\frac{1}{2}$

   b. $\frac{1}{4}$

   c. $\frac{2}{3}$

Fractions of Fractions

Key Ideas

Finding a fraction of a fraction is the same as multiplying the two fractions.

Penny baked a cake for herself and her 3 brothers. She cut it into 5 equal parts and decided that, since she did all of the baking, 2 of the parts would be hers—or $\frac{2}{5}$ of the cake.

Penny then decided to cut her portion of the cake into 7 equal portions, one for each day of the week.

- How much is each day's share of Penny's cake?

Each day's share is 1 of 7 equal portions, or $\frac{1}{7}$.

- How many small pieces of cake will she eat in every $\frac{1}{7}$-portion?

We can see from the picture that she will eat 2 small pieces each day.

After 4 days, Penny had $\frac{3}{7}$ of her cake remaining. (Remember, her portion is $\frac{2}{5}$ of the whole cake.)

- How many small pieces does Penny have left?

There are 6 small pieces.

- How many of Penny's small cake pieces would there have been in the whole cake (before she gave any to her brothers)?

🅔 **Textbook** This lesson is available in the *eTextbook*.

From the picture, you can count that there would have been 35 total pieces.

We can use a fraction to describe the amount of *the whole cake* that Penny has left.

$\dfrac{6}{35}$ ◄——— Penny has this many pieces left. There would be this
◄——— many equal-sized pieces in the whole cake.

So when Penny has $\dfrac{3}{7}$ of $\dfrac{2}{5}$ of the whole cake remaining, she has $\dfrac{6}{35}$ of the whole cake left.

$\dfrac{3}{7}$ of $\dfrac{2}{5} = \dfrac{6}{35}$ ◄——— Notice that this comes from 3×2.
◄——— Notice that this comes from 7×5.

Because this is the same as multiplying the two fractions, we can write a problem like $\dfrac{3}{7}$ of $\dfrac{2}{5}$ as $\dfrac{3}{7} \times \dfrac{2}{5}$.

It makes sense to say that the word *of* means multiplication—multiplying the denominators gives the total number of parts and multiplying the numerators gives the total number of parts considered.

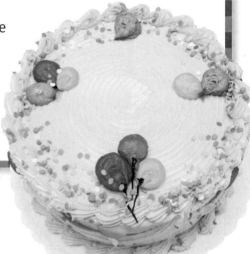

Multiply.

1. $\dfrac{4}{7} \times \dfrac{2}{5} = $ ▢

2. $\dfrac{2}{7} \times \dfrac{2}{5} = $ ▢

3. $\dfrac{7}{7} \times \dfrac{2}{5} = $ ▢

4. $\dfrac{3}{7} \times \dfrac{2}{5} = $ ▢

5. $\dfrac{2}{5} \times \dfrac{4}{7} = $ ▢

6. $\dfrac{3}{5} \times \dfrac{2}{7} = $ ▢

7. $\dfrac{1}{5} \times \dfrac{4}{7} = $ ▢

8. $\dfrac{3}{5} \times \dfrac{5}{7} = $ ▢

9. $\dfrac{1}{5} \times \dfrac{1}{7} = $ ▢

10. $\dfrac{5}{5} \times \dfrac{7}{7} = $ ▢

11. $\dfrac{4}{5} \times \dfrac{3}{7} = $ ▢

12. $\dfrac{3}{5} \times \dfrac{4}{7} = $ ▢

Replace the ▢ to make each statement true.

13. $\dfrac{1}{2} \times $ ▢ $= \dfrac{1}{12}$

14. $\dfrac{3}{4}$ of ▢ $= \dfrac{6}{16}$

15. $\dfrac{4}{5} \times $ ▢ $= \dfrac{8}{45}$

16. $\dfrac{2}{9}$ of ▢ $= \dfrac{8}{45}$

17. $\dfrac{3}{4}$ of ▢ $= \dfrac{6}{12}$

18. $\dfrac{5}{8} \times $ ▢ $= \dfrac{10}{56}$

| Writing + Math ▸ **Journal**

Draw a picture showing how to find $\dfrac{3}{5}$ of $\dfrac{1}{4}$. Write a rule in your own words about how to find a fraction of a fraction.

Key Ideas

Every decimal has an equivalent fraction, but not every fraction has an exact decimal equivalent.

- What is $\frac{1}{2}$ of 4 sandwiches? If we take half of the sandwiches in this group, we will have 2 sandwiches.

- What is $\frac{1}{2}$ of 4?

The halfway point on a number line from 0 to 4 is 2.

$$0 \qquad\qquad 2 \qquad\qquad 4$$

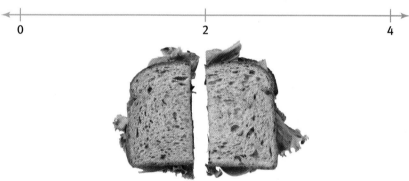

- What is $\frac{1}{2}$ of 1 sandwich? Half of a single sandwich is $\frac{1}{2}$.

- What is $\frac{1}{2}$ of 1?

The middle point on a number line from 0 to 1 is $\frac{1}{2}$.

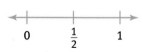

$$0 \qquad \frac{1}{2} \qquad 1$$

As you can see, fractions can be used to name positions on a number line. These positions represent numbers called rational numbers.

A rational number, by definition, can be written as a fraction $\left(\frac{a}{b}\right)$ using any two whole integers (a and b), as long as the denominator (b) is positive. For example, $\frac{1}{2}$, $\frac{4}{5}$, $-\frac{7}{8}$, $\frac{15}{4}$, and $\frac{0}{5}$ are all rational numbers and have a distinct position on the number line.

eTextbook This lesson is available in the *eTextbook*.

But how do we know where any fraction (or rational number) goes on a number line? Let's look at $\frac{1}{2}$ again.

On a number line from 0 to 1, we already know that $\frac{1}{2}$ is the middle point. If we plotted the decimal 0.5, it would also be the middle point.

- What decimal answer do you get if you divide 1 by 2?

$$2\overline{)\begin{array}{l} 0.5 \\ 1.0 \end{array}}$$

So, we can write $\frac{1}{2} = 1 \div 2 = 0.5$. We call 0.5 the decimal equivalent of $\frac{1}{2}$.

To find information about any rational number's place on the number line, you can divide its numerator by its denominator. For many fractions, such as $\frac{1}{2}$, you can find an exact decimal equivalent.

Usually, however, you will not get an exact decimal equivalent when you divide, and you will have to approximate.

- Let's try to find a decimal equivalent of $\frac{1}{3}$ (by dividing 1 by 3).

$$3\overline{)\begin{array}{l} 0.3333333333... \\ 1.0000000000... \end{array}}$$

- Do you think this quotient will ever end?

It will go on and on. We can approximate $\frac{1}{3}$ to as many places as we wish with a decimal. For example, if we approximate to the nearest thousandth, we would say $\frac{1}{3}$ is about 0.333. But we cannot write a decimal that is exactly equal to $\frac{1}{3}$ in the usual way.

For each fraction, give the decimal equivalent or an approximation to the nearest thousandth. To help you check your answers, each fraction is placed above its corresponding point on a number line. Work in groups.

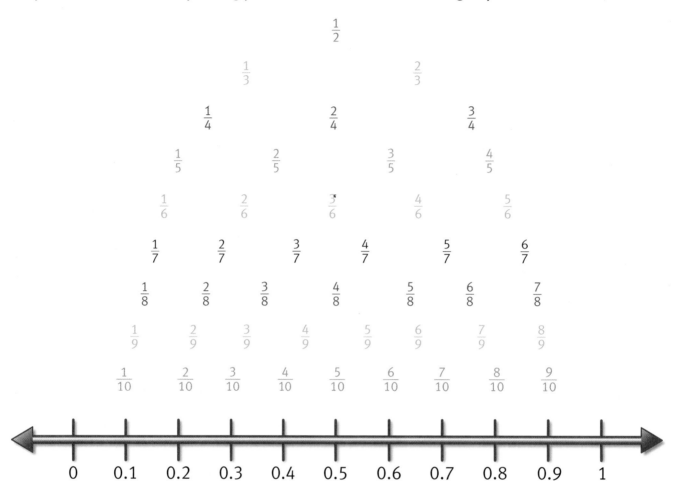

When you are finished, draw a table to organize the fractions and their decimal equivalents or approximations. Save your chart. You will find it useful when you play the **Up to 1 Game.**

252

Game

Decimal Equivalency and Strategies Practice

Up to 1 Game

Players: Two or more

Materials: *Number Cubes* (two 0–5, two 5–10)

Object: To be the last player to pass 1

Math Focus: Comparing and ordering fractions and decimals; finding decimal equivalents of common fractions

HOW TO PLAY

1. For each round, every player should take a turn rolling all four *Number Cubes*.

2. Use any two of the numbers rolled to make a fraction or a decimal less than 1. (For example, if you roll 1, 2, 8, and 7, you could make $\frac{1}{2}$, $\frac{1}{7}$, $\frac{1}{8}$, $\frac{2}{7}$, $\frac{2}{8}$, $\frac{7}{8}$, or any of these decimals: .12, .17, .18, .21, .27, .28, .71, .72, .78, .81, .82, or .87.)

3. For each turn, write the number you make as a decimal. If you make a fraction, record the decimal equivalent (or approximation) to the nearest thousandth, as well as the fraction. You may use a calculator for this if you wish.

4. On each turn, you must write a number greater than the number made on your previous turn.

5. If you cannot write a number less than 1 that is also greater than your previous number, you are out.

6. The last player to go out wins. If all players are unable to go in the same round, then it is a tie.

SAMPLE GAME

Turn	Alex's Record Roll	Number Made	Whitt's Record Roll	Number Made
1	8 10 4 4	0.40 ($\frac{4}{10}$)	8 7 3 2	0.23
2	2 5 3 5	0.60 ($\frac{3}{5}$)	7 1 0 7	0.70
3	1 1 8 10	0.80 ($\frac{8}{10}$)	5 1 8 6	0.75 ($\frac{6}{8}$)
4	10 6 1 5	0.83 ($\frac{5}{6}$)	2 1 6 6	cannot go

Alex won.

LESSON 6.4 Equivalent Fractions

Key Ideas

Fractions that represent the same rational number are called *equivalent fractions.*

Jim and Sally made a pizza. "Okay," said Sally, "do you want to slice it into 8 pieces as usual?"

"No," said Jim. "I don't think we can eat 8 pieces. Just slice it into 4 pieces." Does Jim's answer make sense?

No, it does not. To understand why, think about this question: Which is greater, $\frac{4}{4}$ of the pizza or $\frac{8}{8}$ of the pizza?

Both fractions represent the same amount—the entire pizza.

Later in the week, Jim and some friends made 2 large pizzas. They sliced 1 pizza into 6 equal pieces and the other into 12 equal pieces.

Jim ate 2 pieces from the 6-slice pizza.

Diego ate 4 pieces from the 12-slice pizza.

- Who ate more pizza, Jim or Diego? They ate the same amount. Diego ate more pieces, but his pieces were smaller.

- Which is more, 4 slices from the 6-slice pizza or 8 slices from the 12-slice pizza? Neither is larger. The fractions $\frac{4}{6}$ and $\frac{8}{12}$ are the same amount.

- How many slices of the 12-slice pizza would equal 1 piece of the 6-slice pizza? You can see from the pictures that $\frac{2}{12}$ of a pizza is the same as $\frac{1}{6}$ of a pizza. Therefore, $\frac{2}{12}$ and $\frac{1}{6}$ are equivalent fractions.

If you multiply both the numerator and the denominator of a fraction by the same number, the value of the fraction does not change.

For example: $\frac{1}{6} = \frac{(1 \times 2)}{(6 \times 2)} = \frac{2}{12}$

Think in terms of portions of a circle:

When you multiply the denominator by 2, you are dividing the circle into twice as many parts: $2 \times 6 = 12$. When you multiply the numerator by 2, you are taking twice as many parts.

$1 \times 2 = 2$.

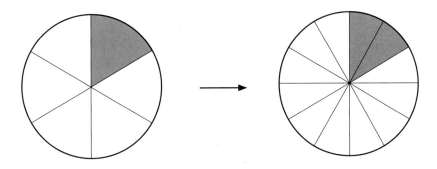

If you look at this process in reverse, you can see that it also works for division.

$\frac{2}{12} = \frac{(2 \div 2)}{(12 \div 2)} = \frac{1}{6}$

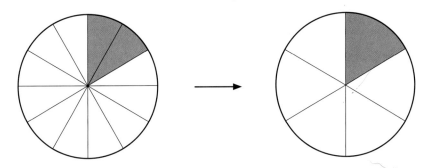

If the numerator *and* the denominator of a fraction are multiplied or divided by the same number, the result will be an equivalent fraction.

This fact means that for *any* fraction, we can make an endless number of equivalent fractions. The fractions $\frac{1}{6}$, $\frac{2}{12}$ ($\times \frac{2}{2}$), $\frac{3}{18}$ ($\times \frac{3}{3}$), $\frac{12}{72}$ ($\times \frac{12}{12}$), and so on are all equivalent fractions.

This fact will be useful when doing arithmetic with fractions or when comparing and ordering them.

Fractions that yield the same amount are equivalent—they represent the same rational number. Let's practice finding equivalent fractions.

- Example:

Find the missing numerator: $\dfrac{3}{4} = \dfrac{\square}{8}$

Since the denominator on the right is 2 times the other, then the numerator on the right must also be 2 times the other. So, the missing numerator is 6.

$$\dfrac{3}{4} = \dfrac{6}{8}$$

- Example:

Find the missing denominator: $\dfrac{8}{\square} = \dfrac{4}{6}$

Since the numerator on the left is 2 times the other, then the denominator on the left must also be 2 times the other. So, the missing denominator is 12.

$$\dfrac{8}{12} = \dfrac{4}{6}$$

Find the missing numerator or denominator.

1. $\dfrac{1}{3} = \dfrac{\square}{12}$

2. $\dfrac{\square}{20} = \dfrac{3}{5}$

3. $\dfrac{2}{3} = \dfrac{10}{\square}$

4. $\dfrac{1}{2} = \dfrac{\square}{18}$

5. $\dfrac{\square}{12} = \dfrac{2}{3}$

6. $\dfrac{\square}{24} = \dfrac{5}{6}$

7. $\dfrac{20}{\square} = \dfrac{2}{3}$

8. $\dfrac{5}{7} = \dfrac{20}{\square}$

9. $\dfrac{3}{4} = \dfrac{\square}{12}$

10. $\dfrac{1}{7} = \dfrac{3}{\square}$

11. $\dfrac{\square}{8} = \dfrac{3}{4}$

12. $\dfrac{1}{\square} = \dfrac{3}{9}$

13. $\dfrac{3}{\square} = \dfrac{1}{5}$

14. $\dfrac{3}{4} = \dfrac{\square}{20}$

15. $\dfrac{1}{2} = \dfrac{\square}{16}$

The fractions $\frac{2}{3}$, $\frac{6}{9}$, $\frac{10}{15}$, $\frac{14}{21}$, $\frac{18}{27}$, and $\frac{22}{33}$ all represent the same rational number. For some purposes, any one of these would work. For other purposes, you might need a particular fraction. Which of the fractions would you prefer if you wanted to compare the number with $\frac{15}{21}$? Which would you prefer if you wanted to compare the number with the fraction $\frac{21}{33}$?

A *common factor* of two numbers is a number that divides into both numbers without leaving a remainder. When a fraction has no common factors in the numerator and denominator (other than 1), we say the fraction has been reduced to *lowest terms*.

To reduce a fraction to lowest terms, divide both the numerator and the denominator by any common factors. For example, to reduce $\frac{22}{33}$ to lowest terms, divide both 22 and 33 by 11 ($\frac{22 \div 11}{33 \div 11} = \frac{2}{3}$) to get $\frac{2}{3}$. To reduce $\frac{18}{27}$ to lowest terms, divide both the numerator and denominator by 9, to get $\frac{2}{3}$.

Reduce each of the following fractions to lowest terms.

16. $\frac{17}{34} = \blacksquare$ 17. $\frac{16}{80} = \blacksquare$ 18. $\frac{16}{64} = \blacksquare$

19. $\frac{9}{27} = \blacksquare$ 20. $\frac{9}{36} = \blacksquare$ 21. $\frac{27}{36} = \blacksquare$

22. $\frac{18}{36} = \blacksquare$ 23. $\frac{12}{30} = \blacksquare$ 24. $\frac{9}{30} = \blacksquare$

25. $\frac{18}{30} = \blacksquare$ 26. $\frac{5}{30} = \blacksquare$ 27. $\frac{5}{35} = \blacksquare$

28. $\frac{15}{35} = \blacksquare$ 29. $\frac{25}{35} = \blacksquare$ 30. $\frac{20}{35} = \blacksquare$

Write three equivalent fractions for each of the following fractions.

31. $\frac{1}{3}$ 36. $\frac{3}{5}$

32. $\frac{1}{5}$ 37. $\frac{3}{7}$

33. $\frac{1}{7}$ 38. $\frac{4}{9}$

34. $\frac{4}{7}$ 39. $\frac{3}{5}$

35. $\frac{1}{4}$ 40. $\frac{5}{9}$

Key Ideas

To add or subtract fractions with the same denominator, simply add or subtract the numerators.

Joe, Carlos, Lee Ann, and Latisha went to Sophie's Pizza Place. They were all hungry, so they ordered 2 large pizzas. When the pizzas were ready, Sophie cut each of them into 12 equal parts. Although the friends were hungry, they could not eat all the pizza. These pictures show what the 2 pizzas looked like when they finished eating.

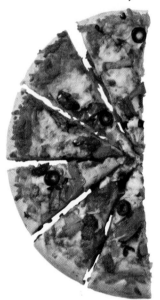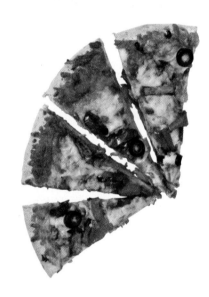

"Boy, there's a lot of pizza left," said Joe. "I wonder whether we needed to order 2. What fraction of a whole pizza is left?"

Latisha said, "There is $\frac{4}{12}$ of this pizza and $\frac{6}{12}$ of that one left. Let's put the pieces on one dish and see what fraction of one pizza it is altogether."

- Adding the remaining slices results in 10 slices. What fraction of a whole pizza would the 10 slices be?
  If each piece is $\frac{1}{12}$ of a pizza, then 10 slices would be $\frac{10}{12}$ of a whole pizza.

The friends also bought a large pitcher of lemonade. Sophie told them that the pitcher held 12 glasses of lemonade.

Joe poured a glassful for each of his friends. Joe, Carlos, and Lee Ann drank their glasses of lemonade, and each poured another glassful.

Latisha said, "I wonder what fraction of the lemonade is left."

ⓔ Textbook This lesson is available in the *eTextbook*.

Carlos said, "That's easy to figure out. We started with 12 glassfuls in the pitcher and poured 4 glassfuls. So, there were 8 glassfuls left, or $\frac{8}{12}$ of the lemonade. Then we poured 3 more glassfuls, or $\frac{3}{12}$ of the lemonade. So, there are 5 more glassfuls left, or $\frac{5}{12}$ of the lemonade."

$\frac{8}{12} - \frac{3}{12} = \frac{5}{12}$. If all 4 friends now fill their glasses again, what fraction of the lemonade will be left?

$\frac{5}{12} - \frac{4}{12} = \frac{1}{12}$, so there will be 1 glass of lemonade left.

To add or subtract fractions with the same denominator, just add or subtract the numerators.

Example: $\frac{4}{7} - \frac{1}{7}$

Let's divide a line segment into sevenths.

This is $\frac{4}{7}$ of the line segment.

This is $\frac{1}{7}$ of the line segment.

$\frac{4}{7} - \frac{1}{7} = \frac{3}{7}$

Example: $\frac{7}{9} - \frac{5}{9}$

The denominators are the same, so we can subtract the numerators.

$\frac{7}{9} - \frac{5}{9} = \frac{2}{9}$

Add or subtract.

1. $\frac{3}{4} + \frac{1}{4} = \blacksquare$

2. $\frac{2}{5} + \frac{2}{5} = \blacksquare$

3. $\frac{4}{8} - \frac{2}{8} = \blacksquare$

4. $\frac{1}{3} + \frac{1}{3} = \blacksquare$

5. $\frac{6}{12} - \frac{2}{12} = \blacksquare$

6. $\frac{2}{3} - \frac{1}{3} = \blacksquare$

7. $\frac{5}{7} + \frac{2}{7} = \blacksquare$

8. $\frac{9}{10} - \frac{4}{10} = \blacksquare$

When you add or subtract fractions, sometimes the answer can be rewritten in lower terms. You should rewrite the answer in lower terms only when it is more convenient for you or for other people. Let's practice how to do this.

Example: $\frac{1}{10} + \frac{3}{10}$

$\frac{1}{10} + \frac{3}{10} = \frac{4}{10}$ The numerator and denominator have a common factor of 2.

$\frac{(4 \div 2)}{(10 \div 2)} = \frac{2}{5}$ Divide both the numerator and the denominator by 2.

So, if we want the answer in lowest terms, $\frac{1}{10} + \frac{3}{10} = \frac{2}{5}$.

Example: $\frac{11}{15} - \frac{8}{15}$

$\frac{11}{15} - \frac{8}{15} = \frac{3}{15}$ The numerator and denominator have a common factor of 3.

$\frac{(3 \div 3)}{(15 \div 3)} = \frac{1}{5}$ Divide both the numerator and the denominator by 3.

So, if we want the answer in lowest terms, $\frac{11}{15} - \frac{8}{15} = \frac{1}{5}$.

Add or subtract. Write answers in lowest terms.

9 $\frac{1}{7} + \frac{2}{7} = \blacksquare$

10 $\frac{5}{6} - \frac{4}{6} = \blacksquare$

11 $\frac{4}{7} - \frac{3}{7} = \blacksquare$

12 $\frac{7}{12} - \frac{6}{12} = \blacksquare$

13 $\frac{3}{6} + \frac{2}{6} = \blacksquare$

14 $\frac{5}{6} - \frac{5}{6} = \blacksquare$

15 $\frac{6}{8} - \frac{3}{8} = \blacksquare$

16 $\frac{4}{12} - \frac{3}{12} = \blacksquare$

17 $\frac{8}{8} - \frac{3}{8} = \blacksquare$

18 $\frac{1}{9} + \frac{2}{9} = \blacksquare$

19 $\frac{6}{9} - \frac{4}{9} = \blacksquare$

20 $\frac{3}{10} + \frac{2}{10} = \blacksquare$

21 $\frac{4}{5} - \frac{2}{5} = \blacksquare$

22 $\frac{6}{6} - \frac{3}{6} = \blacksquare$

23 $\frac{2}{3} + \frac{1}{3} = \blacksquare$

24 $\frac{7}{9} - \frac{4}{9} = \blacksquare$

25 $\frac{8}{15} + \frac{4}{15} = \blacksquare$

26 $\frac{12}{16} + \frac{2}{16} = \blacksquare$

27 $\frac{5}{10} + \frac{3}{10} = \blacksquare$

28 $\frac{5}{11} + \frac{3}{11} = \blacksquare$

29 $\frac{12}{18} - \frac{6}{18} = \blacksquare$

e Textbook This lesson is available in the **eTextbook.**

Solve the following problems.

30 Mike baked a pie and then cut it into 8 equal parts.

    a. What fraction of the whole pie was each part?

    b. Mike ate $\frac{3}{8}$ of the pie, and Ana ate $\frac{2}{8}$ of the pie. How much did they eat altogether?

    c. How much of the pie was left?

31 Mr. and Mrs. Cosby drove across the country. They started in Portland, Maine, and drove to Portland, Oregon, which is about 3,100 miles away. They divided the trip into 10 equal parts and drove 1 part each day.

    a. What fraction of the trip did the Cosbys complete on the first day?

    b. How many miles is that?

    c. What fraction of the trip did the Cosbys complete in 1 week (7 days)?

32 **Extended Response** Bob and 4 friends decided to fill a tub with water from his well. Each of the 5 people brought a bucket full of water. Each bucket had enough water to fill $\frac{1}{4}$ of the tub. How full was the tub after they all poured their buckets into it? Explain.

LESSON 6.6 Practice with Fractions

Key Ideas

It is easier to compare fractions when they have the same denominator.

We often use fractions when measuring lengths with a ruler.

A typical ruler looks something like this:

Look along the length of the ruler, between the 0″ mark and the 1″ mark, at the lines of different lengths. Answer the following questions:

1 What length does the longest of those lines represent?

2 There are two lines that are shorter than the $\frac{1}{2}''$ mark but longer than any of the other lines. What lengths do they stand for?

3 **Extended Response** Find the marks for $\frac{1''}{8}$, $\frac{3''}{8}$, $\frac{5''}{8}$, and $\frac{7''}{8}$ on the ruler. Where are the marks for $\frac{2''}{8}$, $\frac{4''}{8}$, and $\frac{6''}{8}$? How are the odd-numbered eighths different from the even-numbered eighths? Why are they marked this way?

4 The shortest marks on this ruler stand for sixteenths of an inch. For each of the following, tell whether the given mark corresponds to the marks for $\frac{1''}{2}$, $\frac{1''}{4}$, $\frac{1''}{8}$, or whether it is one of the shortest marks:

a. $\frac{1}{16}$　　　　　b. $\frac{2}{16}$　　　　　c. $\frac{3}{16}$

d. $\frac{4}{16}$　　　　　e. $\frac{5}{16}$　　　　　f. $\frac{6}{16}$

g. $\frac{7}{16}$　　　　　h. $\frac{8}{16}$　　　　　i. $\frac{9}{16}$

j. $\frac{10}{16}$　　　　　k. $\frac{11}{16}$　　　　　l. $\frac{12}{16}$

m. $\frac{13}{16}$　　　　　n. $\frac{14}{16}$　　　　　o. $\frac{15}{16}$

ⓔTextbook This lesson is available in the *eTextbook*.

We usually add or subtract fractions that come from measurements. The measurements themselves almost always have the same denominators, or one denominator is a multiple of the other. If you measured two short lines, and one was $\frac{4}{16}''$ and the other was $\frac{2}{16}''$, you would likely report the lengths as $\frac{1}{4}''$ and $\frac{1}{8}''$. However, you can look back at the measuring instrument to see that $\frac{1}{4}''$ corresponds to $\frac{4}{16}''$ or $\frac{2}{8}''$, or you can multiply the numerator and the denominator of $\frac{1}{4}$ by 2.

Decide which fraction in each of the following pairs is greater. Write a $<$, $>$, or $=$ symbol.

5. $\frac{1}{2}$ ⬜ $\frac{3}{4}$

6. $\frac{5}{16}$ ⬜ $\frac{3}{8}$

7. $\frac{7}{8}$ ⬜ $\frac{3}{4}$

8. $\frac{1}{4}$ ⬜ $\frac{1}{2}$

9. $\frac{2}{16}$ ⬜ $\frac{1}{8}$

10. $\frac{15}{16}$ ⬜ $\frac{3}{4}$

11. $\frac{6}{8}$ ⬜ $\frac{11}{16}$

12. $\frac{1}{2}$ ⬜ $\frac{10}{16}$

13. $\frac{2}{4}$ ⬜ $\frac{8}{16}$

14. $\frac{4}{16}$ ⬜ $\frac{2}{8}$

15. $\frac{7}{16}$ ⬜ $\frac{3}{8}$

16. $\frac{7}{16}$ ⬜ $\frac{1}{2}$

17. $\frac{1}{8}$ ⬜ $\frac{3}{16}$

18. $\frac{12}{16}$ ⬜ $\frac{7}{8}$

19. $\frac{7}{8}$ ⬜ $\frac{14}{16}$

20. $\frac{9}{16}$ ⬜ $\frac{1}{2}$

Writing + Math **Journal**

You measure a pencil to be 4 inches long. How many $\frac{1}{2}$ inches is that? $\frac{1}{4}$ inches? $\frac{1}{8}$ inches? $\frac{1}{16}$ inches? Write three rules for changing a measurement from one unit to another (for example, $\frac{1}{2}'' = 2$ quarter inches).

Burrito Bonito offers a variety of burritos on their menu. What fraction of the burritos contain beef?

Rita solved the problem this way:

I Made an Organized List.
I used a system to make sure I listed every possibility.

First I listed all the burritos with beef.	Then I listed all the burritos with chicken.	Then I listed all the burritos with no meat.
beef + cheese + beans	chicken + cheese + beans	beans + cheese
beef + cheese	chicken + cheese	beans only
beef + beans	chicken + beans	cheese only
beef only	chicken only	

Think about Rita's strategy. Answer the following questions.

1. What system did Rita use to help her make the list in an organized way?

2. How does organizing help to make sure that nothing is missed and nothing is listed twice?

3. What answer will Rita get? Why?

DeShawn solved this problem another way:

I Made an Organized List and Used Logical Reasoning.

I listed 7 types of burritos. Because 4 of them have meat, that means $\frac{4}{7}$ of the burritos have meat. Because $\frac{1}{2}$ of the meat burritos have beef, that means $\frac{1}{2}$ of $\frac{4}{7}$ of the burritos have beef.

With meat
meat, cheese, & beans
meat & cheese
meat & beans
meat only

Without meat
beans & cheese
beans only
cheese only

Think about DeShawn's solution. Answer the following questions.

④ How did DeShawn organize his list?

⑤ What answer will DeShawn get if he continues?

⑥ Will DeShawn get the same answer as Rita? Explain.

⑦ Do you agree with DeShawn's statement that $\frac{4}{7}$ of the burritos have meat? Why or why not?

⑧ What is your answer to the problem? Explain.

Solve the following problems. Explain how you solved them.

⑨ Suppose Burrito Bonito now offers two choices of bean filling. Now what fraction of the burritos have beef?

⑩ Do a greater fraction of the burritos have beef now that there are two kinds of beans?

Cumulative Review

Decimals and Money **Lesson 3.1**

Add or subtract.

1 $24.17
  $+ 36.84$

2 $121.83
  $- 87.98$

3 $300.00
  $- 94.87$

Using Number Patterns to Predict **Lesson 4.2**

	If you start at this number	and you keep doing this,	which number or numbers will you hit?
4	10	add 20	a. 100 b. 150 c. 650
5	3	add 6	a. 27 b. 45 c. 72
6	500	subtract 3	a. 400 b. 300 c. 200

Function Machines **Lesson 4.4**

Solve.

7 A function machine gives 10 as the answer when 30 is put in. You could program your calculator to do this in two ways. What are they?

Find the number that came out (*y*) or the function machine rule.

8

17 ⟶ ⬛ ⟶ 9

9

7 ⟶ ×8 ⟶ *y*

Graphing in Four Quadrants Lesson 5.4

Copy and complete these tables on a sheet of paper. Then graph the ordered pairs.

10

$$x \longrightarrow \boxed{-3} \longrightarrow y$$

x	0	2	5	6	−2
y	−3	▪	▪	▪	▪

11

$$x \longrightarrow \boxed{\times 4} \longrightarrow y$$

x	1	2	3	4	5
y	4	▪	▪	▪	▪

Multiplying and Dividing by Powers of 10 Lesson 3.6

Multiply or divide.

12 $3.624 \times 100 = $ ▪

14 $0.6789 \times 1,000 = $ ▪

13 $36.24 \div 100 = $ ▪

15 $9.876 \div 1,000 = $ ▪

Applying Decimals Lesson 3.15

Solve.

16 Nathan buys a hot dog for $2.75, a drink for $1.75, and chips for $1.25 at the ball game.

  A. What is Nathan's change if he pays with a $10 bill?

  B. What is Nathan's change if he pays with a $20 bill?

17 The XYZ Store buys T-shirts in boxes of 100. Each box costs $350. If the shirts are sold for $6 each, how much profit will the store make on each shirt?

Key Ideas

To compare two fractions, you can find equivalent fractions with the same denominator.

Yoshi has $\frac{2}{3}$ of a pizza, and Rosa has $\frac{3}{4}$ of a pizza. Who has more pizza?

$$\frac{2}{3} \quad \boxed{} \quad \frac{3}{4}$$

These fractions do not have the same denominator. How can we compare them?

We want both fractions to have a common denominator. So, we will first replace each fraction with an equivalent fraction. Then we will be able to compare the fractions. The number 12 has both 3 and 4 as factors, so we will choose a denominator of 12:

$$\frac{2}{3} = \frac{\boxed{}}{12} \qquad \frac{3}{4} = \frac{\boxed{}}{12}$$

- Replace $\frac{2}{3}$ with $\frac{8}{12}$ (by multiplying both the numerator and denominator by 4).

$$\frac{2}{3} \times \frac{4}{4} = \frac{(2 \times 4)}{(3 \times 4)} = \frac{8}{12}$$

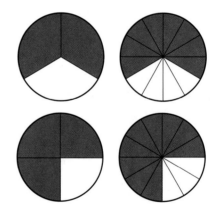

- Replace $\frac{3}{4}$ with $\frac{9}{12}$ (by multiplying both the numerator and denominator by 3).

$$\frac{3}{4} \times \frac{3}{3} = \frac{(3 \times 3)}{(4 \times 3)} = \frac{9}{12}$$

Now that the denominators are the same, we can compare the fractions by comparing the numerators.

Since $\frac{8}{12} < \frac{9}{12}$, it is also true that $\frac{2}{3} < \frac{3}{4}$.

So, Rosa has more pizza than Yoshi.

e **Textbook** This lesson is available in the *eTextbook*.

There is more than one way to find a common denominator.

- One way is to make a list of equivalent fractions for each fraction, and then look for a pair with the same denominator.

Example: Replace $\frac{2}{5}$ and $\frac{1}{4}$ with equivalent fractions that have a common denominator.

$\frac{2}{5} = \frac{4}{10} = \frac{6}{15} = \mathbf{\frac{8}{20}} = \frac{10}{25} = \frac{12}{30} = \frac{14}{35}$ and so on.

$\frac{1}{4} = \frac{2}{8} = \frac{3}{12} = \frac{4}{16} = \mathbf{\frac{5}{20}} = \frac{6}{24} = \frac{7}{28} = \frac{8}{32}$ and so on.

We can say that 20 is a common denominator of $\frac{2}{5}$ and $\frac{1}{4}$.

$\frac{8}{20} > \frac{5}{20}$, so $\frac{2}{5} > \frac{1}{4}$.

- You can always find a common denominator for two fractions by multiplying their denominators.

Example: Find a common denominator for $\frac{5}{6}$ and $\frac{3}{4}$. Multiply 6×4 to get 24. Use 24 as a common denominator.

$\frac{5}{6} = \frac{\blacksquare}{24} = \frac{20}{24}$ $\frac{3}{4} = \frac{\blacksquare}{24} = \frac{18}{24}$

If you use this method, you often would not find the least common denominator. For example, in this case, 12 is also a common denominator.

$\frac{5}{6} = \frac{10}{12}$ $\frac{3}{4} = \frac{9}{12}$

However, whichever common denominator you use, you will be able to make the same correct conclusion.

$\frac{20}{24} > \frac{18}{24}$ $\frac{10}{12} > \frac{9}{12}$

So, $\frac{5}{6} > \frac{3}{4}$.   So, $\frac{5}{6} > \frac{3}{4}$.

Find a common denominator for each of the following pairs of fractions.

1. $\frac{2}{3}, \frac{1}{6}$ 2. $\frac{1}{10}, \frac{3}{5}$ 3. $\frac{1}{2}, \frac{1}{4}$

4. $\frac{1}{8}, \frac{3}{4}$ 5. $\frac{1}{3}, \frac{2}{5}$ 6. $\frac{1}{4}, \frac{2}{3}$

7. $\frac{1}{6}, \frac{3}{8}$ 8. $\frac{4}{9}, \frac{1}{2}$ 9. $\frac{1}{12}, \frac{3}{10}$

10. $\frac{1}{2}, \frac{4}{5}$ 11. $\frac{3}{4}, \frac{1}{6}$ 12. $\frac{1}{4}, \frac{5}{8}$

You can find a common denominator for more than two fractions.

Example: Find a common denominator for $\frac{1}{3}$, $\frac{1}{4}$, and $\frac{2}{7}$.

You need a number that has 3, 4, and 7 among its factors (in other words, a number that is divisible by 3, 4, and 7). The numbers 84, 252, and 1,008 all have factors of 3, 4, and 7, so any of those numbers could be common denominators for this group of fractions. However, the least common denominator is 84.

Find a common denominator for each of the following groups of fractions.

13. $\frac{1}{3}, \frac{5}{6}, \frac{1}{8}$

14. $\frac{5}{9}, \frac{3}{4}, \frac{13}{16}$

15. $\frac{8}{12}, \frac{3}{4}, \frac{1}{2}$

16. $\frac{4}{5}, \frac{3}{15}, \frac{7}{45}$

17. $\frac{1}{6}, \frac{3}{5}, \frac{2}{3}$

18. $\frac{1}{9}, \frac{2}{3}, \frac{4}{27}$

Replace ▢ with either <, >, or = to make each comparison correct.

19. $\frac{1}{3}$ ▢ $\frac{4}{12}$

20. $\frac{1}{3}$ ▢ $\frac{2}{7}$

21. $\frac{2}{3}$ ▢ $\frac{4}{6}$

22. $\frac{11}{22}$ ▢ $\frac{33}{44}$

23. $\frac{1}{6}$ ▢ $\frac{1}{2}$

24. $\frac{8}{13}$ ▢ $\frac{20}{39}$

25. $\frac{2}{6}$ ▢ $\frac{1}{8}$

26. $\frac{3}{4}$ ▢ $\frac{2}{8}$

27. $\frac{1}{7}$ ▢ $\frac{3}{12}$

28. $\frac{1}{3}$ ▢ $\frac{2}{3}$

29. $\frac{2}{9}$ ▢ $\frac{1}{3}$

30. $\frac{9}{12}$ ▢ $\frac{3}{4}$

31. $\frac{2}{9}$ ▢ $\frac{9}{18}$

32. $\frac{1}{2}$ ▢ $\frac{4}{5}$

33. $\frac{3}{4}$ ▢ $\frac{14}{16}$

34. $\frac{2}{6}$ ▢ $\frac{1}{4}$

Textbook This lesson is available in the *eTextbook*.

Order the following sets of fractions from least to greatest.

35 $\frac{1}{2}, \frac{1}{4}, \frac{3}{8}, \frac{5}{8}, \frac{3}{4}$

38 $\frac{1}{15}, \frac{5}{5}, \frac{2}{3}, \frac{7}{15}, \frac{1}{5}$

36 $\frac{7}{10}, \frac{2}{5}, \frac{1}{4}, \frac{4}{5}, \frac{3}{4}$

39 $\frac{3}{16}, \frac{1}{5}, \frac{1}{4}, \frac{7}{16}, \frac{2}{4}$

37 $\frac{7}{9}, \frac{1}{3}, \frac{3}{6}, \frac{2}{3}, \frac{5}{9}$

40 $\frac{5}{10}, \frac{1}{2}, \frac{3}{5}, \frac{4}{10}, \frac{1}{5}$

Solve the following problems.

41 Sara, Mark, and Laura all took the same math test, which had fewer than 50 questions. Sara missed $\frac{1}{5}$ of the questions, Mark missed $\frac{3}{10}$ of the questions, and Laura missed $\frac{1}{8}$ of the questions.

   a. Who had the greatest score?

   b. How many questions were on the test?

42 Rebecca wants to buy $\frac{1}{2}$ of a pie that is divided into 16 equal parts. How many pieces will she get?

43 The Lopez family drove $\frac{1}{3}$ of the way to their vacation spot on Monday and $\frac{3}{8}$ of the way on Tuesday. On which day did they drive farther?

44 Hector usually finishes his homework in $\frac{3}{4}$ of an hour. Sara usually finishes her homework in $\frac{5}{8}$ of an hour. Who takes less time?

45 Pamela read about $\frac{2}{3}$ of a book on Monday and about $\frac{1}{6}$ of the book on Tuesday. On which day did she read more?

Counting Possible Outcomes

Key Ideas

Counting the possible outcomes of an event is important for understanding probability.

Think about an experiment in which a penny, nickel, and dime are flipped one at a time. After all 3 flips, the combinations that the coins can make are as follows:

- 3 heads

- 2 heads and 1 tail

- 1 head and 2 tails

- 3 tails

Do we need to list 1 tail and 2 heads as another combination? No, because it is the same as 2 heads and 1 tail.

In a probability experiment in which we want to see how often something is likely to occur, these combinations are sometimes called *events*.

- How often should each of the 4 events occur?

To find out, look at all the possible outcomes of the coin flips and see how many outcomes fit the description of each of our four events.

One way to see all the possible outcomes is to make a tree diagram. In the diagram, the penny can land on either heads or tails, which are 2 possible outcomes. For each of the penny's 2 outcomes, the nickel can also land on heads or tails—making 4 total outcomes for 2 flips. Finally, for each of the 4 outcomes involving the penny and nickel, the dime can also land on either heads or tails—resulting in 8 total outcomes when flipping the 3 coins.

Each "branch" of the tree diagram, from the first to third flip, is a separate outcome. Do you see why there is a total of $2 \times 2 \times 2 = 8$ outcomes?

ⓔ Textbook This lesson is available in the *eTextbook*.

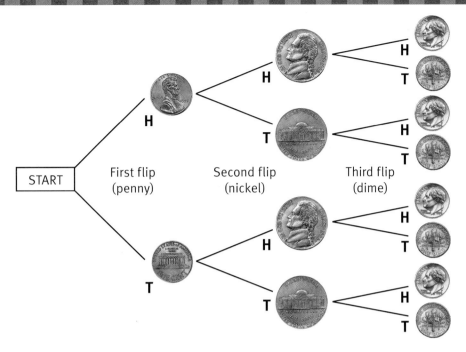

START

First flip (penny) — H / T

Second flip (nickel) — H / T

Third flip (dime) — H / T

Look at the top branch—how many heads flips would you get? That branch, HHH, has 3 heads. Can you find HTH and THH? Both have 2 heads but are separate outcomes since they occupy different branches of the diagram.

Answer the following questions using the tree diagram.

1. How many total outcomes are there for 3 flips?

2. How many outcomes have 3 heads?

3. How many outcomes have 3 tails?

4. How many outcomes have 2 heads and 1 tail? Write the different letter combinations.

5. How many combinations have 1 head and 2 tails? Write the different letter combinations.

6. Which of the following events do you think will occur more often: 3 heads, 2 heads and 1 tail, 1 head and 2 tails, or 3 tails?

7. Would you be surprised if it did not occur?

8. **Extended Response** Try to list all the possible ways that two 0–5 **Number Cubes** could be rolled. You may wish to list outcomes in a logical order (0, 0; 0, 1; 0, 2;...) or by using a tree diagram. (You should start with six branches.)

Keep your list for the outcomes of the experiment using two 0–5 **Number Cubes.** You will need it in the next lesson.

Key Ideas

The probability that an event will occur can be expressed as a fraction.

To determine the probability of an event, start with a list of all possible equally likely outcomes. Count the number of total outcomes as well as the number of outcomes in which the event occurs.

Use this information to create a fraction. The *total* number of outcomes is the denominator and the number of outcomes *for the event* is the numerator. Determining which events are equally likely may be very difficult.

Answer the following questions.

1. How many marbles are in the box?

2. Suppose you choose one marble without looking. Which color are you most likely to choose?

3. Which color are you least likely to choose?

4. How many marbles are red?

5. What is the probability of choosing a red marble?

6. What is the probability of choosing a green marble?

7. What is the probability of choosing a yellow marble?

8. What is the probability of not choosing

    a. a red marble?   **b.** a green marble?   **c.** a yellow marble?

eTextbook This lesson is available in the *eTextbook.*

Perform the probability experiment from Lesson 6.8, again, in which a penny, nickel, and dime are flipped one at a time.

With a partner, flip the three coins 40 times. While one person flips coins, the other person should keep records, like the example table shown. Tally how often you get 3 heads, 2 heads, 1 head, and 0 heads. Write the totals as fractions of 40. After about 20 flips, switch jobs.

Complete the table, and answer the questions.

Event	Tallies	Total	Fraction of 40
3 Heads	卌 ‖	7	$\frac{7}{40}$
2 Heads	卌 卌 卌 ‖	17	$\frac{17}{40}$
1 Head	卌 卌 ‖‖		
0 Heads	‖‖		

9 Which two events happened most often during your experiment? Were these the same two events that happened most often in Lesson 6.8?

10 **Extended Response** Are the results what you expected? Why or why not?

Review the tree diagram for the coin flipping experiment from Lesson 6.8. When we flip three coins, we assume the 8 outcomes—HHH, HHT, HTH, HTT, THH, THT, TTH, and TTT—are all equally likely.

To find the probability of getting 2 heads and 1 tail, we count the number of outcomes with 2 heads, which is 3 (HHT, HTH, and THH). Since there are 8 total possible outcomes when flipping three coins, the probability of having 2 heads and 1 tail when flipping three coins is $\frac{3}{8}$.

Find the probability of the following events when flipping three coins. Write your answers both as a fraction with a denominator of 8 and as an equivalent fraction with a denominator of 40.

⑪ 3 heads

⑫ 1 head and 2 tails

⑬ 3 tails

⑭ 4 heads

⑮ 2 heads or 1 head

⑯ 0 heads, 1 head, 2 heads, or 3 heads

⑰ Use the above information to answer these questions.

   a. What is the least a number can be for a probability?

   b. What is the greatest a number can be for a probability?

⑱ **Extended Response** How did the results of your experiment compare to the calculated probabilities?

Calculate the following probabilities. Use the list you made in Lesson 6.8 for the possible outcomes when rolling two 0–5 *Number Cubes*.

⑲ What is the probability of the two numbers rolled having a sum of

   a. 0?   **g.** 6?

   b. 1?   **h.** 7?

   c. 2?   **i.** 8?

   d. 3?   **j.** 9?

   e. 4?   **k.** 10?

   f. 5?   **l.** 11?

⑳ Why do the middle sums occur more often than the other sums?

Probability and Strategies Practice

Anything But 10 Game

Players: Two or more

Materials: *Number Cubes* (one 0–5, one 5–10)

Object: To score a total of 100 points or more

Math Focus: Addition and probability

HOW TO PLAY

❶ Roll both **Number Cubes.** Find the sum of the two numbers rolled.

❷ If the sum is *not* 10, add the number of points that you rolled to your running score. Keep your turn and roll again, or stop and add those points to your score.

❸ On each turn, players may have as many rolls as they like until they either roll a sum of 10 or choose to stop.

❹ If you roll a sum of 10, you lose your turn, and you also lose any points you may have earned on that turn.

❺ The first player to score 100 points or more is the winner.

SAMPLE GAME

Round	Patti's Roll	Sum	Score	Janel's Roll	Sum	Score
1	7 5	12		9 4	13	
	5 4	9		6 2	8	21
	10 5	15	36	Janel stopped.		
	Patti stopped.					
2	8 3	11		10 4	14	
	7 0	7		8 3	11	
	6 4	10	36	7 1	8	54
	Since 6 + 4 = 10, Patti lost her turn.			Janel stopped.		

After two rounds, Janel was ahead.

Adding Fractions

Key Ideas

The sum of any two fractions can be found by finding equivalent fractions with a common denominator.

Juan knows it is $\frac{3}{4}$ of a mile from his home to school. Matt said that he lives $\frac{1}{10}$ of a mile on the other side of the school. If Juan walks to school and then to Matt's house, how far will he walk?

To add fractions with different denominators,

- replace the fractions with equivalent fractions that have a common denominator.

- add the numerators (keeping the common denominator).

- if you wish, write the sum in lowest terms.

One of the common denominators of the fractions $\frac{1}{10}$ and $\frac{3}{4}$ is 20.

$$\frac{1}{10} \times \frac{2}{2} = \frac{(1 \times 2)}{(10 \times 2)} = \frac{2}{20}$$

$$\frac{3}{4} \times \frac{5}{5} = \frac{(3 \times 5)}{(4 \times 5)} = \frac{15}{20}$$

$$\frac{2}{20} + \frac{15}{20} = \frac{17}{20}$$

So, $\frac{1}{10} + \frac{3}{4} = \frac{17}{20}$.

Add the following fractions. Write your answers in lowest terms.

1. $\frac{1}{4} + \frac{3}{8} = \blacksquare$

2. $\frac{5}{8} + \frac{1}{4} = \blacksquare$

3. $\frac{2}{9} + \frac{3}{6} = \blacksquare$

4. $\frac{3}{10} + \frac{1}{5} = \blacksquare$

5. $\frac{1}{2} + \frac{1}{2} = \blacksquare$

6. $\frac{1}{4} + \frac{1}{2} = \blacksquare$

7. $\frac{4}{15} + \frac{2}{5} = \blacksquare$

8. $\frac{1}{3} + \frac{1}{5} = \blacksquare$

9. $\frac{1}{7} + \frac{1}{2} = \blacksquare$

10. $\frac{3}{5} + \frac{1}{10} = \blacksquare$

11. $\frac{3}{8} + \frac{6}{12} = \blacksquare$

12. $\frac{1}{3} + \frac{1}{4} = \blacksquare$

13. $\frac{7}{15} + \frac{2}{5} = \blacksquare$

14. $\frac{2}{9} + \frac{2}{3} = \blacksquare$

15. $\frac{1}{4} + \frac{1}{8} = \blacksquare$

e Textbook This lesson is available in the *eTextbook*.

16 $\frac{2}{12} + \frac{3}{6} = $ ▭

17 $\frac{3}{7} + \frac{1}{2} = $ ▭

18 $\frac{9}{18} + \frac{1}{9} = $ ▭

19 $\frac{1}{2} + \frac{1}{6} = $ ▭

20 $\frac{2}{9} + \frac{1}{2} = $ ▭

21 $\frac{3}{5} + \frac{1}{6} = $ ▭

22 $\frac{1}{8} + \frac{1}{3} = $ ▭

23 $\frac{4}{7} + \frac{1}{3} = $ ▭

24 $\frac{4}{14} + \frac{2}{7} = $ ▭

Solve the following problems.

25   Mrs. Sanchez walked $\frac{1}{5}$ mile from her house to Route 20 and then $\frac{3}{10}$ mile to her downtown office. How far did she walk altogether?

26   Paul bought $\frac{1}{4}$ pound of peanuts and $\frac{5}{8}$ pound of cashews. How many pounds of nuts did he buy?

27   Javier sold $\frac{2}{5}$ of the tickets to the play at school. Henry sold $\frac{3}{10}$ of the tickets while he was at the skate park. What fraction of the tickets did the two boys sell altogether?

28   Linda needs $\frac{1}{4}$ teaspoon of salt for her rolls and $\frac{1}{8}$ teaspoon of salt to make muffins. How much salt does she need altogether?

29   Doug walked $\frac{1}{2}$ mile to the store and $\frac{1}{3}$ mile farther to the theater. How far has Doug walked?

30   The home team fans filled $\frac{2}{3}$ of the stadium, and the visiting team fans filled $\frac{1}{6}$ of the stadium. How much of the stadium was filled altogether?

Subtracting Fractions

Key Ideas

When you subtract fractions, you can use a common denominator just as you do when you add fractions.

The process for subtracting fractions is very similar to the process for adding fractions. Can you figure out how to subtract fractions that have different denominators?

A recipe calls for $\frac{3}{4}$ of a pound of butter. You estimate that you have already added $\frac{2}{3}$ of a pound. How much more butter do you need to add?

$$\frac{3}{4} = \frac{}{12}$$

$$-\frac{2}{3} = \frac{}{12}$$

Find a common denominator

We can use 12.

Replace each fraction with an equivalent fraction that has a denominator of 12. Then subtract.

$$\frac{3}{4} = \frac{9}{12}$$

$$-\frac{2}{3} = -\frac{8}{12}$$

$$\frac{1}{12}$$

So, you need another $\frac{1}{12}$ of a pound of butter.

Add or subtract. Write answers in lowest terms.

① $\frac{1}{2} + \frac{1}{3} = \blacksquare$

② $\frac{1}{2} - \frac{1}{3} = \blacksquare$

③ $\frac{5}{8} + \frac{1}{4} = \blacksquare$

④ $\frac{5}{8} - \frac{1}{4} = \blacksquare$

⑤ $\frac{3}{5} - \frac{1}{2} = \blacksquare$

⑥ $\frac{3}{5} + \frac{1}{4} = \blacksquare$

⑦ $\frac{5}{6} - \frac{1}{3} = \blacksquare$

⑧ $\frac{5}{6} - \frac{1}{2} = \blacksquare$

⑨ $\frac{4}{7} - \frac{1}{2} = \blacksquare$

⑩ $\frac{2}{7} + \frac{1}{4} = \blacksquare$

⑪ $\frac{5}{9} + \frac{2}{9} = \blacksquare$

⑫ $\frac{3}{7} - \frac{2}{7} = \blacksquare$

e Textbook This lesson is available in the *eTextbook.*

Solve the following problems.

13 **Extended Response** Bob and Roland baked a pie. Each boy cut a slice and ate it. Bob's slice was about $\frac{1}{4}$ of the pie. Roland's slice was about $\frac{1}{3}$ of the pie.

a. About what fraction of the pie did they eat altogether?

b. Suppose someone told you that Hank later ate $\frac{1}{2}$ of the original pie. What would you think?

14 Rayette, Luz, and Patty decided to fill a barrel with water from the lake. Rayette used a pail that holds enough water to fill $\frac{1}{2}$ of the barrel. Luz used a pail that holds enough water to fill $\frac{1}{4}$ of the barrel. Patty used a pail that holds enough water to fill $\frac{1}{3}$ of the barrel.

a. Whose pail holds the most water?

b. Whose pail holds the least water?

c. If all three people filled their pails and emptied them into the barrel, how full would the barrel be?

d. Which two pails together can hold the most water? How full would just those two pails of water fill the barrel?

15 Mrs. Wong began a trip with a full tank of gas. When she was about $\frac{2}{3}$ of the way to her destination, she saw that her gas tank was only $\frac{1}{4}$ full.

a. Do you think she should try to finish the trip without stopping for gas?

b. Suppose she had started the trip with only $\frac{1}{2}$ tank of gas and was about $\frac{2}{3}$ of the way to her destination when she saw that her gas tank was only $\frac{1}{4}$ full. Could she finish the trip without stopping for gas?

16 Anna ate $\frac{3}{8}$ of the pizza, and Luis ate $\frac{1}{2}$ of the pizza.

a. About what fraction of the pizza did they eat altogether?

b. How much of the pizza was left over?

Applying Fractions

Key Ideas

When you use fractions in real situations, always think about what the fractions mean.

Add or subtract.

1 $\frac{2}{3} - \frac{1}{4} = $ ▢

2 $\frac{3}{5} + \frac{1}{5} = $ ▢

3 $\frac{5}{6} + \frac{1}{4} = $ ▢

4 $\frac{1}{3} - \frac{1}{4} = $ ▢

5 $\frac{3}{5} - \frac{2}{5} = $ ▢

6 $\frac{1}{2} - \frac{1}{3} = $ ▢

7 $\frac{5}{6} - \frac{3}{7} = $ ▢

8 $\frac{1}{5} + \frac{5}{7} = $ ▢

9 $\frac{3}{6} + \frac{1}{5} = $ ▢

10 $\frac{1}{3} - \frac{1}{8} = $ ▢

11 $\frac{1}{2} + \frac{1}{3} = $ ▢

12 $\frac{5}{6} - \frac{6}{9} = $ ▢

Solve the following problems.

13 Annette promised to give $\frac{1}{4}$ of her pencils to Percy, $\frac{2}{3}$ to Inez, and $\frac{1}{4}$ to James. Can she keep this promise?

14 Ms. Dixon is driving from Springfield to Princeton and back. She started with a full tank of gasoline. She is halfway to Princeton and has $\frac{1}{4}$ of a tank of gasoline left.

a. What fraction of a tank of gas has Ms. Dixon used so far?

b. If she fills the tank, what fraction of a tank of gas will she have left when she gets to Princeton?

c. About how many tanks of gas will Ms. Dixon use in getting from Springfield to Princeton?

d. About how many tanks of gas will she use for the entire round trip?

15 Mrs. Lindsey had a piece of birch wood that was $\frac{2}{3}$ foot long. She cut off $\frac{1}{6}$ foot to use as the pedestal for a model airplane. How much wood is left?

16 Erin has $\frac{3}{4}$ pound of jelly beans. Shannon has $\frac{2}{8}$ pound of jelly beans. How much do they have altogether?

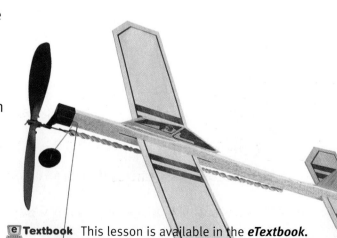

e Textbook This lesson is available in the *eTextbook*.

Game

Applying Fractions and Strategies Practice

Fractured Fractions Game

Players: Two

Materials: *Number Cubes:* (two 0–5), Fractured Fractions sheet

Object: To "capture" the most circles by coloring more than half of a circle in the player's color

Math Focus: Equivalent fractions and mental addition of common fractions

HOW TO PLAY

1 Players should take turns rolling the two *Number Cubes* and making a fraction that is less than or equal to 1 using the two numbers rolled. If a zero is rolled on either cube, the player should roll that cube again.

2 The player should color segments of circles that have a total equal to his or her fraction. The player may also substitute any equivalent fraction or sum of fractions that have a total equal to the original fraction rolled and color those segments of circles instead.

3 For example, a roll of $\frac{3}{4}$ may be used to shade 3 segments on the fourths circle or 5 segments on the tenths circle, plus 2 segments on the eighths circle (since $\frac{3}{4} = \frac{2}{4} + \frac{1}{4} = \frac{5}{10} + \frac{2}{8}$). A player may not color less than a whole segment. If a player cannot find a way to use the entire fraction rolled, he or she forfeits the turn.

4 Players must state in advance what segments they will be coloring, and both players must agree that the choices are correct. It is acceptable to color an uncolored segment of a circle that has already been captured.

SAMPLE GAME

Players are Blue and Red. Red goes first.

Red: (1, 5); colors $\frac{1}{5}$ of the fifths circle

Blue: (3, 3); colors $\frac{2}{3}$ of the thirds circle (capturing it), plus $\frac{3}{9}$ of the ninths circle

R: (2, 4); colors $\frac{4}{8}$ of the eighths circle

B: (0, 1); rerolls

B: (3, 2); colors $\frac{3}{9}$ of the ninths circle (capturing it), plus $\frac{2}{6}$ of the sixths circle

R: (5, 4); colors $\frac{2}{5}$ of the fifths circle (capturing it), plus $\frac{4}{10}$ of the tenths circle

Blue is leading by 2 circles (thirds and ninths) to Red's 1 circle (fifths).

Exploring 💡 Problem Solving

Tasting the World

St. Paul, Minn. Eat a few lunches at Highwood Hills Elementary School and you might think you were traveling around the world. Today the aroma of cilantro and garlic filled the room as the cooks prepared a Somali dish called chicken suqaar. On other days, students experience the flavors of Mexico, Thailand, or Laos. It's all part of the city's effort to reflect the diversity of the student body in St. Paul schools.

Adding an authentic ethnic dish to the menu is no easy task. It can take a full year for a recipe to be approved. The meal must meet standards for nutritional value, and it must be affordable. To become part of the menu, the recipe cannot call for overly expensive ingredients or too much preparation. And, of course, it must taste good!

Before offering a new dish to more than 40,000 students, the district tests the recipe at a few schools. Because it has 60 Somali students, Highwood Hills Elementary School was an easy choice to help decide if the district's version of chicken suqaar was on target.

Cilantro and garlic help give chicken suqaar its distinctive flavor and aroma.

When a dish is added to the menu, there must be enough ingredients on hand to feed thousands of students. That can call for large quantities of ingredients and large pots in which to cook them.

The following recipe for chicken suqaar serves 8 people. Imagine how much of each ingredient is needed to serve the whole school district.

A pressure cooker, such as the one on the right, is used to cook food very quickly through the use of high-temperature steam under pressure.

Chicken Suqaar (yields 8 servings)

1 lb or 4 cups	cooked chicken, diced
$\frac{1}{4}$ cup	cilantro, chopped
$\frac{3}{4}$ cup	onion, chopped
1 cup	carrots, frozen or fresh, sliced
1 cup	green pepper, chopped
1 tsp	chicken base
1 tsp	garlic, minced
$\frac{1}{8}$ cup	vegetable oil

Saute all ingredients except chicken in oil until tender. Add chicken. Mix well. Heat ingredients to 165 degrees.

Each school orders just enough ingredients to prepare the number of servings that will be needed that day.

Answer and discuss the following questions.

1 How many cups of carrots are in each serving of chicken suqaar?

2 How many cups of carrots would be needed to make 800 servings of chicken suqaar?

3 How many cups of diced cooked chicken are in a single serving? How many pounds is that?

4 How many pounds of diced cooked chicken would be needed to make 800 servings of chicken suqaar?

5 If the diced cooked chicken comes in 10-pound bags, how many bags would be needed for 800 servings?

Exploring Problem Solving

Imagine you are in charge of ordering food for your school cafeteria. You are ordering ingredients to make Hmong beef fried rice.

Hmong Beef Fried Rice
(yields approximately 7 one-cup servings)

ground beef	1 lb
garlic powder	2 tbsp
sugar	1 tsp
salt	$\frac{1}{2}$ tsp
rice, cooked	4 cups
eggs	2

For toppings or garnish, use cilantro sprigs, peas, and chopped scallions.

You know that about $\frac{2}{3}$ of the students in the school will order Hmong beef fried rice when it is on the menu. There are 1,054 students in the school.

To help order the rice, assume the following:

- $\frac{1}{3}$ cup of dry rice makes 1 cup of cooked rice
- 1 cup of dry rice weighs about $\frac{1}{2}$ pound

Work in groups to solve the following problems.

6. Copy and complete the order form.

7. Explain how you figured out how much of each item to order.

8. Create your own problem based on the information on this page and page 285. Exchange your problem with a classmate.

Item	Quantity
10-pound bag of ground beef	
carton of 48 eggs	
25-pound bag of dry rice	

Cumulative Review

Multiplying and Dividing Integers Lesson 4.9

Multiply or divide.

① $-9 \times 4 = $ ▢

② $-8 \times (-4) = $ ▢

③ $-6 \times (-7) = $ ▢

④ $28 \div (-4) = $ ▢

⑤ $48 \div (-8) = $ ▢

⑥ $-56 \div -7 = $ ▢

Functions and Ordered Pairs Lesson 5.2

Copy each list of ordered pairs, but replace the *x* or *y* with the correct number.

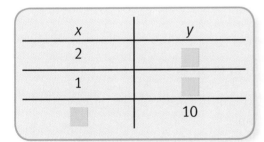

⑦ $(12, 7)$; $(15, y)$; $(x, 5)$; $(0, y)$; $(-1, y)$

⑧ $(12, 4)$; $(21, y)$; $(x, 5)$; $(0, x)$; $(x, 8)$; $(-6, y)$

Composite Functions in Standard Notation Lesson 5.11

Complete each function table and graph the ordered pairs for each.

⑨ $y = 3x + 1$

x	y
2	▢
1	▢
▢	10

⑩ $y = \frac{x}{2} - 1$

x	y
10	▢
0	▢
▢	2

Cumulative Review

Linear Equations Lesson 5.12

Evaluate each equation by solving for either *x* or *y*.

⑪ $3x - 5 = 25$

⑫ $5x + 2 = 42$

⑬ $11(3) - 22 = y$

⑭ $\frac{x}{7} \times 6 = 30$

⑮ $4(x) + 7 = 23$

⑯ $\frac{85}{5} - 20 = y$

Fractions of a Whole Lesson 6.1

Solve for *n*.

⑰ $\frac{1}{3}$ of $30 = n$

⑱ $\frac{2}{3}$ of $60 = n$

⑲ $\frac{3}{4}$ of $100 = n$

⑳ $\frac{4}{5}$ of $80 = n$

Decimal Equivalents of Fractions Lesson 6.3

For each fraction, give the decimal equivalent or approximation correct to three decimal places (to the nearest thousandth).

㉑ $\frac{2}{3}$

㉒ $\frac{1}{8}$

㉓ $\frac{3}{7}$

㉔ $\frac{4}{9}$

㉕ $\frac{1}{6}$

㉖ $\frac{2}{5}$

e)Textbook This lesson is available in the *eTextbook*.

Key Ideas Review

CHAPTER 6

In this chapter you explored various features of fractions.

You learned how to express fractional equivalents and how to add and subtract fractions.

You learned how to use fractions to demonstrate probabilities.

Complete the following exercises.

1 $\frac{2}{9}$ of 54 = ▢

2 $\frac{2}{3} + \frac{1}{4} =$ ▢

3 $\frac{2}{3} - \frac{1}{2} =$ ▢

4 $\frac{4}{8} \times \frac{2}{8} =$ ▢

Answer the following questions.

5 Create a number line with the following fractions, listed from least to greatest and having the same denominator.

$\frac{1}{2}, \frac{6}{8}, \frac{4}{4}, \frac{4}{16},$ and $\frac{0}{7}$

6 Explain why all decimals can be written as fractions, but not all fractions can be written as decimals.

List three equivalent fractions for each number.

7 $\frac{3}{9}$

8 $\frac{4}{7}$

Use the sums from the two spinners to answer the following questions.

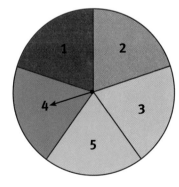
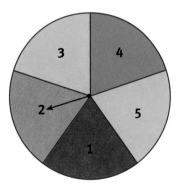

Suppose you spun both spinners and added the two numbers together.

9 What is the probability of spinning a sum that is an even number?

10 What is the probability of spinning a sum that is a multiple of 3?

Real Math • Chapter 6

289

Chapter Review

Lesson 6.1 Solve.

1. $\frac{1}{4}$ of $20 = n$

2. $\frac{3}{4}$ of $20 = n$

3. $\frac{1}{3}$ of $45 = n$

4. $\frac{3}{5}$ of $45 = n$

5. $\frac{1}{6}$ of $18 = n$

6. $\frac{5}{6}$ of $30 = n$

Lesson 6.2 Multiply.

7. $\frac{4}{7} \times \frac{2}{9} = \blacksquare$

9. $\frac{2}{5} \times \frac{3}{7} = \blacksquare$

8. $\frac{2}{3} \times \frac{2}{5} = \blacksquare$

10. $\frac{2}{3} \times \frac{4}{7} = \blacksquare$

Replace the ▦ to make each statement true.

11. $\frac{1}{3} \times \blacksquare = \frac{1}{12}$

13. $\frac{3}{5} \times \blacksquare = \frac{9}{25}$

12. $\frac{3}{4}$ of $\blacksquare = \frac{6}{12}$

14. $\frac{2}{7}$ of $\blacksquare = \frac{8}{35}$

Lesson 6.4 Find the missing numerator or denominator.

15. $\frac{2}{5} = \frac{10}{\blacksquare}$

17. $\frac{5}{7} = \frac{15}{\blacksquare}$

16. $\frac{1}{2} = \frac{\blacksquare}{16}$

18. $\frac{1}{6} = \frac{\blacksquare}{24}$

Lesson 6.7 Order the fractions from least to greatest.

19. $\frac{1}{3}, \frac{1}{2}, \frac{5}{6}, \frac{2}{3}, \frac{1}{6}$

20. $\frac{5}{8}, \frac{1}{4}, \frac{3}{4}, \frac{1}{2}, \frac{3}{8}$

21. $\frac{4}{15}, \frac{5}{5}, \frac{2}{3}, \frac{11}{15}, \frac{1}{5}$

22. $\frac{3}{10}, \frac{1}{2}, \frac{4}{5}, \frac{7}{10}, \frac{3}{5}$

e Textbook This lesson is available in the *eTextbook*.

Lesson 6.9 Solve.

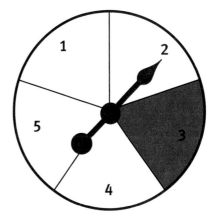

23 A spinner with the numbers 1–5 has an equal
chance of landing on any number. What is the
probability of

   a. landing on a number less than 2?

   b. landing on a number greater than 3?

   c. landing on an odd number?

24 What is the probability of landing on a number greater than 5?

   a. $\frac{1}{5}$

   b. $\frac{1}{2}$

   c. 0

Lessons 6.10–6.11 Add or subtract. Write your answers in lowest terms.

25 $\frac{1}{2} + \frac{3}{7} = $ ▢   27 $\frac{1}{3} + \frac{1}{5} = $ ▢

26 $\frac{4}{5} - \frac{3}{10} = $ ▢   28 $\frac{11}{12} - \frac{1}{4} = $ ▢

Lesson 6.12 Solve.

29 Krystin started the day with $\frac{3}{4}$ of a tank of gas in her car. She
used $\frac{1}{8}$ to go to work and another $\frac{1}{16}$ to drive to the store. How
much gas did she have left when she got to the store?

30 Kobe lives $\frac{5}{6}$ of a mile from school. On the way home, he stopped
at a friend's house $\frac{1}{2}$ mile from school. How far from home was
Kobe?

Practice Test

Find the missing numerator or denominator.

1. $\dfrac{3}{4} = \dfrac{\square}{20}$

2. $\dfrac{21}{\square} = \dfrac{7}{8}$

3. $\dfrac{3}{7} = \dfrac{15}{\square}$

4. $\dfrac{\square}{25} = \dfrac{1}{5}$

5. $\dfrac{4}{5} = \dfrac{\square}{30}$

6. $\dfrac{5}{6} = \dfrac{15}{\square}$

7. $\dfrac{7}{9} = \dfrac{42}{\square}$

8. $\dfrac{1}{9} = \dfrac{\square}{36}$

Solve for n. Write your answer in lowest terms.

9. $\dfrac{3}{5} + \dfrac{1}{3} = n$

10. $\dfrac{1}{4} + \dfrac{4}{8} = n$

11. $\dfrac{3}{4} - \dfrac{2}{16} = n$

12. $\dfrac{1}{4} \times \dfrac{2}{7} = n$

13. $\dfrac{1}{2} \times \dfrac{3}{4} = n$

14. $\dfrac{2}{5} + \dfrac{5}{9} = n$

15. $\dfrac{5}{7} - \dfrac{1}{4} = n$

16. $\dfrac{3}{8} \times \dfrac{4}{6} = n$

Decide which fraction in each of the following pairs is greater. Replace $\square$ with $<$, $>$, or $=$.

17. $\dfrac{3}{10} \,\square\, \dfrac{5}{12}$

18. $\dfrac{1}{4} \,\square\, \dfrac{1}{5}$

19. $\dfrac{2}{5} \,\square\, \dfrac{4}{10}$

20. $\dfrac{5}{7} \,\square\, \dfrac{2}{3}$

21. $\dfrac{9}{18} \,\square\, \dfrac{1}{2}$

22. $\dfrac{4}{6} \,\square\, \dfrac{12}{18}$

23. $\dfrac{1}{2} \,\square\, \dfrac{1}{4}$

24. $\dfrac{6}{20} \,\square\, \dfrac{10}{24}$

Choose the correct answer.

25. Which decimal is equivalent to the fraction $\frac{2}{5}$?

    (A) 0.2

    (B) 0.4

    (C) 0.5

    (D) 0.7

26. Hilton has $\frac{3}{4}$ of his drink left, and Evelyn has $\frac{1}{5}$ of her drink left. How much more of his drink does Hilton have than Evelyn has?

    (A) $\frac{2}{5}$

    (B) $\frac{4}{7}$

    (C) $\frac{11}{20}$

    (D) $\frac{19}{20}$

27. Ms. Ying has 12 flowers in her window box. There are 4 marigolds, 3 petunias, and the rest are pansies. What fraction of the flowers are pansies?

    (A) $\frac{1}{12}$

    (B) $\frac{3}{12}$

    (C) $\frac{4}{12}$

    (D) $\frac{5}{12}$

28. Which fraction is equivalent to $\frac{3}{8}$?

    (A) $\frac{4}{9}$

    (B) $\frac{6}{11}$

    (C) $\frac{6}{16}$

    (D) $\frac{11}{16}$

29. Which of the following shows the fractions in order from greatest to least?

    (A) $\frac{5}{6}, \frac{4}{5}, \frac{1}{2}, \frac{1}{3}$

    (B) $\frac{4}{5}, \frac{5}{6}, \frac{1}{3}, \frac{1}{2}$

    (C) $\frac{1}{3}, \frac{1}{2}, \frac{4}{5}, \frac{5}{6}$

    (D) $\frac{1}{2}, \frac{1}{3}, \frac{4}{5}, \frac{5}{6}$

30. Quinn put 6 colored counters into a bag; 2 are red, 1 is blue, and 3 are green. What is the probability that Quinn will pull out a blue counter?

    (A) $\frac{6}{6}$

    (B) $\frac{3}{6}$

    (C) $\frac{2}{6}$

    (D) $\frac{1}{6}$

31. What fraction will make the following statement true?

    $$\frac{4}{5} \times \boxed{} = \frac{8}{15}$$

    (A) $\frac{4}{10}$

    (B) $\frac{2}{3}$

    (C) $\frac{2}{10}$

    (D) $\frac{4}{3}$

32. Devon put $\frac{2}{3}$ of her vacation pictures into a photo album and framed $\frac{1}{5}$ of them. What fraction of her pictures did not go into the album or get framed?

    (A) $\frac{2}{15}$

    (B) $\frac{3}{8}$

    (C) $\frac{1}{2}$

    (D) $\frac{13}{15}$

33. What is a common denominator for the following fractions?

$$\frac{4}{5}, \frac{6}{7}, \frac{1}{2}$$

Ⓐ 10   Ⓑ 14

Ⓒ 35   Ⓓ 70

34. What is $\frac{4}{5} \times \frac{7}{8}$?

Ⓐ $\frac{11}{13}$ Ⓑ $\frac{14}{20}$

Ⓒ $\frac{19}{40}$ Ⓓ $\frac{3}{3}$

35. The rule for a function machine is subtract 3. If 7 comes out of the function machine, which number went in?

Ⓐ 4   Ⓑ 6

Ⓒ 10   Ⓓ 21

36. $3x - 4 = y$. If y is 20, what is x?

Ⓐ $x = 5$ Ⓑ $x = 8$

Ⓒ $x = 20$ Ⓓ $x = 56$

37. Which number is greatest?

Ⓐ 100,101   Ⓑ 101,001

Ⓒ 110,100   Ⓓ 101,011

38. Felicia spent $25.50 on 5 jump ropes. How much did each jump rope cost?

Ⓐ $5.50   Ⓑ $5.10

Ⓒ $4.10   Ⓓ $4.01

39. $x \longrightarrow \boxed{\times 2} \longrightarrow n \longrightarrow \boxed{-8} \longrightarrow y$

If x is 3, what is y?

Ⓐ $y = -2$ Ⓑ $y = 2$

Ⓒ $y = 5.5$ Ⓓ $y = 14$

40. $350 \times 1,000 = \boxed{}$

Ⓐ 35   Ⓑ 3,500

Ⓒ 35,000   Ⓓ 350,000

41. What is 79.174 rounded to the nearest hundredth?

Ⓐ 79   Ⓑ 79.1

Ⓒ 79.17   Ⓓ 79.18

42. If you start at the point (1, 4) and move right 2 steps and down 2 steps, at what point would you be?

Ⓐ (4, 1)   Ⓑ (3, 2)

Ⓒ (2, 3)   Ⓓ (−1, 2)

Answer the following questions.

43. This tree diagram shows the outcomes of tossing two pennies and rolling one 0–5 **Number Cube**.

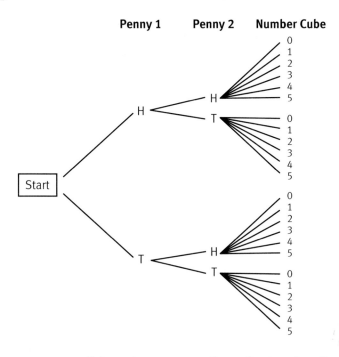

   a. How many possible outcomes are there for tossing 2 pennies and rolling the number cube?

   b. How many outcomes have 2 heads? Write the combinations.

   c. How many outcomes have 1 head, 1 tail, and the number 1? Write the combinations.

   d. What is the probability (in lowest terms) of rolling a 2?

   e. What is the probability of tossing 2 heads and rolling an even number? Write your answer in lowest terms.

   f. What is the probability of tossing a head, a tail, and rolling an odd number? Write your answer with a denominator of 24 and also in lowest terms.

44. Which would you expect to happen more frequently: 2 heads and a 1 or a head, a tail, and a 1? Explain why.

In This Chapter You Will Learn

- how to relate mixed numbers and improper fractions.
- how to add and subtract mixed numbers.
- how to divide fractions.

Problem Solving

SOCIAL STUDIES

On an April night in 1775, two lanterns glowed in the steeple of the Old North Church in Boston. Patriots across the river in Charlestown saw the faint lights. The men set in motion the plans laid out by Paul Revere and others to spread the word of an impending British assault.

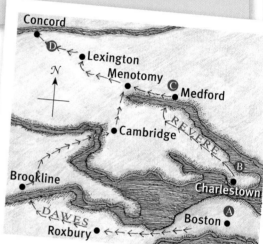

A **April 18, 10:00 P.M.** Revere orders the lantern signal to be sent.

10:15 P.M. Revere hurries from his house and heads to Charlestown.

B **11:00 P.M.** Revere sets off for Lexington.

C **11:30 P.M.** Revere reaches Medford and awakens the captain of the Minute Men.

D **April 19, 12:05 A.M.** Revere reaches Lexington. Another messenger, William Dawes, arrives about $\frac{1}{2}$ hour after Revere. The two riders soon set off for Concord together.

Look at this record of the British march to Concord and back.

From	To	Distance	Time
Lechmere Point	Lexington	11 miles	3–4 hours
Lexington	Concord	6–7 miles	2–3 hours
Concord	Lexington	6–7 miles	2–3 hours
Lexington	Charlestown	11 miles	3–4 hours

1 What are the least and the greatest total distances that the British soldiers could have marched?

2 What are the least and the greatest total times that the British soldiers marched?

3 What can you say about the average speed of the British soldiers?

Key Ideas

We can use fractions to refer to numbers greater than 1.

Numbers that combine a whole number with a fraction, such as $3\frac{1}{2}$, $2\frac{4}{5}$, and $1\frac{2}{3}$, are sometimes called mixed numbers.

- $2\frac{1}{2}$ watermelons

- $4\frac{3}{4}$ inches

A fraction like $\frac{5}{3}$ is sometimes called an improper fraction. An improper fraction has a numerator that is greater than its denominator.

- There are many situations in which it is useful to replace a mixed number with an improper fraction that represents the same amount.

Example: Change $2\frac{3}{4}$ to an improper fraction.

Think:

- How many fourths are in 2? $2 \times 4 = 8$

- How many fourths are in $\frac{3}{4}$?   3

- How many fourths are in all? $2\frac{3}{4} = \frac{8}{4} + \frac{3}{4} = \frac{11}{4}$.

ⓔ Textbook This lesson is available in the *eTextbook*.

- If we started with an improper fraction, how could we replace it with an equivalent mixed number?

Example: Change $\frac{14}{3}$ to a mixed number.

$$\begin{array}{r} 4\ R2 \\ 3\overline{)14} \end{array}$$

Divide 14 by 3 to see how many wholes there are. The remainder tells you how many thirds are left over.

from the quotient

So, $\frac{14}{3} = 4\frac{2}{3}$. ← from the remainder ← from the divisor

Complete each expression with an equivalent improper fraction or mixed number.

1. $2\frac{1}{3} = \square$

2. $2\frac{3}{5} = \square$

3. $1\frac{1}{2} = \square$

4. $3\frac{2}{3} = \square$

5. $\frac{7}{4} = \square$

6. $\frac{11}{6} = \square$

7. $\frac{8}{3} = \square$

8. $\frac{5}{4} = \square$

Solve.

9. **Extended Response** Taylor is counting distance markers along the highway. She has counted 33 of them so far. Her parents told her there is $\frac{1}{10}$ of a mile between each marker. How many miles has Taylor traveled since she started counting? Explain why the answer is not $\frac{33}{10}$.

10. Ms. Blair is conducting an experiment with her chemistry class. Each pair of students needs $\frac{1}{4}$ meter of plastic tubing. If there are 11 pairs of students, how much tubing does Ms. Blair need for the whole class? Give your answer as both a mixed number and an improper fraction.

Writing + Math · Journal

Which is greater, $3\frac{2}{3}$ or $2\frac{5}{3}$? Draw a picture that shows your answer.

Multiplying Mixed Numbers

Key Ideas

To multiply mixed numbers, you can change them to improper fractions and multiply them the same way you multiply other fractions.

- Example: $3\frac{1}{3} \times 2\frac{1}{2} = $ ▨

Change $3\frac{1}{3}$ to an improper fraction.

$3\frac{1}{3} = \frac{10}{3}$

Change $2\frac{1}{2}$ to an improper fraction.

$2\frac{1}{2} = \frac{5}{2}$

Because $3 \times 2 = 6$ and $4 \times 3 = 12$, the answer should be between 6 and 12.

Multiply.

$\frac{10}{3} \times \frac{5}{2} = \frac{50}{6}$

The answer is $\frac{50}{6}$.

You may change $\frac{50}{6}$ to a simpler equivalent fraction: $\frac{25}{3}$.

Then change $\frac{25}{3}$ to a mixed number: $8\frac{1}{3}$.

So, the answer could be written as $8\frac{1}{3}$.

- Example: $\frac{5}{8} \times 4\frac{1}{3} = $ ▨

$\frac{5}{8} \times 4\frac{1}{3} = \frac{5}{8} \times \frac{13}{3} = \frac{65}{24} = 2\frac{17}{24}$

When multiplying by a whole number, first change it to an improper fraction. You may do this by writing it with a denominator of 1.

- Example: $5\frac{2}{3} \times 4 = $ ▨

$5\frac{2}{3} \times 4 = \frac{17}{3} \times \frac{4}{1} = \frac{68}{3} = 22\frac{2}{3}$

ⓔ Textbook This lesson is available in the *eTextbook*.

Always check your answers to see that they make sense. Here is a way to check your answers when multiplying mixed numbers.

- $3\frac{1}{3} \times 2\frac{1}{2} = 8\frac{1}{3}$

Check: $3\frac{1}{3}$ is between 3 and 4.

$2\frac{1}{2}$ is between 2 and 3.

Therefore, $3\frac{1}{3} \times 2\frac{1}{2}$ must be between 3×2 and 4×3.

Is the answer ($8\frac{1}{3}$) between 6 and 12?

Yes, so the answer makes sense.

Multiply. Check to see that your answers make sense.

1. $2\frac{1}{3} \times 5\frac{2}{7} = \blacksquare$
2. $\frac{7}{8} \times 2\frac{1}{6} = \blacksquare$
3. $2\frac{2}{5} \times 4\frac{1}{6} = \blacksquare$
4. $3\frac{1}{8} \times 2\frac{1}{6} = \blacksquare$
5. $1\frac{2}{3} \times 2\frac{1}{6} = \blacksquare$
6. $\frac{4}{7} \times 5\frac{1}{4} = \blacksquare$
7. $4\frac{1}{3} \times 3\frac{4}{7} = \blacksquare$
8. $3\frac{4}{5} \times \frac{5}{7} = \blacksquare$

9. $1\frac{3}{4} \times 2\frac{2}{7} = \blacksquare$
10. $1\frac{1}{2} \times 2\frac{1}{4} = \blacksquare$
11. $\frac{2}{3} \times \frac{3}{8} = \blacksquare$
12. $\frac{2}{3} \times 3\frac{3}{8} = \blacksquare$
13. $\frac{2}{3} \times \frac{2}{5} = \blacksquare$
14. $2\frac{2}{3} \times 1\frac{1}{6} = \blacksquare$
15. $\frac{3}{4} \times \frac{2}{3} = \blacksquare$
16. $1\frac{3}{4} \times 1\frac{2}{3} = \blacksquare$

Solve the following problems.

17. Lee worked $1\frac{1}{2}$ hours overtime on each of 3 days last week. How many overtime hours did Lee work altogether last week?

18. Mark went to the local indoor rock-climbing facility. His first 3 climbs were each $16\frac{3}{4}$ feet. How many total feet did Mark climb on his first 3 attempts?

Adding Mixed Numbers

Key Ideas

Adding mixed numbers is similar to adding proper fractions.

$$2\frac{4}{5} + 4\frac{1}{3} = \boxed{}$$

$$\begin{array}{r} 2\frac{4}{5} \\ + 4\frac{1}{3} \\ \hline \end{array}$$

Add the fraction parts.

We cannot add them yet because $\frac{4}{5}$ and $\frac{1}{3}$ have different denominators.

Choose a common denominator.

$$\begin{array}{rcl} 2\frac{4}{5} & = & 2\frac{?}{15} \\ + 4\frac{1}{3} & = & + 4\frac{?}{15} \\ \hline \end{array}$$

$$\begin{array}{rcl} 2\frac{4}{5} & = & 2\frac{12}{15} \\ + 4\frac{1}{3} & = & + 4\frac{5}{15} \\ \hline \end{array}$$

Replace $\frac{4}{5}$ with $\frac{12}{15}$.

Replace $\frac{1}{3}$ with $\frac{5}{15}$.

$$\begin{array}{rcl} 2\frac{4}{5} & = & 2\frac{12}{15} \\ + 4\frac{1}{3} & = & + 4\frac{5}{15} \\ \hline & & \frac{17}{15} \end{array}$$

Now the fraction parts can be added.

$$\frac{12}{15} + \frac{5}{15} = \frac{17}{15}$$

$$\begin{array}{rcl} 2\frac{4}{5} & = & 2\frac{12}{15} \\ + 4\frac{1}{3} & = & + 4\frac{5}{15} \\ \hline & & 6\frac{17}{15} \\ & & 7\frac{2}{15} \end{array}$$

Add the whole numbers.

$2 + 4 = 6$

Change $\frac{17}{15}$ to $1\frac{2}{15}$. Add $1\frac{2}{15}$ to 6. $6 + 1\frac{2}{15} = 7\frac{2}{15}$

Rewrite the answer.

Does the answer make sense?

The answer should be greater than $2 + 4$, or 6, and less than $3 + 5$, or 8.
The answer is greater than 6 and less than 8, so the answer makes sense.

e Textbook This lesson is available in the *eTextbook*.

You may also add two mixed numbers as two improper fractions.

Example: $4\frac{3}{4} + 5\frac{3}{8} = \boxed{}$

$\begin{array}{c} 4\frac{3}{4} \\ + 5\frac{3}{8} \\ \hline \end{array}$ $\longrightarrow$ $\begin{array}{c} 4\frac{3}{4} = \frac{19}{4} \\ + 5\frac{3}{8} = \frac{43}{8} \\ \hline \end{array}$ $\longrightarrow$ $\begin{array}{c} \frac{19}{4} = \frac{?}{8} \\ + \frac{43}{8} = \frac{43}{8} \\ \hline \end{array}$ $\longrightarrow$ $\begin{array}{c} \frac{38}{8} \\ + \frac{43}{8} \\ \hline \frac{81}{8} = 10\frac{1}{8} \end{array}$

Add.

1. $3\frac{5}{8} + 1\frac{1}{4} = \boxed{}$

2. $5\frac{1}{2} + 2\frac{2}{3} = \boxed{}$

3. $4\frac{3}{4} + 1\frac{5}{6} = \boxed{}$

4. $1\frac{1}{3} + 3\frac{2}{3} = \boxed{}$

5. $3\frac{1}{2} + 2\frac{3}{4} = \boxed{}$

6. $3\frac{6}{7} + 4\frac{1}{4} = \boxed{}$

7. $1\frac{1}{2} + 2\frac{4}{5} = \boxed{}$

8. $4\frac{1}{6} + 2\frac{2}{3} = \boxed{}$

9. $4\frac{3}{4} + 3\frac{3}{4} = \boxed{}$

10. $5\frac{2}{3} + 3\frac{1}{3} = \boxed{}$

11. $4\frac{11}{15} + 5\frac{2}{3} = \boxed{}$

12. $5\frac{2}{3} + 3\frac{2}{3} = \boxed{}$

13. $12\frac{2}{3} + 4\frac{2}{9} = \boxed{}$

Solve.

14. A plumber bought 5 pipes. Two were $3\frac{1}{2}$ feet long, and the others were $1\frac{3}{8}$ feet. What was the total length of pipe purchased?

15. For a school project, Drew needs $4\frac{1}{4}$ feet of rope, and Owen needs $5\frac{2}{3}$ feet of rope. How much rope do they need altogether?

16. Clara had $5\frac{3}{4}$ cups of blueberries and $2\frac{5}{8}$ cups of strawberries. How many cups of berries did she have altogether?

Subtracting Mixed Numbers

Key Ideas

Subtracting mixed numbers is similar to subtracting fractions less than 1. It is even more similar to adding mixed numbers.

To subtract fractions with *different* denominators, replace one or both of the fractions with an equivalent fraction so that the denominators will be the same.

Example: $5\frac{2}{3} - 3\frac{1}{4} = 5\frac{8}{12} - 3\frac{3}{12}$

$$\begin{array}{r} 5\frac{8}{12} \\ -\ 3\frac{3}{12} \\ \hline 2\frac{5}{12} \end{array}$$

Now that the denominators are the same, you may subtract the fractions and the whole numbers.

$$5\frac{2}{3} - 3\frac{1}{4} = 2\frac{5}{12}$$

If the fractional part of the number you are subtracting is greater than the fractional part of the number from which you are subtracting, regroup before subtracting.

Example: $7\frac{1}{3} - 4\frac{3}{4} = 7\frac{4}{12} - 4\frac{9}{12}$

$$\begin{array}{r} 6\frac{12}{12} \\ 7\frac{4}{12} \\ -\ 4\frac{9}{12} \\ \hline \end{array}$$

Since $\frac{12}{12} = 1$, we can regroup 7 as $6\frac{12}{12}$. The $\frac{12}{12}$ is added to $\frac{4}{12}$, so that $7\frac{4}{12}$ is regrouped as $6\frac{16}{12}$.

$$\begin{array}{r} 6\frac{16}{12} \\ -\ 4\frac{9}{12} \\ \hline 2\frac{7}{12} \end{array}$$

Rewrite the problem. Subtract the fractional parts and the whole numbers as before.

$$7\frac{1}{3} - 4\frac{3}{4} = 2\frac{7}{12}$$

- Does the answer make sense? The answer should be greater than $7 - 5$, or 2, and less than $8 - 4$, or 4. The answer is greater than 2 and less than 4, so the answer makes sense.

e Textbook This lesson is available in the *eTextbook*.

Subtract.

1. $5\frac{7}{9} - 3\frac{4}{6} = \boxed{}$

2. $4\frac{5}{7} - 2\frac{1}{2} = \boxed{}$

3. $3\frac{1}{4} - 2\frac{5}{8} = \boxed{}$

4. $3\frac{1}{2} - 2\frac{1}{4} = \boxed{}$

5. $5\frac{2}{7} - 3\frac{6}{7} = \boxed{}$

6. $8\frac{5}{6} - 3\frac{1}{3} = \boxed{}$

7. $5\frac{3}{5} - 2\frac{1}{3} = \boxed{}$

8. $2\frac{4}{5} - 1\frac{1}{2} = \boxed{}$

9. $4\frac{1}{6} - 2\frac{2}{3} = \boxed{}$

10. $5\frac{6}{10} - 1\frac{1}{5} = \boxed{}$

11. $5\frac{2}{3} - 3\frac{1}{3} = \boxed{}$

12. $3\frac{2}{3} - 1\frac{1}{3} = \boxed{}$

13. $7\frac{2}{3} - 2\frac{1}{4} = \boxed{}$

14. $5\frac{2}{3} - 3\frac{2}{3} = \boxed{}$

Add or subtract.

15. $5\frac{4}{9} + 2\frac{2}{3} = \boxed{}$

16. $15\frac{1}{3} - \frac{2}{3} = \boxed{}$

17. $1\frac{7}{8} + 3\frac{1}{4} = \boxed{}$

18. $3\frac{1}{4} + 1\frac{7}{8} = \boxed{}$

19. $10\frac{1}{2} + 10\frac{1}{2} = \boxed{}$

20. $2\frac{1}{2} + 3\frac{4}{7} = \boxed{}$

21. $5\frac{4}{9} - 2\frac{2}{3} = \boxed{}$

22. $15\frac{1}{3} - 1\frac{2}{3} = \boxed{}$

Solve the following problems.

23. Tom weighs $142\frac{1}{2}$ pounds. His wrestling opponent weighs $140\frac{3}{4}$ pounds. By how much does Tom outweigh his opponent?

24. Amy lives $1\frac{3}{4}$ miles from the baseball field. Tony lives $1\frac{2}{3}$ miles from the same field. How much farther is Amy's round trip than Tony's round trip?

25. Daniel ran $7\frac{1}{2}$ miles on Monday and $8\frac{3}{4}$ miles on Tuesday. How much farther did Daniel run on Tuesday?

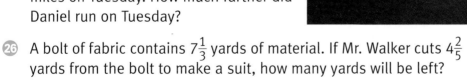

26. A bolt of fabric contains $7\frac{1}{3}$ yards of material. If Mr. Walker cuts $4\frac{2}{5}$ yards from the bolt to make a suit, how many yards will be left?

Addition and Subtraction Applications

Key Ideas

Knowledge of fractions can be used in many practical situations.

Abigail is making a piece of furniture that will be 30 inches tall. The base, or bottom portion, and the crown, or top portion, are each to be $4\frac{1}{2}$ inches high. There will be 4 drawers and 3 spaces between the drawers. The spaces between the drawers will each be $\frac{1}{4}$ inch high.

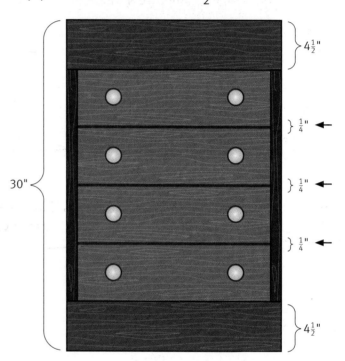

Solve.

1. How much space is left for drawers?

2. If the 2 bottom drawers are each $4\frac{1}{4}$ inches high, how much space is left for the other 2 drawers?

3. If the bottom 3 drawers are each $4\frac{1}{4}$ inches high, how much space is left for the top drawer?

4. **Extended Response** If the bottom 3 drawers are each 7 inches high, how much space is left for the top drawer? Explain.

5. If all 4 drawers are equal in height, how high should each of them be?

ⓔ Textbook This lesson is available in the *eTextbook*.

Solve the following problems.

6 If it is a quarter after 2 now, what time will it be in $3\frac{1}{2}$ hours?

7 Lia is $10\frac{1}{2}$ years old. In how many years will she be 18 years old?

8 Mrs. Harris earns $8 per hour. She gets time and a half for overtime. That means she is paid $1\frac{1}{2}$ times her usual wage when she works overtime.

    a. How much does Mrs. Harris earn per hour when she works overtime?

    b. Last week, Mrs. Harris worked 40 hours at her regular hourly rate, plus 10 hours of overtime. How much money did she earn last week?

    c. This week, Mrs. Harris worked 40 hours at her regular hourly rate, and $12\frac{1}{2}$ hours of overtime. How much did she earn?

    d. Mrs. Harris usually works until 4:30 P.M. Today she worked until 8:00 P.M. How many hours of overtime did she put in today?

    e. Mrs. Harris worked until 6:30 P.M. on Thursday and until 7:00 P.M. on Friday. How many hours of overtime did she work in those two days?

9 Both Maria and Derek collect miniature cars. Maria has $1\frac{1}{2}$ times as many cars as Derek does. If Derek has 20 cars, how many does Maria have?

10 Diego gets a $\frac{1}{2}$-hour lunch and a 20-minute break each day at his job. How many hours of break time does he get during his 5-day work week?

Exploring Problem Solving

Stan is building a model of Paul Revere's house. The instructions say that if you measure and cut very carefully, the seven pieces listed below can be cut from a single 16-inch by 12-inch sheet of foam board. How can that be done?

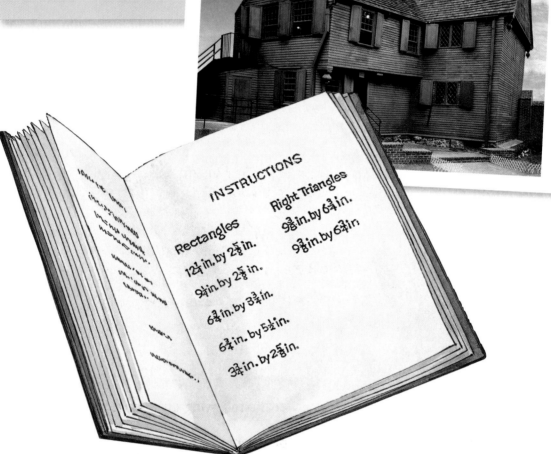

INSTRUCTIONS

Rectangles
$12\frac{1}{4}$ in. by $2\frac{5}{8}$ in.
$9\frac{1}{4}$ in. by $2\frac{5}{8}$ in.
$6\frac{3}{4}$ in. by $3\frac{3}{4}$ in.
$6\frac{3}{4}$ in. by $5\frac{1}{2}$ in.
$3\frac{3}{4}$ in. by $2\frac{5}{8}$ in.

Right Triangles
$9\frac{3}{8}$ in. by $6\frac{1}{4}$ in.
$9\frac{3}{8}$ in. by $6\frac{1}{4}$ in.

Olivia solved the problem this way:

I decided to Make a Physical Model.
I decided to cut the pieces from two sheets of cardboard.
Then I looked at a photo of the house and glued the pieces together.

Think about Olivia's strategy, and answer these questions.

1 Why doesn't Olivia need to make her model from a 16 inch × 12 inch piece of cardboard?

2 How can Olivia use her model to try to solve the problem?

3 Would you use Olivia's strategy? Why or why not?

Diego solved the problem another way:

I decided to Break the Problem into Parts, Use Logical Reasoning, and Make a Diagram.

First, I figured out what to do with the triangles. Next, I looked for pieces that have the same length or same width. Then, I looked for measurements that added up to whole numbers, especially 12 or 16.

Think about Diego's strategy, and answer the following questions.

4 How do you think the triangles should be arranged?

5 Why might it help to find pieces that have a side the same length?

6 Why might it help to find measurements that add up to whole numbers?

7 Would you use Diego's strategy? Why or why not?

8 Solve the problem. Use any strategy you think will work.

9 What strategy did you use? Why?

10 Write a problem like the one on page 308. Then trade with a partner and solve.

Cumulative Review

Using Composite Functions Lesson 5.8

Solve.

Livio opened a lemonade stand. He purchased a large jug of lemonade for $20, and sold glasses at $1.25 apiece.

1 Write a function rule to calculate Livio's profit (y) if he sells x glasses.

2 What will his profit or loss be if he sells 10 glasses?

3 What will his profit or loss be if he sells 20 glasses?

Equivalent Fractions Lesson 6.4

Reduce each of the following fractions to lowest terms.

4 $\frac{35}{49}$

5 $\frac{54}{63}$

6 $\frac{48}{72}$

For each of the following fractions, write three equivalent fractions.

7 $\frac{3}{4}$

8 $\frac{2}{5}$

9 $\frac{1}{6}$

10 $\frac{5}{7}$

Counting Possible Outcomes Lesson 6.8

If the spinner is spun 3 times, how many ways can the combination be

11 red, white, and blue?

12 red, red, and blue?

13 red, red, and red?

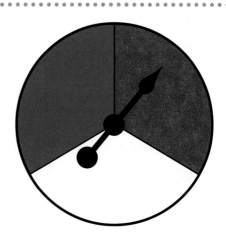

Addition and Subtraction of Fractions Lessons 6.10 and 6.11

Add or subtract.

⑭ $\frac{1}{2} + \frac{1}{3} = \boxed{}$

⑮ $\frac{2}{3} - \frac{1}{4} = \boxed{}$

⑯ $\frac{1}{4} + \frac{1}{6} = \boxed{}$

⑰ $\frac{1}{2} - \frac{1}{3} = \boxed{}$

⑱ $\frac{3}{8} + \frac{1}{3} = \boxed{}$

⑲ $\frac{1}{6} - \frac{1}{8} = \boxed{}$

⑳ $\frac{1}{2} + \frac{1}{4} = \boxed{}$

㉑ $\frac{3}{5} + \frac{1}{3} = \boxed{}$

㉒ $\frac{5}{9} - \frac{3}{8} = \boxed{}$

㉓ $\frac{4}{7} - \frac{1}{2} = \boxed{}$

㉔ $\frac{1}{8} + \frac{1}{4} = \boxed{}$

㉕ Abu walked $\frac{1}{4}$ mile to school and $\frac{3}{10}$ mile to the store. How far did he walk altogether?

Multiplying Decimals by Whole Numbers Lesson 3.9

Multiply.

㉖ $648.25 \times 43 = \boxed{}$

㉗ $869 \times 51.6 = \boxed{}$

㉘ $9{,}755 \times 54.2 = \boxed{}$

㉙ $865.4 \times 997 = \boxed{}$

㉚ $23.65 \times 51 = \boxed{}$

㉛ $341.88 \times 62 = \boxed{}$

㉜ $156 \times 96.3 = \boxed{}$

㉝ $369 \times 45.32 = \boxed{}$

㉞ $574.09 \times 68 = \boxed{}$

㉟ If 1 lunch costs $4.98, how much would 75 lunches cost?

Key Ideas

There are different ways to divide by a fraction. One way uses the fact that multiplication and division are inverse operations. Another way uses common denominators.

Recall that multiplication and division are inverse operations. If you multiply a number, such as 60, by $\frac{3}{4}$ (to get 45), then you can multiply 45 by the inverse of $\frac{3}{4}$ $\left(\frac{4}{3}\right)$ to get 60.

$$60 \longrightarrow \left(\times\frac{3}{4}\right) \longrightarrow 45$$

$$60 \longleftarrow \left(\div\frac{3}{4}\right) \longrightarrow 45$$

$$60 \longleftarrow \left(\times\frac{4}{3}\right) \longrightarrow 45$$

- When dividing fractions, you can multiply by the inverse of the second fraction:

$$6\frac{1}{2} \div 1\frac{1}{3} = \frac{13}{2} \div \frac{4}{3} = \frac{13}{2} \times \frac{3}{4} = \frac{39}{8} \text{ or } 4\frac{7}{8}$$

To check your answer, multiply:

$$\frac{39}{8} \times \frac{4}{3} = \frac{156}{24} \text{ or } 6\frac{1}{2}$$

- A second way to divide is to find a common denominator for both fractions and divide the numerators:

$$6\frac{1}{2} \div 1\frac{1}{3} = \frac{13}{2} \div \frac{4}{3} = \left(\frac{13}{2} \times \frac{3}{3}\right) \div \left(\frac{4}{3} \times \frac{2}{2}\right) = \frac{39}{6} \div \frac{8}{6}$$

$$39 \div 8 = 4\frac{7}{8}$$

Divide. Reduce whenever possible.

1 $12 \div \frac{2}{3} = \blacksquare$

2 $\frac{1}{2} \div \frac{1}{3} = \blacksquare$

3 $16 \div \frac{4}{5} = \blacksquare$

4 $\frac{2}{5} \div \frac{3}{7} = \blacksquare$

5 $\frac{5}{8} \div \frac{5}{4} = \blacksquare$

6 $\frac{5}{12} \div \frac{10}{3} = \blacksquare$

ⓔ **Textbook** This lesson is available in the *eTextbook*.

Replace ▦ in each of the following to make a correct statement.

7 $\dfrac{7}{5} \times \dfrac{2}{3} =$ ▦

8 $\dfrac{14}{15} \div \dfrac{7}{5} =$ ▦

9 $\dfrac{14}{15} \div \dfrac{2}{3} =$ ▦

10 $6\dfrac{1}{4} \div$ ▦ $= 3\dfrac{3}{4}$

11 ▦ $\div 4\dfrac{1}{3} = \dfrac{33}{65}$

12 $8\dfrac{1}{3} \div$ ▦ $= 5$

Answer the following questions.

13 Reuben teaches art in an elementary school. He has $2\dfrac{1}{2}$ large containers of blue acrylic paint for his students to use. If about $\dfrac{3}{10}$ of a container is used for each day's lesson, about how many lessons can Reuben teach with the paint available?

14 **Extended Response** Orlando needed to measure salt for a recipe. The recipe called for $\dfrac{1}{4}$ teaspoon of salt, but Orlando did not have a measuring spoon that small. Instead he used two $\dfrac{1}{2}$-teaspoons of salt. Was this correct? Explain why Orlando might have done that.

Writing + Math Journal

Choose any three of the statements you completed in Problems 7–12. Make up a realistic word problem that can be solved using the information given in the statement.

Key Ideas

Calculators are a convenient way to check answers when adding or subtracting rational numbers.

We know we can add or subtract two fractions by finding a common denominator.

$\frac{1}{4} + \frac{2}{3} = \frac{3}{12} + \frac{8}{12} = \frac{11}{12}$

How would you use a calculator to quickly check this answer? Most calculators cannot display fractions. If you want to solve a problem like this with a calculator, you must first replace the fractions with decimal approximations or equivalents.

- Find the decimal equivalent of $\frac{1}{4}$ by dividing: $1 \div 4$

  Push **1**, **÷**, **4**, **=** ⟶ | 0.25 |

- Find a decimal approximation of $\frac{2}{3}$ by dividing: $2 \div 3$

  Push **2**, **÷**, **3**, **=** ⟶ | 0.6666666 |

- Add: $0.25 + 0.6666666 = 0.9166666$

If you use a calculator, you will find that $\frac{11}{12}$ (**1**, **1**, **÷**, **1**, **2**) is approximately equivalent to 0.9166666.

Here are some more examples:

$\frac{1}{5} + \frac{1}{3} = \frac{3}{15} + \frac{5}{15} = \frac{8}{15}$

$\frac{1}{5} + \frac{1}{3}$ ⟶ $0.2 + 0.3333333 =$ | 0.53333333 |

$\left(\text{Is } \frac{8}{15} \approx 0.53333333?\right)$

$\frac{3}{7} - \frac{1}{8} = \frac{24}{56} - \frac{7}{56} = \frac{17}{56}$

$\frac{3}{7} - \frac{1}{8}$ ⟶ $0.4285714 - 0.125 =$ | 0.3035714 |

$\left(\text{Is } \frac{17}{56} \approx 0.3035714?\right)$

Some calculators leave off digits instead of rounding correctly. For $\frac{2}{3}$ ($2 \div 3$), they might show 0.6666666 instead of 0.6666667.

Some fractions are used so often that it is useful to remember their decimal equivalents or approximations. That way, you will not always have to divide to find their values. Even when you are using a calculator, you can save time if you already know the decimal equivalent or approximation.

In the table below, each number across the top stands for the numerator. Each number down the left side stands for the denominator.

Copy the table and fill in the blanks. Find the decimal equivalents or approximations and round to the nearest thousandth.

			Numerator								
		1	2	3	4	5	6	7	8	9	10
Denominator	1										
	2										
	3										
	4				1					2.25	
	5										
	6										
	7	0.143									
	8			0.375							
	9								0.889		
	10										

Keep your table. It will be useful as you solve problems in this chapter and when you play the **Up to 2 Game** (page 319).

Solve the following problems in two ways—by finding a common denominator and by using decimals to approximate. For each problem, show that the two answers you get are equivalent or nearly equivalent.

1 $\frac{2}{5} - \frac{1}{3} = \boxed{}$

2 $\frac{2}{3} - \frac{1}{6} = \boxed{}$

3 $\frac{5}{9} - \frac{1}{3} = \boxed{}$

4 $\frac{4}{4} - \frac{3}{4} = \boxed{}$

5 $\frac{3}{8} - \frac{1}{4} = \boxed{}$

6 $\frac{1}{2} - \frac{1}{4} = \boxed{}$

7 $\frac{1}{3} + \frac{5}{9} = \boxed{}$

8 $\frac{2}{3} - \frac{3}{5} = \boxed{}$

Decimal Equivalents of Rational Numbers

Key Ideas

Calculators are a convenient way to approximate or check the answer for addition and subtraction of mixed numbers.

When measurements are given as mixed numbers, you add them to find the total. You subtract mixed numbers to compare or find out how much is left.

In this lesson, you will learn to use decimals (with a calculator) to approximate and check the addition and subtraction of mixed numbers.

Example: $2\frac{2}{3} + 4\frac{1}{2} = \blacksquare$

Here are two ways to solve this problem:

- Find a common denominator.

$$2\frac{2}{3} = 2\frac{4}{6} \qquad \longrightarrow \qquad 2\frac{4}{6}$$
$$+ 4\frac{1}{2} = 4\frac{3}{6} \qquad \longrightarrow \qquad + 4\frac{3}{6}$$
$$\overline{\qquad\qquad\qquad\qquad} \qquad \overline{\qquad\qquad}$$
$$6\frac{7}{6} = 7\frac{1}{6}$$

The answer is $7\frac{1}{6}$.

- Use a calculator to find decimal equivalents or approximations.

$2\frac{2}{3}$	$4\frac{1}{2}$
$\frac{2}{3}$ is about 0.6666667.	$\frac{1}{2}$ is 0.5.
$2\frac{2}{3}$ is about 2.6666667.	$4\frac{1}{2}$ is 4.5.

$2.6666667 + 4.5 = 7.1666667$

The answer is 7.1666667.

Are the answers for the two methods approximately equivalent?

Yes, because the fraction $\frac{1}{6}$ is about 0.1666667, $7\frac{1}{6}$ is about 7.1666667.

Example: $5\frac{2}{9} - 3\frac{5}{6} = \blacksquare$

Here are two ways to solve this problem:

- Find a common denominator.

$$5\frac{2}{9} = 5\frac{4}{18} = 4\frac{22}{18} \longrightarrow \quad 4\frac{22}{18}$$
$$-3\frac{5}{6} = 3\frac{15}{18} = 3\frac{15}{18} \longrightarrow \quad -3\frac{15}{18}$$
$$\overline{} \qquad \overline{}$$
$$1\frac{7}{18}$$

The answer is $1\frac{7}{18}$.

- Use a calculator to find decimal equivalents or approximations.

$$5\frac{2}{9} - 3\frac{5}{6} = 5.2222222 - 3.8333333 = 1.3888889$$

Are the two answers about equivalent?

Yes. The fraction $\frac{7}{18}$ is about 0.3888889 (if you round correctly), so $1\frac{7}{18}$ is about 1.3888889.

Solve the following problems in two ways. For each problem, check to see that your two answers are equivalent or about equivalent. Round your answers to four decimal places, if necessary.

1. $1\frac{4}{9} + 3\frac{1}{3} = \blacksquare$

2. $2\frac{1}{3} + \frac{5}{6} = \blacksquare$

3. $5\frac{8}{9} + 8\frac{1}{6} = \blacksquare$

4. $7\frac{3}{8} + 6\frac{1}{2} = \blacksquare$

5. $6\frac{3}{4} - 4\frac{1}{2} = \blacksquare$

6. $\frac{4}{5} + \frac{1}{3} = \blacksquare$

7. $9\frac{1}{4} - 4\frac{2}{3} = \blacksquare$

8. $8\frac{2}{3} - 2\frac{2}{5} = \blacksquare$

9. $3\frac{1}{6} - 2\frac{2}{3} = \blacksquare$

10. $1\frac{4}{5} - \frac{1}{3} = \blacksquare$

11. $8\frac{5}{6} + 3\frac{1}{3} = \blacksquare$

12. $1\frac{3}{8} + 1\frac{3}{4} = \blacksquare$

13. $4\frac{3}{5} - 2\frac{7}{10} = \blacksquare$

14. $6\frac{1}{9} + 2\frac{8}{9} = \blacksquare$

15. $4\frac{2}{3} - 2\frac{3}{4} = \blacksquare$

16. $8\frac{5}{9} + 6\frac{2}{3} = \blacksquare$

17. $5\frac{3}{8} + \frac{5}{6} = \blacksquare$

18. $6\frac{3}{8} + 1\frac{1}{4} = \blacksquare$

19. $5\frac{1}{4} - 2\frac{11}{12} = \blacksquare$

20. $5\frac{1}{3} - 3\frac{4}{9} = \blacksquare$

You may recall the **Up to 1 Game.** To play that game, you made a number line table that related decimals and fractions less than or equal to 1. The **Up to 2 Game** involves numbers less than or equal to 2.

Make a number line table like the one below. For each fraction, write the decimal equivalent or approximation to the nearest thousandth. Each fraction is placed above its corresponding point on the number line. Work in small groups. Use a calculator when you need it. The table on page 315 should also help.

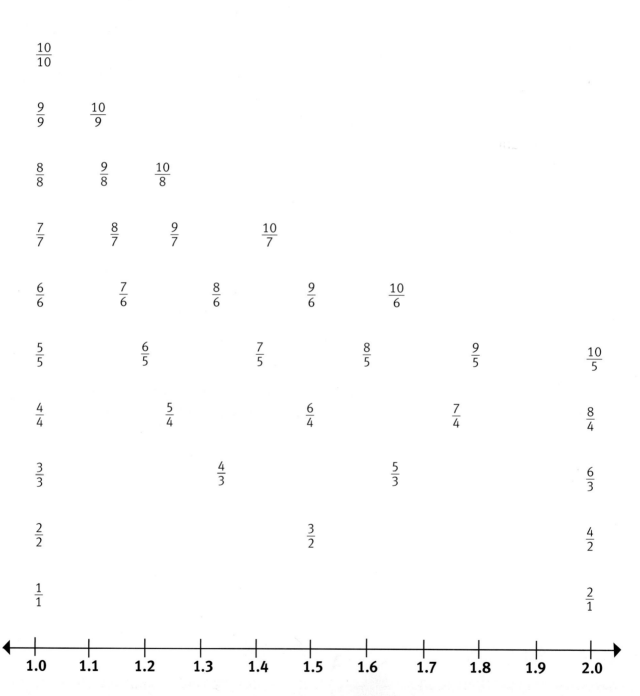

📱**Textbook** This lesson is available in the *eTextbook.*

Decimal Equivalency Strategies and Practice

Up to 2 Game

Players: Two or more

Materials: *Number Cubes* (two 0–5, two 5–10)

Object: To be the last player to get to 2

Math Focus: Comparing and ordering fractions and decimals, finding decimal equivalents of common fractions

HOW TO PLAY

1 Each round, every player takes a turn rolling all four cubes.

2 Use any two of the numbers you roll to make a fraction or a decimal less than or equal to 2 but greater than your last number. (For example, if you roll a 3, 3, 5, and 10, you could make $\frac{3}{3}, \frac{3}{5}, \frac{3}{10}, \frac{5}{3}, \frac{5}{10}, \frac{10}{5}$, or any of the following decimals: 0.103, 0.105, 0.310, 0.33, 0.35, 0.510, 0.53, 1.03, 1.05. Notice that you may place the decimal point between the 1 and the 0 if you roll a 10.)

3 For each turn, write the amount you make as a decimal. If you make a fraction, record the decimal equivalent (or an approximation) to the nearest hundredth, as well as the fraction. You may use a calculator for this or your table from page 315, if you wish.

4 On each turn, you must write a number greater than or equal to the number made on your previous turn. You cannot make a number greater than 2.

5 On any turn that you cannot write a number less than or equal to 2 that is greater than your previous turn, you are out.

6 The last player to go out wins; if all players are unable to go in the same round, then the game ends in a tie.

Using Mixed Numbers

Key Ideas

Mixed numbers can be used in many situations.

Solve the following problems.

1. Mindy charges $20.00 per hour for tutoring high-school students in algebra. She tutored Gerald twice this week, once for $\frac{3}{4}$ hour, and once for $\frac{1}{2}$ hour. How much money does Gerald owe Mindy?

2. Mr. LaRue earns about $37,000 per year. He spends about $120 each week on groceries. About what fraction of his income is spent on groceries?

3. Ava was downloading a program to her computer. It took 12 minutes to download $\frac{3}{4}$ of the program. At that rate, how many more minutes will it take to finish downloading?

4. **Extended Response** Judy's grades put her in the top $\frac{1}{5}$ of her graduating class. If there were 125 students in the class, could she have had the 30th highest grade average? Explain.

5. **Extended Response** Juanita was told to practice her piano lessons for at least 5 hours each week.

   a. If she practices for $\frac{3}{4}$ hour each day, will she have practiced at least 5 hours? Explain.

   b. If she practices $1\frac{1}{4}$ hour each day, will she have practiced at least 5 hours? Explain.

e Textbook This lesson is available in the *eTextbook*.

6 **Extended Response** Janice, Patti, and Becky worked together in their garden for about $\frac{1}{2}$ hour each day, sharing the work equally. At the end of the week, about what fraction of the work did Becky do? Explain.

7 **Extended Response** The Palaez family was driving from Hartville to Mason City, a distance of about 64 miles. When they had driven about 40 miles, Juanita exclaimed that they were $\frac{8}{5}$ of the way there. Could Juanita be right? Why or why not? If not, what mistake did she likely make?

8 Ms. Yonteff's fifth-grade class raised money so they could go on a trip to Bunker Hill. Their goal was to raise $9,000. They were able to raise $10,000. About what fraction of their goal did they reach?

9 Thornwell Elementary School sought donations so that they could purchase new computers. The goal was to raise $30,000. At the end of the year, the principal reported that they had raised $\frac{5}{4}$ of their goal. Is that possible? If so, about how much did they raise?

10 Mr. Pickwick's job is to sell dishes, pots, pans, and glasses to restaurants. He earns $\frac{1}{20}$ of his total sales as a commission. He also has a sales goal. If he reaches the sales goal, he receives a bonus of $5,000. If he reaches $\frac{12}{10}$ of the goal, he earns an additional bonus of $10,000.

   a. If Mr. Pickwick's sales goal is $200,000, how much will he earn if he reaches his goal?

   b. How much will he earn if he reaches $\frac{12}{10}$ of his goal?

Racing to Boston

April 20 An explosive dash in the final seconds catapulted Louise Sauvage to a Boston Marathon victory on a day honoring the beginning of America's fight for independence.

Reaching speeds of more than 35 miles per hour, Sauvage kept battling seven-time champion Jean Driscoll for the lead. At one point, Sauvage trailed so far behind she could not even see Driscoll in front of her. But with only 70 yards left in the 26.2-mile race, Sauvage lunged to the most thrilling finish in marathon history—so close that both racers ended with the same official time of 1:41:19.

In 1975, Boston became the first major marathon to allow wheelchair athletes to compete. Within 20 years, the wheelchair division has grown to include more than 100 racers.

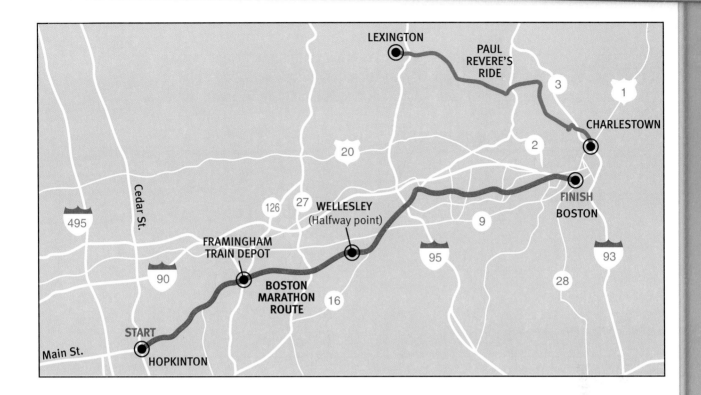

Answer these questions. Use the information on pages 322 and 323.

1 How could Louise Sauvage have won even though both racers finished with the same official time? Explain with an example.

2 What is the greatest amount of time that Sauvage could have won by?

3 Is the last 70 yards more or less than $\frac{1}{50}$ of the entire 26.2-mile marathon? How do you know?

4 About what fraction of the Boston Marathon distance was Paul Revere's ride from Charlestown to Lexington?

Exploring Problem Solving

Marathon racing has its ups and downs, as you can see from this graph of the Boston Marathon course. Whether running or propelling a wheelchair, going uphill is a lot harder than going downhill. One uphill stretch of the Boston course is so grueling, it is called Heartbreak Hill.

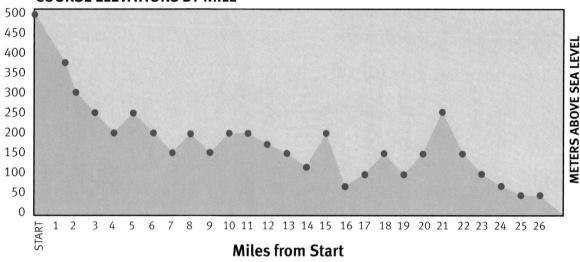

COURSE ELEVATIONS BY MILE

Miles from Start

METERS ABOVE SEA LEVEL

How much do hills affect runners? To find out, you can use this graph and the table. The table shows the approximate times for the lead runners at different points of the 104th Boston Marathon.

Mile Mark	Time	Place Name
2	12:09	Ashland
$4\frac{1}{3}$	12:20	Uphill
5	12:24	Framingham
$7\frac{2}{5}$	12:36	Natick
$10\frac{1}{10}$	12:49	Natick Center
$12\frac{2}{5}$	1:00	Wellesley College
$15\frac{2}{5}$	1:15	Wellesley Hills
$16\frac{3}{5}$	1:21	Route 128 Crossing
$17\frac{1}{2}$	1:25	Newton Hills
$20\frac{3}{5}$	1:40	Top of Heartbreak Hill
21	1:42	Boston College
$22\frac{1}{5}$	1:48	Cleveland Circle
$23\frac{1}{3}$	1:53	Coolidge Corner

Work in groups to discuss and solve these problems.

5. Based on the graph, on which part of the Boston Marathon course do you think racers go the slowest? Why?

6. Based on the graph, on which part are racers fastest? Why?

7. Use the table to find and compare speeds on the two parts of the course you selected for Problems 5 and 6.

8. Did your results match what you expected? Explain.

Cumulative Review

Solve.

The relationship between degrees Fahrenheit and degrees Celsius
can be written as a function rule:

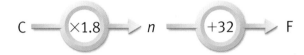

C ─── ($\times 1.8$) ──▸ *n* ─── ($+32$) ──▸ F

① Which temperature in degrees Celsius would you expect in a classroom?

    a. 10

    b. 20

    c. 45

② Which temperature in degrees Celsius is closest to 100°F?

    a. 20

    b. 30

    c. 40

③ What is the inverse of the function rule given above?

④ Which temperature in degrees Fahrenheit is closest to 5°C?

    a. 40

    b. 32

    c. 50

⑤ If a thermometer reads 86°F, what is the same temperature in degrees Celsius?

Probability and Fractions Lesson 6.9
Solve.

A game of pool uses balls that are numbered 1–15. Suppose the balls are mixed up and you pick one. What is the probability that the number of the ball is

6 greater than 9?

7 an even number?

8 a multiple of 4?

Adding and Subtracting Mixed Numbers Lessons 7.3 and 7.4

9 $1\frac{7}{8} + 3\frac{1}{4} =$

10 $4\frac{1}{4} - 2\frac{1}{3} =$

11 $2\frac{1}{3} + 3\frac{4}{5} =$

12 $5\frac{1}{6} - 4\frac{3}{4} =$

Graphing in Four Quadrants Lesson 5.4
Write the coordinates of the following points.

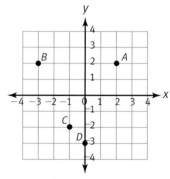

13 *A*

14 *B*

15 *C*

16 *D*

17 If you can only walk along the grid lines, which is closer to *D*, *A* or *B*?

18 If you can only walk along the grid lines, which is closer to *C*, *A* or *B*?

Key Ideas Review

In this chapter you explored mixed numbers.

You learned how to convert mixed numbers to improper fractions and improper fractions to mixed numbers.

You learned how to compute with mixed numbers and to express mixed numbers as decimals.

· ·

Answer the following questions.

1. Explain how to convert a mixed number to an improper fraction and provide an example.

2. Solve the following expression:

$$\blacksquare \div \frac{2}{3} = 7\frac{1}{4}$$

Explain how you found your answer.

Write the decimal equivalent of the following fractions.

3. $9\frac{5}{10} = \blacksquare$

4. $3\frac{6}{8} = \blacksquare$

5. $7\frac{5}{8} = \blacksquare$

Solve the following exercises by providing the answer as a fraction and decimal equivalent or approximation.

6. $2\frac{2}{3} \times 1\frac{1}{2} = \blacksquare$

7. $4\frac{3}{9} + 5\frac{1}{4} = \blacksquare$

8. $10\frac{4}{6} - 8\frac{1}{2} = \blacksquare$

9. $\frac{1}{2} \div \frac{3}{9} = \blacksquare$

10. $3\frac{3}{4} \times 2\frac{3}{6} = \blacksquare$

Chapter Review

Lesson 7.1 **Replace** each mixed number with an equivalent improper fraction.

1 $2\frac{1}{6}$ **2** $1\frac{1}{8}$ **3** $4\frac{1}{5}$

4 $3\frac{5}{7}$ **5** $7\frac{1}{8}$ **6** $6\frac{1}{7}$

Replace each improper fraction with a mixed number.

7 $\frac{5}{2}$ **8** $\frac{7}{3}$ **9** $\frac{11}{3}$

10 $\frac{9}{4}$ **11** $\frac{10}{7}$ **12** $\frac{21}{5}$

Lesson 7.2 **Multiply.** Check to see that your answers make sense.

13 $3\frac{1}{3} \times 4\frac{2}{7} = \blacksquare$ **15** $1\frac{2}{5} \times 3\frac{1}{7} = \blacksquare$

14 $1\frac{5}{8} \times 1\frac{3}{5} = \blacksquare$ **16** $4\frac{1}{2} \times 3\frac{1}{9} = \blacksquare$

Lesson 7.3 **Add.**

17 $3\frac{5}{8} + 1\frac{1}{4} = \blacksquare$ **19** $4\frac{3}{4} + 1\frac{5}{6} = \blacksquare$

18 $5\frac{1}{2} + 2\frac{2}{3} = \blacksquare$ **20** $4\frac{3}{5} + 1\frac{1}{3} = \blacksquare$

Lesson 7.4 **Subtract.**

21 $5\frac{7}{9} - 3\frac{4}{6} = \blacksquare$ **23** $3\frac{1}{5} - 1\frac{2}{3} = \blacksquare$

22 $4\frac{1}{4} - 2\frac{3}{8} = \blacksquare$ **24** $5\frac{4}{5} - 2\frac{1}{6} = \blacksquare$

Lesson 7.6 Divide. Reduce when possible.

25 $12 \div \frac{2}{3} = $ ▢

27 $2\frac{1}{5} \div 3\frac{2}{3} = $ ▢

26 $1\frac{3}{4} \div 2\frac{1}{3} = $ ▢

28 $3 \div \frac{2}{3} = $ ▢

Lesson 7.8 Complete each exercise and write the answer as a mixed number and as a decimal. For each exercise, check to see that your two answers are equivalent or almost equivalent. Round your answers to four decimal places if necessary.

29 $1\frac{2}{7} + 3\frac{1}{3} = $ ▢

30 $2\frac{3}{8} + 5\frac{3}{4} = $ ▢

31 $1\frac{3}{5} + 4\frac{1}{5} = $ ▢

32 $4\frac{1}{5} + 2\frac{2}{9} = $ ▢

Lesson 7.9 Solve.

33 Lilla earns $10 per hour doing errands. On Monday, she worked $2\frac{1}{4}$ hours and on Friday she worked $1\frac{1}{2}$ hours. How much did Lilla earn for those 2 days?

34 Abby walks to raise money. After 6 miles, she had completed $\frac{3}{5}$ of the walk. How many miles were left to go?

35 Gil starts each work week with $50. He spends about $3 each day on lunches. About what fraction of his weekly money is spent on lunch?

Write each improper fraction as a mixed number.

1. $\frac{7}{4}$

2. $\frac{21}{5}$

3. $\frac{15}{2}$

Write each mixed number as an improper fraction.

4. $3\frac{3}{5}$

5. $2\frac{5}{6}$

6. $5\frac{8}{9}$

Solve for *n*. Watch the signs. Reduce when possible.

7. $2\frac{3}{5} + 3\frac{2}{3} = n$

8. $\frac{3}{4} \div \frac{3}{8} = n$

9. $2\frac{5}{6} - 2\frac{1}{8} = n$

10. $4\frac{1}{4} \times \frac{2}{9} = n$

11. $4\frac{1}{2} \times 3\frac{2}{3} = n$

12. $1\frac{5}{7} + 4\frac{3}{5} = n$

13. $1\frac{5}{6} \div 4 = n$

14. $6\frac{2}{5} - 2\frac{3}{4} = n$

15. $3\frac{9}{10} + 1\frac{1}{4} = n$

16. $2\frac{1}{5} \times 1\frac{3}{5} = n$

Textbook This lesson is available in the *eTextbook*.

Choose the correct answer.

17. Sangi ate $4\frac{3}{4}$ graham crackers with his lunch and $2\frac{1}{2}$ more as a snack. How many graham crackers did Sangi eat?

    Ⓐ $2\frac{1}{4}$ Ⓑ $6\frac{1}{4}$

    Ⓒ $6\frac{2}{3}$ Ⓓ $7\frac{1}{4}$

18. Travis used $2\frac{2}{3}$ cups of milk to make a batch of 8 cupcakes. How many cups of milk are in each cupcake?

    Ⓐ $\frac{1}{3}$ cup   Ⓑ $\frac{6}{15}$ cup

    Ⓒ $5\frac{2}{3}$ cups   Ⓓ $8\frac{1}{3}$ cups

19. Which decimal approximation is equivalent to the sum of $\frac{7}{10}$ and $\frac{2}{3}$?

    Ⓐ 1.4   Ⓑ 1.367

    Ⓒ 0.692   Ⓓ 0.033

20. Beth's cat weighs 9 pounds. Her dog weighs $25\frac{1}{2}$ pounds. How many times as heavy as her cat is her dog?

    Ⓐ $229\frac{1}{2}$ Ⓑ $16\frac{1}{2}$

    Ⓒ $2\frac{5}{6}$ Ⓓ $1\frac{7}{18}$

21. Mike works $5\frac{3}{4}$ hours 4 days a week. How many hours does he work in 2 weeks?

    Ⓐ $11\frac{1}{2}$ Ⓑ $19\frac{1}{2}$

    Ⓒ 23   Ⓓ 46

22. Which mixed number will make the following statement true?

    $$\frac{4}{5} \times \boxed{} = 1\frac{1}{15}$$

    Ⓐ $1\frac{5}{12}$ Ⓑ $1\frac{1}{3}$

    Ⓒ $\frac{2}{3}$ Ⓓ $\frac{4}{15}$

23. The Pifalos are sailing their boat in a race from Marblehead, MA, to Halifax, Nova Scotia. If they have sailed $210\frac{5}{8}$ nautical miles and the race is 360 nautical miles long, how many more miles do they have to sail?

    Ⓐ $149\frac{3}{8}$ Ⓑ $150\frac{3}{8}$

    Ⓒ $569\frac{5}{8}$ Ⓓ $570\frac{3}{8}$

Practice Test

24. The historical society needs to raise $25,000 to restore an old home. They raised $1\frac{1}{8}$ of their goal. How much money did they raise?

   Ⓐ $31,250   Ⓑ $28,125

   Ⓒ $21,875   Ⓓ $3,125

25. $3\frac{4}{5} \times 3\frac{7}{8} = $ ▢

   Ⓐ $9\frac{7}{10}$ Ⓑ $14\frac{7}{10}$

   Ⓒ $14\frac{29}{40}$ Ⓓ 15

26. Josiah did some computation and got a rounded answer of 6.2667. Which exercise did he solve?

   Ⓐ $6 + \frac{2}{3}$ Ⓑ $8\frac{2}{3} - 2\frac{2}{5}$

   Ⓒ $8\frac{2}{5} - 2\frac{4}{15}$ Ⓓ $3\frac{3}{5} + 3\frac{4}{15}$

27. Which of the following equations matches this composite function?

   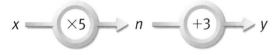

   Ⓐ $y = \frac{x}{5} + 3$ Ⓑ $y = 5x + 3$

   Ⓒ $y = \frac{x}{3} + 5$ Ⓓ $y = 3x + 5$

28. Which of the following numbers is a common denominator for the fractions $\frac{1}{4}$, $\frac{5}{8}$, and $\frac{5}{6}$?

   Ⓐ 16   Ⓑ 24

   Ⓒ 32   Ⓓ 42

29. If you start at 100 on a calculator and keep subtracting 6, which number will you hit?

   Ⓐ 90   Ⓑ 80

   Ⓒ 70   Ⓓ 60

30. Subtract: $7 - (10) = n$.

   Ⓐ $n = 17$ Ⓑ $n = 3$

   Ⓒ $n = -3$ Ⓓ $n = -17$

31. Which of the following fractions is equivalent to $\frac{15}{40}$?

   Ⓐ $\frac{3}{8}$ Ⓑ $\frac{1}{3}$

   Ⓒ $\frac{3}{10}$ Ⓓ $\frac{5}{8}$

32. Ellen rolled a **Number Cube** labeled with the numbers 5 through 10. What is the probability that she rolled an even number?

   Ⓐ $\frac{6}{6}$ Ⓑ $\frac{3}{6}$

   Ⓒ $\frac{2}{6}$ Ⓓ $\frac{1}{6}$

33. Paint spilled on Gene's paper. Which answer could be the correct product?

   Ⓐ 126,000   Ⓑ 123,804

   Ⓒ 76,000   Ⓓ 75

34. Jen sells advertisement space in the newspaper. She earns $\frac{1}{15}$ of her total sales as a commission. She also has a sales goal every month. If she reaches her goal, she receives a bonus of $3,000. If she reaches $\frac{5}{4}$ of her goal, she receives an additional $1,000.

    a. If her sales goal is $120,000, how much will Jen earn if she reaches her goal? Explain your answer.

    b. How much will Jen earn if she sells $\frac{5}{4}$ of her goal? Explain your answer.

35. Keith had the plans to construct this bookcase. All the measurements are shown below, but the measurement for the heights of the wooden separators, which are equal, are missing.

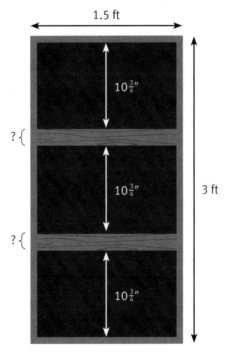

    a. How could you find the missing measurements? Explain.

    b. What is the height of each separator?

CHAPTER 8

Division and Ratios

In This Chapter You Will Learn

- how to compute batting averages.
- how to divide by two- and three-digit numbers.
- how to solve problems using rates and ratios.

Problem Solving

In June 1780, the British marched across New Jersey and prepared to attack. The Jersey Brigade was outnumbered. Upon hearing the news, George Washington gave orders to General Stirling, who then sent a message to the brigade's officers. Suppose the message was sent in a code in which each letter of the alphabet stands for a different letter. So, the letter *B* might stand for *T*, the letter *Q* for *L*, and so on.

JYVES NMFS YXX FSW RLVEW QLH EYU JHPFWV. YUULQ FSW WUWJQ YP JHES YP ZLPPMKXW. YF FSW PYJW FMJW QLH YVW VWQHWPFWO ULF FL HPW YJJHUMFMLU HUUWEPPYVMXQ. PSLLF LUXQ NSWU QLH SYCW Y PHVW FYVBWF. FVQ FL PFYQ MU FSW NLLOP RLV KWFFWV OWRWUPW YBYMUPF YFFYET LU SLVPWKYET.

In any language, some letters occur more often than others, as the following graph shows.

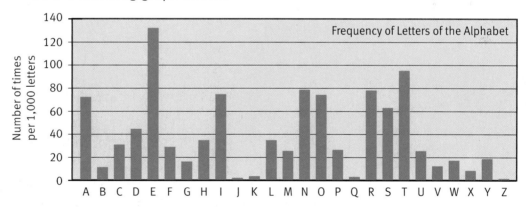

Work in groups to solve the following problems.

1. Make a tally of the number of times each letter appears in the message. Use the graph to help you decode the secret message.

2. Did the number of times each letter appeared in the message exactly match the average numbers from the graph? Why do you think that happened?

Averages

Key Ideas

An average is a value we use to represent a typical value in a set of data.

You have probably heard the word *average* many times. Perhaps you've heard someone say, "His batting average is .265 this season," or "I spend an average of two hours doing homework every day."

The average, or mean, of a set of numbers is the number you get if you subtract amounts from the greater numbers in the set and add those amounts to the smaller numbers until the numbers are all the same. You can also find the average, or mean, by adding all the numbers, and then dividing that sum by how many numbers there are altogether. For example, the average of 4, 6, 8, and 2 is 5 because $4 + 6 + 8 + 2 = 20$, and $20 \div 4 = 5$.

Find the averages.

1. 4, 3, 5, 9, 4
2. 12, 15, 18, 15
3. 2, 3, 8, 7
4. 9, 10, 11, 12, 13
5. 22, 21, 25, 20
6. 4, 6, 6, 10, 10
7. 20, 30, 40, 50
8. 2, 4, 6, 8, 10
9. 32, 34, 36, 38, 40

10. 52, 54, 56, 58, 60
11. 72, 74, 76, 78, 80
12. 100, 107, 109, 113
13. 10, 18, 19, 23, 26
14. 15, 25, 30, 40
15. 75, 85, 86, 90, 92

e Textbook This lesson is available in the *eTextbook*.

Amalia kept a record of her test scores at school and recorded them on the following table. On all tests a perfect score is 100.

Test Scores September–December

Date	Test Subject	Score
9/10	mathematics	91
9/14	spelling	48
9/30	history	65
10/15	mathematics	95
10/19	spelling	53
11/2	spelling	49
11/4	history	75
11/6	mathematics	97
11/20	history	79
12/1	spelling	55
12/4	mathematics	100
12/7	history	90
12/15	mathematics	96
12/16	spelling	60
12/17	history	95
12/18	mathematics	96

Answer the following questions, rounding to the nearest tenth.

16 What was the average of all of Amalia's test scores?

17 **Extended Response** How well does the average describe Amalia's test results?

18 What was Amalia's average score in mathematics?

19 What was her average score in history?

20 What was Amalia's average score in spelling?

21 **Extended Response** How well do the individual averages describe Amalia's test results? If you were her teacher, how would you report Amalia's results?

Amalia decided to make a table for her test scores in each subject. This is what her table for history looked like:

History Test Scores

Date	Score
9/30	65
11/4	75
11/20	79
12/7	90
12/17	95

Study Amalia's test scores. Round your answers to the nearest tenth.

22 **Extended Response** Do you think the average score tells how well Amalia is doing in history? Why or why not?

23 **Extended Response** If you were Amalia's teacher, what grade would you give her in history? Explain your answer.

24 What score would Amalia need on her next spelling test to have an average of 60 on her spelling tests?

25 What is the greatest average on mathematics tests she could have after her next test?

26 **Extended Response** Sarah received scores of 75, 80, 82, and 87 on four quizzes. She estimates her average to be 80. Is she correct? Why or why not?

27 Alan is reading a book for his geography project. He read 32 pages the first night, 24 pages the next night, 28 pages the third night, and 36 pages the fourth night. What is the average number of pages Alan read each night?

28 Juan's times, in minutes and seconds (MM:SS), to get home from school this week were 12:00, 9:25, 10:40, 8:35, and 11:20. What was his average time in minutes and seconds?

eTextbook This lesson is available in the *eTextbook*.

Game

Averaging and Strategies Practice

Cube Averaging Game

Players: Two

Materials: *Number Cubes* (one 0–5)

Object: To get the greater average

Math Focus: Finding averages, mental arithmetic (addition and division), and mathematical reasoning

HOW TO PLAY

1 The first player rolls the cube no more than five times and writes down each number as it is rolled.

2 The second player may tell the first player to stop after three or four rolls, or he or she may allow the first player to roll five times.

3 The first player calculates the average of the three, four, or five numbers rolled.

4 The players reverse roles.

5 For each round the player with the greater average is the winner and must be the second player to roll the cube in the next game.

SAMPLE GAME

Rita rolled: `3` `2` `3` `1`

José told her to stop.

Rita calculated her average:

$3 + 2 + 3 + 1 = 9$

$$4{\overline{)9.00}}^{\,2.25}$$

José rolled: `2` `3` `1`

Rita told him to stop.

José calculated his average:

$2 + 3 + 1 = 6$

$$3{\overline{)6}}^{\,2}$$

Rita won the round because her average (2.25) was greater than José's (2).

Mean, Median, Mode, and Range

Key Ideas

When a set of numbers is arranged in numerical order, the middle number is called the median. The mode is the number that appears most often, and the range is the difference between the greatest and least numbers.

When the numbers in a set are written in numerical order, there will be as many numbers to the left of the median as to the right. If there is no middle number, the mean of the two middle values is the median.

The Great Long-Jump Contest

Tomeo and Barry had a contest to see who could jump farther. They took five jumps each. The winner would have the longest average of the five jumps.

Study the contest results. Then answer the questions that follow.

Jump Number	Distance of Jump (measured to the nearest centimeter)	
Jump	Tomeo	Barry
1	140	143
2	141	158
3	139	144
4	143	102
5	138	149

1. What was the average distance of Tomeo's jumps?

2. What was the average distance of Barry's jumps?

3. Who won the contest, Tomeo or Barry?

4. Do you think the averages describe how well Tomeo and Barry can jump?

5. If Tomeo and Barry were to have a second contest with only one jump each, who would be more likely to win?

6. **Extended Response** What information did you use to answer the previous question?

7. **Extended Response** How could you make the judging more favorable for Barry?

eTextbook This lesson is available in the *eTextbook*.

As part of a research project to learn about students' study habits, Tom conducted a survey of the 61 fifth-grade students in his school. All students were given survey forms that asked how many hours they spent on homework each week, and whether they were A students, B students, C students, or students who usually had grades lower than a C.

Fifty-four students returned their surveys. Tom recorded his results in this way:

8-B, 10-L, 12-A, 6-C, 12-A, 12-A, 8-C, 7-B, 2-B, 15-B, 12-A, 8-C, 5-B, 9-L, 13-A, 9-C, 9-B, 9-A, 3-C, 10-A, 6-C, 8-B, 8-C, 8-A, 10-B, 13-A, 1-L, 8-B, 9-C, 7-A, 10-C, 10-A, 9-B, 12-A, 8-C, 2-L, 7-C, 7-B, 6-C, 9-L, 8-C, 8-B, 9-B, 9-A, 13-A, 17-A, 1-L, 5-C, 8-B, 5-C, 14-A, 8-L, 13-B, 6-C

8 According to Tom's results, what do you think 10-A means?

9 What does 2-L mean?

10 What does 5-C mean?

11 **Extended Response** Was this a useful way for Tom to record his results? What are some other ways?

Tom decided to find out how much homework A students did. He separated the surveys of the A students and recorded the time they spent on homework each week this way:

12, 12, 12, 12, 13, 9, 10, 8, 13, 7, 10, 12, 9, 13, 17, 14

12 How many students thought of themselves as A students?

13 On average, how many hours a week did they say they do homework?

In order from least to greatest, the numbers are:

7, 8, 9, 9, 10, 10, 12, 12, 12, 12, 12, 13, 13, 13, 14, 17

14 What is the median?

Still another way to describe the time spent on homework by A students is to tell which number appears the most. That number is called the mode. Here 12 is the mode. Sometimes data can have two or more modes. If every number appears the same number of times, there is no mode.

We can also describe the time spent on homework by A students by finding the range of hours. The range is the difference between the greatest and least values in a set. In this case, the range is 10 hours (7–17). Sometimes we use a *clipped range*, in which we omit the greatest and least values. The clipped range for Tom's data is 6 hours (8–14).

Complete this table by using data from Tom's survey. Use a calculator to find the mean. Round answers to the nearest tenth. Then discuss the meaning of the results.

Hours Spent on Homework

	A Students	B Students	C Students	Lower Than C Students	All Students
Number of Students	16	15	16	7	54
Mean	11.4	▢	▢	▢	▢
Median	12	▢	▢	▢	▢
Mode	12	▢	▢	▢	▢
Range	10 (7–17)	▢	▢	▢	▢
Clipped Range	6 (8–14)	▢	▢	▢	▢

15 **Extended Response** Which method gives the best description of the results of Tom's survey? Explain your answer.

16 **Extended Response** If you wanted to find out about the study habits of students in your school, how would you conduct your survey? How would you report the results?

Writing + Math **Journal**

Describe a situation in which it would be a good idea to use a clipped range. Why do you think this is better than another method?

e Textbook This lesson is available in the *eTextbook*.

Game

Averaging and Strategies Practice

Golf Game

Players: One or more

Materials: *Number Cubes* (two 0–5, two 5–10)

Object: To get the lowest average number of rolls for the given number of turns

Math Focus: Finding averages, mental arithmetic, and mathematical reasoning

HOW TO PLAY

1 Decide how many turns each player will get. (Five turns are recommended.)

2 Each player begins a turn with a score of 1,000, and continues rolling until he or she reaches a score of 0.

3 For each roll, the player chooses which of the four cubes to roll. You may roll zero, one, two, three, or four cubes.

4 After the cubes have been rolled, use all the digits showing to make a number. If you roll a 10, you must keep the 1 and 0 together in that order, but if you roll a 0 you can place it anywhere, including as the first digit.

5 Between rolls, either subtract the number you make from your running score or add it to your running score. If it is not possible to subtract it without falling below −10, you must add it. If you choose not to roll, you may instead add or subtract either 1 or 2 to or from your running score.

6 Record the number of rolls each player takes in each turn.

7 When all players have completed their turns, each player computes his or her average number of rolls per turn. The player with the least average wins.

SAMPLE GAME (one turn):

Steve rolled 10, 3, and 7. The least number he could make was 1,037, which cannot be subtracted from 1,000 to get a number greater than −10, so he had to add.
Next he rolled two 10s and 0. He made 01010 and subtracted.
On his third try, Steve rolled 10, 9, and 2 and subtracted 1,029, getting −2.
In place of a fourth roll, he added 2.
Because it took him 4 rolls to reach 0, Steve's score for that turn was 4. He took four more turns and found the average score of all five turns.

$$
\begin{array}{r}
1000 \\
+\ 1037 \\
\hline
2037 \\
-\ 01010 \\
\hline
1027 \\
-\ 1029 \\
\hline
-\ 2 \\
+\ 2 \\
\hline
0
\end{array}
$$

Interpreting Averages

Key Ideas

When summarizing data, you should always think about whether mean, median, mode, or none of these should be used.

The Census Bureau of Humboldt County says that the average number of children per family is 1.8.

1 Is it possible for one family to have 1.8 children?

2 Is it possible for 100 families to have an average of 1.8 children per family?

3 About how many children would you expect there to be if you surveyed 100 families in Humboldt County?

The Census Bureau of Shelby County says that the average number of children per family is 3.4.

4 Is it possible for one family to have 3.4 children?

5 Is it possible for a number of families to have an average of 3.4 children each?

6 About how many children would you expect there to be if you surveyed 100 families in Shelby County?

Suppose a family from each of those counties were to visit you.

7 Which family do you think would probably have more children? Can you be certain without knowing the families?

Suppose 10 families from each county were to visit you.

8 Which group would probably have more children? Would you be surprised if they didn't?

There are 10,578 families in Orange County. They have 23,269 children altogether.

9 What would you suppose is the average number of children per family? What is the actual average number of children per family? (Use a calculator. Give the answer to the nearest tenth.)

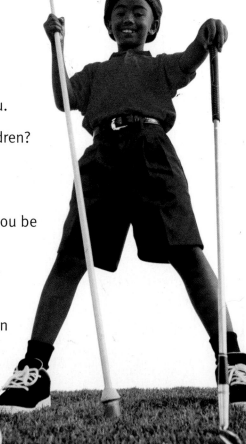

For each situation, decide whether the mean, median, or mode would be most appropriate. Explain your answer.

10 **Extended Response** The Rockville Rockets basketball team has players with the following heights: 5'9", 5'9", 6'11", 5'8", 5'7", 5'8", 5'7", 5'9", 5'7", and 5'8". A newspaper wants the average height of the players. If you were a reporter, how might you report the average height, and why?

11 In order to install a traffic light at an intersection, a city requires an average of 5,000 vehicles to pass through the intersection each day. In one week the following numbers of vehicles were counted: Sunday–1,812; Monday–6,213; Tuesday–5,935; Wednesday–6,086; Thursday–6,113; Friday–6,184; Saturday–2,593. The city claims the average number of cars is approximately 4,991, so the intersection does not need a light. A neighborhood group claims the average number of cars is 6,086, and that there should be a light. How is each group finding its average?

12 **Extended Response** A magazine columnist conducted a survey to find the average number of hours her readers watched television each day. Based on the responses, how might she find the average? Explain your reasoning.

13 A school district wants to report the average number of school days cancelled due to bad weather each year for the past decade. Over the past 10 years, school has been cancelled 0, 2, 1, 0, 1, 7, 1, 1, 1, and 0 days. What method would you suggest to the district for reporting the average number of days that were missed?

14 Douglas played three games of miniature golf. His score was 57 in the first game, 63 in the second game, and 63 in the third game. Which method of finding the average would give him the smallest average score, and what is that score?

15 **Extended Response** Michiko has kept track of her grades on her last five math tests. Her scores were 85, 87, 84, 43, and 86. (She accidentally skipped a page on her fourth test.) What would be the best average to use in predicting her score on her next test? What would you predict her next score to be?

Writing + Math **Journal**

Review Problem 11. Suppose there is a third group claiming that the data is meaningless because it does not show the times of day when the intersection is used the most. Who is correct? Explain your reasoning.

Ratios and Rates

Key Ideas

There are many ways to compare numbers. One way is to use ratios.

A *ratio* is the comparison of two numbers using division.

You may have heard people talk about the ratio of students to teachers in a school or the ratio of sunny days to rainy days during the year.

We usually compare numbers in one of the following ways:

- We find the difference between the numbers by subtracting.

- We find the quotient (or ratio) of the numbers by dividing.

- We simply report the numbers and don't do any calculations.

Suppose Nituna ran 6 kilometers and Mike ran 4 kilometers.

We might find the difference ($6 - 4 = 2$, or $4 - 6 = -2$) and say:

"Nituna ran 2 kilometers farther than Mike," or "Mike ran 2 kilometers less than Nituna."

We might find the ratio $\left(\frac{6}{4} = \frac{3}{2} = 1\frac{1}{2} \text{ or } \frac{4}{6} = \frac{2}{3}\right)$ and say:

"Nituna ran $1\frac{1}{2}$ times as far as Mike," or "Mike ran $\frac{2}{3}$ as far as Nituna."

We could report the numbers and not find the difference or the ratio. Then we would simply say:

"Nituna ran 6 kilometers, and Mike ran 4 kilometers."

Notice that in the last statement we do not lose information, but we don't really compare the numbers.

How we choose to compare numbers depends on the kind of information we are trying to stress and how the information will be used. But just giving a number or numbers is not enough. You must give the number in a sentence or phrase to show what it means (for example, "Mike ran $\frac{2}{3}$ as far as Nituna").

ⓔ Textbook This lesson is available in the *eTextbook.*

In the example with Nituna and Mike, we gave five sentences. Each sentence provided information that compared how far each person ran. Now consider the following statements. Think of ways in which you could report and compare the information. Discuss which ways would be most useful.

Decide on a way to report the information in each statement.

1. Sam bought a sports card for 5¢ and sold it for 10¢.

2. Harry bought a lot of sports cards for 5¢ each and sold them for 10¢ each.

3. It costs Mrs. Wu 15¢ per kilometer to drive her small car and 45¢ per kilometer to drive her large car.

4. Cindy is 140 centimeters tall, and Nikki is 138 centimeters tall.

5. It takes Kevin 10 minutes to walk home from school. It takes Brian 15 minutes to walk home from school.

6. A math book has 640 pages. A geography book has 520 pages.

7. Rishi spent 25¢ for his bottle of water, which he bought in bulk. Vahagn paid $1 for his bottle of water from the vending machine.

8. Aileen made $15 delivering papers to her 25 customers for 6 days this week. Justin made $2.50 for delivering to the same customers on Sunday.

There are special kinds of ratios called rates, which are commonly used to report certain kinds of information.

A rate is a ratio written with units. Rates often relate two quantities with different types of units and are sometimes called *mixed ratios*.

Often a rate is written so that the second number is 1, as in 20 miles per hour (20 miles per 1 hour).

Example: Mr. Delgado drove 240 kilometers in 3 hours. On the average, how fast did he drive? (In other words, how far would he have gone in 1 hour if he had driven at the same speed for the whole trip?)

We can set up this ratio to relate the distance Mr. Delgado traveled to the time it took:

$$\frac{240 \text{ kilometers}}{3 \text{ hours}}$$

Since $\frac{240}{3} = 80$, we can say that Mr. Delgado's average speed was 80 $\frac{\text{km}}{\text{hr}}$ (80 kilometers per hour, or 80 kilometers for each hour).

We can check this. We ask, "If Mr. Delgado drove at 80 kilometers per hour for 3 hours, how far did he go?"

$$3 \times 80 = 240$$

So Mr. Delgado drove 240 kilometers in 3 hours. This checks with the original information.

Example: A box of Better Bran cereal costs $1.05 for 350 grams. How much does it cost per gram?

We can set up this ratio to compare the weight and price of the cereal:

$$\frac{105¢}{350 \text{ grams}}$$

Since $\frac{105}{350} = 0.3$, we can say that the box of Better Bran cereal costs $\frac{0.3¢}{\text{gram}}$ (0.3¢ per gram, or 0.3¢ for each gram).

We can check this by asking how much 350 grams of Better Bran cereal at 0.3¢ per gram would cost.

$$350 \times 0.3¢ = \$1.05$$

That checks with the original information.

Use a calculator if needed. Check your answers to see that they make sense.

9 A 750-gram box of Crunchy Corn cereal costs $2.10, and a 500-gram box costs $1.50.

   a. How much per gram is the cereal in the 750-gram box?

   b. How much per gram is the cereal in the 500-gram box?

   c. Which box is the better buy?

10 Miss Carroll drove about 800 kilometers in 12 hours and used 70 liters of gasoline.

   a. What was her average speed?

   b. On average, about how many kilometers per liter of gasoline did she get?

   c. If she continued at the same speed, about how far could she have gone in 15 hours?

   d. About how much more gasoline would Miss Carroll need to drive 200 kilometers further if she continued using gas at the same rate?

   e. **Extended Response** How did you figure this out?

11 Jeff's car gets 25 miles per gallon of gasoline. His cabin is 190 miles away, and he wants to drive directly there without stopping for gas.

   a. How many gallons of gas will he need to get there?

   b. **Extended Response** Suppose his friend's sport utility vehicle gets 19 miles per gallon and has 9 gallons of gas in it. Jeff's car has only 8 gallons of gas. Does it matter whose car they take? Explain.

12 An office supply store sells 3 pencils for 96¢. If the rate remains the same, how much will 10 pencils cost?

Journal

Describe a time during the last week in which ratios or rates were useful to you.

240 km

Comparing Ratios

Key Ideas

Comparing two ratios is like comparing two rational numbers.

An advertisement reads, "This model gets more miles per gallon than any other car its size." How can you tell if that is true?

We often use ratios to compare things like gasoline consumption, unit cost, or win/loss records. Sometimes deciding the greater of two ratios is simple, but sometimes it requires computation.

Example A: The Chelsea Chiefs won 7 out of 11 games, and the Burnside Bombers won 6 out of 10. Which team has the better record?

Example B: Latoya's car used 18 gallons of gasoline to go 300 miles. Meg's car needed 16 gallons to go 280 miles. Which car got more miles per gallon?

Example C: A 5-kilogram bag of Canine Cuisine dog food costs $7.98 at one store. At another store, a 6-kilogram bag of the same dog food costs $7.98. Which store has the better buy?

Example D: In Mrs. Carter's class, 12 of the 25 students are boys. In Mr. D'Angelo's class, 14 of the 26 students are boys. Which class has a greater ratio of boys to all students?

 Textbook This lesson is available in the *eTextbook*.

You can compare two ratios by using division to convert them to decimals. This is easy if you have a calculator. You can also compare ratios in other ways, and, in some cases, it is faster without a calculator. Here is how you might compare the ratios in Examples A, B, C, and D.

Example A: Chiefs' record: $\frac{7}{11} = 0.636$ (rounded to the nearest thousandth)

Bombers' record: $\frac{6}{10} = 0.600$

The Chiefs have the better record (0.636 is greater than 0.600).

Example B: Latoya: $\frac{300}{18} = 16.67 \frac{mi}{gal}$ (rounded to the nearest hundredth)

Meg: $\frac{280}{16} = 17.5 \frac{mi}{gal}$

Meg's car got more miles per gallon (17.5 is greater than 16.67).

Example C: In this example, it is easier not to use the calculator. The price is the same for both bags, but one bag has more dog food in it than the other. So the bag that has more is the least expensive.

Example D: The fraction of boys in Mrs. Carter's class is $\frac{12}{25}$. The fraction of boys in Mr. D'Angelo's class is $\frac{14}{26}$. The fraction of boys in Mrs. Carter's class is less than $\frac{1}{2}$ because half of 25 is $12\frac{1}{2}$, while the fraction of boys in Mr. D'Angelo's class is greater than $\frac{1}{2}$ because half of 26 is 13. So Mr. D'Angelo's class has the greater ratio of boys.

① Mark wrote $\frac{3}{4}$ of his history paper over the weekend. Doug wrote $\frac{2}{3}$ of his history paper over the weekend. Who finished more of the assignment? If they both needed to write a 12-page paper, how many pages did each person write?

② Which team has the better record, the Whitewater Blue Sox with 21 wins out of 43 games or the Prairie Creek Pups with 17 wins out of 33 games? How many more games will the team with the lesser record need to win to beat the other team's record?

③ According to the meteorologist, it has been snowing at a rate of 2 inches per hour for the past 12 hours and is expected to continue doing so for the next 12 hours. How many inches of snow have fallen in the past 12 hours? How many inches will have fallen in 24 hours if the meteorologist's prediction is correct?

Here are some ways to compare two ratios:

- If the denominators are the same, the ratio with the greater numerator is greater. For example: $\frac{5}{7} > \frac{4}{7}$

- If the numerators are the same, the ratio with the smaller denominator is greater. For example: $\frac{6}{12} > \frac{6}{13}$ (Because $\frac{1}{13}$ is less than $\frac{1}{12}$, $\frac{6}{13}$ is less than $\frac{6}{12}$.)

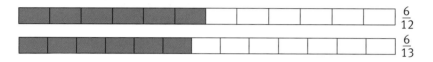

- If one ratio is less than $\frac{1}{2}$ and the other is greater than $\frac{1}{2}$, the one that is greater than $\frac{1}{2}$ is greater. For example: $\frac{205}{400} > \frac{49}{100}$

- If you cannot use any of the first three methods, it is probably easiest to divide (using a calculator if you have one). Then compare the quotients. For example: to compare $\frac{7}{12}$ and $\frac{11}{19}$, find $7 \div 12$ and $11 \div 19$.

$$\frac{7}{12} = 0.583 \text{ (to the nearest thousandth)}$$

$$\frac{11}{19} = 0.579 \text{ (to the nearest thousandth)}$$

So $\frac{7}{12} > \frac{11}{19}$ (because $0.583 > 0.579$).

Copy each pair of ratios below. Replace ▨ with $<$, $=$, or $>$.
Use a calculator only when necessary.

4 $\frac{3}{7}$ ▨ $\frac{4}{7}$ 5 $\frac{3}{8}$ ▨ $\frac{3}{9}$ 6 $\frac{7}{15}$ ▨ $\frac{9}{16}$

7 $\frac{4}{9}$ ▨ $\frac{4}{7}$ 8 $\frac{5}{6}$ ▨ $\frac{4}{6}$ 9 $\frac{3}{5}$ ▨ $\frac{4}{9}$

10 $\frac{1}{3}$ ▨ $\frac{1}{4}$ 11 $\frac{1}{2}$ ▨ $\frac{13}{27}$ 12 $\frac{1}{2}$ ▨ $\frac{14}{28}$

13 $\frac{1}{4}$ ▨ $\frac{3}{7}$ 14 $\frac{1}{2}$ ▨ $\frac{15}{29}$ 15 $\frac{13}{27}$ ▨ $\frac{14}{28}$

16 $\frac{38}{47}$ ▨ $\frac{39}{48}$ 17 $\frac{23}{39}$ ▨ $\frac{24}{40}$ 18 $\frac{71}{89}$ ▨ $\frac{72}{88}$

🅔 **Textbook** This lesson is available in the *eTextbook.*

19 $\dfrac{16}{22}$ ■ $\dfrac{12}{25}$ **20** $\dfrac{51}{101}$ ■ $\dfrac{60}{100}$ **21** $\dfrac{58}{61}$ ■ $\dfrac{45}{90}$

You have just learned some methods to compare ratios. You can use the same methods to compare answers in other division problems.

Example: Which is greater, $9 \div 3$ or $9 \div 4$?

Think of $9 \div 3$ as $\dfrac{9}{3}$ and $9 \div 4$ as $\dfrac{9}{4}$. Since both ratios have the same numerator, the one with the smaller denominator is greater.

So $\dfrac{9}{3} > \dfrac{9}{4}$, and $9 \div 3 > 9 \div 4$.

Replace ■ with $<$, $=$, or $>$ as you copy each statement below. Compare the division problems as you would compare ratios. You do not have to calculate the quotients.

22 $8 \div 2$ ■ $8 \div 3$

23 $6 \div 4$ ■ $6 \div 3$

24 $60 \div 4$ ■ $60 \div 3$

25 $517 \div 4$ ■ $517 \div 3$

26 $517 \div 4$ ■ $517 \div 7$

27 $1{,}000 \div 9$ ■ $1{,}000 \div 10$

28 $1{,}000 \div 28$ ■ $1{,}000 \div 26$

29 $6 \div 2$ ■ $8 \div 2$

30 $12 \div 3$ ■ $14 \div 3$

31 $427 \div 3$ ■ $421 \div 3$

32 $1{,}000 \div 17$ ■ $2{,}000 \div 17$

33 $9 \div 5$ ■ $13 \div 6$

34 $19 \div 13$ ■ $14 \div 18$

35 $10 \div 7$ ■ $100 \div 42$

36 $100 \div 47$ ■ $1{,}000 \div 620$

37 $212 \div 31$ ■ $612 \div 31$

38 **Extended Response** Which is the least expensive per kilogram, 2 kilograms of Kitty Kitchen cat food for $2.50 or 1 kilogram of Kitty Kitchen for $1.29? If you needed only 3 kilograms, what would you do and why?

Writing + Math **Journal**

In your own words, explain how you know when it is convenient to use a calculator to compare two ratios.

Using Approximate Quotients

Key Ideas

Sometimes all you need is an answer that is close rather than the exact answer. When we use our common sense and available information to make this kind of educated guess, it is called an *approximation*.

We approximate the answer to a problem when we need to find it quickly without a calculator or when finding the exact answer is not appropriate.

Suppose you were thinking of opening a grocery store in Redhill. You might want to know the ratio of people to grocery stores. The numbers are given in the table on page 355.

Redhill: 25,075 people ÷ 19 grocery stores (25,075 ÷ 19)

Think: 19 × *what* is 25,075?

One way to approximate 25,075 ÷ 19, is to round the divisor to make it easier to work with. Round 19 to 20.

20 × *what* is about 25,075?

20 × 6 is 120.

20 × 12 is 240.

20 × 120 is 2,400.

20 × 1,200 is 24,000.

20 × 1,300 is 26,000.

The answer is between 1,200 and 1,300. Because there are really fewer than 20 stores, a good approximation would be about 1,300 people per grocery store.

---

① In Whitetree, about how many people are there for each grocery store? In Bluefield?

② 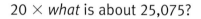 In which town do you think a new grocery store would have the best chance of success? How did you decide?

③ **Extended Response** Why do you think this is a good piece of information on which to base your decision?

④ **Extended Response** What other types of information might be helpful in making a decision on where to build a new grocery store?

Textbook This lesson is available in the *eTextbook*.

This table tells how many people, houses, and certain kinds of businesses are in each of three towns: Redhill, Whitetree, and Bluefield.

Some Facts about Three Towns

Type of Information	Redhill	Whitetree	Bluefield
Population	25,075	20,455	9,800
Houses (including apartment buildings)	2,054	4,123	1,987
Automobile service stations	32	37	10
Grocery stores	19	18	4
Restaurants	42	29	18

5 About how many people are there per restaurant in Redhill? In Whitetree? In Bluefield?

6 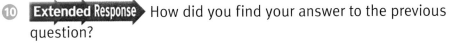 Extended Response How did you find your answer to Problem 5?

7 Extended Response In which town do you think a new restaurant would have the best chance of success? How did you decide?

8 Extended Response In which town do you think a new service station would have the best chance of success? How did you decide?

9 In which town, on the average, is the highest ratio of people per house?

10 Extended Response How did you find your answer to the previous question?

11 Extended Response Which town do you think has the most apartment buildings? Why?

Write a division problem that you could use to approximate ratios in the following situations. Show the corresponding multiplication problem.

12. Suppose you and your 4 friends had 21 party favors. How could you split them fairly?

13. How could you seat 178 people at 30 equally-sized tables?

14. A vendor had 422 hot dogs to sell. How could she distribute them to her 6 workers?

15. There were only 5 water fountains for a group of 251 tourists. How many people were there per water fountain?

16. How would you distribute 2,411 bottles of water among 800 relief workers?

17. If 29 boys and 20 girls went on an egg hunt for 603 eggs, what was the average number of eggs found by each child?

18. A casserole had 225 grams of fat and contained 20 servings in all. How many fat grams were there per serving?

Journal

Make up and discuss your own questions about Redhill, Whitetree, and Bluefield. Be sure to include solutions.

Textbook This lesson is available in the *eTextbook*.

Multidigit Division and Strategies Practice

Roll-a-Problem (Division) Game

Players: Two or more

Materials: *Number Cubes* (one 0–5), a calculator

Object: To get the greatest quotient

Math Focus: Multidigit division, place value, and mathematical reasoning

HOW TO PLAY

1 Outline a division problem on your paper, like this:

2 The lead player rolls the cube. Each player writes the number rolled in any of his or her five blanks.

3 The lead player rolls the *Number Cube* again. Each player writes the number rolled in any of the remaining blanks. The number 0 may be written in any blank, but if the divisor is 00, the player is eliminated because division by 0 is not possible.

4 Repeat step three until all the blanks are filled.

5 Estimate the division of the three-digit number by the two-digit number. In the case of a dispute, carry out the division on a calculator to see who has the greatest quotient.

6 The player with the greatest quotient wins.

OTHER WAYS TO PLAY THIS GAME

1 For additional multidigit practice, instead of estimating, divide the three-digit number by the two-digit number in Step 5. In this case, no calculator is necessary.

2 Change the number of digits in the divisor or the dividend.

3 Use a 5–10 *Number Cube.* Roll again if a 10 is rolled.

4 Try to get the smallest quotient.

Approximating Quotients

Key Ideas

When dividing by a two-digit divisor, rounding to a multiple of 10 can give us a quick and easy approximation.

Mrs. Wong drove 613 miles and used about 22 gallons of gas. What is the average number of miles she traveled per gallon of gas?

To find out, you need to divide 613 by 22. How?

You could use a calculator. You could work it out with pencil and paper if you had time. Or you could approximate the answer.

Here is another way to get an approximate answer to 613 ÷ 22.

A. Round the divisor so it has only zeros after the first digit.

$$22 \longrightarrow 20$$

B. Divide 20 by 10 to get a number between 1 and 10. (Remember that dividing by 10 is the same as moving the decimal point one place to the left.)

$$613 \div 20 \longrightarrow 61.3 \div 2$$

C. Because $61.3 \div 2$ is about 30 or 31, $613 \div 22$ is about 30 or 31.

So, Mrs. Wong's car goes about 30 or 31 miles for each gallon of gas.

If you use a calculator to divide 613 by 22, the answer will be a bit less than 27.9. Your approximation was slightly larger because the divisor was rounded down.

Find approximate answers.

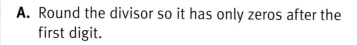

1. 44 ÷ 20
2. 920 ÷ 19
3. 158 ÷ 37
4. 280 ÷ 71

5. 180 ÷ 60
6. 542 ÷ 9
7. 1,600 ÷ 40
8. 728 ÷ 91

9. 48 ÷ 24
10. 8,015 ÷ 51
11. 341 ÷ 19
12. 512 ÷ 32

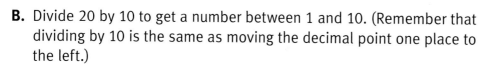

13. 732 ÷ 16
14. 121 ÷ 31
15. 198 ÷ 21
16. 486 ÷ 98

e Textbook This lesson is available in the *eTextbook*.

Work in groups. You can do these problems without finding exact answers. When you have finished discussing and solving each problem, write an explanation for each answer on your own.

⑰ **Extended Response** Mr. Cruz owns a grocery store. On an average day, he sells about 35 boxes of Big Oats cereal. He has 725 boxes of this cereal in stock, and his next shipment will arrive in 2 weeks. Is he likely to run out of stock on this item? (Mr. Cruz's store is open 6 days a week.) How do you know?

⑱ **Extended Response** Mr. Watkins wants to drive from New York City to San Francisco, California, a distance of 4,753 kilometers. He plans to drive about 700 kilometers each day. If he leaves New York City on Wednesday morning, will he be in San Francisco in time to have dinner on Saturday evening of the same week? How do you know?

⑲ **Extended Response** Miss Flores owns a restaurant. On an average day, she sells about 18 sirloin steaks. She has 272 of these steaks in the freezer, and her next shipment will arrive in 3 weeks. If the restaurant is open 7 days per week, is she likely to run out of sirloin steaks before her next shipment? How do you know?

⑳ Julie's parents agreed to let her work at her uncle's farm over the summer. She worked weekdays from 3 P.M.–5 P.M. for 3 weeks in a row. Her uncle paid her $148.67, the cost of a new snowboard she wanted.

   a. How many hours did Julie work?

   b. About how much did she make per hour?

   c. What multiplication or division equation did you use to figure this out?

Writing + Math **Journal**

Explain why approximation is a useful skill.

Dividing by a Two-Digit Number

Key Ideas

Dividing by a two-digit number is similar to dividing by a one-digit number.

Mr. Littman's fifth-grade class has $5,783 to divide equally among themselves. They have 5 $1,000 bills, 7 $100 bills, 8 $10 bills, and 3 $1 bills. There are 23 students in the class. How can they divide the money fairly?

Beth noticed that there were exactly 23 bills. She suggested that each person take one bill. Max suggested they go to the bank and exchange all the bills for $1 bills, and then distribute the bills one at a time. However, the bank didn't have that many $1 bills. They also discovered that the bank had only $1,000 bills, $100 bills, $10 bills, $1 bills, dimes, and pennies.

They exchanged the 5 $1,000 bills for $100 bills.

- How many $100 bills did they have altogether after the exchange?

They determined that each student could take two of the 57 $100 bills, and they would still have some left over. They decided to keep a record of what they had done by putting a 2 in the hundreds place.

$$
\begin{array}{r}
2 \\
23\overline{)5783} \\
-46 \\
\hline
11
\end{array}
$$

number of students ⟶ 23)5783 — each student received · total money

- How many $100 bills are left after each student takes 2?

They exchanged the 11 $100 bills for $10 bills.

- How many $10 bills will they have now? How many will each student get? How many will be left?

The students recorded the distribution of the 118 $10 bills (5 for each person with 3 left over) by putting a 5 in the tens place:

$$
\begin{array}{r}
25 \\
23\overline{)5783} \\
-46 \\
\hline
118 \\
-115 \\
\hline
3
\end{array}
$$

number of students ⟶ 23)5783 — each student received · total money

Next, they went back to the bank and exchanged the 3 $10 dollar bills for 30 $1 bills and each took 1. In their record, they wrote a 1 in the ones place. At this point, 10 $1 bills remained. They decided to exchange those for dimes (the bank had no quarters), so each student took 4 dimes and a 4 was recorded in the tenths place. Finally, they exchanged the dimes they had left for pennies, and divided them equally.

- How many dimes were left? How many pennies does each student have? What should they do with the remaining 11¢?

Dividing up the dimes left 8 remaining, which were exchanged for pennies. There were 3 pennies per student.

$$
\begin{array}{r}
251.43 \\
23\overline{)5783.00} \\
-46 \\
\hline
118 \\
-115 \\
\hline
33 \\
-23 \\
\hline
100 \\
-92 \\
\hline
80 \\
-69 \\
\hline
11
\end{array}
$$

number of students ⟶ (points to 23)

⟵ each student received (points to 251.43)
⟵ total money (points to 5783.00)

The above record shows what happened with each step, but without the decimal point, it looks as if each person received $25,143! They used a decimal point to show where the ones place is in both the original amount of money (the dividend) and in the amount each person received (the quotient, or answer). Therefore, each person received $251.43.

After incorporating the decimal point, this seems like a fair way to divide the money. It records all necessary information and keeps a record of what happened.

Before you do a long division problem, approximate the answer. That may help you catch any mistakes you make. After you divide, check your answer to see that it makes sense. It should be fairly close to your approximate answer. For example find the answer to $73\overline{)5745}$, to the nearest whole number.

● Approximate.

We can round the divisor from 73 to 70 and then divide both numbers by 10:

$$73\overline{)5745} \longrightarrow 70\overline{)5745} \longrightarrow 7\overline{)574}^{82} \quad \text{or} \quad 7\overline{)575}^{82}$$

Because we rounded down, the answer should be less than 82, or about 80.

● Divide.

$$\begin{array}{r} 78.6 \\ 73\overline{)5745.0} \\ -511 \\ \hline 635 \\ -584 \\ \hline 51.0 \\ -43.8 \end{array}$$

Check:
79 is close to 80
(the approximate answer),
so it makes sense.

It is also possible to check the division by multiplication, if you really want to be sure of the answer. $78 \times 73 = 5{,}694$. Add 51 (the exact remainder) to get 5,745. Since 5,745 is the dividend, the answer checks.

For each problem, approximate an answer, and then do the long division. (Round answers to the nearest whole number.)

1. $62\overline{)4973}$
2. $38\overline{)3960}$
3. $23\overline{)966}$
4. $12\overline{)3237}$
5. $81\overline{)7412}$
6. $56\overline{)23128}$
7. $78\overline{)2140}$
8. $35\overline{)3810}$
9. $41\overline{)33456}$
10. $37\overline{)3293}$
11. $15\overline{)4620}$
12. $21\overline{)1466}$
13. $52\overline{)25614}$
14. $77\overline{)1008}$
15. $46\overline{)2342}$

In each exercise, two of the answers are clearly wrong and one is correct. Choose the correct answer.

16 $54\overline{)47088}$

 a. 82   **b.** 872   **c.** 8,722

17 $54\overline{)2646}$

 a. 9   **b.** 49   **c.** 409

18 $7\overline{)6909}$

 a. 97   **b.** 987   **c.** 9,087

19 $43\overline{)199133}$

 a. 41   **b.** 461   **c.** 4,631

20 $654\overline{)5437356}$

 a. 834   **b.** 8,314   **c.** 83,614

21 $111\overline{)83583}$

 a. 73   **b.** 753   **c.** 7,543

22 $9\overline{)394434}$

 a. 486   **b.** 4,386   **c.** 43,826

23 $43826\overline{)394434}$

 a. 9   **b.** 89   **c.** 889

24 $872\overline{)47088}$

 a. 4   **b.** 54   **c.** 504

25 $49\overline{)26460}$

 a. 40   **b.** 540   **c.** 4,540

26 $3\overline{)369669}$ **a.** 232 **b.** 1,232   **c.** 123,223   **d.** 123,223.5

27 The 1910 census reported that about 92,200,000 people lived in the United States. The debt of the United States government at that time was about $1,100,000,000. Approximately what was the debt per person?

 a. $1   **b.** $12   **c.** $120   **d.** $1,200   **e.** $12,000

28 The 1940 census reported that about 132,200,000 people lived in the United States. The debt of the U.S. government at that time was about $43,000,000,000. Approximately what was the debt per person?

 a. $3   **b.** $32   **c.** $325   **d.** $3,250   **e.** $32,500

29 The 1980 census reported that about 226,500,000 people lived in the United States. The debt of the U.S. government at that time was about $907,700,000,000. Approximately what was the debt per person?

 a. $4   **b.** $40   **c.** $400   **d.** $4,000   **e.** $40,000

30 The 2000 census reported that about 281,400,000 people lived in the United States. The debt of the U.S. government at that time was about $5,628,700,000,000. Approximately what was the debt per person?

 a. $2   **b.** $20   **c.** $200   **d.** $2,000   **e.** $20,000

Exploring Problem Solving

Imagine you are a code breaker assigned to decode the three-word phrase below. You know the number 1 stands for *A*, 2 for *B*, 3 for *C*, and so on. But there are no numbers on the paper, only a table that gives clues about the numbers.

Message:

___ ___ ___ ___   ___ ___ ___ ___ ___   ___ ___ ___ ___ ___

Letters of	Mean	Median	Mode	Range
1st word	$15\frac{3}{4}$	$14\frac{1}{2}$	none	12
2nd word	$19\frac{3}{4}$	$19\frac{1}{2}$	none	10
3rd word	10	10	none	9

 Wei solved the problem this way:

I used the Guess, Check, and Adjust Strategy.
I'll start with the first word.
I'll guess some easy letters.

Guess	Mean	Mode	Range	Result
A, B, C, D 1 2 3 4	$1 + 2 + 3 + 4 = 10$ $\frac{10}{4} = 2\frac{1}{2}$			Mean is way too low.
M, A, T, H 13, 1, 21, 8	$13 + 1 + 21 + 8 = 43$ $\frac{43}{4} = 10\frac{3}{4}$			Mean is still too low.

364

Think about Wei's strategy. Answer the following questions.

1. Is there only one combination of 4 numbers with a mean of $15\frac{3}{4}$?

2. What will Wei need to check once she finds 4 numbers with a mean of $15\frac{3}{4}$?

3. Would you use Wei's strategy? Why or why not?

Kareem solved the problem another way.

I Used Logical Reasoning and Number Sense.
First word:

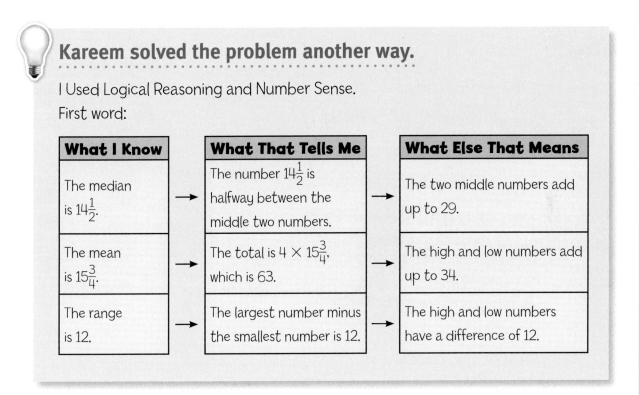

What I Know	What That Tells Me	What Else That Means
The median is $14\frac{1}{2}$.	The number $14\frac{1}{2}$ is halfway between the middle two numbers.	The two middle numbers add up to 29.
The mean is $15\frac{3}{4}$.	The total is $4 \times 15\frac{3}{4}$, which is 63.	The high and low numbers add up to 34.
The range is 12.	The largest number minus the smallest number is 12.	The high and low numbers have a difference of 12.

Think about Kareem's strategy. Answer the following questions.

4. What do you think Kareem means when he writes "middle numbers"? How does he know that these numbers add up to 29?

5. How does Kareem know that the high and low numbers add up to 34?

6. What conclusion can you draw from the fact that there is no mode for any of the words?

7. Why do you think Kareem's strategy will or will not work?

8. Solve the problem by decoding the phrase. Use any strategy you think will work. What strategy did you use? Why?

Cumulative Review

Adding and Subtracting Decimals Lesson 3.4

Solve for *n*. Watch the signs.

① $28.4 + 13.9 = n$

③ $187.82 - 105.5 = n$

② $28.4 - 13.9 = n$

④ $67.99 + 49.14 = n$

Repeated Operations: Savings Plans Lesson 4.3

Solve.

Each week, Enrique earns $20 and spends $13.

⑤ How many weeks will it take for Enrique to save $100?

⑥ How many weeks will it take for Enrique to save $300?

Adding and Subtracting Integers Lesson 4.8

Complete each of the following exercises.

⑦ $(-5) + (-9) =$ ☐   ⑧ $(-8) - (-4) =$ ☐   ⑨ $5 + 11 =$ ☐   ⑩ $7 - 10 =$ ☐

⑪ $|-8| =$ ☐   ⑫ $|-6| - |-9| =$ ☐   ⑬ $|7| - |-6| =$ ☐   ⑭ $|-6| + |-5| =$ ☐

Patterns Lesson 4.10

Write the missing numbers in each pattern. Then tell what the pattern is.

⑮ 14, 11, ☐, ☐, 2, ☐, ☐, −7, −10

⑯ −64, 32, −16, ☐, −4, 2, ☐

Linear Equations **Lesson 5.12**

Evaluate each equation by solving for either *x* or *y*.

17 $7x - 7 = 35$

19 $11(4) - 34 = y$

18 $2x + 27 = 49$

20 $\frac{x}{2} \times 6 = 42$

....

Fractions of Fractions **Lesson 6.2**

21 $\frac{1}{2} \times \blacksquare = \frac{1}{10}$

22 $\frac{3}{4}$ of $\blacksquare = \frac{6}{20}$

23 $\frac{4}{5} \times \blacksquare = \frac{8}{35}$

24 $\frac{2}{9}$ of $\blacksquare = \frac{6}{36}$

25 $\frac{3}{4}$ of $\blacksquare = \frac{9}{16}$

26 $\frac{5}{6} \times \blacksquare = \frac{10}{42}$

....

Practice with Fractions **Lesson 6.6**

Solve.

Mrs. May's fifth-grade class was assigned a book to read. So far, Josh has read $\frac{2}{3}$ of the book, Chen has read $\frac{3}{4}$, and Tai has read $\frac{7}{10}$.

27 Who has read the most pages? 28 Who has read the fewest pages?

Decide which fraction in each of the following pairs is greater. Replace the $\blacksquare$ with a $<$, $>$, or $=$ symbol.

29 $\frac{1}{3}$ $\blacksquare$ $\frac{1}{4}$

31 $\frac{5}{8}$ $\blacksquare$ $\frac{3}{4}$

30 $\frac{9}{16}$ $\blacksquare$ $\frac{1}{2}$

32 $\frac{1}{3}$ $\blacksquare$ $\frac{2}{5}$

....

Multiplying Mixed Numbers **Lesson 7.2**

Multiply. Check to be sure your answers make sense.

33 $3\frac{2}{3} \times 1\frac{1}{7} = \blacksquare$

35 $3\frac{2}{5} \times 1\frac{2}{6} = \blacksquare$

34 $\frac{5}{6} \times 4\frac{1}{3} = \blacksquare$

36 $3\frac{1}{8} \times 1\frac{1}{5} = \blacksquare$

Practice with Division

Key Ideas

Being able to divide quickly and accurately is useful, but thinking and approximating may sometimes save time and allow you to avoid using a longer, more precise method.

Suppose your older brother wanted to buy a new car for $19,561 in cash. If he saved $250 per month under his mattress, would he have saved enough to buy the car after 5 years? How long would it take him?

First, 19,561 ÷ 250 is about 79, so it would take him about 79 months.

Next, since there are 12 months in a year and 6 × 12 = 72, it would take him about 6 years and 7 months (79 − 72 = 7) to save up the amount.

You may notice that he will save $1,000 in 4 months, which yields $3,000 per year. In 5 years, he will therefore save $15,000, but it would take him between 6 years ($18,000) and 7 years ($21,000) to save $19,561.

In each problem, two of the answers are clearly wrong and one is correct. Choose the correct answer.

1. $26\overline{)1352}$ **a.** 520   **b.** 52   **c.** 5.2

2. $25\overline{)1625}$ **a.** 65   **b.** 100   **c.** 6.5

3. $5\overline{)1005}$ **a.** 201   **b.** 202   **c.** 203

4. $12\overline{)1632}$ **a.** 1,360   **b.** 13.6   **c.** 136

5. $8\overline{)1168}$ **a.** 200   **b.** 146   **c.** 14.6

6. $10\overline{)2160}$ **a.** 200   **b.** 216   **c.** 217

7. $26\overline{)1794}$ **a.** 6.9   **b.** 69   **c.** 690

8. $15\overline{)2355}$ **a.** 156   **b.** 157   **c.** 158

ⓔ **Textbook** This lesson is available in the *eTextbook*.

9 Create eight more multiple-choice division questions of your own, using Exercises 1–8 on the previous page as a guide. Include three answer choices for each question.

Remember that one answer must be correct. You must be able to see that the other two answers are wrong, but don't make the problems too easy.

10 The total weight of 12 people is 1,560 pounds. What is their average weight?

11 Mr. Jackson drove his car 14,062 miles last year. His car averaged 23 miles per gallon of gas. About how many gallons of gas did his car use during that year?

12 Thirty-six people can ride the roller coaster at one time.

a. How many times does the roller coaster have to run in order to give rides to 432 people?

b. Extended Response If there were 450 people, how many trips would be necessary? Explain your answer.

Writing + Math **Journal**

Write your own word problem that requires division by a two-digit divisor. What is the answer? What mistakes might someone make while answering this problem?

Dividing by a Three-Digit Number

Key Ideas

Dividing by a three-digit number is very similar to dividing by a two-digit number.

Mrs. Brown wants to join the health club. The daily cost to use the club is $4. An annual membership costs $1,533.

"Something is wrong with those prices," she thought.

Can you find out what is wrong with the prices?

If you go every day, paying by the day costs only $1,460 ($4 × 365). It is more expensive to become an annual member.

Mrs. Brown wanted to know the cost per day if she became an annual member and used the club for each of the 365 days in a year.

How much is $365\overline{)1533}$?

- First, estimate. We can round 1,533 ÷ 365 to 1,600 ÷ 400, which is about 4.

- Now let's calculate the precise amount.

$$\begin{array}{r} 4.2 \\ 365\overline{)1533.0} \\ -\,1460. \\ \hline 73.0 \\ -\,73.0 \\ \hline 0 \end{array}$$

Write the answer as dollars and cents: $4.20. So, yearly membership costs: $4.20 per day if a member goes every day of the year.

Solve the following problems.

① Approximate the daily cost of becoming a yearly member and using the club the following number of times.

   a. once a week (assume 52 weeks in 1 year)

   b. twice a week

   c. 5 times a month

   d. 10 times a month

   e. every other day

Textbook This lesson is available in the *eTextbook*.

Approximate first, then divide. Round quotients to the nearest whole number.

2   52)1508   3   245)6370   4   28)3154

5   46)1426   6   173)2595   7   122)427

8   162)1134   9   205)1291   10 107)3436

11 115)690   12 216)1080   13 314)7065

14 315)2116   15 459)9785   16 136)1455

17 **Extended Response** A box of 144 pencils costs $21.60. What is the cost of one pencil? If a box of 25 pencils costs $4.98 and you need only a limited number of pencils, when would it be more cost effective to buy the larger box?

18 The running track is an oval that is exactly 440 yards around. There are 1,760 yards in 1 mile. How many times must Sarah run around the track to run 2 miles?

19 It costs $125 to buy an evergreen tree that is 10 feet tall. The Chang family has $730 in their budget to buy new trees this year. How many evergreens can they buy at this price?

20 Rob did yard work after school, on weekends, and during vacation last spring and summer and earned $3,648. He knows he worked 105 days. On average, about how much did he earn per day? Round to the nearest dollar.

21 A city telephone book has 48,415 names. There are about 323 names on each page in the book. About how many pages are there altogether?

22 **Extended Response** Jenna's last 4 math test scores were 87, 89, 92, and 88. What score does she need on the 5th test to have an average of 90? Explain how you got your answer.

> **Writing + Math** **Journal**
>
> Movie tickets are being offered as a prize for the best river clean-up idea. The tickets must be able to be divided equally among 2, 3, 4, or 5 winners. What is the least number of tickets that could be offered as a prize? Write about your problem-solving strategy.

Batting Averages and Other Division Applications

Key Ideas

Finding batting averages and making price comparisons are two of the many practical applications of division.

Luis, Lamont, and Chris played on a baseball team last summer. They kept records of how many hits each player got and how many times each was at bat.

Player	Official Times at Bat	Hits
Luis	62	27
Lamont	72	27
Chris	90	29

"I got the most hits," Chris said, as they filled out their table.

"That's because you were at bat the most," said Lamont. "I don't think your batting average is as high as mine."

"Or mine," said Luis.

"Well," said Chris, "let's figure them out."

Do you know, or can you figure out, how a baseball player's average is calculated?

You can create a ratio by dividing the number of hits by the number of official times at bat. The division is rounded to three decimal places.

Who do you think had the highest batting average?

Who do you think had the lowest batting average?

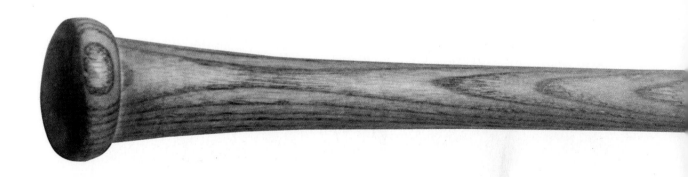

Textbook This lesson is available in the *eTextbook*.

To calculate a batting average, divide the number of hits by the number of official times at bat, and round to the nearest thousandth. Here's how to calculate Luis's batting average.

Divide the number of Luis's hits (27) by the number of his official times at bat (62).

27 ÷ 62

Carry the division to four decimal places.

```
      0.4354
62 ) 27.0000
    −248
      220
     −186
      340
     −310
       300
      −248
```

Round to the nearest thousandth: 0.4354 ⟶ 0.435

Batting averages are usually reported without the 0 to the left of the decimal point because they can only be between 0 and 1. That means Luis's official batting average is .435.

Solve the following.

1. Approximate the batting averages for Lamont and Chris.

2. Now calculate their batting averages. Carry out the division to four decimal places, then round to the nearest thousandth.

As you can see, Luis has the greatest batting average.

Setting up a ratio by dividing is sometimes useful for choosing the better buy when shopping. Look at the following bags of dog food.

Which bag is least expensive per kilogram?

$$\frac{\$6.25}{5 \text{ kg}} = \frac{1.25 \text{ dollars}}{\text{kilogram}}$$

(rounded to the nearest cent)

$$\frac{\$3.58}{3 \text{ kg}} = \frac{1.19 \text{ dollars}}{\text{kilogram}}$$

(rounded to the nearest cent)

Therefore, the 3-kilogram bag costs about 6 cents less per kilogram than the 5-kilogram bag.

Solve the following problems.

For $118, you can get a season pass to use the Wakefield skating rink. If you don't have a pass, you have to pay $2.95 each time you use the rink.

Suppose you expect to use the rink about 30 times during the season.

❸ Which is cheaper—to buy a season pass or to pay each time?

❹ About how much would you save per visit if you used the cheaper method? (Hint: Find the ratio of cost to visits in each case.)

Suppose you use the rink only 24 times.

❺ Which method is cheaper?

❻ How much cheaper is it per visit?

Suppose you use the rink 80 times during the season.

❼ Which method is cheaper?

❽ By how much per visit?

For each exercise, approximate an answer, divide, then check your answer by multiplying. (Round answers to the nearest whole number.)

❾ 36)2478

❿ 91)4588

⓫ 53)8139

⓬ 21)287

⓭ 13)2547

⓮ 78)6324

 Textbook This lesson is available in the *eTextbook.*

15. A bottle of Slow-Red Ketchup contains 280 grams and costs $1.35. A bottle of Thick-Tomato Ketchup contains 200 grams and costs $1.08.

   a. Which brand costs less per gram?

   b. How much cheaper is it per gram?

16. Cho is driving from Boston, Massachusetts, to Washington, D.C., a distance of about 690 miles. She wants to make the trip in 13 hours.

   a. About how many miles per hour must Cho average?

   b. After 5 hours of travel Cho has gone 300 miles. Must she go faster for the rest of the trip, or can she go slower and still get there in 13 hours?

17. The team's new player has 37 hits. In his other 86 times at bat, he was out.

   a. What fraction of his times at bat has he made hits?

   b. What is his batting average?

18. What is the batting average of a player who has 44 hits and who has been out 106 times?

19. What is the batting average of a player who has been at bat 20 times and has made 12 hits?

20. **Extended Response** Melissa needs 8 ballpoint pens. She can buy a package of 8 pens for $14.96, or she can buy the same pens for $1.75 each. How can she determine which is the better buy? What is the better buy?

Writing + Math **Journal**

What is the batting average for someone who has only been up to bat once and got 1 hit? Does that mean he or she is a better player than someone with a .275 average? Explain.

Average Heights

Key Ideas

Averages are often used when summarizing large amounts of data.

The students in Latoya's class have measured their heights again and made a new table.

Name	Height (cm)	Name	Height (cm)	Name	Height (cm)	Name	Height (cm)
Judy	135	Aretha	143	Latoya	146	Melba	150
Chen	135	Joan	144	Kareem	145	Donna	151
Tami	136	Marco	144	Frank	145	Herb	152
Myra	137	Carlos	144	Pedro	146	Gene	153
Florence	138	Steve	145	Melvin	147	Min-ja	153
José	140	Liz	146	Lance	145	Ana	154
Marie	142	Carmen	147	Tiwa	150		

❶ What was the average height of the students in Latoya's class at the beginning of the year? (See the table on page 6.)

❷ What was the range in heights at the beginning of the year? Remember, the range of a set of numbers is the difference between the greatest and least values.

❸ Inspect the tables on this page and on page 6. Who grew the most? Who grew the least?

❹ Estimate the average amount of growth during this period.

❺ What is the range of heights in Latoya's class now?

❻ Make an estimate of the average height of Latoya's class now.

eTextbook This lesson is available in the *eTextbook*.

Latoya has made another bar graph to show her classmates' heights.

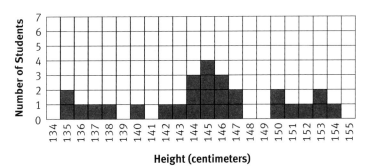

Height (centimeters)

7 **Extended Response** How is the new graph like the one Latoya made at the beginning of the year? (See page 6.) How is it different?

Work in groups. Measure each person's height to the nearest centimeter.

8 Make a table and record the height of each person in your class.

9 Compare your table with the one you made at the beginning of the year (when you completed page 6).

   a. What was the average height of the students in your class at the beginning of the year?

   b. What was the range in heights of the students in your class at the beginning of the year?

   c. Who has grown the most? Who has grown the least? Estimate the average amount of growth since the beginning of the year.

   d. What is the range of heights in your class now?

   e. Estimate the average height of your class now. Does your estimate make sense?

10 Use your table to make a bar graph of the heights of the students in your class now.

Use your new graph to answer Problems 11–14.

11 How many students are below the class's average height? Above the class's average height?

12 How many students are the same height as the class's average height?

13 **Extended Response** How is the new graph similar to the one you made earlier in the year?

14 **Extended Response** How is the new graph different from the earlier one?

⑮ Look at the graphs of Latoya's class and of your class.

    a. Can you determine the mean of the heights by looking at the graphs?

    b. Can you tell the median of the heights from the graphs?

    c. Can you tell the mode of the heights from the graphs?

    d. **Extended Response** Suppose you included your teacher's height in the graph for your class. Which would be affected the most—the mean, median, mode, or range? Would any of these stay the same?

Latoya's friend Sergio also collected information from his class. The heights, in centimeters, of the 25 students in Sergio's class are in the following list.

135	138	142	146	147
136	138	144	146	147
137	138	145	146	148
137	140	145	146	150
137	141	145	146	155

Use the table above to answer the following questions.

⑯ Find the median, mode, and range of these heights.

⑰ **Extended Response** Do you think the mean of the heights of the students in Sergio's class will be the same as the mean of the heights of the students in Latoya's class? Why or why not?

⑱ Make a graph of the heights in Sergio's class like the graph Latoya made of the heights in her class.

⑲ Based on the graph you made, do you think the mean of the heights in Sergio's class will be greater than, less than, or about the same as the mean of the heights in your class?

     e Textbook This lesson is available in the *eTextbook*.

There are errors in four of the nine problems below. Find the errors, and then do each calculation correctly.

20.
```
        2.92
   21)61.32
     -42
      193
     -189
       42
      -42
        0
```

21.
```
        2.08
   32)62.56
     -64
      256
     -256
        0
```

22.
```
        3.04
   46)139.84
     -138
       18
       -0
      184
     -184
        0
```

23.
```
        1.11
   25)52.50
     -25
      27
     -25
      25
     -25
       0
```

24.
```
        2.35
   17)39.95
     -34
      59
     -51
      85
     -85
       0
```

25.
```
        99
   99)9801
     -891
      891
     -891
        0
```

26.
```
        3.825
   16)47.320
     -48
      132
     -132
        0
```

27.
```
        3.02
   24)36.48
     -36
      48
     -48
       0
```

28.
```
        2.45
   52)127.40
     -104
      234
     -208
      260
     -260
        0
```

Writing + Math ⟩ **Journal**

Summarize the change in the class's heights since your measurement in Chapter 1. How did the average height change? Did the range change? Would you have expected it to change?

Using Rates to Make Predictions

Key Ideas

We can use mathematics to help us predict the future based on the past.

Suppose you have been riding in a car for 7 hours and have traveled 371 miles. Your average speed has been about 53 miles per hour. About how far will you have gone after 10 hours if you continue at the same rate?

If you keep going at about the same rate, you will go about 53 miles every hour. So you will have gone about 530 miles after 10 hours, since $10 \times 53 = 530$.

However, in a real situation you may not keep going at about the same rate. The road conditions may get better, so you may travel faster. The road conditions may get worse, so you may go more slowly. You may run out of gas. Or you may stop for lunch or to look at the scenery.

Even though conditions can change, it is often useful to know what would happen if something did continue at about the same rate.

Answer the following questions about continuing at the same rate.

Miss Bluehouse has been driving for 6 hours and has gone 331 miles.

1. At about what average speed is Miss Bluehouse traveling?

2. About how far do you think she will have driven altogether after 10 hours?

3. About how far will she have driven after 8 hours?

4. About how far do you think Miss Bluehouse drove in the first 4 hours?

5. If Miss Bluehouse was traveling at an average speed of 45 miles per hour, about how far would she have driven after 10 hours? After 8 hours?

Solve these problems.

⑥ Jill's car went 371 miles after she filled the gas tank. Then she stopped at a station and filled the tank again. It took 17 gallons of gas to fill the tank.

    a. About how many miles per gallon did Jill's car travel?

    b. Jill's tank holds 20 gallons of gas. If she starts with a full tank, about how far can Jill go before the car runs out of gas?

    c. Jill has driven 250 miles since she last bought gas. About how many gallons of gas has she used?

    d. Jill has a half tank of gas in her car. Can she drive the 230 miles to the state capital without stopping for gas?

To find the *daily mean temperature* for a community, we find the average of the high and low temperatures for the day.

⑦ If the high temperature in Jamestown today was 7°C and the low was 1°C, what was the daily mean temperature in Jamestown?

⑧ If the high temperature in Kingsville today was 28°C and the low was 20°C, what was the daily mean temperature in Kingsville?

⑨ If the high temperature in Greensburg today was 15°F and the low was −5°F, what was the daily mean temperature in Greensburg?

⑩ If the high temperature in Portstown today was 81°F and the low was 52°F, what was the daily mean temperature in Portstown?

⑪ If the high temperature in Fairbanks was −15°F and the low was −40°F, what was the daily mean temperature in Fairbanks?

To find the *average mean temperature* for a month, we add all the daily mean temperatures, and then divide by the number of days in the month. Here are the daily mean temperatures (in °C) for January in Jamestown:

0, 2, 1, 6, 1, 0, 3, 7, 8, 10, 4, 0, 0, 1, 1, 1, 3, 7, 12, 15, 16, 4, 2, 3, 5, 4, 2, 1, 1, 6, 0

⑫ What was the average mean temperature in Jamestown in January to the nearest tenth of a degree?

Try to decide whether average values are useful in the situations described below. Discuss your decisions with other students.

⑬ **Extended Response** Mr. Miller is planning a trip to New York City in October. He learns that the temperature during October averages about 15°C. Knowing this, Mr. Miller decides not to take a warm coat.

a. Does Mr. Miller have enough information to make a sound decision?

b. If so, did he make a good decision? If not, what are some other kinds of information he could use?

⑭ **Extended Response** Mrs. Soo lives in New York City. To help plan her household budget for October, she wants to estimate the cost for heating her home. Will knowing the average temperature for October in New York City help Mrs. Soo? Explain your answer.

⑮ **Extended Response** The visitor's center in New York City created a poster inviting people to spend their vacations enjoying what the city has to offer. On the poster, the average temperature for the summer months is given as 24.8°C. Is this enough information to help people decide what types of clothing to pack when planning a trip to New York City? Explain your answer.

This lesson is available in the *eTextbook*.

For the following problems, refer to the **Golf Game** in Lesson 8.2, on page 343.

16 Suppose Steve had nine more turns with scores of 3, 5, 6, 3, 4, 12, 6, 5, and 4. What are the mean, median, mode, and range for this set of 10 scores (including the 9 from the first turn)? How would you decide what the mode is? Are there several? How many? If the median is found to be two numbers, remember that we use the average of those two numbers.

17 Three other players played the **Golf Game.** The other players got the following scores:

Player	Scores	Mean	Median	Mode	Range
Andaiye	5, 5, 6, 4, 4, 3, 4, 3, 7, 3				
Yan-Ping	6, 5, 4, 6, 7, 5, 7, 4, 6, 3				
Cuneyt	5, 9, 4, 5, 7, 7, 8, 5, 6, 8				

Copy and complete the table above by calculating the mean, median, mode, and range for each set of scores.

18 If the four players were competing for the lowest score, who would win if they used means? Who would win if they used medians? Who would win if they used modes? Who would win if they used the smallest range?

19 Extended Response ▶ If you had to decide in advance whether to use the mode, median, or mean to decide the winner, which do you think would be the most reasonable to use? Why?

20 Play the game with ten turns. Keep track of the ten scores. Calculate the mean, median, mode, and range. Compare these figures with the mean, median, mode, and range that your friends got. Who had the best average? Does it matter whether you used the mean, median, or mode?

Writing + Math ▶ **Journal**

Of the three characterizations of data we are using (mean, median, and mode), which seems most stable? That is, which is least affected by small changes in the data? Explain why.

LESSON 8.14 Population Density

Key Ideas

One useful example of ratios or rates is the population density for a geographical area.

Classes at Centerville School

Teacher	Number of Students	Number of Tables	Number of Chairs	Students per Table	Chairs per Table	Students per Chair
Mr. Burke	22	5	24			
Ms. Ruiz	25	6	28			
Miss Stamos	18	6	24			
Mrs. Davis	20	5	21			
Mr. Asari	23	5	22			
Mr. Gomez	25	5	25			
Ms. Golden	24	6	24			

Use a calculator to solve the following problems. Give your answers to the nearest hundredth.

1. In Ms. Golden's class, how many students are there per table? How many chairs are there per table? How many students are there per chair?

2. In Mr. Burke's class, how many students are there per table? How many chairs are there per table? How many students are there per chair?

3. Copy the table above and complete the last three columns. Round numbers to the nearest hundredth.

4. Determine the total number of students in Centerville School. What is the average number of students per class?

5. **Extended Response** Is there anything else you can observe about classes in Centerville School based on the table?

According to the 2000 census, the population of Alaska was 626,932, and its area was 571,951 square miles. The population of the District of Columbia was 572,059, and its area was 61 square miles.

Use this information to answer the following questions.

6 Which was more crowded, Alaska or the District of Columbia—that is, which had more people per square mile?

7 About how many people were there per square mile in Alaska?

8 Is that more or less than 1 person per square mile?

9 About how many people were there per square mile in the District of Columbia?

10 Is that more or less than 10,000 people per square mile?

11 Look at the table below. Write the names of the states and the population density (number of people per square mile) for each state on a separate sheet of paper. Then, rank the states in order from greatest to least population density. Round to the nearest tenth.

State	2000 Population	Area in Square Miles	Population Density	Rank
California	33,871,648	155,959	▢	▢
Georgia	8,186,453	57,906	▢	▢
Massachusetts	6,349,097	7,840	▢	▢
New York	18,976,457	47,214	▢	▢
Rhode Island	1,048,319	1,045	▢	▢
Texas	20,851,820	261,797	▢	▢
Wyoming	493,782	97,100	▢	▢

12 According to the 2000 census, the population of the United States was 281,421,906 and its area was 3,537,438 square miles. About how many people were there per square mile in the United States in 2000?

Writing + Math **Journal**

Five new students need to be assigned to Mr. Gomez's and Ms. Golden's classes. How many students should go to each class? Why?

Key Ideas

We often use ratios to compare physical objects in a scientific setting.

How might a scientist be able to guess whether an animal lived in water, on land, or flew in the air by looking at its skeleton?

Solve the following problems.

1. Michael is 178 centimeters tall. When he holds out his arms, the distance from fingertip to fingertip is 182 centimeters. What is the ratio of the distance between his fingertips to his height?

2. Sarah is 65 inches tall. When she holds out her arms, the distance from fingertip to fingertip is 63 inches. What is the ratio of the distance between her fingertips to her height?

3. Measure your height and fingertip distance. Find the ratio of your fingertip distance to your height.

4. Find full-body pictures of some animals that walk on land (for example, a cat, a dog, a gerbil).

   a. Measure the fingertip distance up one front leg or arm, across the shoulder, and down the other front leg or arm.

   b. Measure each animal's length by starting at the tip of the nose and measure along the back to the tip of the tail.

   c. What is the ratio of the fingertip distance to the length for each walking animal you measured?

5. Find some full-body pictures of flying animals (a bird or a bat, for example).

   a. Measure the fingertip distance from the tip of one wing, across the back, to the tip of the other wing.

   b. Measure the length from the tip of the beak or head, along the back, to the tip of the tail.

   c. Find the ratio of the fingertip distance to the length for each flying animal you measured.

ⓔ Textbook This lesson is available in the *eTextbook*.

6. Find some full-body pictures of swimming animals (such as a fish, a dolphin, or a whale).

   a. Measure the fingertip distance from the tip of one flipper, fin, or front leg across the back to the other flipper, fin, or front leg.

   b. Measure the length from the tip of the head to the tip of the tail.

   c. What is the ratio of fingertip distance to length for each swimming animal you measured?

7. Work in groups to organize the data you collected. Make separate tables showing animals with ratios less than, greater than, and equal to 1.

8. **Extended Response** What do the animals in each table have in common?

9. Suppose you found the skeleton of an animal that had a fingertip distance of 342 cm and a length of 351 cm. From those measurements, what could you tell about how the animal moved?

10. If five animals had the dimensions shown in this table, what could you conclude about how they moved?

Animal	A	B	C	D	E
Fingertip Distance (cm)	72	41	145	25	104
Length (cm)	74	10	141	92	33

 **Journal**

Describe what you learned today about ratios of different animals' fingertip distance and length. Explain why you think each type of animal has the ratio that it does.

Exploring 💡 Problem Solving

Welcome to *Mixed Messages: The History of Codes*. Today we journey back to the American Revolution to see why our founding fathers might also be called our *confounding* fathers. They, like the British, used a variety of methods to make sure their secrets were safe even if their letters fell into the wrong hands.

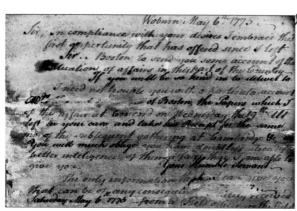

George Washington liked to use invisible ink to conceal messages between the lines of an innocent letter. Placing the paper over a candle or treating it with a chemical would reveal the hidden writing—as long as the letter didn't burst into flames first.

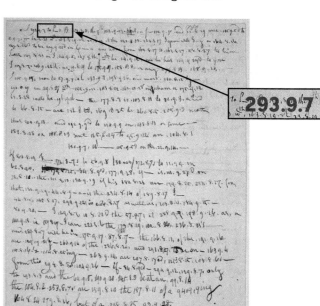

Benedict Arnold based his code on a published book. Arnold would search in this "key" book for each word he wanted to use. Then, instead of writing the word, he wrote the page number, line number, and the position of the word from the left. For example, the second word in this letter of July 12, 1780, is "293.9.7" which stands for "wrote."

At times, the British would use a trick called a *mask* to hide their secrets. To send a message, they would follow these three steps.

1. Start with a mask: a sheet of paper with a cutout.

2. Write the secret letter in that exact shape.

3. Now comes the tricky part. Add words to the left and right to change the meaning of the entire letter.

If anyone intercepted the note, it would look and read like an ordinary letter. In fact, it might intentionally give false information.

But place the mask over the page and you can easily read the secret message within the letter.

Answer the following questions. Use the information on both pages.

1. If you had the key book, how would you decode the numbers 136. 14. 2 in one of Benedict Arnold's letters?

2. Solve this puzzle: in the key book, which word do you think is physically closer to the word in Problem 1—136.29.3 or 137.13.19?

3. How could a masked letter be used to send false information?

Time to put your code-breaking talents to use. Imagine you have intercepted a masked letter without the mask.

You have, however, found clues for creating and positioning the rectangular mask opening.

- Each pair of numbers is a dividend and divisor.

- The remainder tells the number of inches.

mask opening	
width	266, 44
height	318, 35
distance from top	381, 76
distance from left	451, 28

You will have heard, Dear Sir, long before this letter has made its way to you, that our Sir. W. Howe has gone, as the Rebels are aware, Eastward to the Chesapeak bay with great hopes. Washington has now taken all the greatest part of the Rebels to Philadelphia to fight Wm's army. I hear that he has now returned, finding that none of our troops landed but am not certain. I am sure such marching has tired them. I'm left to command with more men than needed but still I have too small a force to make an invasion. Their army is small, simply a diversion for you. I'll therefore send Sir W. 4 or 5 battalions to try something at any rate. I can spare him 1,500 men. By the way, I think Sir W's moves lately are excellent and Washington's are the worst he could make in every respect. Sincerely and with much joy on your success, I am with great sincerity,

     H.C.

Work in groups to discuss and solve the following problems. Compare your answers with other groups.

4. What are the dimensions of the mask opening?

5. How should the mask opening be placed over the letter?

6. What is the secret message hidden in the letter?

7. Create and exchange your own masked letter message with other groups.

Cumulative Review

Subtraction Rules and Negative Numbers Lesson 4.7

Add or subtract. Do not use a calculator. Watch for negative numbers.

1 $40 + 15 =$ ▢

2 $(-40) + 39 =$ ▢

3 $0 - 15 =$ ▢

4 $15 - 20 =$ ▢

5 $35 - 25 =$ ▢

6 $0 + 10 =$ ▢

7 $(-3) + 4 =$ ▢

8 $(-6) + 5 =$ ▢

Multiplying and Dividing Integers Lesson 4.9

Complete the following exercises.

9 $(-5) \times (-6) =$ ▢

10 $(-7) \times 8 =$ ▢

11 $5 \times (-2) =$ ▢

12 $16 \div (-4) =$ ▢

13 $-24 \div (-6) =$ ▢

14 $-6 \div 6 =$ ▢

Decimal Equivalents of Fractions Lesson 6.3

For each fraction, give the decimal equivalent or approximation correct to three decimal places.

15 $\frac{6}{9} =$ ▢

16 $\frac{4}{8} =$ ▢

17 $\frac{2}{5} =$ ▢

18 $\frac{7}{9} =$ ▢

19 $\frac{1}{4} =$ ▢

20 $\frac{2}{7} =$ ▢

Comparing Fractions Lesson 6.7

Order the following sets of fractions from least to greatest.

21 $\frac{2}{3}, \frac{1}{2}, \frac{5}{6}, \frac{1}{3}, \frac{1}{6}$

22 $\frac{3}{10}, \frac{1}{5}, \frac{1}{2}, \frac{2}{5}, \frac{1}{4}$

Replace ⬜ **with either** $<$, $>$, **or** $=$.

㉓ $\dfrac{1}{4}$ ⬜ $\dfrac{3}{12}$ ㉕ $\dfrac{2}{7}$ ⬜ $\dfrac{5}{14}$

㉔ $\dfrac{1}{5}$ ⬜ $\dfrac{2}{9}$ ㉖ $\dfrac{5}{6}$ ⬜ $\dfrac{8}{10}$

- -

Applying Fractions Lesson 6.12

Solve the following problems.

The James family needed 3 days to drive from Ohio to California. They drove $\dfrac{3}{10}$ of the way on Friday and $\dfrac{1}{3}$ of the way on Saturday.

㉗ On which day did they drive a greater distance?

㉘ How much of the trip was left to drive on Sunday?

㉙ Suppose 3 friends are sharing a pizza. If 2 boys each wanted $\dfrac{1}{4}$ of the pizza and 1 wanted $\dfrac{2}{5}$, is that possible? If so, how much of the pizza is unclaimed?

- -

Dividing Fractions Lesson 7.6

Divide. Reduce when possible.

㉚ $12 \div \dfrac{2}{3} =$ ⬜   ㉛ $\dfrac{1}{2} \div \dfrac{1}{3} =$ ⬜   ㉜ $16 \div \dfrac{4}{5} =$ ⬜

㉝ $\dfrac{2}{5} \div \dfrac{3}{7} =$ ⬜   ㉞ $\dfrac{5}{8} \div \dfrac{5}{4} =$ ⬜   ㉟ $\dfrac{5}{12} \div \dfrac{10}{3} =$ ⬜

- -

Averages Lesson 8.1

Find the average of the following sets of numbers.

㊱ 8, 11, 15, 26   ㊲ -5, 4, 10, 15

Solve.

㊳ Kelli had scores of 85, 87, and 90 on her first 3 math tests. She thought that if she scored a 94 on her next test, she could raise her average to a 90 and get an A. Was Kelli right? What would her average be?

               ⓔ **Textbook** This lesson is available in the *eTextbook*.

CHAPTER
8

Key Ideas Review

In this chapter, you learned about division and ratios.

You learned how to divide multidigit numbers within the context of real-world situations. You learned how to analyze data using ratios, mean, median, mode, and range.

· ·

Solve.

1 $1,974 \div 42 = $ ▢

2 $38,586 \div 354 = $ ▢

3 What do the terms *range* and *mode* refer to?

4 Jorge is a linebacker. The table below shows the number of tackles he made for the first six games of the season.

Game	Number of Tackles
1	8
2	12
3	8
4	15
5	9
6	11

What is Jorge's average number of tackles for each game?

5 Explain two ways to compare ratios.

Chapter Review

Lesson 8.1 **Solve.**

1. Chu scored 80, 88, 90, and 94 on his last 4 spelling tests. What was his average?

2. Chu wants to bring his average up to 90. Could he do that after his next test? If so, what is the minimum score he would need?

Lesson 8.2 **Solve.**

Mrs. Long's second-grade class had the following scores on their math tests: 88, 73, 95, 78, 86, 84, 67, 90, 78, 95, and 82.

3. Find the mean, mode, median, and range of the data.

Lesson 8.4 **Solve.**

Abby drove from Columbus, Ohio, to St. Louis, Missouri. Her trip was approximately 410 miles.

4. Abby drove the first 240 miles in 4 hours. What was her average rate of speed?

5. The rest of the trip took $2\frac{1}{2}$ hours. What was Abby's average speed for the entire trip?

Lesson 8.5 **Copy** each pair of ratios below. Replace ▮ with $<$, $>$, or $=$. Use a calculator only when necessary.

6. $\frac{5}{9}$ ▮ $\frac{5}{8}$ 7. $\frac{3}{11}$ ▮ $\frac{3}{13}$ 8. $\frac{4}{12}$ ▮ $\frac{8}{15}$ 9. $\frac{4}{5}$ ▮ $\frac{7}{8}$

Lesson 8.7 **Find** approximate answers.

10. $62 \div 20 =$ ▮   11. $480 \div 19 =$ ▮   12. $498 \div 101 =$ ▮

13. $560 \div 71 =$ ▮   14. $150 \div 29 =$ ▮   15. $1,400 \div 20 =$ ▮

Lesson 8.8 Solve.

16 For the school fund-raiser, 27 students raised $810. What was the average amount raised per student?

17 Jacque saved all his allowance for 35 weeks and accumulated $525. What was his weekly allowance?

Lesson 8.10 Divide.

18 $3,640 \div 325 = \boxed{}$

20 $54,926 \div 947 = \boxed{}$

19 $18,306 \div 678 = \boxed{}$

21 $4,879 \div 170 = \boxed{}$

Lesson 8.11 Solve.

Ted is the leading batter on his Little League team with 14 hits in 20 at bats.

22 What is Ted's batting average up to this point?

23 If Ted gets 6 hits in his next 10 at bats, what will his overall average be?

Lesson 8.13 Solve.

Peg needs to get to her uncle's house by 5:00 P.M. for dinner. He lives 320 miles away.

24 If she leaves at noon and does not stop, what is the slowest speed she could average and still arrive on time?

25 If Peg averaged only 59 miles per hour, how many miles from her uncle's house would she be at 5:00?

Practice Test

Solve the following problems.

Gali took a survey to see how many miles from school her classmates lived. Here are the results: 5, 7, 8, 10, 2, 1.5, 6, 4.5, 5, and 12.

1. What is the mean of the distances?

2. What is the median of the distances?

3. What is the mode of the distances?

4. What is the range of the data?

Replace ▮ with <, >, or =.

5. $\frac{1}{5}$ ▮ $\frac{1}{3}$

6. $16 \div 7$ ▮ $15 \div 11$

7. $\frac{15}{17}$ ▮ $\frac{15}{18}$

8. $35 \div 14$ ▮ $25 \div 10$

Find approximate answers.

9. $1,005 \div 203$

10. $189 \div 20$

11. $7,321 \div 12$

For each problem, approximate an answer, and then do the division. Round answers to the nearest whole number.

12. $18\overline{)1405}$

13. $131\overline{)380}$

14. $455\overline{)3640}$

15. $28\overline{)483}$

Choose the correct answer.

16. Find the mean of 43, 25, 46, 17, and 89.

    Ⓐ 220   Ⓑ 55

    Ⓒ 44   Ⓓ 43

17. The town of Dashire reports an average family size of 3.12. About how many people would you expect there to be in 20 families?

    Ⓐ 3.12   Ⓑ 31

    Ⓒ 47   Ⓓ 62

18. Jackie's car drove 312 miles on 12 gallons of gas. How many miles per gallon is that?

    Ⓐ 26   Ⓑ 31.2

    Ⓒ 300   Ⓓ 3744

19. Which ratio of girls to all students is greatest?

    Ⓐ 11 to 21   Ⓑ 12 to 25

    Ⓒ 11 to 23   Ⓓ 10 to 20

20. How many tables would you need to seat 184 people if each table could fit a maximum of 5 people?

    Ⓐ 36   Ⓑ 37

    Ⓒ 40   Ⓓ 41

21. The United States Mint produced 6,836,000,000 pennies in the year 2004. Approximately how many pennies is that per month?

    Ⓐ 6,000,000,000

    Ⓑ 600,000,000

    Ⓒ 6,000,000

    Ⓓ 600,000

22. Which batter has the best batting average?

    Ⓐ Jim: 12 hits in 38 at bats

    Ⓑ John: 11 hits in 35 at bats

    Ⓒ Jana: 14 hits in 40 at bats

    Ⓓ Jessie: 15 hits in 50 at bats

23. Divide: $27\overline{)8505}$

    Ⓐ 315   Ⓑ 31.5

    Ⓒ 3.15   Ⓓ 0.315

Practice Test

Choose the correct answer.

24. The class sizes at the Greater Elementary School are as follows: 22, 25, 21, 20, 22, 15, and 23. Which method of finding the average results in the lowest average class size?

   Ⓐ mean   Ⓑ median

   Ⓒ mode   Ⓓ they are equal

25. Naomi drove 495 miles in 9 hours. What was her average speed?

   Ⓐ 65 mph   Ⓑ 60 mph

   Ⓒ 55 mph   Ⓓ 50 mph

26. Approximately 12,150 people take public transportation every morning between the hours of 7 A.M. and 10 A.M. About how many people is that per hour?

   Ⓐ 4   Ⓑ 40

   Ⓒ 400   Ⓓ 4,000

27. $1\frac{4}{5} \times 3\frac{1}{8} = $ ▭

   Ⓐ $\frac{1}{10}$ Ⓑ $3\frac{1}{10}$

   Ⓒ $5\frac{5}{8}$ Ⓓ $5\frac{7}{8}$

28. Which fraction is equivalent to $\frac{12}{20}$?

   Ⓐ $\frac{6}{14}$ Ⓑ $\frac{3}{5}$

   Ⓒ $\frac{2}{10}$ Ⓓ $\frac{3}{4}$

29. Which unit of measurement should be used to measure the length of a paper clip?

   Ⓐ centimeters   Ⓑ miles

   Ⓒ grams   Ⓓ feet

30. Misha runs $1\frac{3}{4}$ miles 4 days a week. How many miles does she run in 3 weeks?

   Ⓐ $5\frac{1}{4}$ Ⓑ 7

   Ⓒ $10\frac{1}{2}$ Ⓓ 21

31. The rule for a function machine is "subtract 8." If −3 comes out of the function machine, which number went in?

   Ⓐ −11   Ⓑ −5

   Ⓒ 5   Ⓓ 11

32. Solve for *n*.

   $15 - (2 \times 7) = n$

   Ⓐ 1   Ⓑ 16

   Ⓒ 23   Ⓓ 91

ⓔ **Textbook** This lesson is available in the *eTextbook*.

33. Daily sales for a retail store are shown below. Use the information in the table to answer the following questions.

Monday	Tuesday	Wednesday	Thursday	Friday	Saturday	Sunday
$12,450	$10,005	$4,550	$16,900	$10,600	$12,345	$15,230

    a. On his weekly report, the store manager reported a daily average income of $12,345. How did he find this average? Show your work.

    b. During the week, there was a snowstorm and the store had to close early. On which day do you think the storm occurred? Why?

    c. The next week, the store manager calculated the mean sales to be $13,420. Is this greater or less than this week's mean sales, and by how much?

34. Suppose two different stores sold copies of the same book.

    a. If Read-o-rama sold 30 books for $388.50 and Bookworm sold 25 books for $337.50, which store had the lowest price per book?

    b. Suppose you wanted to buy 14 copies of this book for your reading group at the lowest possible price. If Read-o-rama also sold 5-packs of the book at $50 each, how many 5-packs or individual copies should you buy? Explain.

Geometry

In This Chapter You Will

- learn how to measure angles.
- study properties of plane figures.
- learn to use scales to represent larger areas.

Problem Solving

Like people around the world, Native Americans used materials available to them to create comfortable and safe living environments. What shapes do you see in the structures shown on these two pages? Are some shapes more rigid than others? Try this activity to find out.

REAL WORLD

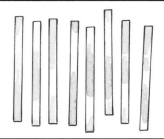

A. Cut out 8 strips of the same length cardboard.

B. Make a triangle frame and a square frame. Compare to see which shape is more rigid.

Answer the following questions.

1 Which frame is more rigid?

2 How can you make the weaker frame more rigid?

3 Will you get the same result if you use strips of different lengths? Try it.

4 How many different-shaped triangles can you make with 3 strips?

5 How many different 4-sided shapes can you make with 4 strips?

6 How do your answers to Problems 4 and 5 help explain why one shape is more rigid than the other?

Key Ideas

Angles can be classified according to the size of the rotation they represent. There are different ways to identify an angle in a figure.

Plans for building or designing houses often include angles. Sailors use angles to navigate their ships. These are only two of the many ways people use angles. An angle always has one vertex, which is a point shared by two sides. The sides of an angle can be rays, lines, or line segments.

An angle that forms a square corner (or quarter turn) is called a *right angle*. Examples of right angles include the following:

An angle that is smaller than a right angle is called an *acute angle*. The following are some examples of acute angles:

An angle that is larger than a right angle and less than a straight angle is called an *obtuse angle*. The following are some examples of obtuse angles:

  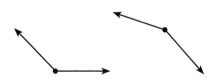

The angle pictured below is called a straight angle because its sides lie along a straight line.

vertex

ⓔ **Textbook** This lesson is available in the *eTextbook*.

Each angle below is labeled with a letter at the vertex. Identify each angle as *acute*, *right*, *obtuse*, or *straight*.

1

6

2

7

3

8

4

9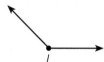

5

10

Sometimes we can identify an angle with one letter, which represents the vertex. In other cases, we use three letters, one of which is the vertex and the other two are points, one on each of the two sides.

To name or label an angle, we can use the vertex (corner point) of the angle. In this drawing, the highlighted vertex is labeled *B*, so this angle can be called *angle B* or *ABC*.

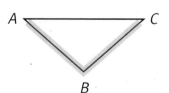

11 What are the angles in this triangle called?

Angles in nature

The branches of a tree form angles. As shown in the photograph of cedar trees, we usually study the angle formed by the trunk and the top of the branches, or the angle between a large branch and the top of the smaller branches. We'll call these the *top angles*.

Use the photograph to solve the following problems.

12 Make a list of right angles and near right angles.

13 Make a list of acute angles.

14 Make a list of obtuse angles.

15 Select four angles to order from least to greatest. Estimate their measures.

eTextbook This lesson is available in the *eTextbook*.

Now study the angles formed by the trunk and the bottom of the branches. These are the *bottom angles*.

16. Make three lists.

    a. One list of right or near right angles.

    b. One list of acute angles.

    c. One list of obtuse angles.

17. Order four of the angles from least to greatest. Estimate their measure.

18. **Extended Response** Compare the lists you made for the top angles with the lists you made for the bottom angles. Describe any patterns that emerge.

 **Journal**

Name other examples of obtuse, acute, and right angles that can be found outside the classroom.

Key Ideas

One common way to measure angles is with a unit called the *degree*.

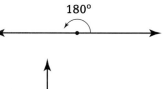

There are 360 degrees in a complete turn.

A *straight angle* has 180 degrees because its sides lie along a straight line, and its distance is half of a full turn.

We usually talk about angles that are less than 180 degrees. A *right angle* is one-fourth of a complete turn. Since $360 \div 4 = 90$, there are 90 degrees in a right angle.

An *acute angle* has less than 90 degrees, and an *obtuse angle* has a measure between 90 and 180 degrees.

The symbol for degree is a small circle written above and to the right of the number.

For example: 90° means "90 degrees." 37° means "37 degrees."

To measure an angle in degrees, we use a protractor (just as we use a ruler to measure distance).

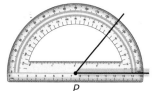

Position your protractor so that the little hole is on the vertex (or corner) of the angle and the dotted line is on one side of the angle.

The other side of the angle lines up with a number that tells you how many degrees are in that angle.

What is the measure of angle *P*?

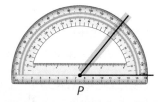

Is the answer 50° or 130°?

Since angle *P* is an acute angle and the measure of an acute angle must be less than 90°, the correct measure of angle *P* is 50°.

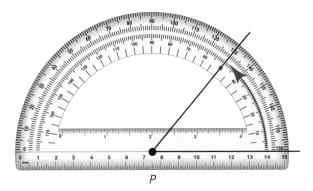

P

Why are there two scales on the protractor?

Look at angle *Q*. Suppose we place a protractor over angle *Q* to measure it, like this:

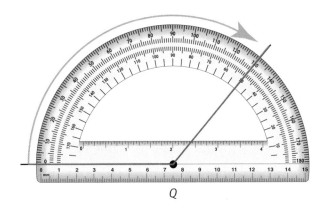

Q

One side of the angle lines up with the same numbers that the side of angle *P* lined up with. On a protractor, one side measures the angle to the right and the other side measures the angle to the left.

Can the measure of angle *Q* be 50°?

No, you can tell by looking at angle *Q* that it is obtuse. So, its measure must be between 90° and 180°. In this instance, the angle is 130°.

Indicate whether each angle is *acute*, *obtuse*, or *right*. Give the measure of each angle using degrees.

1

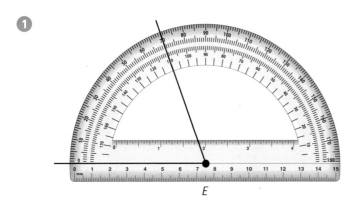

E

2

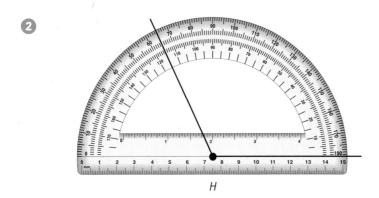

H

3 On a piece of paper, sketch angle *ABC* with the measure 180°. What is this type of angle called?

4 How many degrees are in an acute angle?

5 How many degrees are in an obtuse angle?

This lesson is available in the *eTextbook*.

Measure each angle. (Some figures may have more than one angle.)
Write the name of each angle and its measure. To make it easier to read
each angle's measure with your protractor, you can trace the angle and
extend its sides with your ruler.

6

7

8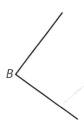

9

10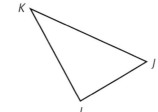

11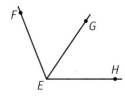

12 **Extended Response** Explain how to decide which scale to use
on a protractor.

13 **Extended Response** Draw two intersecting perpendicular lines. Add the
measures of the four angles formed. Do they add up to 360°? Explain
why or why not.

14 Choose two of the angles you drew in Problem 13 that are adjacent to
one another (they share a side). If you add the measures of these two
angles, what is the total measure? Does it matter which two adjacent
angles you choose?

15 How many degrees are in a quarter turn? In a half turn? In three-fourths
of a turn? In a full turn?

> **Writing + Math** **Journal**
>
> Write a step-by-step explanation of how to measure an angle with a
> protractor.

Angles and Sides of a Triangle

Key Ideas

The sum of the angle measures of any triangle is 180°. Given the lengths of any two sides of a triangle, you can determine a range of possible lengths for the third side.

The following are a few types of special triangles we often use in geometry.

Triangles that have a right angle are called **right** triangles.	Triangles that have two sides of equal length are called **isosceles** triangles.	Triangles that have three sides of equal length are called **equilateral** triangles.

We call triangles with three different side lengths **scalene** triangles. We do not want to confuse them with special triangles.

e Textbook This lesson is available in the *eTextbook*.

Just as there is a relationship between the sizes of the angles in a triangle, there is a relationship between the lengths of the sides of a triangle.

Suppose there is a triangle with sides measuring 3 and 10 units.

What could you conclude about the third side?

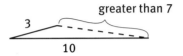

greater than 7

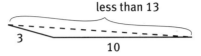

less than 13

We can see from these diagrams that there is a range of possible values for the length of the third side. For example, if one side of a triangle is 10 units and another is 3 units, the third side will not reach between the ends of the first two sides unless it is greater than 7 units long.

If the third side were 13 or more units long it would reach too far to meet the ends of the first two sides. So, in the triangle above, not every choice for the length of the third side would work.

Measure the three angles of each triangle, and then find the sum of the measures. Indicate which, if any, of the triangles are *right, isosceles,* or *equilateral.*

①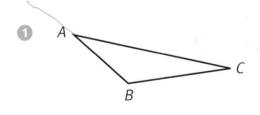

②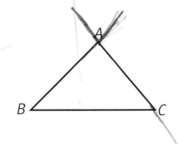

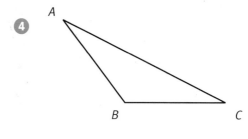

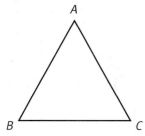

7 State which of the following triples of side lengths can be used to form a triangle:

a. 2, 6, 5

b. 10, 2, 3

c. 13, 24, 11

8 **Extended Response** Is the sum of the angle measures of each triangle about the same? If not, why might they be different?

9 **Extended Response** Do you think it is possible to have an equilateral triangle that is not an isosceles triangle? Explain.

10 **Extended Response** Is it possible to have a triangle with more than one obtuse angle? Why or why not?

Writing + Math **Journal**

What interesting fact did you find about the angles in triangles? Did you notice anything special about isosceles or equilateral triangles while you were measuring their angles?

Textbook This lesson is available in the *eTextbook*.

Triangle Game

Players: Two or more

Materials: *Number Cubes* (two 0–5 and two 5–10)

Object: To make as many triangles as possible

Math Focus: Drawing triangles and mathematical reasoning

HOW TO PLAY

❶ Take turns rolling all four *Number Cubes*.

❷ Each number rolled represents a number of centimeters.

❸ Think of as many triangles as you can, using combinations of the numbers rolled as side lengths.

❹ The player who can make the most triangles wins the round.

SAMPLE GAME

Lelani rolled:

| 8 | 5 | 7 | 4 |

She could make four triangles:

8, 7, 5

8, 7, 4

8, 5, 4

7, 5, 4

Pedro rolled:

| 2 | 3 | 6 | 10 |

He could not make any triangles.

Lelani won this round.

Drawing Triangles

Solve.

1 Draw triangle *ABC* with your ruler and protractor so that

    a. angle *C* measures 90°.

    b. side *AC* is 8 centimeters long.

    c. side *BC* is 6 centimeters long.

Compare your triangle with a triangle that somebody else has drawn. Do they look the same? Cut out the two triangles to see if they fit on top of each other.

Measure side *AB* on your triangle. Compare the length of your side *AB* with the lengths of sides *AB* that other students have drawn.

Measure angles *A* and *C*. Compare the measures of your angles *A* and *C* with the measures of angles *A* and *C* that others have drawn.

2 Are all the triangles the same?

3 Draw triangle *DEF* with your ruler and protractor so that

    a. angle *D* measures 60˚.

    b. side *DE* is 10 centimeters long.

    c. side *DF* is 10 centimeters long.

4 Measure angles *E* and *F*. Measure side *EF*. How did your measures compare to the measures of others in the class? What type of triangle is this?

5 Draw triangle *GHI* with your ruler and protractor so that

    a. angle *H* measures 45°.

    b. side *GH* is 14 centimeters long.

    c. side *HI* is 10 centimeters long.

     ⓔ Textbook This lesson is available in the *eTextbook*.

Solve.

6 What is the measure of angle *I*? Angle *G*? What is the length of side *GI*? Did everyone get the same answers?

7 Draw triangle *JKL* with your ruler and protractor so that

   a. angle *J* measures 30°.

   b. side *JK* is 7 centimeters long.

   c. side *KL* is 8 centimeters long.

One way to do this is to first draw side *JK* and angle *J*, and then extend the other side of angle *J*. Place the 0 centimeter mark of your ruler at point *K* and swing the ruler until the 8 centimeter mark hits the other side of angle *J*. The point where they meet is point *L*.

8 Measure angles *K* and *L* and side *JL*. Compare your answers with the answers of others in the class. Does everyone have the same answers?

9 Draw triangle *MNP* with your ruler and protractor so that

   a. angle *M* measures 30°.

   b. side *MN* is 7 centimeters long.

   c. side *NP* is 3 centimeters long.

10 Measure angles *N* and *P* and side *MP*. Compare your measurements with the answers of others in the class. Does everyone have the same measurements?

11 Draw triangle *QRS* with your ruler and protractor so that

   a. angle *Q* measures 30°.

   b. side *QR* is 7 centimeters long.

   c. side *RS* is 5 centimeters long.

12 **Extended Response** Measure angles *R* and *S* and side *QS*. Compare your answers with classmates' answers. Does everyone have the same answers? If so, try to follow these steps to draw a triangle that would give different answers.

Key Ideas

Congruent figures have exactly the same shape and size. **Similar** figures have the same shape but may or may not be different in size.

When we draw diagrams of triangles, we often name each vertex with capital letters, such as A, B, and C. We name the side opposite a given vertex with the corresponding lowercase letter. For example, in triangle ABC, the side opposite angle A is named side a.

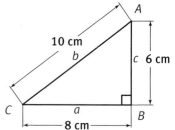

In triangle ABC

- side c (sometimes called AB) is 6 centimeters.

- side a (also known as BC) is 8 centimeters.

- side b (also known as CA) is 10 centimeters.

- the measure of angle A is 53°.

- the measure of angle B is 90°.

- the measure of angle C is 37°.

Draw the triangle as described below and then answer the questions.

① Draw a triangle and label it A'B'C' so that

- angle A' has the same measure as angle A (in the above example).

- angle B' has the same measure as angle B.

- angle C' has the same measure as angle C.

Make side a' (B'C') twice as long as side a (BC).
(Make a' 16 centimeters long.)

  a. How long is side c' (A'B')?

  b. Is that twice as long as side c (AB)?

  c. How long is side b' (C'A')?

  d. Is triangle A'B'C' the same size as triangle ABC? Is it the same shape?

2 Suppose you drew triangle A″B″C″ to be the same shape, but this time you made side c″ half as long as side c.

   a. How long would side a″ be?

   b. How long would side b″ be?

   c. Now draw triangle A″B″C″. Measure sides a″ and b″ to check your answers to parts a and b.

   d. Is triangle A″B″C″ the same size as triangle ABC? Is it the same shape?

Look at the following triangles:

Since they have the same size and shape, we say that triangles ABC and A′B′C′ are congruent.

Notice that corresponding parts of the triangles are the same size. For example, angles A and A′ both have the same measurement, and sides a and a′ both have the same length.

Any two figures that have the same size and shape are congruent.

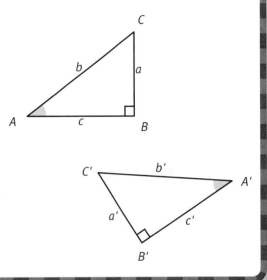

Select the figure that is congruent to the first figure.

3   **a.**   **b.**   **c.**   **d.**

4   **a.**   **b.**   **c.**   **d.**

5   **a.**   **b.**   **c.**   **d.**

Look at the following triangles.

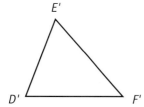

Where is side *f* in this diagram? Where are sides *d*, *e*, *d'*, *e'*, and *f'*?

Since they have exactly the same shape but different sizes, we say that these triangles are *similar*.

Corresponding angles of similar triangles have the same measures. For instance, angle *E* has the same measure as angle *E'*. However, corresponding sides of similar triangles are not necessarily the same. For example, angles *D* and *D'* have the same measure, but sides *f* and *f'* are not the same length.

However, the ratios of the lengths of corresponding sides of similar triangles will be equal.

$$\frac{f}{f'} = \frac{d}{d'} = \frac{e}{e'}$$

We say that corresponding sides of similar triangles are proportional. Measurements that form equal ratios are proportional.

Answer the following questions.

6 What are some examples of congruent figures or objects?

7 What are some examples of similar figures or objects?

8 If two figures are congruent, are they also similar? (Do they have the same shape?)

Complete the following items.

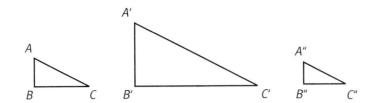

9 All the triangles above are the same shape. They are similar. Record each of the following measurements to the nearest millimeter.

$c = $ ▢ mm $c' = $ ▢ mm

$a = $ ▢ mm $a' = $ ▢ mm

$b = $ ▢ mm $b' = $ ▢ mm

Find the following ratios. Use a calculator if necessary. Round to the nearest hundredth.

10 $\dfrac{c}{a} = $ ▢   **11** $\dfrac{c'}{a'} = $ ▢

$\dfrac{c}{b} = $ ▢ $\dfrac{c'}{b'} = $ ▢

$\dfrac{b}{a} = $ ▢ $\dfrac{b'}{a'} = $ ▢

12 Estimate the following ratios. Then compute each one after making the appropriate measurements.

$\dfrac{c''}{a''} = $ ▢

$\dfrac{c''}{b''} = $ ▢

$\dfrac{b''}{a''} = $ ▢

13 Suppose triangle *QRS* is similar to triangle *Q'R'S'*.

 a. If angle *Q* is 55°, what is the measure of angle *Q'*?

 b. If angle *R* is 35°, what is the measure of angle *S'*? (Hint: First find the measure of angle *S*.)

 c. **Extended Response** If *q* (side *RS*) is 50 millimeters, can you find the length of *q'*? If so, what is it? If not, why not?

Key Ideas

Using symbols and notation makes it easier to discuss geometric figures.

Here are some short ways to write some of the things we have discussed. We will use these short forms when they are convenient. You may use them if you wish.

Symbol	Meaning
$\triangle ABC$	triangle ABC
$\angle A$	angle A
$\angle BAC$	angle BAC (A is the vertex, B is a point on one side of the angle, and C is a point on the other side of the angle.)
$\angle A = 37°$	The measure of $\angle A$ is 37°.
$\angle A = \angle D$	The measure of $\angle A$ is equal to the measure of $\angle D$.
c	In a triangle, this is a shorter name for the side that is opposite angle C.
$c = 10$ cm or $AB = 10$ cm	The length of side c (or side AB) is 10 centimeters.
$c = c'$ or $AB = A'B'$	The length of side c (or side AB) is equal to the length of side c' (or side $A'B'$).
$\triangle ABC \cong \triangle A'B'C'$	Triangle ABC is congruent to triangle $A'B'C'$ (point A corresponds to point A', point B to point B', and point C to point C').
$\triangle ABC \sim \triangle A'B'C'$	Triangle ABC is similar to triangle $A'B'C'$ (here, too, point A corresponds to point A', and so on).

ⓔ Textbook This lesson is available in the *eTextbook.*

For each pair of triangles, write whether the triangles are similar or congruent. Also write which corresponding parts are equal. Use symbols and make sure the letters of each triangle are in the proper order. The first one is done for you.

1

$\angle A = \angle P$
$\angle B = \angle Q$
$\angle C = \angle R$
$\triangle ABC \sim \triangle PQR$

2

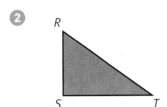 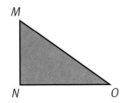

3

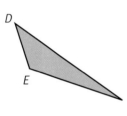 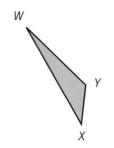

4

 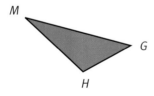

Answer the following questions.

5 In △ABC, ∠A = 35° and ∠B = 100°. Without measuring, find the measure of ∠C.

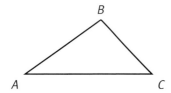

6 **Extended Response** In △DEF ~ △GHI, f = 8 cm, d = 6 cm, e = 12 cm, g = 3 cm, and ∠D = 27°. Without measuring, find the length of i, the length of h, and the measure of ∠G. Explain how you found your answer.

e Textbook This lesson is available in the *eTextbook*.

7 Consider figures *A*, *B*, *C*, *D*, *E*, *F*, and *G* below. Which appear to be congruent to each other? Which appear to be similar but not congruent?

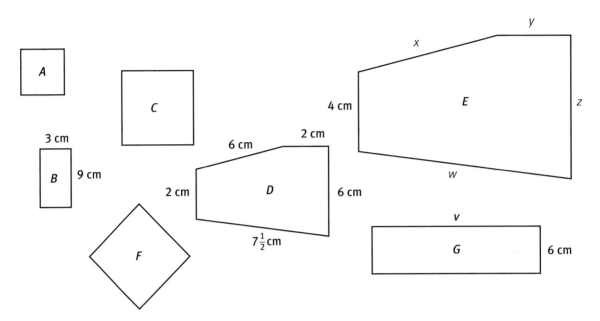

8 Assuming figures *D* and *E* are similar to each other and the measurements given for their sides are correct, what is the value of *x*? Of *y*? Of *z*? Of *w*?

9 Suppose the length of one side of square *A* is 1 centimeter. What is the area of square *A*? What is the perimeter of square *A*?

10 If the side of square *C* is 2 centimeters long, what is the area of square *C*? What is the perimeter of square *C*?

11 If the side of a square is 3 centimeters long, what is the area of the square? What is the perimeter of the square?

12 **Extended Response** Assume that figure *B* is similar to figure *G*. Find the length of *v*. Find the perimeter of *G*. If the side labeled 6 centimeters in figure *G* was really supposed to be 18 centimeters, how would the perimeter change? Why?

 **Journal**

Are all equilateral triangles congruent to each other? Are they all similar to each other? Explain your reasoning.

Key Ideas

If you know the lengths of the sides and all of the angles of one triangle ABC and the length of one side of a similar triangle A'B'C', you can determine the other two sides of A'B'C' and all its angles.

You may want to draw pictures to help you solve the problems on this page.

① $\triangle ABC \cong \triangle DEF$. $c = 9$ cm, $a = 10$ cm, $b = 15$ cm. $\angle A = 39°$, $\angle B = 104°$.

a. What is the measure of $\angle C$?

b. What is the measure of $\angle D$?

c. What is the measure of $\angle E$?

d. What is the measure of $\angle F$?

e. What is the length of f?

f. What is the length of d?

g. What is the length of e?

h. What is the length of FD?

② $\triangle ABC \sim \triangle GHI$. $\triangle ABC$ is the same triangle as in Problem 1. The length of side $i = 27$ cm. Find the measures of each of the angles and the length of each of the sides.

a. $\angle G$ **b.** $\angle I$ **c.** g **d.** $\angle H$ **e.** GH **f.** h

③ $\triangle GHI \sim \triangle JKL$. $\triangle GHI$ is the same triangle as in Problem 2. The length of side $k = 5$ cm. Find the measure of each of the angles and the lengths of each of the sides.

a. $\angle J$ **b.** $\angle L$ **c.** j **d.** $\angle K$ **e.** l **f.** JL

Solve the following.

④ In △MNP, ∠M = 47° and ∠N = 83°. ∠P = ▢

⑤ In △QRS, ∠Q = 60° and ∠R = ∠Q. ∠S = ▢

⑥ In △TUV, ∠T = 40° and ∠U = ∠V. ∠V = ▢

Ms. Walker is using an overhead projector to project a triangle on the wall. The triangle on the wall is similar to the triangle she has drawn.

Eleanor and Pablo are measuring the sides of the triangle on the wall. They find that AC = 260 centimeters, BC = 208 centimeters, and AB = 156 centimeters.

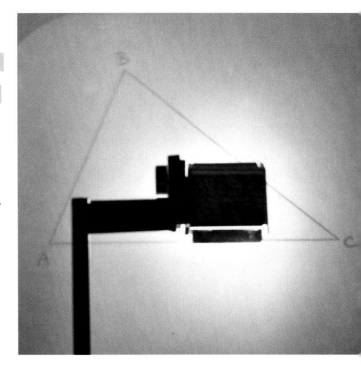

⑦ Which side of the small triangle is the longest?

⑧ Which side of the small triangle is the shortest?

⑨ Eleanor measures side AC of the small triangle. It is about 5 centimeters long. About how many times longer is side AC of the big triangle?

⑩ Find the length of sides AB and BC in the small triangle.

⑪ How many times longer than the sides of the small triangle are the corresponding sides of the big triangle?

⑫ **Extended Response** Which is greater, the measure of angle A on the wall or in the drawing? How do you know?

Writing + Math **Journal**

Are all right triangles similar to each other? Explain how you know.

Exploring Problem Solving

Imagine you and your friends are designing and building a playhouse. You have just learned about a Native American tribe called the Hidatsa and decide to make your playhouse like a Hidatsa earth lodge. You will use 12 logs of the same length to form the outer support of the roof. What will be the measure of the angle formed by a pair of adjoining logs?

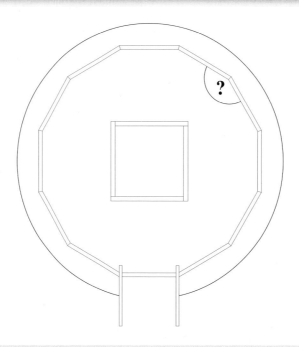

 Samira solved the problem this way:

I decided to Use a Model.

I looked at the wall clock in the classroom and imagined the clockface with a 12-sided polygon on top of it.

 ⓔ Textbook This lesson appears in the *eTextbook*.

Think about Samira's strategy. Answer the following questions.

① How is the face of a clock like the layout of the earth lodge? How is it different?

② Samira borrowed a toy clock that first graders use to learn to tell time. How can she use the clock to solve the problem?

③ Suppose Samira did not use a clock. How could she still use her strategy to solve the problem?

Ananda solved the problem another way.

I decided to Make a Diagram and Use Geometric Reasoning.

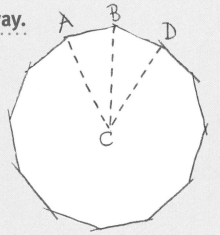

Think about Ananda's strategy. Answer the following questions.

④ Which angle's measure is the problem asking for?

⑤ If Ananda divided the whole figure into triangles the same size as △ABC and △BCD, how many triangles would there be altogether?

⑥ Would all those triangles be congruent? How do you know?

⑦ If Ananda knew the measure of ∠ACB, what would that tell him about other angles in the diagram?

⑧ How could Ananda use that information about other angles to solve the problem?

⑨ Solve the problem. Use any strategy you think will work. What strategy did you use? Why?

⑩ What would the answer be if you used only 8 logs instead of 12 for the roof support?

Cumulative Review

Probability and Fractions Lesson 6.9

Solve.

Two standard dice, numbered 1–6, are rolled. What is the probability that

① the roll is a double?

② the sum of the rolls is less than 4?

③ the sum of the rolls is greater than 9?

. . . .

Adding Mixed Numbers Lesson 7.3

Add.

④ $3\frac{5}{8} + 1\frac{1}{4} = $ ▢   ⑥ $4\frac{3}{4} + 1\frac{5}{6} = $ ▢

⑤ $5\frac{1}{2} + 2\frac{2}{3} = $ ▢   ⑦ $1\frac{1}{3} + 3\frac{2}{3} = $ ▢

Solve.

⑧ Renee left school, walked $\frac{3}{4}$ mile to her friend's house, and then walked $1\frac{1}{5}$ miles home. How far did she walk altogether?

. . . .

Finding Mean, Median, Mode, and Range Lesson 8.2

Answer.

Chico's scores on his last 5 spelling tests were 75, 90, 84, 82, and 89.

⑨ What was the mean of his scores?   ⑪ What was the range of his scores?

⑩ What was the median of his scores?   ⑫ Was there a mode? If so, what was it?

ⓔ **Textbook** This lesson is available in the *eTextbook*.

Approximating Quotients Lesson 8.7

Solve.

A half-gallon jug (64 ounces) of lemonade is used to fill glasses.

⑬ About how many 10-ounce glasses can be filled?

⑭ If 7-ounce glasses are used instead, how many can be filled?

⑮ Lloyd is saving $22 per week until he has $321 to buy a bicycle. About how many weeks will it take him to save enough money to buy the bicycle?

· ·

Dividing By a Two-Digit Number Lesson 8.8

Solve.

⑯ Jen drove her car 330 miles and used 18 gallons of gas. Pablo's car went 360 miles and used 17 gallons. Whose car got better gas mileage? By about how much?

Divide.

⑰ $45\overline{)14049}$ ⑱ $25\overline{)6465}$ ⑲ $46\overline{)1932}$

· ·

Angles Lesson 9.1

Find the measurements of the following angles. Use a protractor if necessary.

⑳ 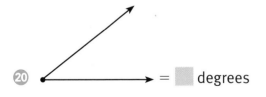 = ▮ degrees   ㉒  = ▮ degrees

㉑  = ▮ degrees   ㉓  = ▮ degrees

LESSON 9.8 Scale Drawings

Key Ideas

Scale drawings represent real objects. They are the same shape as the real objects, but they differ in size. The ratio of the size of the drawing to the size of the object is called the *scale*.

Usually, a scale is given to tell how much larger or smaller lengths are in the drawing than in the real object.

The next page shows part of a scale drawing of a classroom. The scale is 1 cm = 50 cm, which means that 1 centimeter on the drawing represents 50 centimeters in the actual classroom. Every distance in the drawing is $\frac{1}{50}$ of the corresponding distance in the real classroom.

Answer the following questions as accurately as you can.

1. How long is the actual chalkboard?

2. How long and how wide are the actual student desks?

3. What is the diameter of the actual wastebasket?

4. How high is the actual ceiling?

5. How long and how wide is the top of the actual teacher's desk?

6. What is the area of the top of the actual teacher's desk?

7. What is the area of the actual art table?

8. What is the area of the actual chalkboard?

9. Suppose a rectangular reading table is moved into the room. The tabletop is 1.5 meters long and 0.5 meter wide. How long and how wide would the reading table be in the drawing?

10. How long and how wide is the actual classroom?

430

e Textbook This lesson is available in the *eTextbook*.

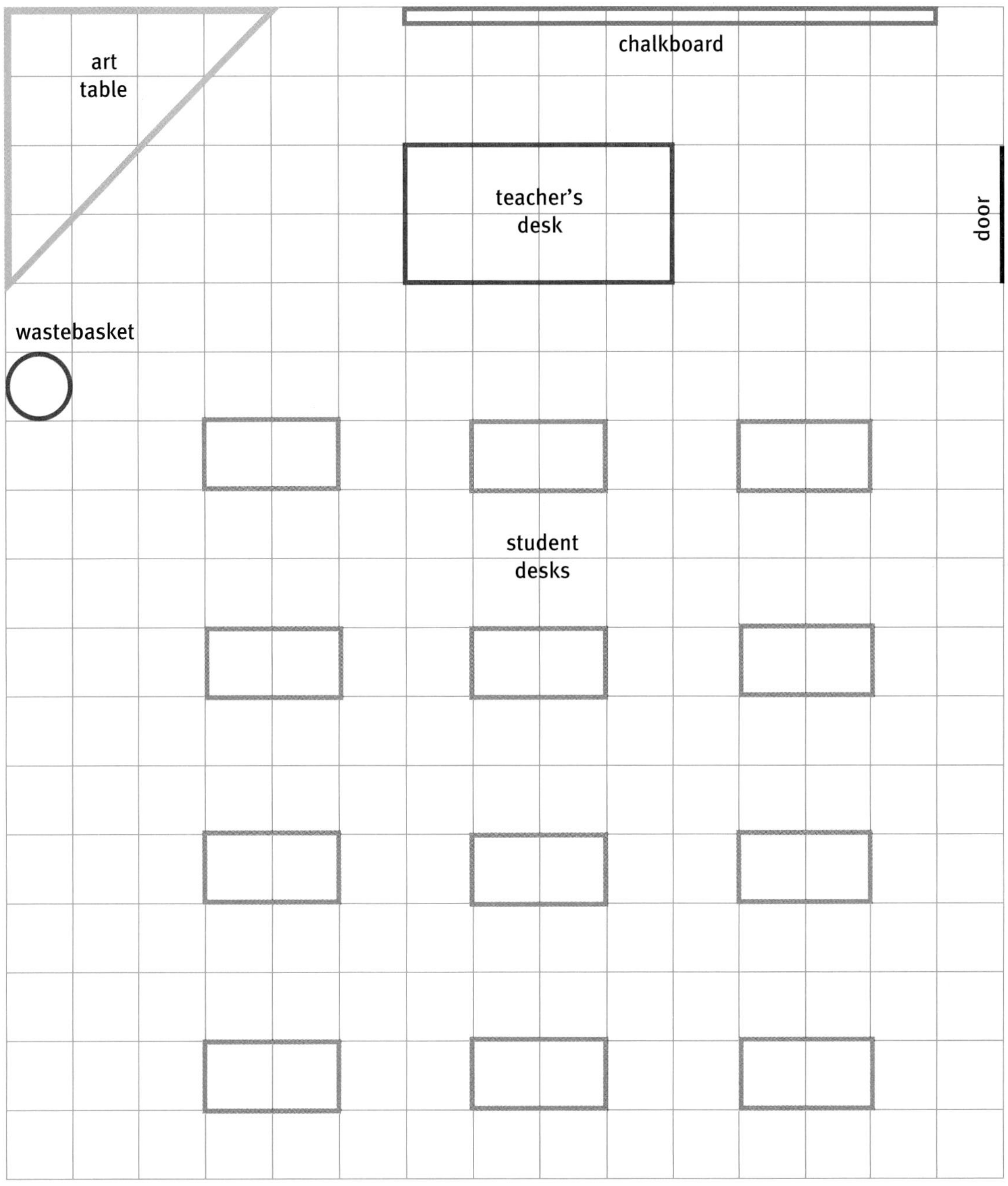

art
table

chalkboard

teacher's
desk

door

wastebasket

student
desks

Scale: 1 cm = 50 cm

The Denizens made a scale drawing of their living room. They decided to use a scale in which 1 unit on the drawing stood for 1 foot in the actual room.

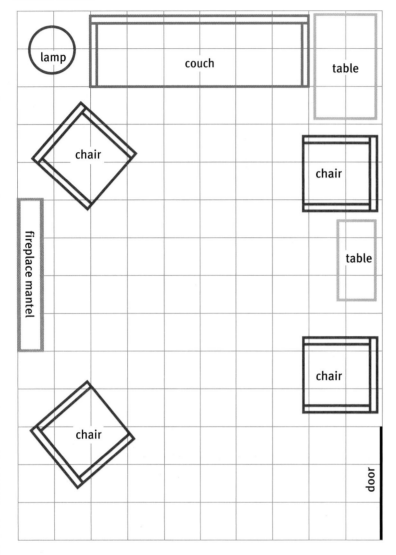

Scale: 1 unit = 1 ft

Answer the following questions as accurately as you can, based on the scale drawing.

⓫ What are the dimensions of the living room?

⓬ How long is the fireplace mantel?

⓭ How long is the couch?

⓮ What are the dimensions of the larger table? What are the dimensions of the smaller table?

The Denizens made a scale drawing of their bedroom. They decided to use the same scale, where 1 unit on the drawing stood for 1 foot in the actual room.

Scale: 1 unit = 1 ft

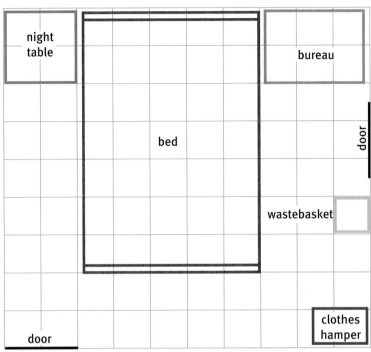

Scale: 1 unit = 1 ft

Answer the following questions as accurately as you can, based on the scale drawing.

15 What are the dimensions of the bedroom?

16 What are the dimensions of the bed?

17 What are the dimensions of the bureau?

18 What are the dimensions of the clothes hamper?

19 What are the dimensions of the wastebasket?

20 **Extended Response** Could the bureau be moved to the wall by the foot of the bed? Explain your answer.

Using a Map Scale

Key Ideas

Like scale drawings, maps are usually drawn using a scale that shows how distances between places on the map represent the actual distances between those places.

Most maps and blueprints are drawn to scale. For a map of an entire country, 1 inch could stand for 50 miles. For a map of a state, 1 inch could stand for only 10 miles. For a map of a city, 1 inch could stand for only 1 mile.

Sometimes an = sign is used to show the scale. For example,
Scale: 1 in. = 50 mi.

Of course, 1 inch is not equal to 50 miles. The = symbol here means "stands for." When you see the = symbol used to show the scale of a map or drawing, remember that it means "stands for," not "equals."

Sometimes a colon (:) is used instead of the = symbol. For example,
Scale 1 in.: 50 mi.

Solve.

1 Suppose the scale of a map is 1 cm = 20 km, and the distance between Summerville and Winter City is about 7 centimeters on the map. About how far apart are the towns in real life?

Use the map to approximate the number of kilometers between the following cities.

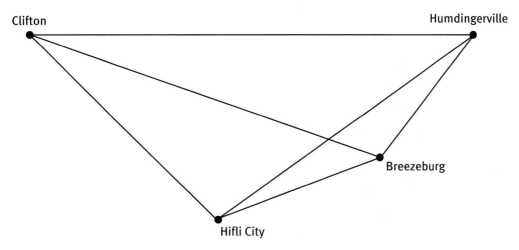

Kite County   Scale: 1 cm = 20 km

Clifton   Humdingerville

                                        Breezeburg

                    Hifli City

2 Clifton to Humdingerville

3 Clifton to Breezeburg

4 Clifton to Hifli City

5 Hifli City to Clifton

6 Hifli City to Humdingerville

7 Hifli City to Breezeburg

8 Humdingerville to Breezeburg

9 Breezeburg to Humdingerville

On the map, how long of a line segment would you need to draw to represent each of the following distances?

10 20 km

11 80 km

12 30 km

13 5 km

14 40 km

15 10 km

16 50 km

17 60 km

18 What fraction of a real distance is the corresponding distance on the map?

Using the scale and map below, estimate the number of air miles between the following cities.

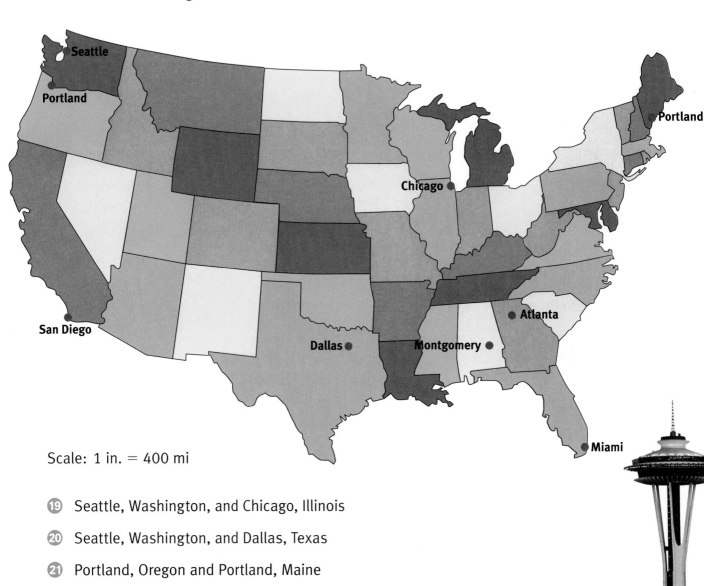

Scale: 1 in. = 400 mi

⑲ Seattle, Washington, and Chicago, Illinois

⑳ Seattle, Washington, and Dallas, Texas

㉑ Portland, Oregon and Portland, Maine

㉒ Seattle, Washington, and Miami, Florida

㉓ Montgomery, Alabama, and Atlanta, Georgia

㉔ Dallas, Texas, and Miami, Florida

㉕ Montgomery, Alabama, and Chicago, Illinois

㉖ Portland, Maine and San Diego, California

㉗ Montgomery, Alabama, and Miami, Florida

㉘ San Diego, California, and Portland, Maine

ⓔ **Textbook** This lesson is available in the *eTextbook*.

Solve.

29 Marcus draws $\triangle PQR$ so that $PQ = 7$ inches, $QR = 11$ inches, and $RP = 8$ inches. Then he projects the drawing on a wall so that PQ on the wall is about 84 inches long. What are the lengths of the other sides of the triangle on the wall?

30 On a map of the United States, the scale is 1 cm = 90 km. The distances on the map between pairs of cities are given below. What is the distance, in kilometers, between each pair of cities?

  a. Duluth to New Orleans: 21 cm

  b. Chicago to Omaha: 8 cm

  c. Salt Lake City to Los Angeles: 10.5 cm

  d. Little Rock to Atlanta: 8 cm

  e. Baton Rouge to Portland, Maine: 26 cm

  f. Seattle to San Antonio: 32 cm

  g. Omaha to Salt Lake City: 12.5 cm

  h. Chicago to New York City: 13 cm

  i. Portland, Maine to Portland, Oregon: 46 cm

 **Journal**

In your own words, explain how to find actual distances between places using a map scale.

Key Ideas

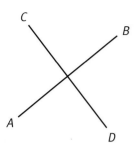

Two lines are **perpendicular** if they form right angles when they meet or intersect within the same plane. Lines *AB* and *CD* are perpendicular.

Two lines are parallel if they go in the same direction and never intersect within the same plane. Lines *EF* and *GH* are parallel.

If two lines are not parallel and they lie in the same plane, they must cross each other. Sometimes we can see where they cross, but sometimes we cannot. In this example, lines *IJ* and *KL* are neither parallel nor perpendicular.

If we extend each of these lines, we can see that they cross or intersect at exactly one point.

For each pair of lines, write whether the lines are *perpendicular*, *parallel*, or *neither*.

1   **2**   **3**   **4**

5   **6**   **7**   **8**

e Textbook This lesson is available in the *eTextbook*.

Solve the following problems.

(9) List at least two pairs of perpendicular lines in your classroom.

(10) List at least two pairs of parallel lines in your classroom.

Sometimes, in pictures, lines that look parallel are drawn as though they would actually meet at some point. This is because when we see parallel lines going off into the distance, they appear to get closer together, even though we know they really do not.

(11) In the pictures shown below, find at least two pairs of lines that look as though they are parallel.

(12) In the pictures shown below, find at least two pairs of lines that look as though they are perpendicular.

Solve using the quadrilateral.

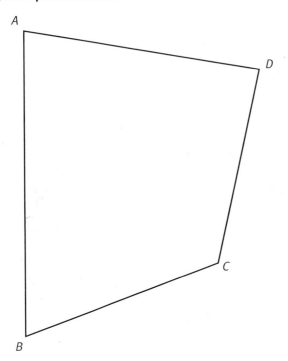

A figure with four sides is called a *quadrilateral*. (*Quadri-* means "four," and *lateral* means "side.")

13 Measure each of the four angles of quadrilateral *ABCD*. Add the measures together. What is the sum of the angle measures of this quadrilateral?

14 Draw a quadrilateral on a new sheet of paper. Measure its four angles. What is the sum of the four measures?

15 Can you draw a quadrilateral that has four acute angles?

16 Can you draw a quadrilateral that has four obtuse angles?

e **Textbook** This lesson is available in the *eTextbook.*

Solve the following.

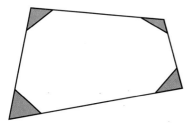

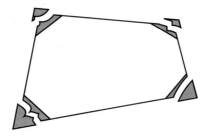

17 **Extended Response** Cut out the quadrilateral you drew in Problem 14. Tear off the four angles. Put the vertices of the four angles together so that the sides touch without overlapping. What do you notice? What does that tell you about the sum of the angles in your quadrilateral?

18 Draw a quadrilateral *EFGH*. Then draw a diagonal line segment *EG* through the quadrilateral. Look at △*EFG* in your figure.

   a. List the three angles in △*EFG*.

   b. What is the sum of their measures?

   c. Look at △*EGH*. List the three angles in △*EGH*.

   d. What is the sum of their measures?

   e. Look at the six angles you listed. Which two add up to ∠*FEH*?

   f. Which two add up to ∠*FGH*?

Writing + Math **Journal**

Looking at Problem 18, how can you prove that the measures of the angles in a quadrilateral add up to 360°?

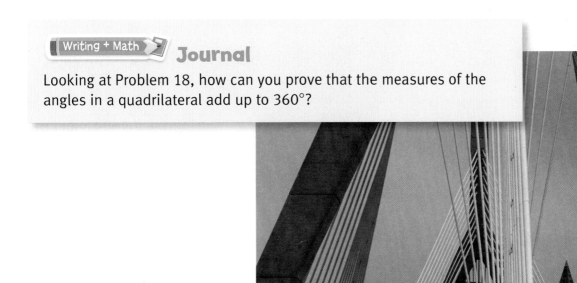

Parallelograms

Key Ideas

A parallelogram is a special kind of quadrilateral. The opposite sides of all parallelograms are parallel.

Make sketches, if you wish, to help you supply the missing information.

1. In quadrilateral $ABCD$, $\angle A = 70°$, $\angle B = 90°$, and $\angle D = 120°$. $\angle C = $ ▢

2. In quadrilateral $ABCD$, $\angle A = 90°$, $\angle B = \angle A$, and $\angle C = \angle B$. $\angle D = $ ▢

3. In quadrilateral $ABCD$, $\angle A = \angle B = \angle C = \angle D$. $\angle A = $ ▢

4. In quadrilateral $ABCD$, $\angle A = 40°$, $\angle B = 140°$, and $\angle B = \angle D$. $\angle C = $ ▢

5. In quadrilateral $ABCD$, $\angle A = \angle C$, $\angle B = \angle D$, and $\angle A = 120°$. $\angle B = $ ▢

6. Use a protractor to draw each of the figures described in Problems 1–5.

ⓔ Textbook This lesson is available in the *eTextbook*.

Solve the following.

7 Look at your figures for Problems 4 and 5 on page 442. What do you notice about the opposite sides of each of those figures?

Quadrilaterals whose opposite sides are parallel are called *parallelograms.* In parallelograms, opposite sides also have the same length.

8 Look at your figures for Problems 2 and 3 on page 442. Are the opposite sides in each figure parallel? Are the figures parallelograms? What is special about the angles of each of those two figures?

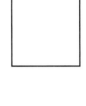

Quadrilaterals in which all four angles are right angles are special parallelograms called *rectangles.*

9 What do we call a rectangle with four equal angles whose sides all have the same length?

There are names for various kinds of quadrilaterals. For example, a parallelogram in which all four sides are the same length is called a *rhombus*.

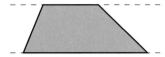 

A quadrilateral that has only one pair of parallel sides is called a *trapezoid* (but if the quadrilateral has two pairs of parallel sides, it is not called a trapezoid).

Give the standard name for each of the following figures.

10  11  12

13  14  15

16  17  18

19   20  21

ⓔ Textbook This lesson is available in the *eTextbook*.

Answer the following questions.

22 Draw a parallelogram with a right angle. What is the name for the figure you drew?

23 Can you draw a parallelogram with a right angle that is not a rectangle?

24 Draw a trapezoid with one right angle.

25 How many right angles can a trapezoid have and still be a trapezoid?

26 Draw a parallelogram in which a pair of adjacent (touching) sides are of equal length. What is this figure called?

27 **Extended Response** Give a description of a square using the name of one other figure, such as quadrilateral, parallelogram, and so on. Make your description as concise as possible. Do this again using the name of a different quadrilateral.

Name each of the following quadrilaterals. Write *trapezoid*, *parallelogram*, *rectangle*, *rhombus*, or *square*.

28

29

30

31

32

Key Ideas

The words concave and convex are used to describe the shape of closed plane figures. They are also used to describe the shapes of lenses and other space figures.

Make a sketch of a quadrilateral called *ABCD* so that $\angle A = \angle B = \angle C = 30°$ and $\angle D = 270°$. In what way is this quadrilateral different from those we have seen?

If you can find a line segment between two points of a figure that contains a point outside the figure, then the figure is said to have a *concave* shape.

Otherwise, we say the figure has a *convex* shape. A convex figure is one in which every line segment between two points of the figure remains entirely inside the figure.

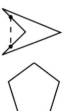

Tell whether each of these closed figures has a *concave* or a *convex* shape. If you know the names for any of the figures, include them in your answer.

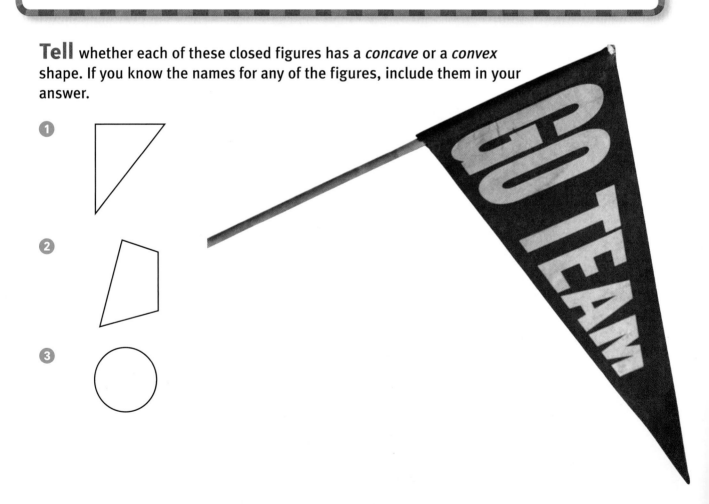

1

2

3

ⓔTextbook This lesson is available in the *eTextbook*.

Write whether each of these figures is *concave* or *convex*. If you know the names for any of the figures, include them in your answer.

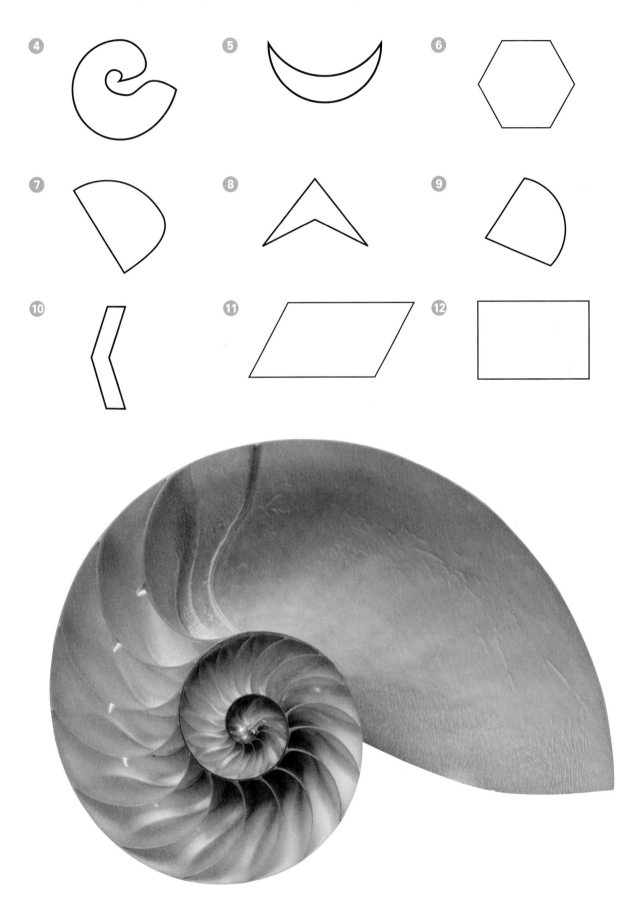

④

⑤

⑥

⑦

⑧

⑨

⑩

⑪

⑫

Answer the following questions.

Suki and Elise told Ana to describe a figure for them and they would each draw it. They wanted to see whether they would make the same figure for each description.

Ana said, "Draw a triangle with angles that measure 30°, 60°, and 90°."

Suki drew a triangle like this:

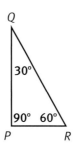

This is what Elise's triangle looked like:

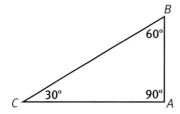

Suki said, "I drew my triangle correctly, but it's not like yours, Elise."

Elise said, "Both triangles are drawn correctly. They're similar triangles."

⓭ Is Elise correct?

Ana said, "You both are correct. Here's a harder one. Draw a triangle with angles that measure 50°, 70°, and 80°."

Suki started to work with her straightedge and protractor. Elise looked at Ana and said, "That's not hard; that's impossible."

⓮ Is Elise correct? Why?

📱 **Textbook** This lesson is available in the *eTextbook*.

Try to draw each of the following figures. If you believe it is impossible to draw the figure described, try to explain why.

15. a triangle with angles that measure 50° and 40°; the side between those two angles is 10 centimeters long

16. a quadrilateral with a convex shape

17. a quadrilateral with a concave shape

18. a triangle with a convex shape

19. a triangle with a concave shape

20. a quadrilateral with four angles that each measure 90° and all sides of the same length

21. a quadrilateral with angles that measure 120°, 120°, 60°, and 60°

22. a quadrilateral with angles that measure 60°, 60°, 70°, and 80°

23. a triangle with sides that measure 6, 8, and 10 centimeters long

24. a triangle with sides that are each 10 centimeters long

25. a triangle with sides that measure 5, 10, and 16 centimeters long

26. a triangle with sides that measure 5, 10, and 15 centimeters long

27. a triangle with sides that measure 5, 10, and 14 centimeters long

28. a quadrilateral with sides that measure 2, 5, 10, and 16 centimeters long

29. Scott lives 1 mile from Chen. Chen lives 2 miles from their school. Could Scott live 4 miles from the school?

30. Could Scott live 0.5 mile from the school?

 **Journal**

Explain your answers to Problems 29 and 30.

Exploring Some Properties of Polygons II

Key Ideas

Polygons are closed plane figures created with a chain of line segments (at least three) that do not cross each other and that touch only at their endpoints. You can draw a polygon by starting at a point and drawing a chain of straight line segments, each starting at the last one's endpoint before ending at your starting point.

Try drawing polygons. Any shape you make will be a polygon as long as you follow the rules above.

For each of the following figures, determine if it is a polygon. If not, explain why. If it *is* a polygon, state whether it is concave or convex.

Answer the following questions.

A polygon whose sides are all equal in length and whose interior angles are all equal in measure is called a *regular polygon.* A regular polygon can be described as *equilateral* (having equal sides), and *equiangular* (having equal angles).

7 What do you call a four-sided regular polygon? What do you call an irregular four-sided polygon?

Name these other regular polygons.

8   **9**   **10**

11 **Extended Response** Can you have an irregular octagon with all sides the same length? If so, sketch one and explain why it is not regular.

12 **Extended Response** Are all regular hexagons congruent? Are they similar? Explain.

13 Complete the following table for angle measures in polygons.

Number of Sides	Name	Measure of a Regular Interior Angle	Total Interior Angle Measure
3	▪	▪	▪
4	▪	▪	▪
5	▪	108°	▪
6	▪	▪	▪
7	heptagon	about 128.57°	▪
8	▪	▪	1,080°
▪	nonagon	▪	1,260°
▪	decagon	144°	▪

14 **Extended Response** Describe a pattern you found in the sum of the interior angle measures in the polygons listed above.

Native American Museum Opens on the National Mall

Washington, D.C.

Tens of thousands of Native Americans celebrated the opening of the long-awaited museum they helped design. In keeping with the spirit of Native American architecture, the National Museum of the American Indian (NMAI) stands in harmony with nature. The curving limestone walls appear shaped by the forces of wind and water. Features throughout the building highlight the interplay of the earth, the moon, and the sun.

As one of the builders described the windswept shape of the museum, "There isn't a straight line anywhere—not one square corner."

Nearly 500 different Native Nations joined a procession along the National Mall to celebrate the opening.

"Like many Indian dwellings, the new museum faces east, toward the rising sun. We can say that the sun is rising on Indian country," said President George W. Bush, in a speech honoring the museum's opening.

Inside the museum, a 120-foot-high gathering space displays the angles of the sun at special times of the year. Prisms set into a southern wall disperse the sun's rays into a spectrum of colors.

e Textbook This lesson appears in the *eTextbook*.

The NMAI filled the last building spot on the National Mall, a 4.25-acre site visible in this satellite photo taken during the museum's construction. To honor the Native American reverence for the earth, more than 33,000 plants of 150 species surround the museum, modeling the natural environment that existed before the arrival of Europeans.

This image shows the location for the site of the NMAI before it was built.

This image shows a close up of the NMAI construction site.

Answer the following questions. Use the information on both pages.

1. How does the appearance of the NMAI remind you of the other Native American dwellings?

2. Based on what you can see in the photos, do you agree with the statement on page 452 about there not being a straight line or corner in the museum? Why or why not?

3. How would you describe the shape of the site on which the museum was built?

Imagine you are designing a full-sized replica of a Creek town house for the National Museum of the American Indian. These meeting places ranged in size from 30 to 60 feet in diameter and could seat up to 500 people.

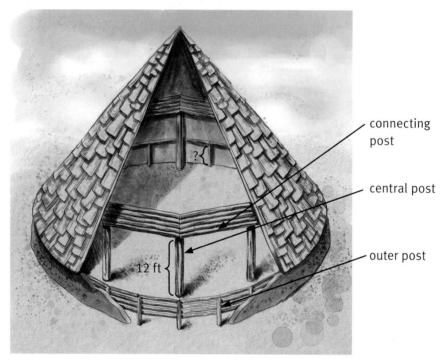

connecting post

central post

outer post

12 ft

Your replica will be 54 feet wide. Each of the eight central posts will

- rise 12 feet above the ground.

- be 36 feet from the opposite central post.

You want the peak of the roof to be 30 feet above the ground.

Work in groups to discuss and solve the following problems.

4 What will be the measure of the angle between two adjacent connecting posts? Hint: Think of a problem you may have already solved.

5 How high above the ground should each outer post rise? Hint: You can make a scale drawing.

e Textbook This lesson appears in the *eTextbook.*

Cumulative Review

Subtracting Mixed Numbers Lesson 7.4

Solve the following problems.

1. Randy lives $1\frac{7}{8}$ miles from school. Anthony lives $1\frac{2}{3}$ miles from the same school. How much farther is Randy's round trip than Anthony's round trip?

2. David ran $4\frac{1}{3}$ miles on Saturday and $6\frac{3}{5}$ miles on Sunday. How much farther did David run on Sunday?

3. $7\frac{7}{9} - 4\frac{4}{6} = \blacksquare$

4. $6\frac{5}{7} - 3\frac{1}{2} = \blacksquare$

. . . .

Decimal Equivalents of Rational Numbers Lesson 7.8

Solve each problem with fractions and decimals. For each problem, check to see that your two answers are equivalent. Round your answers to three decimal places.

5. $3\frac{4}{8} + 4\frac{1}{4} = \blacksquare$

6. $3\frac{1}{5} + 1\frac{3}{6} = \blacksquare$

7. $4\frac{1}{6} - 1\frac{2}{3} = \blacksquare$

8. $6\frac{3}{8} + 1\frac{3}{4} = \blacksquare$

. . . .

Ratios and Rates Lesson 8.4

Solve.

Car A and Car B leave to go on a 390-mile trip. Car A drives slightly faster than Car B and averages about 65 miles per hour. Car B averages about 60 miles per hour. Car A makes a 40-minute stop, and Car B drives without stopping.

9. Which car will arrive first?

10. How much later will the other car arrive?

The Quik-Mart sells 12-packs of juice for $7.44, and the One-Stop Shop sells the same juice in 8-packs for $5.20.

11. How much does 1 container cost at each store?

12. What is the cheapest way to buy 48 containers?

Batting Averages and Other Division Applications Lesson 8.11

Solve.

In the first half of the Little League season, Chad started poorly and had only 8 hits in 32 at bats. For the second half, Chad improved and had 12 hits in 28 at bats.

What was Chad's batting average for

⑬ the first half of the season?

⑭ the second half of the season?

⑮ the whole season?

⑯ Jelly is sold in 10-ounce and 15-ounce jars, which cost $1.99 and $3.09, respectively. Which is the better buy?

Angles and Sides of a Triangle Lesson 9.3
Solve.

⑰ Which of the following could be the measures of the angles in a triangle?

    a. 50, 70, 90   **b.** 60, 60, 80

    c. 50, 100, 30 **d.** 70, 70, 70

⑱ Which of the following could be the measures of the angles in an isosceles triangle?

    a. 50, 50, 90   **b.** 65, 65, 50

    c. 100, 50, 30 **d.** 40, 40, 60

Fractions of a Whole Lesson 6.1
Solve for *n*.

⑲ $\frac{2}{3}$ of 15 = n ⑳ $\frac{3}{4}$ of 16 = n ㉑ $\frac{3}{3}$ of 17 = n

㉒ $\frac{4}{7}$ of 28 = n ㉓ $\frac{3}{5}$ of 30 = n ㉔ $\frac{3}{8}$ of 64 = n

Ⓔ **Textbook** This lesson is available in the *eTextbook*.

Key Ideas Review

In this chapter, you explored the components of geometrical figures.

You learned how to measure angles and compare figures to identify them as congruent or similar.

You learned how to use ratios for scales of maps and drawings.

Label the angles below as *acute, obtuse, right,* or *straight.*

1

2

3

Use the map to answer the following problems. Estimate all distances by air.

Scale: 1 inch = 400 miles

4 What is the distance from Montgomery, Alabama, to Chicago, Illinois?

5 How far is it from Miami, Florida, to Portland, Maine?

Solve the following problem.

6 Explain how these triangles are congruent by finding the measures of the angles and the lengths of the sides.

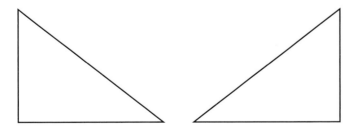

Chapter Review

Lesson 9.1 **Solve.**

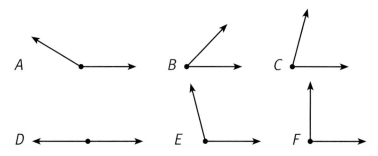

Which of the above angles are

① acute? ② straight? ③ right? ④ obtuse?

Which of the above angles could measure

⑤ 75°? ⑥ 105°? ⑦ 45°? ⑧ 90°?

Lesson 9.3 **Determine** if the following sets of numbers could be the lengths of the sides of a triangle.

⑨ 10, 10, and 8 ⑩ 11, 7, and 19 ⑪ 5, 7, and 11.5 ⑫ 6, 8, and 15

Answer the questions below.

⑬ An isosceles triangle has two known sides that measure 4 feet and 9 feet. What is the measure of the third side?

⑭ Suppose the sum of the lengths of the two sides of an equilateral triangle is 15 inches. What is the length of the third side?

Lesson 9.5 **Solve.**

⑮ Triangles *ABC* and *A'B'C'* are similar. The length of *AB* is 3, of *BC* is 8, and of *AC* is 6. If the length of *A'B'* is 9, what are the lengths of the other two sides of triangle *A'B'C'*?

Lesson 9.7 The scale on the grid of city blocks is 1 centimeter = $\frac{1}{4}$ mile. If you can travel only along grid lines, how far is it from

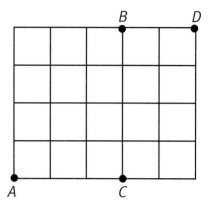

⑯ *A* to *C* and back?

⑰ *C* to *D* and back?

⑱ *A* to *D* to *B*?

Lessons 9.11–9.13 **Draw** an example of each of the following.

⑲ trapezoid

⑳ parallelogram

㉑ concave pentagon

㉒ concave quadrilateral

㉓ rhombus

㉔ square

For each pair of lines, tell whether the lines are perpendicular, parallel, or neither.

1.

2.

3.

Draw a triangle according to the clues, and then answer the questions.

4. Draw a triangle *RST* with your ruler and protractor so that

   a. side *RS* measures 5 centimeters.

   b. side *RT* measures 3 centimeters.

   c. angle *S* measures 37°.

5. How long is side *TS*?

6. What is the measure of angle *R*?

Write whether the triangles are similar or congruent. Also write which corresponding parts are equal.

7.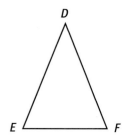

Use this figure to solve the problems.

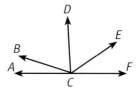

8. Name a straight angle in the figure.

9. Name two obtuse angles in the figure.

Write the correct answer.

10. Which is the missing angle measurement?

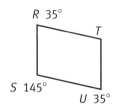

R 35°
T
S 145°
U 35°

Ⓐ 145° Ⓑ 135°

Ⓒ 45° Ⓓ 35°

11. What kind of angle is shown below?

Ⓐ straight Ⓑ obtuse

Ⓒ right Ⓓ acute

12. Which set of numbers could represent the length in centimeters of the three sides of a triangle?

Ⓐ 4, 5, 1 Ⓑ 4, 2, 5

Ⓒ 5, 6, 11 Ⓓ 5, 3, 4

13. Which figure is convex?

Ⓐ 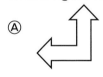 Ⓑ

Ⓒ   Ⓓ

Use this information to answer questions 14–16.

$\triangle RST \sim \triangle XYZ$, $r = 3$ cm, $s = 5$ cm, $t = 7$ cm, and $x = 6$ cm. $\angle S = 30°$

14. What is the measure of side y?

Ⓐ 14 cm Ⓑ 10 cm

Ⓒ 6 cm Ⓓ 5 cm

15. What is the measure of $\angle Y$?

Ⓐ 30° Ⓑ 45°

Ⓒ 60° Ⓓ 90°

16. If the measure of $\angle Z = 130°$, what is the measure of $\angle R$?

Ⓐ 130° Ⓑ 120°

Ⓒ 30° Ⓓ 20°

17. Which of the following is a trapezoid?

Ⓐ   Ⓑ

Ⓒ  Ⓓ

18. What is the name of the right angle?

E
D F

Ⓐ ∠FED Ⓑ ∠EDF

Ⓒ ∠DEF Ⓓ ∠DFE

19. Which is a concave shape?

Ⓐ

Ⓑ

Ⓒ

Ⓓ

20. The scale on a map is 1 inch = 15 miles. A highway on this map measures 5 inches. How many miles is the highway?

Ⓐ 5 miles   Ⓑ 15 miles

Ⓒ 60 miles   Ⓓ 75 miles

21. Find the mean. 12, 15, 15, 7, 8, 10, 10.

Ⓐ 17   Ⓑ 11

Ⓒ 10   Ⓓ 7

22. Carlos changes the tires on his car every 10,000 miles. He needs to change the tires when the odometer says 63,700. The car has 57,250 miles on it. How many more miles can he drive before he will need to change the tires?

Ⓐ 6,300   Ⓑ 6,450

Ⓒ 10,000   Ⓓ 67,250

23. Which decimal is equivalent to the fraction $\frac{4}{5}$?

Ⓐ 0.2   Ⓑ 0.4

Ⓒ 0.5   Ⓓ 0.8

24. The temperature is 0°C. What is the temperature in Fahrenheit?

Ⓐ 0°F   Ⓑ 16°F

Ⓒ 32°F   Ⓓ 60°F

25. Divide. $49\overline{)24{,}549}$

Ⓐ 501   Ⓑ 451

Ⓒ 51   Ⓓ 45

26. $5x - 2 = y$. If y is 18, what is x?

Ⓐ $x = 88$ Ⓑ $x = 20$

Ⓒ $x = 4$ Ⓓ $x = 3$

27. If you start at the ordered pair (0, 2) and move right 2 steps and then down 2 steps, at what ordered pair are you now?

Ⓐ (0, 0)   Ⓑ (2, 0)

Ⓒ (0, −2)   Ⓓ (−2, 2)

28. Which improper fraction is equivalent to $4\frac{1}{3}$?

Ⓐ $\frac{41}{3}$ Ⓑ $\frac{4}{3}$

Ⓒ $\frac{5}{3}$ Ⓓ $\frac{13}{3}$

Ⓔ **Textbook** This lesson is available in the *eTextbook*.

Use this scale drawing of a classroom to solve the problems.

Scale: 1 cm = 30 cm

29. a. What is the length and width of the teacher's desk?

   b. Four students sit at each group of student desks. About how much space does each student have?

   c. Suppose the teacher put a wastepaper basket by her desk. It measures 15 cm by 30 cm. What would be the dimensions of the basket in the drawing?

30. a. The teacher has another triangular table similar to the one in the classroom, but $\frac{1}{2}$ the size. What are the dimensions of the smaller table?

   b. What kind of triangle is the table?

Geometry and Measurement

In This Chapter You Will Learn

- how to find the area of almost any figure in a plane.
- how to make an equilateral triangle without using a ruler.
- how to make paper deltahedra (space figures) without using a ruler.

Problem Solving

Most homestead sites were simple squares. But odd-shaped pieces of property could require a lot of effort to describe and even more to understand. In an old deed, you may see units of measure that aren't used anymore, such as poles, rods, and chains. In the property descriptions below, can you tell which property is larger?

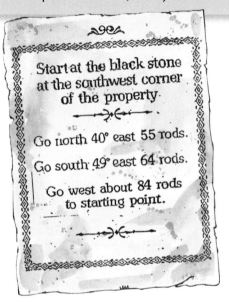

Start at the black stone at the southwest corner of the property.

Go north 40° east 55 rods.

Go south 49° east 64 rods.

Go west about 84 rods to starting point.

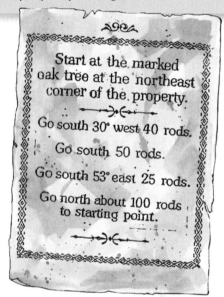

Start at the marked oak tree at the northeast corner of the property.

Go south 30° west 40 rods.

Go south 50 rods.

Go south 53° east 25 rods.

Go north about 100 rods to starting point.

Try this activity, and then answer the questions below.

Make a scale drawing of each property and compare areas. You may trace and cut the diagrams to help you.

1. What shape is each property?

2. Do you need to know the length of a rod in order to find out which property has a greater area?

3. Which property is larger?

4. How can you convince someone that your answer is correct?

Circles: Finding Circumference

Key Ideas

In every circle, the **circumference** and the **diameter** have the same relationship. Sometimes we say that a circle's circumference and diameter are proportional, are proportionate, or have the same proportion.

Jim and Kurt measured three circular objects using centimeters and recorded their results. They used a tape measure to measure the distance around the objects. Since they had a calculator, they decided to do some arithmetic to see if they could find any interesting relationships between the distances they measured. Their results are recorded in the chart below.

Circular object	Diameter d	Circumference C	$C + d$	$C - d$	$C \times d$	$C \div d$
Film reel	27.5	86.5	114.0	59.0	2,378.75	3.145
Small bottle of correction fluid	2.8	8.7	11.5			
Foam cup	8.0	25.0		17.0		

A chord is a (straight) line segment joining two points on a circle. It is not necessarily a diameter.

Copy the table above. Work in a small group to finish Jim and Kurt's calculations. Find two circular objects and measure their diameter (length of a chord through the center) and circumference (distance around). Use a calculator to complete the table.

1 Do you see anything interesting? What?

2 Do the numbers in the last four columns of your table seem about the same for each object, or do they change a great deal from object to object? What is the average of all five quotients? What is the average of the quotients for the entire class?

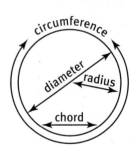

ⓔ Textbook This lesson is available in the *eTextbook.*

When we discuss circles, we often use the following terminology:

- *r* stands for the length of the radius of a circle.
- *d* stands for the length of the diameter of a circle ($d = 2r$).
- *C* stands for the length of the circumference of a circle.

The Greek letter π, pronounced "pi," is usually used to indicate the ratio of the circumference to the diameter of a circle. π cannot be written as one whole number divided by another. However, the number 3.14159 is a good approximation of π. Both 3.14 and $3\frac{1}{7}$ are used to approximate π.

$\pi = \frac{C}{d}$ or equivalently $C = \pi d$.

③ Assuming that 3.14159 is the best approximation of π to the nearest hundred thousandth, is 3.14 or $3\frac{1}{7}$ a closer approximation of π? What is the decimal approximation of $3\frac{1}{7}$ to the nearest hundred thousandth?

Suppose a circle's diameter is about 27.5 cm. The circumference can be calculated by multiplying $3\frac{1}{7}$ times 27.5.

$3\frac{1}{7} \times 27\frac{1}{2} = 86\frac{3}{7} = 86.43$ (approximately)

If we use 3.14 for π instead, we will get $3.14 \times 27.5 = 86.35$. For most purposes, either result would be satisfactory.

Given the following measures for the diameter of a circle, what is each circumference (to the nearest whole unit)?

④ 15 cm   ⑤ 21 ft   ⑥ 14 cm   ⑦ 8 mm

⑧ 12 in.   ⑨ 42 cm   ⑩ 100 cm   ⑪ 20 in.

Given the following measures for the circumference of a circle, what is the diameter (to the nearest whole unit)?

⑫ 31 mi   ⑬ 22 ft   ⑭ 308 cm   ⑮ 19 mi

| Writing + Math | **Journal** |

Explain how a circle's diameter and circumference are related.

Area of Parallelograms

Key Ideas

We can find the area of a parallelogram from its height and length.

Follow these steps to find the area of a parallelogram.

  a. Trace this parallelogram on a sheet of paper and carefully cut out the figure.

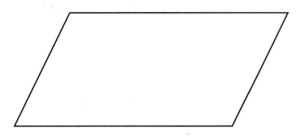

  b. Imagine or draw a line segment from one vertex that is perpendicular to the opposite side.

  c. Cut along the line segment.

  d. Move the triangle to the other side.

Answer the following questions.

① **a.** What special type of parallelogram have you made?

   b. What are the lengths of the base and height of the new figure?

② What is the area of the new figure you made?

③ What is the area of the original parallelogram?

④ **Extended Response** How could you have found the area of the original parallelogram without cutting it?

ⓔ **Textbook** This lesson is available in the *eTextbook*.

The area of a parallelogram can be calculated by multiplying the length of one of the bases by the height.

Find the area of each parallelogram.

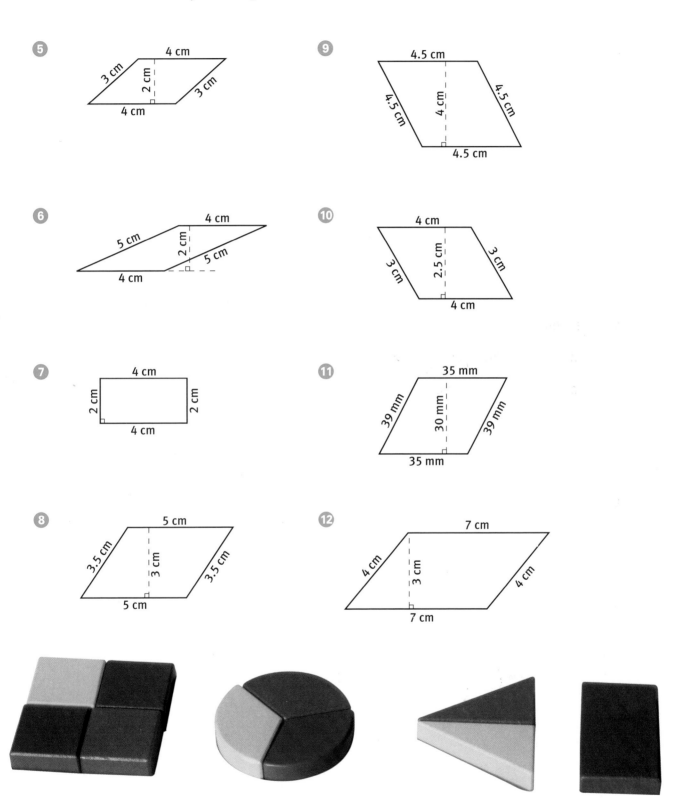

5
3 cm 4 cm 2 cm 3 cm
4 cm

9
4.5 cm 4.5 cm 4 cm 4.5 cm
4.5 cm

6
5 cm 4 cm 2 cm 5 cm
4 cm

10
4 cm 3 cm 2.5 cm 3 cm
4 cm

7
4 cm 2 cm 2 cm
4 cm

11
35 mm 39 mm 30 mm 39 mm
35 mm

8
5 cm 3.5 cm 3 cm 3.5 cm
5 cm

12
7 cm 4 cm 3 cm 4 cm
7 cm

Area of Triangles

Key Ideas

You can find the area of any triangle by finding its base and corresponding height and thinking about the area of a parallelogram.

Follow these steps to find the area of a right triangle.

a. Draw or trace this right triangle.

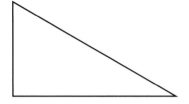

b. Draw or trace another triangle that is congruent to your first one.

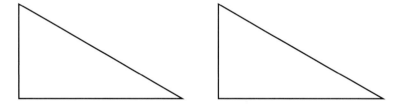

c. Cut out the triangles, and put them together to make a rectangle.

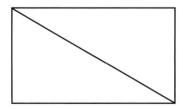

d. Measure the base and height of your rectangle in centimeters.

e. Find the area of your rectangle in square centimeters.

f. The area of each triangle is one half the area of the rectangle.

❶ What is the area of the rectangle above? What is the area of each triangle?

❷ **Extended Response** How could you have found the area of your original triangle without making a copy and cutting? Explain your answer.

ⓔTextbook This lesson is available in the *eTextbook*.

Base and height can describe measurements of a triangle just as they describe measurements of a parallelogram. We choose one side of the triangle as the base. The height is the length of the line segment drawn perpendicular to the base from the opposite vertex. In a right triangle, we can choose the base and height as the sides of the right angle.

These are right triangles.

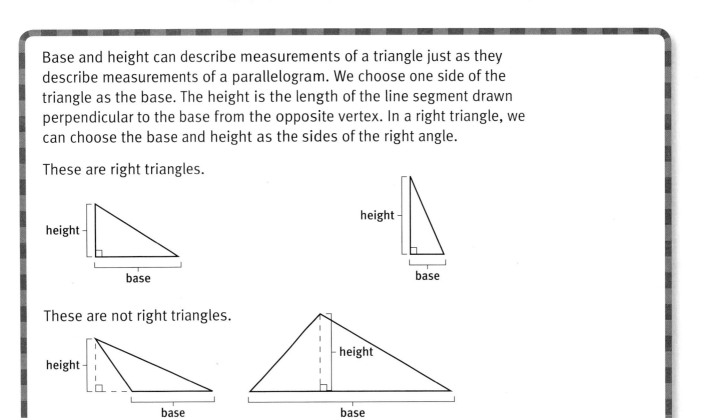

These are not right triangles.

Find the area of these right triangles. You may choose any convenient side as the base.

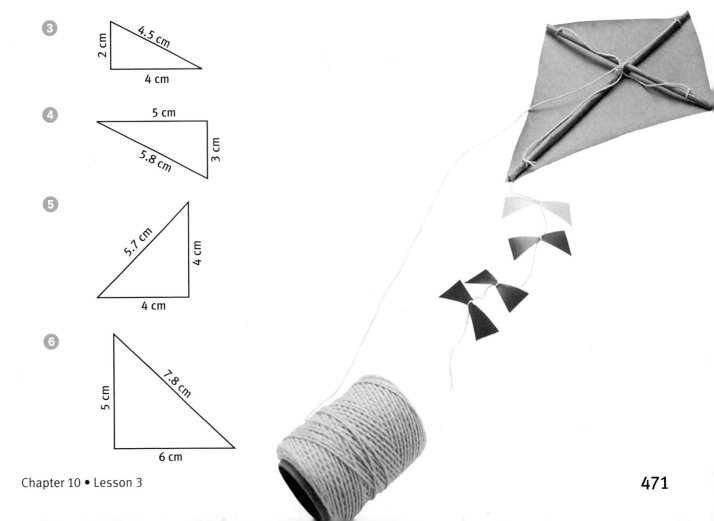

3
4.5 cm
2 cm
4 cm

4
5 cm
5.8 cm
3 cm

5
5.7 cm
4 cm
4 cm

6
5 cm
7.8 cm
6 cm

Follow these steps to find the area of any triangle.

a. Draw any triangle. Label it *ABC*, with *BC* as the base and *AD* as the height. For example,

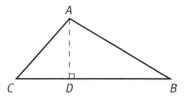

b. Use your triangle to draw a parallelogram (*AEBC*) with *BC* as the base and *AC* as a side. For example,

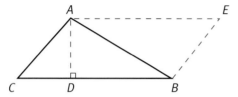

Area of a triangle: The area of a triangle is one half the product of the length of its base and its height. This is sometimes written as:

$$A = \tfrac{1}{2}b \times h$$

Or

$$A = \tfrac{1}{2}bh$$

⑦ Is the area of your parallelogram *AEBC* equal to the length of its base *BC* times its height *AD*?

⑧ In your drawing, is △*ABC* congruent to △*BAE*? If so, then the area of △*ABC* must be half the area of parallelogram *AEBC*.

ⓔ Textbook This lesson is available in the *eTextbook*.

Find the area of each figure.

9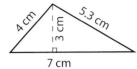

12

10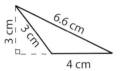

13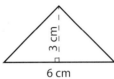

11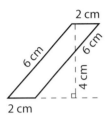

14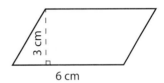

Solve.

15 The Great Pyramid at Giza has four triangular faces that meet at the top. The base of one of these surfaces is about 745 feet and the height of the triangular face is about 450 feet. Find the area of one face of the pyramid.

16 **Extended Response** ▶ Find the area of the shaded region in this figure. How did you find it?

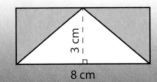

Area of a Circle

Key Ideas

The area of a circle is determined by its radius.

We can estimate the area of a circle by drawing the circle on graph paper and counting the squares that seem to be mostly inside the circle.

Look at the circles and squares surrounding them in Figures 1 and 2. Each square in the graph has sides 1 cm long. Answer the following questions.

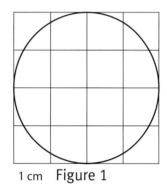

1 cm   Figure 1

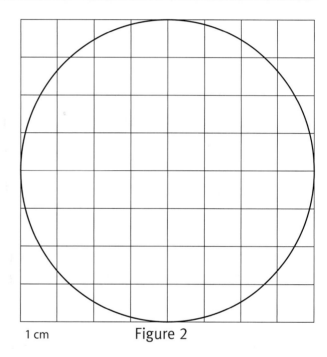

1 cm   Figure 2

1 Consider Figure 1.

a. What is the length of a side of the big square? What is the radius of the circle? (Remember, the radius is half the diameter.) What is the circumference of the circle?

b. How many of the little squares are entirely inside the circle? Mostly inside the circle? Mostly outside the circle?

c. What is the area of the big square?

d. About what would you estimate the area of the circle to be?

2 Consider Figure 2.

a. What is the length of a side of the big square? What is the radius of the circle? What is the circumference of the circle?

b. Count the little squares that are entirely inside the circle, mostly inside, about half inside, and mostly outside of the circle.

c. What is the area of the big square? Estimate the area of the circle.

This circle has been divided into 12 equal pie-shaped pieces called *sectors*. The 12 sectors have been cut out and rearranged below the circle. They form a figure that resembles a parallelogram.

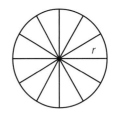

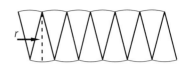

3 About what is the height of that figure?

4 What is the circumference *C* of a circle with radius *r*?

5 Is the base of your figure about half the circumference of the circle or πr?

6 What is the approximate area of your figure? How did you determine this?

7 If we assume the area of a circle is πr^2,

a. about what is the area of the circle in Figure 1 on page 474?

b. about what is the area of the circle in Figure 2?

c. are these areas approximately the same as the areas you estimated for the circles from the squares in the figures?

The area of a circle is given by the formula: $A = \pi \times r \times r = \pi r^2$. Using an estimate of 3.14 for π, find the circumference and area of each circle.

8 $r = 3$ cm

9 $r = 30$ cm

10 $r = 300$ cm

11 $r = 3,000$ cm

12 $r = 7$ cm

13 $r = 70$ cm

14 If you double the radius of a circle, what happens to the circumference? What happens to the area?

15 If you multiply the radius of a circle by 10, what happens to the circumference? What happens to the area?

Algebra **16** If you multiply the radius of a circle by any number, *n*, what happens to the circumference? What happens to the area?

Key Ideas

We can find the area of unusual figures by breaking them into parts for which we know how to find the areas.

Or, we may be able to find the area of a larger figure and then subtract an area we can calculate. We may imagine moving figures together so that we can use formulas we know.

Solve.

1. **Extended Response** In Figure A, the top and bottom segments are parallel. What is the distance between them? See how many different ways you can figure out the area. Do all the methods give the same answer? Describe two different methods.

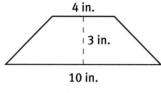

Figure A

2. In Figure B, what is the length of the entire figure? What is the length of the base (top missing line segment) of the missing triangle? What is the height of the entire figure? What is the height of the missing triangle? Find the area of Figure B.

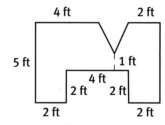

Figure B

e Textbook This lesson is available in the *eTextbook*.

Find the areas of the figures below to the nearest hundredth of a square unit. Use π = 3.14.

3

3 ft

6 ft

3 ft

6 ft

7
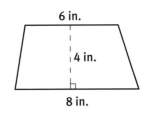

6 in.

4 in.

8 in.

4

8 in.

2 in.

2 in.

6 in.

2 in.

8
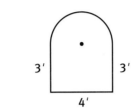

3 '

3 '

4 '

5

6 m

4 m

8 m

9
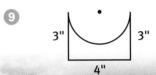

3"

3"

4"

6 Find the perimeter of the figure in Problem 3.

10 Find the perimeter of the figure in Problem 8.

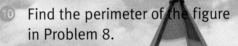

Although homesteaders came from many different cultural backgrounds, most of them practiced the art of quilting. They sewed pieces of cloth into colorful blankets that often displayed geometric patterns.

Imagine you are making a reproduction of this 1882 quilt. You will sew the red, blue, and yellow design onto 4-inch white squares. You have a rectangular piece of blue cloth 12 inches by 15 inches and a rectangular piece of red cloth 18 inches by 24 inches.

Do you have enough red and blue cloth to make 100 quilt squares?

Scale 1:2

Keila solved the problem this way:

I Made a Plan.

A. Think of the design as a combination of figures with simple shapes.
B. Measure the dimensions of the figures in the photo.
C. Calculate the area of each figure.
D. Figure out how much of each color I need.
E. See if I have enough square inches of each color.

Think about Keila's strategy, and answer these questions.

1 What simple figures could you use for this design?

2 What are the dimensions of one of those figures on the actual quilt?

3 How would you find the area of that figure?

4 Do you think Keila's strategy will work? Explain.

Tyler solved the problem another way:

I also decided to Make a Plan. Part of my plan was to Make a Scale Drawing.

A. Make a scale drawing of the design on grid paper.
B. Count squares to find out the area of each part of the design.
C. Figure out how much of each color I need.
D. See if I have enough square inches of each color.

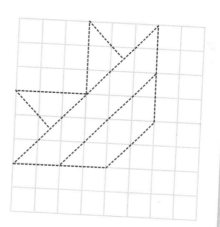

Think about Tyler's strategy, and answer the following questions.

5 About how many squares are in the smaller of the two trapezoids Tyler has drawn so far?

6 How many inches does each space on the diagram represent?

7 How many square inches does each square on the diagram represent?

8 About how many square inches of red cloth does the smaller trapezoid represent?

9 Do you think Tyler's strategy will work? Explain.

10 Solve the problem. Use any strategy you think will work. What strategy did you use? Why?

Cumulative Review

Complete the following sentences by telling whether the answer is *positive* or *negative*.

1 If a negative number is subtracted from a negative number with smaller absolute value, the answer is ▢.

2 If a negative number is subtracted from a negative number with greater absolute value, the answer is ▢.

3 If a negative number is added to a positive number with smaller absolute value, the answer is ▢.

Solve.

4 $(-7) + |-8| = $ ▢   **5** $(-5) - (-9) = $ ▢   **6** $10 - |-12| = $ ▢   **7** $-3 - |7| = $ ▢

Patterns Lesson 4.10

Complete the pattern and state the pattern rule.

8 $-8, -4, 0, $ ▢, ▢, ▢, ▢, 20

9 $-\frac{1}{16}, -\frac{1}{4}, -1, $ ▢, ▢, ▢, -256

10 $81, 27, 9, 3, $ ▢, ▢, ▢, ▢, $\frac{1}{81}$

Decimals and Money Lesson 3.1

Solve.

Ali is in a department store and chooses a jacket for $89.99, 2 shirts that cost $19.99 each, and a pair of pants for $27.50. He has $150 to spend.

11 Does Ali have enough money to pay for what he has selected?

12 If he is short, how much more money does Ali need? If he has enough, how much does he have left?

Decimals and Money **Lesson 3.1**

Solve.

⑬ Pat buys cat food when it is on sale. The current sale is "buy 3 cans, get 1 free." If the price per can is $1.25, how much money does Pat need to purchase 12 cans?

⑭ At the school cafeteria, Janie bought a sandwich for $2.09, a salad for $1.19, and fruit for $0.79. She had 3 one-dollar bills, 3 quarters, and 3 dimes. Did she have enough money for her lunch? If not, what did she need?

Standard Notation for Functions **Lesson 5.10**

Complete each function table, and graph the ordered pairs for each.

⑮ $y = 3x - 4$

x	y
0	▨
1	▨
▨	2

⑯ $y = \frac{x}{3} + 2$

x	y
6	▨
▨	5
12	▨

Dividing Fractions **Lesson 7.6**

Divide. Reduce when possible.

⑰ $16 \div \frac{4}{3} = $ ▨

⑱ $\frac{1}{2} \div \frac{1}{4} = $ ▨

⑲ $9 \div \frac{3}{5} = $ ▨

Solve.

⑳ A 12-foot piece of lumber needs to be split into pieces that are about $1\frac{1}{4}$ feet long. How many of those pieces can be cut from it?

Key Ideas

There are three ways we can modify a figure to obtain a congruent figure. They are rotation, translation, and reflection.

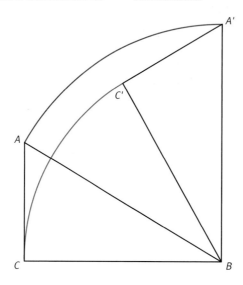

If we rotate $\triangle ABC$ around point B, each point of the triangle moves to a new point. In this figure, A goes to A', and C goes to C'. You can think of this as tracing $\triangle ABC$ on a sheet of tracing paper directly on top of the triangle. Stick a tack through the tracing paper at point B. Turn the tracing paper, and the traced triangle will be where $\triangle A'B'C'$ is in the figure above.

Is $\triangle A'B'C' \cong \triangle ABC$?

Yes, when a figure is rotated around a point in this way, the resulting figure is congruent to the original.

If we slide or translate the tracing along a line in a particular direction without turning or rotating it at all, we would still have a congruent figure as in the picture on the next page. Here the triangle slid along a straight line to the right a distance of $3\frac{1}{2}$ inches. The resulting triangle, $\triangle A''B''C''$, is congruent to the original $\triangle ABC$. This is called a *translation*.

e Textbook This lesson is available in the *eTextbook*.

Using nothing but rotations and translations, you can move many figures to fit on top of figures to which they are congruent.

There are usually many different ways to combine translations and rotations to show that one figure fits on top of another congruent figure. Possible examples of a translation and rotation that can fit $\triangle ABC$ on top of $\triangle EFG$ include the following:

- We can first slide, or translate, $\triangle ABC$ to a place where C is on top of G. Then $\triangle A'B'C'$ can be rotated clockwise about point G until B' is on F and A' is on E,

OR

- we could have translated C to G and then rotated the triangle clockwise around G until A was on E and B was on F.

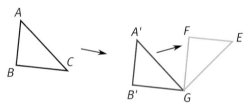

Extended Response **For** each of the following pairs of congruent figures, describe a combined translation and rotation that would place one figure on top of the other.

1

2

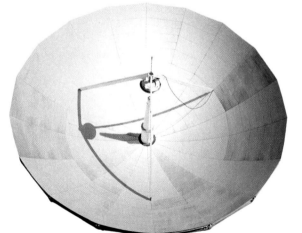

Extended Response **For** each of the following pairs of congruent figures, describe a combined translation and rotation that would place one figure on top of the other.

3

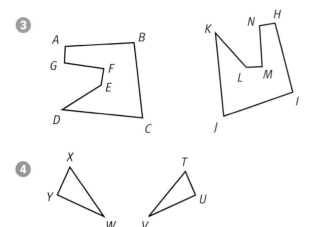

4

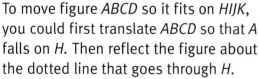

5 Were you able to describe a translation and rotation that would place △*XYW* on top of △*TUV*? Do the two triangles appear to be congruent? What is the difficulty?

When two figures are mirror images of each other, we usually can't make one fit on top of the other using just translations and rotations. We need one more kind of movement. We can change the location of a figure by flipping it over to get its mirror image. This is called a *reflection*.

To move figure *ABCD* so it fits on *HIJK*, you could first translate *ABCD* so that *A* falls on *H*. Then reflect the figure about the dotted line that goes through *H*.

Textbook This lesson is available in the *eTextbook*.

For Problems 6–10, trace or copy the object onto your paper and perform the actions described. Draw your result.

6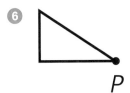

Rotate half a turn clockwise about point *P*.

7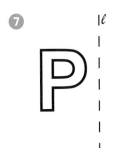

Reflect about line *ℓ*.

8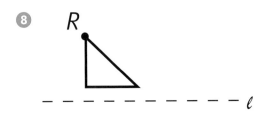

Reflect about line *ℓ*. Then translate down 0.5 in.

9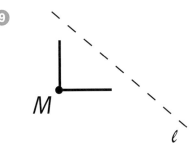

Reflect about line *ℓ*. Then rotate a quarter turn about point *M'*.

10 **Extended Response** Describe another way to translate, rotate, or reflect the figure in Problem 6 that yields the same result.

Symmetry

Key Ideas

If you can fold a plane figure along a line so that the two resulting parts match exactly, then that line is called a *line of symmetry*. If you can rotate a figure about a central point, called the *center of rotation*, for less than a full turn and get that same figure, the figure has rotational symmetry.

Look at the face. If you place a mirror on line *AB* and look at the face from the side, do the drawing and the mirror image match? We say an image like that has *symmetry*.

Every point on one side of line *AB* has a corresponding point on the other side that is exactly the same distance from *AB*. Line *AB* is called a *line of symmetry*, and this kind of symmetry is called *line symmetry*.

There are other kinds of symmetry. A plane figure has *rotational symmetry* if you can rotate it about its center less than a full turn and it looks exactly as it did at the start.

A square has 4 lines of symmetry which are labeled in the diagram to the right.

The square can be rotated to fit on top of itself.

$\frac{1}{4}$ of a circle (90°)

$\frac{1}{2}$ of a circle (180°)

$\frac{3}{4}$ of a circle (270°)

full circle (360°)

The smallest angle by which we can rotate a square and have it look the same is a quarter turn, or 90°, so a square's angle of rotation is 90°. If there is no angle of rotation less than 360°, the figure has an angle of rotation of 0°.

e Textbook This lesson is available in the *eTextbook*.

For each of the following figures, copy the figure, and draw the lines of symmetry. Then write the number of lines of symmetry and the smallest angle of rotation beneath the figure.

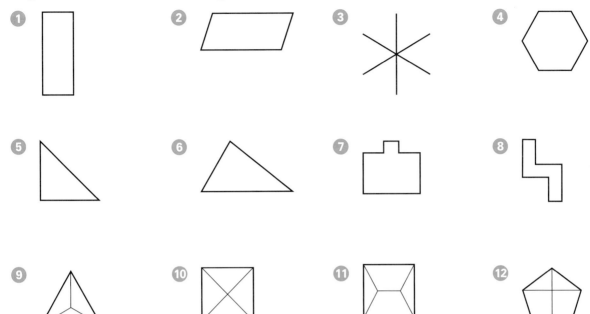

1. 2. 3. 4.

5. 6. 7. 8.

9. 10. 11. 12.

Writing + Math **Journal**

Can a plane figure have more than one center of rotation? Draw a picture or explain your reasoning.

Key Ideas

Models of regular figures can be created using nothing more than a long strip of paper.

Begin with a long strip of gummed tape or receipt paper and fold the paper as shown below. These creases are known as mountain folds because they bend up like a mountain. If you are using gummed tape, start with the gummed side up.

Step 1

Step 2

Step 3

Step 4

Step 5

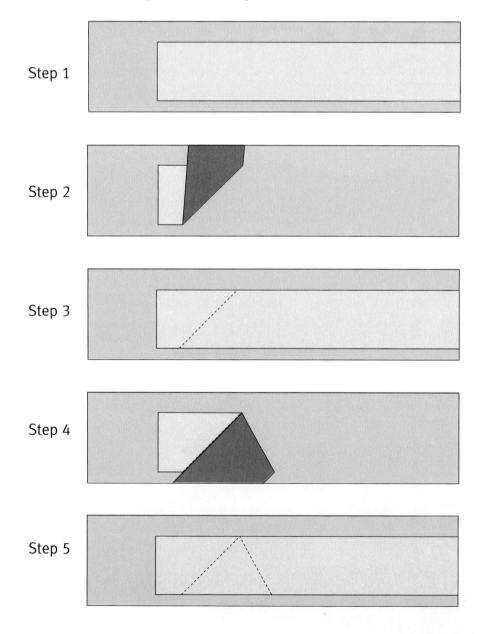

eTextbook This lesson is available in the *eTextbook*.

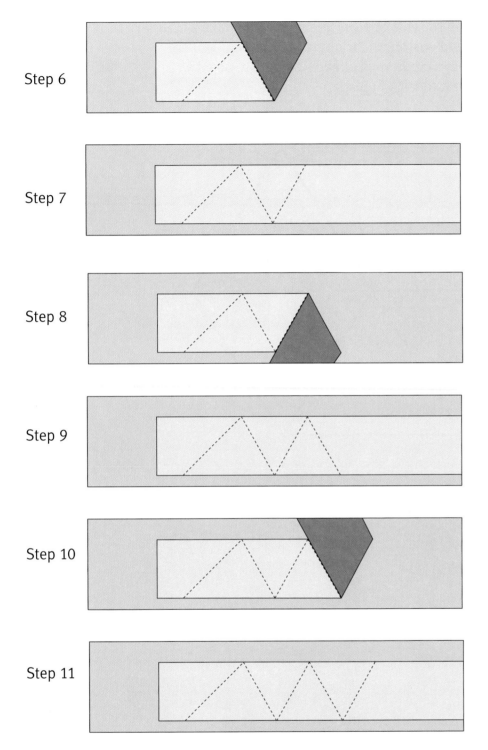

Step 6

Step 7

Step 8

Step 9

Step 10

Step 11

Continue folding to make a long string of triangles (at least 50).

Answer the following questions.

1. What kind of triangle is the first one in Step 5?

2. What kind of triangle does the triangle in step 11 look like?

3. What do you suppose would happen if you kept folding like this?

Experiment and play with these triangles. See if you can make a hexagon like this by folding and pasting the triangles together. If you are using gummed tape, remember that there is already glue on it, so all you need to do is moisten it to get it to stick in place.

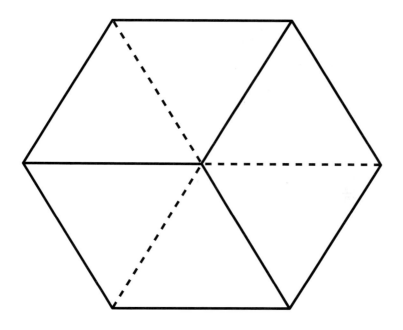

ⓔTextbook This lesson is available in the *eTextbook*.

See if you can fold the triangles into one big triangle like the one below.

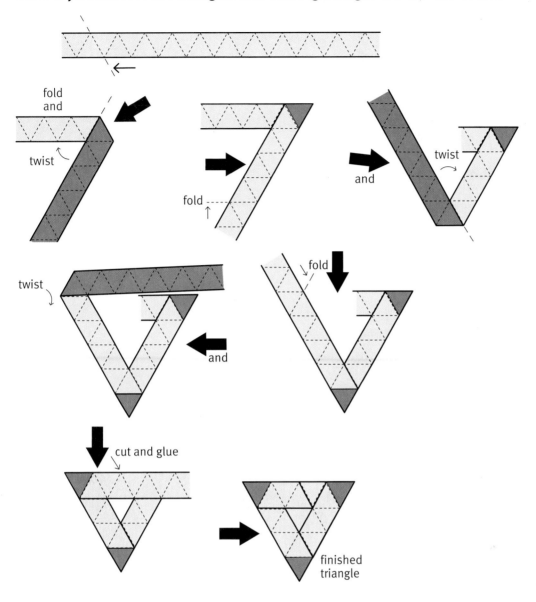

fold and

twist

fold

and twist

twist and

fold

cut and glue

finished triangle

Extended Response ▶ Answer the following questions.

④ What was the hardest part of making these figures?

⑤ Is the big triangle equilateral? How do you know?

Key Ideas

Flexagons are interesting figures that can help us in our study of symmetry.

Building your flexagon

- Take a strip of ten equilateral triangles. Crease each fold line firmly in both directions and mark the first and last triangle with a star as shown.

- Using the guide your teacher gives you, place your strip of triangles on the guide as shown. Then fold the strip as shown in the next three figures, without lifting the triangle from the guide.

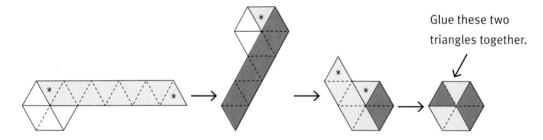

Glue these two triangles together.

- Glue the two starred triangles together.

Flex your flexagon by completing the following steps:

- Place the flexagon back on the guide (matching the folds on the guide so that the two overlapping triangles are at the top).

- Gently lift it off the guide, and bring the three alternative corners at A, B, and C together UNDER the flexagon.

- The top of the flexagon will pop open, revealing a new face with no design on it.

e Textbook This lesson is available in the *eTextbook*.

Draw a design on this new face. Remember that the design affects its symmetry. Here are some possibilities to get you started, but try to think of some designs of your own.

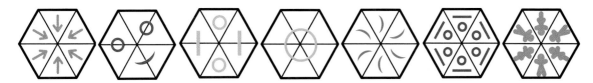

Continue to flex your flexagon by bringing the three alternate corners together below the flexagon. If you try this and it doesn't open, don't force it. Flatten it out and try again with another set of alternate corners. You will soon be an expert at this.

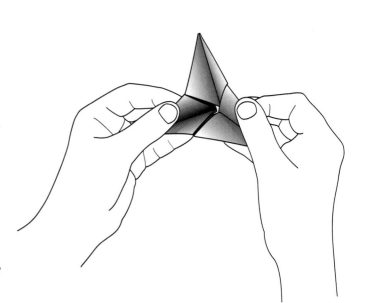

Examine the flexagon you created.

1. Does your original design still have the same number of lines of symmetry when it reappears? If not, how did they change?

2. Does the overall design still have the same rotational symmetry? If not, how did it change?

3. Build more flexagons, and make designs on them that have

    a. 6 lines of symmetry and 60° rotational symmetry.

    b. 3 lines of symmetry and 120° rotational symmetry.

    c. 2 lines of symmetry and 180° rotational symmetry.

4. Build a flexagon that has all of the above symmetries on it.

 **Journal**

Is there any way to make a flexagon that has more than 6 lines of symmetry or a rotational symmetry of less than 60°? Explain why or why not.

Space Figures

Key Ideas

Figures such as polygons and circles are flat, and we can think of them lying entirely in an endless flat surface called a *plane*. We will call figures that do not fit in a single plane *space figures*.

Here are some of the polyhedra (polygons joined together to form a closed surface) with which you may be familiar.

A **pyramid** is a figure formed by connecting all points on the boundary of a polygon to a point not in the plane of the polygon.

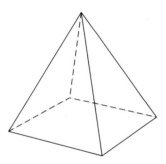 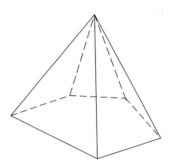

A **prism** has two congruent polygonal bases that are parallel, connected by parallelograms.

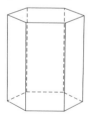 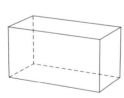 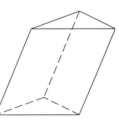 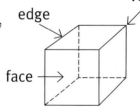

All polyhedra have some number of vertices, edges, and faces.

A **face** refers to one of the polygons in the space figure.

An **edge** is a line segment where two faces meet.

A **vertex** is a point where three or more edges meet.

Another name for a triangular pyramid (a pyramid where all the faces are triangles) is a *tetrahedron*.

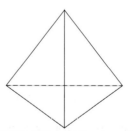

ⓔTextbook This lesson is available in the *eTextbook*.

How many faces, edges, and vertices does it have?

As you can see from the diagram, it has 4 faces (3 slanted faces and a base), 6 edges, and 4 vertices.

Space figures can have symmetry just like plane figures do, but they rotate about axes of symmetry instead of a center point. An **axis of symmetry** is an imaginary line through the center of a figure, around which the parts are symmetrically arranged. In the same way that the earth has an axis about which it rotates, we can rotate space figures about an axis of symmetry.

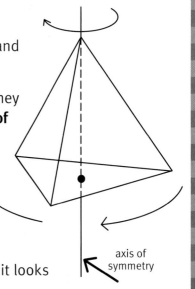

axis of symmetry

In the tetrahedron shown, all of the faces are eqilateral triangles. The order of the axis of symmetry shown is 3. Another way to say this is that if you rotate the object $\frac{1}{3}$ of a turn, or 120°, it looks exactly the same as when you started.

Solve.

1. What is another name for a prism with squares for all faces?

2. How many faces, edges, and vertices does it have?

3. Name and describe some other polyhedron from previous lessons.

Use these drawings of other space figures to answer the following questions.

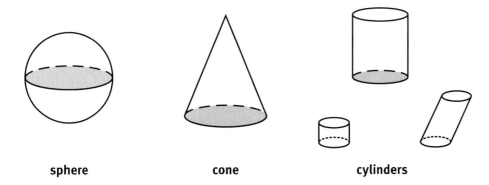

| sphere | cone | cylinders |

4. What do a cone and a pyramid have in common?

5. What do a prism and a cylinder have in common?

6. What do a cone and a cylinder have in common?

Sometimes we make space figures by cutting out plane figures and folding them or sticking them together. These plane figures are sometimes called *nets*.

Trace the nets on pages 496. Cut along the solid lines and fold along any dashed lines. For each figure you create, give its name and tell how many vertices, edges, and faces it has.

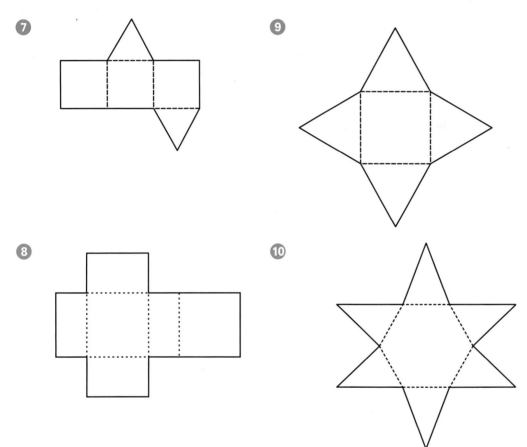

7

9

8

10

ⓔ Textbook This lesson is available in the *eTextbook*.

Answer the following questions.

⑪ Can you draw a net for a sphere?

⑫ Can you draw a net for a cube?

Try to make a net for a three-dimensional figure, cut it out, fold and stick it together along its edges to make the figure. Then count its vertices, edges, and faces and answer the following questions.

⑬ Do all the models you made satisfy the equation $V + F = E + 2$ where V represents the number of vertices, F represents the number of faces, and E represents the number of edges in the figure?

⑭ Which space figures have an axis about which you can rotate the figure $\frac{1}{2}$ of a turn and have the object look exactly the same as before?

⑮ Which models have an axis about which you can rotate the model $\frac{1}{3}$ of a turn and have the object look the same? $\frac{1}{4}$ of a turn? $\frac{1}{5}$ of a turn?

⑯ **Extended Response** Describe the figure below using correct mathematical language.

Building Deltahedra

Key Ideas

Models of space figures can be created using nets.

In Lesson 10.8, you folded strips of paper into strings of equilateral triangles. In this lesson, you will use these strips to make a pentagonal dipyramid.

Constructing a Pentagonal Dipyramid

With the dull side of the tape facing you, take two strips of 6 triangles each, and lay them over each other so that they look like this.

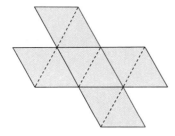

Mark every other side of the boundary as shown.

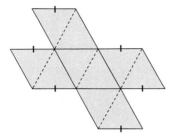

From the remainder of your folded tape, cut 6 double triangle pieces like this.

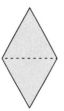

e Textbook This lesson is available in the *eTextbook*.

Connect the model by matching up each marked edge with an unmarked edge beside it and gluing the two together with one of the six double triangle pieces. Glue one of the triangles on the double triangle to one of the meeting faces so that the other triangle of the double triangle hangs over the edge (where the faces are to meet). Then connect the other triangle to the other meeting face. Continue doing this until all of the double triangles have been used and all of the open edges are covered.

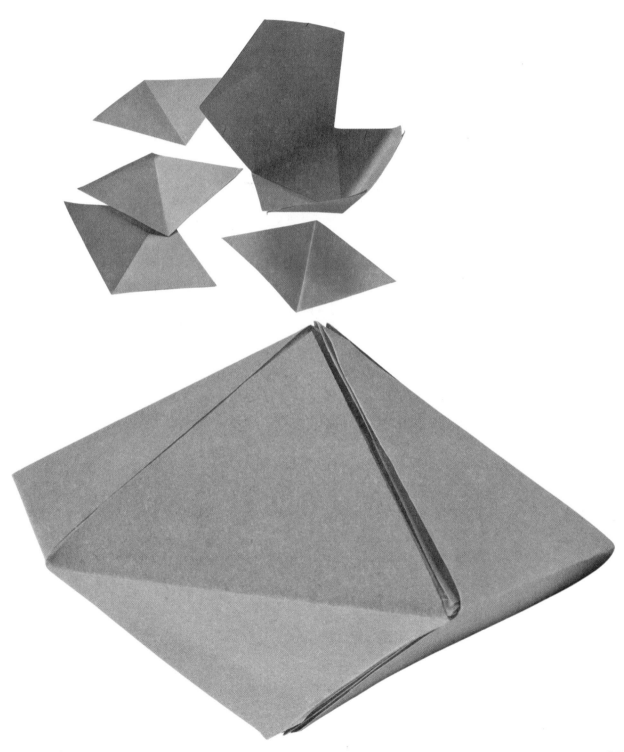

If all the faces of a polyhedron (a space figure made of polygons) are equilateral triangles, that polyhedron is called a deltahedron. This is because the Greek capital letter Δ (delta) is shaped like an equilateral triangle. On this and the next page are eight drawings of deltahedra (plural form of deltahedron), accompanied by their net diagrams. (Remember, a net is a representation of the faces of a space figure in a plane.) See how many of these you can make with your equilateral triangles.

The pictures on this page and the next may give you ideas about how to use the net diagrams to build these deltahedra with the folded tape. You do not have to use these; they are simply examples of configurations that will work. Be creative and devise your own methods. Experiment to find ways to glue pieces of tape together to construct either the deltahedra shown or those you create yourself.

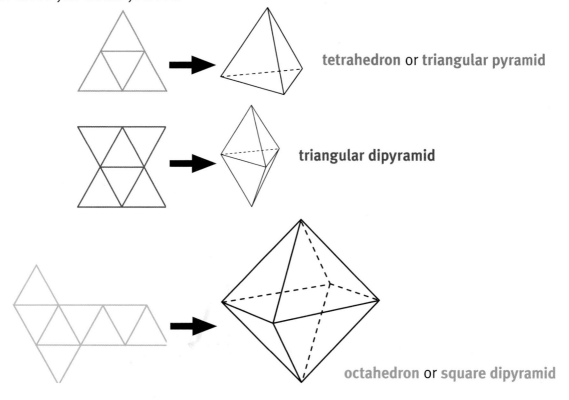

tetrahedron or triangular pyramid

triangular dipyramid

octahedron or square dipyramid

Here are some examples of deltahedra and their nets.

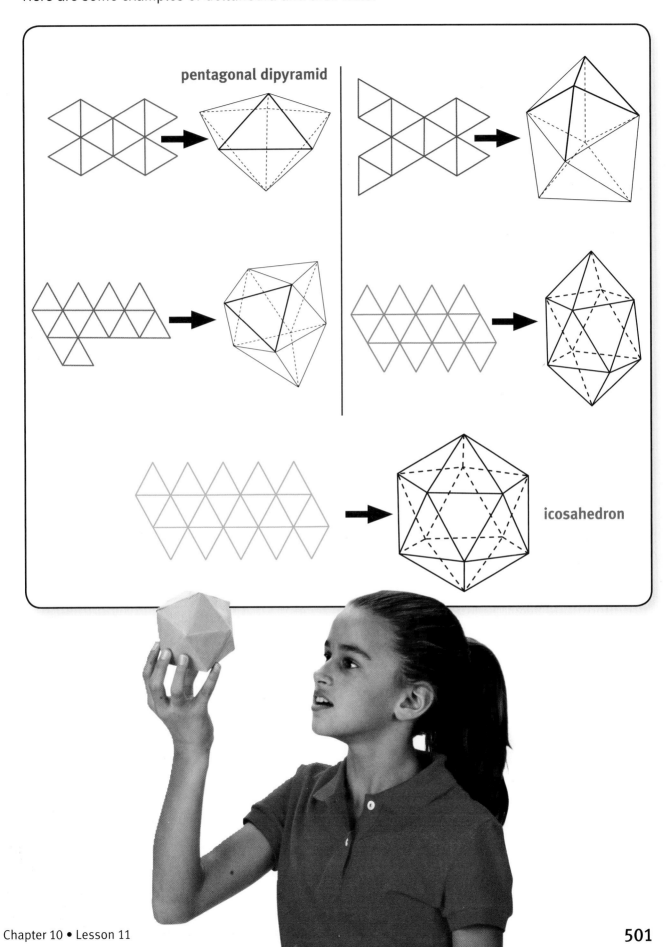

pentagonal dipyramid

icosahedron

Key Ideas

Surface area is the sum of the areas of all the surfaces on a space figure.

In other words, if you needed to wrap an object in paper, the surface area would tell you the minimum amount of paper you would need to cover the entire surface of the object. If you think about the net that could be folded to make a certain space figure, you can calculate the surface area of that space figure easily.

Find the surface area of the boxes made from these nets. Remember to write the units in your answers.

1
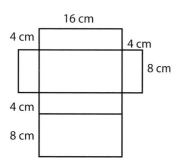
16 cm
4 cm
4 cm
8 cm
4 cm
8 cm

2
5"
5"
5"
5"
5"

4
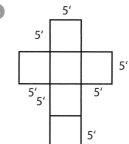
5′
5′
5′
5′
5′
5′

5
1 m
1 m   4 m   1 m
3 m
4 m
1 m

3
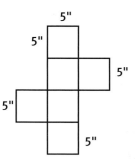
4"   16"   4"
4"
4"
4"
4"

6
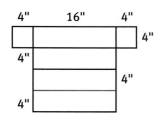
s   s
s
s
s
s
s

eTextbook This lesson is available in the *eTextbook*.

For each of the following nets, decide whether it would make a closed box if you cut it out and folded along the remaining line segments. If so, give the total surface area of the box. If not, write *no*.

7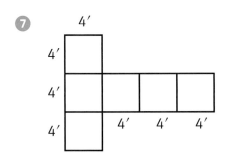

10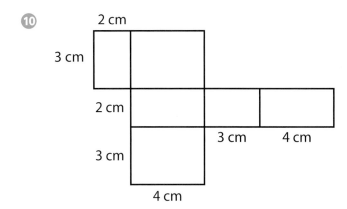

8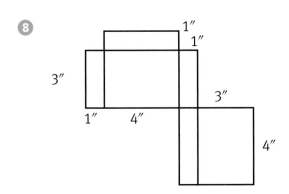

11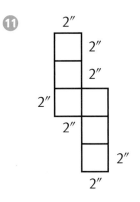

9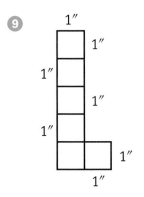

12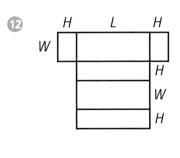

Draw a net for the figures in Problems 13–16. Calculate the total surface area for each space figure.

13 A cube 5 centimeter on a side

14 A cube 3 centimeter on a side

15 A rectangular box that is 3″ by 4″ by 5″

16 A rectangular box that is 3″ by 3″ by 5″

Calculate the total surface area. Draw a net if it helps.

17 A rectangular box that is $\frac{1}{2}$″ by 1″ by 2″

18 A cube that is $\frac{1}{2}$ inch on a side

19 A cube that is 0.5 centimeter on a side

20 A rectangular box that is 0.7 cm by 0.3 cm by 1.2 cm

21 A rectangular box that is 1.25 cm by 2.5 cm by 3 cm

22 A rectangular box that is $1\frac{1}{4}$″ by $2\frac{1}{2}$″ by 3″

In order to answer the following questions, you may want to put cubes together to make the space figures. Calculating the total length of all the edges may seem easier if you look at the actual figure rather than the net.

23. If the edges of a cube are each 1 unit long, what is the total length of all of the edges? What is the total surface area of the cube? What is the volume of the cube?

24. If the edges of a cube are each 2 units long, what is the total length of all of the edges? What is the total surface area of the cube? What is the volume of the cube?

25. If the edges of a cube are each 3 units long, what is the total length of all of the edges? What is the total surface area of the cube? What is the volume of the cube?

26. Using the information from Problems 23, 24, and 25, copy and complete the following chart.

Length of one edge:	1 unit	2 units	3 units
Total length of all edges:	12 units	▨	▨
Surface area:	▨	24 units²	▨
Volume:	▨	▨	27 units³

27. Look at your chart. By what could you multiply the numbers for the first cube in order to find the corresponding numbers for the second cube's total length of the edges, surface area, and volume?

28. By what could you multiply the numbers for the first cube in order to find the corresponding numbers for the third cube's total length of the edges, surface area, and volume?

 Journal

What patterns do you see in Problems 26–28? What would total edges, surface area and volume be for a 4-unit cube?

Volume

Key Ideas

The volume of a space figure is the amount of space occupied by that figure. Volume can be measured in cubic units.

The area of a plane figure is the number of square units of the region inside it. The perimeter of a plane figure is the sum of the lengths of all its sides.

The cubic centimeter (abbreviated cm³) is a unit of volume.

This cube has a volume of one cubic centimeter (1 cm³). Each of its edges is one centimeter long. When we measure liquid volume or capacity in the metric system, we use fractions of liters.

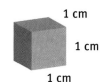

1 ml = 1 cm³

Therefore, if we filled the cube with water, it would contain 1 milliliter.

Other units of volume include cubic meters (m³), cubic feet (ft³), cubic inches (in.³), and cubic yards (yd³).

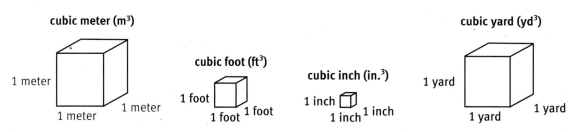

Find the volume of each solid.

1

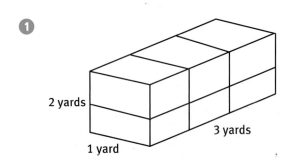

2

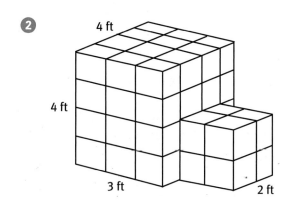

What is the volume of each of these rectangular boxes?

3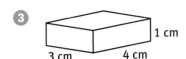
3 cm   4 cm   1 cm

5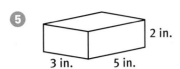
3 in.   5 in.   2 in.

4
2 m   2 m   2 m

6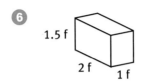
1.5 f   2 f   1 f

What is the volume of each box?

7 4 in. by 3 in. by 3 in.

8 3 ft by 3 ft by 3 ft

9 3 in. by 12 in. by 0.5 in.

10 5 in. by 4 in. by 1 ft

Solve the following problems. Be sure to use correct units.

11 What is the volume in liters of a water-filled cube 10 cm on each side?

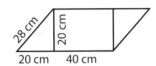
28 cm   20 cm   20 cm   40 cm

12 **Extended Response** Brent and Sarah are helping to make scenery for a school play. They need six figures like the one above. They are going to cut the figures from a large rectangular sheet of purple paper that is 40 centimeters wide and 100 centimeters long.

a. Sarah says they will need more paper. How could she know this?

b. Draw a picture to find out how many figures Brent and Sarah can cut from the single sheet of purple paper.

c. How many sheets of paper do Brent and Sarah need?

13 Mr. Chan has a rectangular garden that he wants to fertilize. The garden is 20 meters long and 18 meters wide. Each bag of fertilizer can cover 100 square meters.

a. What is the area of Mr. Chan's garden?

b. How many bags of fertilizer should he buy? Will he have any fertilizer left over?

The bulletin board in Mrs. Ruiz's classroom is a rectangle that is 3 meters long and 1 meter high. She wants to display students' drawings. Each picture is on a sheet of paper 20 centimeters long and 20 centimeters wide.

⓮ Can she display a picture from every one of the 30 students without the pictures overlapping?

⓯ What is the greatest number of pictures she could display without overlapping?

Find the area and perimeter of each figure.

⓰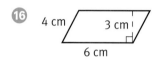

⓱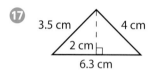

⓲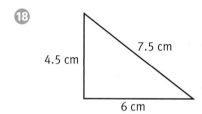

Solve the following problems. Be sure to use correct units.

⓳ Draw a rectangle with an area of 15 cm² and a perimeter of 16 cm.

⓴ Liang works at Waterworld and wants to figure out how much water the new dolphin's swimming pool will hold. It measures 320 meters long, 150 meters wide, and 11 meters deep. How many cubic meters of water would it hold if it were filled to the top?

㉑ Ms. Jain built a wooden storage shed in her backyard, and she wants to paint the outside of it. The shed is 6 feet tall, 8 feet wide, and 10 feet deep. She needs to paint the 4 sides (including the door) and the flat roof, and she wants to use 2 coats of paint. She is using cans of paint that cover 100 square feet each. How many cans will she need?

📧 **Textbook** This lesson is available in the *eTextbook*.

22 The Sanfords are planning to fence in their backyard. The yard is 56 feet across and 25 feet from front to back. Their house is 42 feet across and 31 feet from front to back. They would like the fence to start at a back corner of the house, run to the side of the yard, go around the sides and back of the yard, and run back to the house. How much fencing must they buy?

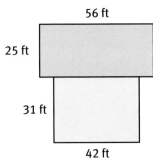

23 Jabari is looking for an apartment. He needs a lot of space in his bedroom (130 square feet), so he wants to check to make sure each apartment he spends time visiting has a large enough bedroom. If the apartment manager at BareBones apartments says the bedroom in apartment A is 11 feet long, 10 feet wide, and 10 feet tall, will there be enough space? Explain your answer.

24 Holly needs to find a storage container for her cousin's toy blocks. If each block is a 4 centimeter by 4 centimeter by 4 centimeter cube,

   a. how much storage space does she need to hold 30 blocks?

   b. will they fit in a container that is 40 centimeters by 10 centimeters by 4 centimeters?

   c. **Extended Response** If Holly's container is 100 centimeters long, 10 centimeters wide, and 3 centimeters tall, will the blocks fit? Explain.

25 Igor has 32 feet of fence to make a pen for his pet goose, Gurtrude. If he makes a rectangular pen, what is the greatest amount of area in which Gurtrude can roam? What should the dimensions of the pen be?

After the Revolutionary War the government gave the land it had promised to soldiers and others. Surveyors of public lands at this time were pioneers, venturing into new and sometimes dangerous territory. Because methods used to describe property boundaries were very confusing, Thomas Jefferson proposed a new square-based system,

known as the *Public Land Survey System*. This System made it easier to describe and keep track of millions of pieces of land. Any square of land could be located by the name of the township it was in, the section of that township, the part of that section, and so on. See the diagram below.

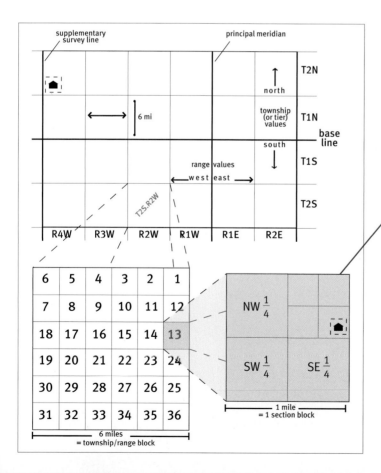

This homestead would be described as the southeast quarter of the southeast quarter of the northeast quarter, section 13, township 2 south, range 2 west or simply:

SE $\frac{1}{4}$, SE $\frac{1}{4}$, NW $\frac{1}{4}$, sec. 13, T2S, R2W.

📱 Textbook This lesson is available in the *eTextbook.*

Think about and discuss these questions.

1 How is the public land survey System like a standard coordinate grid? How is it different?

2 In this system, how would you describe the location of the block marked with the house?

3 How many acres of land are represented by one of the small squares outlined in red in the diagram? (One square mile is 640 acres.)

4 How many yards of fencing would it take to enclose a piece of land described as NW $\frac{1}{4}$, SE $\frac{1}{4}$, sec. 9 of T1N, R3W?

Imagine you are one of four contestants on a game show.

Welcome to *Homesteader's Challenge,* where land is up for grabs and the usual rules of homesteading do not apply. On our show, you can acquire a piece of earth just by walking around it. Here's how we play:

We'll drop off our four contestants somewhere out west and let them start walking at 8 A.M. They'd better come prepared with food, water, and a good plan, because whoever walks around the most land in 10 hours keeps it.

The show begins. Here is what the other contestants do.

Exploring Problem Solving

Name	Plan	Result
Luka	Walk straight until 1 P.M. Then walk east until 3:30 P.M. Then head straight back to the starting point.	Enclosed 0 square miles
Sylvia	I'll walk in a small circle to make sure I get back to start. Then, if there's time, I'll walk in another circle. Just keep walking in circles until time runs out.	Made 4 complete circles
Tyrese	I know I can walk 30 miles in one day, so I'll walk west 14 miles, then walk south, then east, and then north.	Made it back after exactly 30 miles

Solve these problems.

5 Why didn't Luka's plan work?

6 Would Luka's plan work if he walked twice as fast the whole day?

7 Could Sylvia have enclosed only one circular piece of land? Explain.

8 What are some possible shapes that Sylvia's path could have enclosed?

9 How many square miles did Tyrese's path enclose?

10 How could Tyrese have enclosed more land and still have walked west, south, east, and north for a total of 30 miles?

11 What will your plan be? Why?

12 What is the most land you could win by walking a total of 30 miles?

eTextbook This lesson is available in the *eTextbook*.

Cumulative Review

Multiplying and Dividing Integers Lesson 4.9

Multiply or divide.

① $-5 \times 4 = $ ▨

② $-5 \times (-4) = $ ▨

③ $3 \times (-8) = $ ▨

④ $-24 \div 8 = $ ▨

⑤ $56 \div (-8) = $ ▨

⑥ $-30 \div (-6) = $ ▨

⑦ $16 \div (-4) = $ ▨

⑧ $-49 \div 7 = $ ▨

Linear Equations Lesson 5.12

Solve for *x* or *y*.

⑨ $\frac{x}{2} + 12 = 17$

⑩ $3x + 150 = 0$

⑪ $-6x + (-19.3) = -50.5$

⑫ $100 - 3(16) = y$

⑬ $\frac{y}{3} + 60 = 30$

⑭ $15(5) - 69 = y$

Multiplying Mixed Numbers Lesson 7.2

Multiply. Check to see that your answers make sense.

⑮ $2\frac{2}{5} \times 4\frac{1}{6} = $ ▨

⑱ $\frac{3}{4} \times 6\frac{1}{2} = $ ▨

⑯ $3\frac{1}{2} \times 3\frac{1}{7} = $ ▨

⑲ $2\frac{1}{4} \times 5\frac{1}{7} = $ ▨

⑰ $1\frac{1}{3} \times 2\frac{1}{6} = $ ▨

⑳ $\frac{7}{8} \times 1\frac{1}{4} = $ ▨

Using Mixed Numbers Lesson 7.9

Solve.

㉑ Rick's school held a fund-raiser with the goal of raising $7,000.

So far, they have reached $1\frac{2}{5}$ of their goal. How much money has the school raised?

㉒ Suki, Jojo, and Rita each spent time working on a group project. If Suki has spent 2 hours, Jojo has spent $2\frac{1}{4}$ hours, and Rita has spent $1\frac{3}{4}$ hours on the project, what fraction of the work has been done so far by Jojo?

Cumulative Review

Averages Lesson 8.1

Solve.

23 Benny and José had already bowled 3 games. Benny's average was 115 and José's was 121. If José then bowled a 117 in his last game, what would Benny have to bowl in his last game to finish with a higher average than José?

24 Micah received grades of 75, 89, and 85 on his first three English papers. On his next paper, he received an 84. Did his average go up or down?

Comparing Ratios Lesson 8.5

25 Which camp basketball team has the better record—the red team with 11 wins out of 23 games or the blue team with 15 wins out of 29 games? How many more games will the team with fewer wins need to win in a row to beat the other team's record?

26 Flour comes in 3-pound and 5-pound bags. If the smaller bag sells for $1.89 and the larger bag costs $2.99, which is the better buy?

Area of Parallelograms Lesson 10.2

27 If the area of parallelogram *ABCD* is 30 square inches, what could the dimensions of base and height be?

   a. 5 in. $\times$ 10 in.

   b. 6 in. $\times$ 6 in.

   c. 5 in. $\times$ 6 in.

28 What is the area of parallelogram *EFGH* with a base of 8 meters, height of 4 meters, and side length of 5 meters?

Area of a Circle Lesson 10.4

29 What is the area of a circle (to the nearest whole unit) if its radius is equal to 10 meters?

30 A large pie is 10 inches in diameter, and a small pie is 6 inches in diameter. Is the large pie more than twice as big (in area) as the small pie? Show your work.

Key Ideas Review

In this chapter, you learned how to find the area of many types of figures, measured the movement of figures, and studied space figures.

You learned how to compute the area of circles, parallelograms, triangles, irregular figures, and the area of surfaces of space figures.

You learned characteristics of space figures, such as deltahedra and flexagons.

Find the area of each figure.

①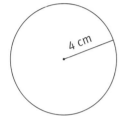
4 cm

②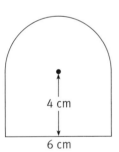
4 cm
6 cm

③ Find the volume of the cube below.

5
5
5

④ Compute the surface area of the square pyramid.

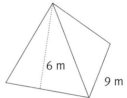
6 m
9 m

⑤ What figure does the net create?

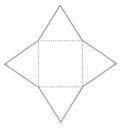

⑥ Describe a combined translation and rotation that would place one of the congruent figures on top of the other.

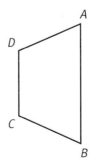
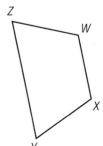
A
D
C
B
Z
W
X
Y

Lesson 10.1 **Given** the following measures for the diameter of a circle, find the circumference (to the nearest whole unit).

1 21 feet   **2** 200 centimeters   **3** 10 miles

4 If you know the circumference of a circle is 110 centimeters, what is the diameter (to the nearest whole unit)?

5 If the circumference of a circle is 62.8 miles, what is its radius (to the nearest whole unit)?

Lessons 10.2–10.3 **Find** the area of each figure.

6
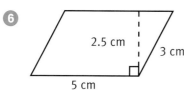

8
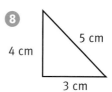

7
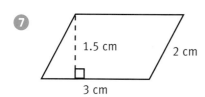

9
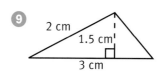

Lesson 10.4 **Using** 3.14 for π, find the circumference and area of each circle.

10 radius = 40 centimeters

11 diameter = 1 centimeter

Lesson 10.5

Find the area of the irregular figures below. Use 3.14 for π.

 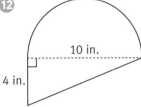

10 in.

4 in.

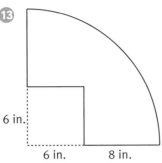

6 in.

6 in.   8 in.

Lesson 10.7

For each of the following letters, answer the following: How many lines of symmetry does it have? Does it have rotational symmetry? If so, give the angle of rotation.

⑭ H

⑮ T

⑯ J

Lesson 10.10

Look at the following nets. Can they be folded into a space figure? If so, write the figure's number of edges, vertices, and faces.

⑰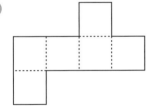

⑱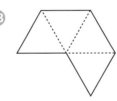

Lessons 10.12–10.13

Find the volume and surface area of each box.

⑲ 5 inches by 3 inches by 2 inches

⑳ 5 centimeters by 5 centimeters by 5 centimeters

Find the circumference and area of each circle given the radius. Use 3.14 for π.

1. $r = 9$ centimeters

2. $r = 3.5$ centimeters

Find the area of each figure.

3.

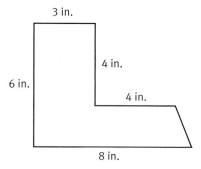

4.

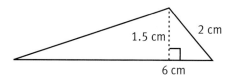

5.

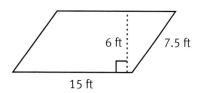

6.

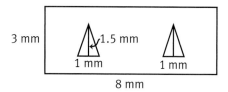

Identify the figure made by each net.

7.

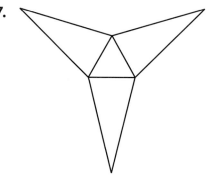

8.

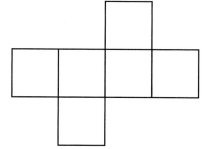

9.

e **Textbook** This lesson is available in the *eTextbook*.

Choose the correct answer.

10. Which shows a rotation of this figure?

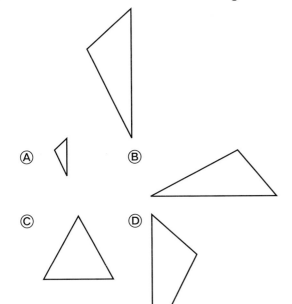

Ⓐ   Ⓑ

Ⓒ   Ⓓ

11. How many faces does a square pyramid have?

  Ⓐ 8   Ⓑ 7

  Ⓒ 6   Ⓓ 5

12. Which figure has rotational symmetry?

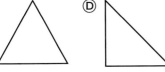

13. Which figure is a cylinder?

14. What is the volume of a box measuring 4 inches × 6 inches × 6 inches?

  Ⓐ 144 in.^{3} Ⓑ 10 in.^{3}

  Ⓒ 24 in.^{3} Ⓓ 5 in.^{3}

15. What is the diameter of a circle with a circumference of 111 feet?

  Ⓐ about 107.86 ft   Ⓑ about 55.5 ft

  Ⓒ about 35.35 ft   Ⓓ about 27.75 ft

16. Which shows a reflection of this figure?

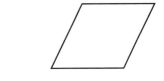

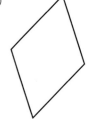
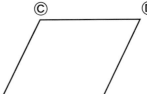

17. Which of the following is a triangular prism?

Ⓐ  Ⓑ

Ⓒ 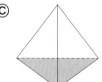 Ⓓ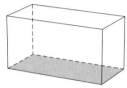

18. How many lines of symmetry does this figure have?

Ⓐ 5 Ⓑ 3

Ⓒ 2 Ⓓ 1

19. The measures of two angles in a triangle are 125° and 15°. What is the measure of the third angle?

Ⓐ 50° Ⓑ 40°

Ⓒ 10° Ⓓ 5°

20. Which ordered pair does not satisfy this function rule?

Ⓐ (20, 18) Ⓑ (15, 13)

Ⓒ (10, 8) Ⓓ (−6, −4)

21. The scale on a map is 1 inch = 25 miles. The distance between two towns measures 5.5 inches. How many miles are between the two towns?

Ⓐ 50 Ⓑ 75

Ⓒ 125 Ⓓ 137.5

22. Owen ate $\frac{1}{4}$ of his sandwich for a snack and shared $\frac{1}{5}$ of it with a friend. What fraction of his sandwich does he have left?

Ⓐ $\frac{2}{5}$ Ⓑ $\frac{1}{2}$

Ⓒ $\frac{11}{20}$ Ⓓ $\frac{19}{20}$

23. Which of the following is a trapezoid?

Ⓐ 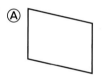 Ⓑ

Ⓒ 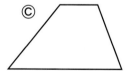 Ⓓ

Extended Response Solve.

24. Describe a series of translations, rotations, and reflections that will make △*DEF* fit on top of the △*ABC*.

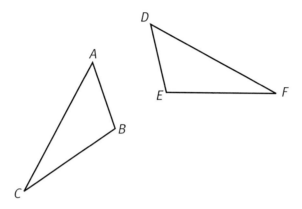

25. The wall in Mr. Taylor's classroom is 6 meters long and 3 meters high. The wall has a window that is 0.5 meter wide and 1 meter high. He wants to cover the wall with colorful paper that his students have decorated. Each picture is 25 centimeters by 25 centimeters.

   a. What is the area, in square centimeters, of the wall that Mr. Taylor can cover with the paper?

   b. How many uncut pieces of colorful paper could Mr. Taylor fit? Explain.

CHAPTER 11

Rational Number and Percent Applications

In This Chapter You Will Learn

- how to multiply decimals.
- how to compute with percents to find discounted prices and interest.
- how to divide decimals.

Imagine you are searching for a sunken ship. After studying the ship's logs and other records, you have narrowed the search to a rectangle $5\frac{9}{10}$ miles long and $2\frac{3}{10}$ miles wide. Somewhere at the bottom of the ocean, within that rectangle, lies the vessel you seek.

You know how much area you can cover each hour. In order to estimate how much time the search could take, you want to approximate the area of the rectangle. You make a diagram to help you.

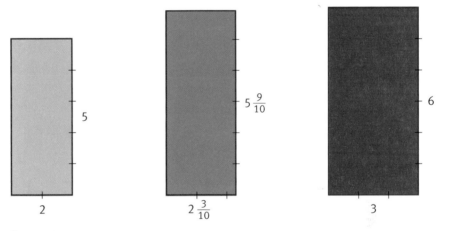

Work in groups to answer the following questions.

1. How can you use your diagram to approximate the area of the search?

2. How could you use the diagram to approximate the product of 5.9×2.3?

3. Without calculating the exact area, do you think the search area is closer to the area of the green rectangle or the area of the red rectangle?

4. Check your estimate. Find a way to determine the exact area of the search region, and then compare it to the areas of the red and green rectangles.

Approximating Products of Decimals

Key Ideas

The product of two decimals can be approximated by multiplying the whole numbers nearest to the decimals.

"This calculator isn't working right," said Ying. "It doesn't show decimal points. But it does everything else right."

"Let me see," said Dean, taking the calculator. "I'll multiply 2.3 by 4.8."

Dean pushed

The display showed 1104.

"You see," said Ying. "The calculator is useless."

"I don't think so," Dean said. "We can put in the decimal point ourselves."

"Okay," Ying said, looking at the digits in 1104. "I'll put it between the two 1s. The answer is 1.104."

"You can't just put it anywhere," Dean told her. "You have to figure out where it goes."

"How?" Ying asked.

"Look at the problem again," said Dean, as he wrote 2.3 × 4.8.

"We know that 2.3 is more than 2, and 4.8 is more than 4. So the answer must be more than 2 × 4, or 8."

"I get it," Ying shouted. "We also know that 2.3 is less than 3, and 4.8 is less than 5, so the answer is less than 3 × 5, or 15."

"That's right," said Dean. "And if the answer is more than 8 and less than 15. We can put the decimal point in only one place."

"Right," said Ying, and she wrote 11.04.

e Textbook This lesson is available in the *eTextbook*.

Replace ▢ with <, >, or = as you copy each problem below.

1. 3.4×2.2 ▢ 3×2
2. 3.8×2.8 ▢ 3×2
3. 2×3 ▢ 3.95×2.95
4. 4×3 ▢ 3.95×2.95
5. 6.1×8.9 ▢ 7×9
6. 1.8×0.6 ▢ 2×1

7. 10.25×7.5 ▢ 10×7
8. 7.5×10.25 ▢ 11×8
9. 1.5×1.5 ▢ 2×2
10. 1×1 ▢ 1.5×1.5
11. 0.75×14.2 ▢ 1×15
12. 0.25×5.5 ▢ 1×6

These problems were done on Ying's broken calculator. Copy each answer, and insert the decimal point in the correct place.

13. $3.7 \times 1.8 = 666$
14. $0.45 \times 45 = 2025$
15. $4.1 \times 8.7 = 3567$
16. $3.5 \times 3.5 = 1225$
17. $35 \times 3.5 = 1225$
18. $1.08 \times 5.4 = 5832$

19. $32.6 \times 2.3 = 7498$
20. $35 \times 0.035 = 1225$
21. $32.6 \times 23 = 7498$
22. $2.5 \times 2.5 = 625$
23. $32.6 \times 0.23 = 7498$
24. $25 \times 0.25 = 625$

Without using a pencil and paper or a calculator, decide which is correct. In each case, only one answer is correct.

25. $5.3 \times 4.2 =$ ▢
   a. 12.16
   b. 22.26
   c. 32.26

26. $2.25 \times 2.25 =$ ▢
   a. 5.0625
   b. 3.9165
   c. 10.615

27. $10.5 \times 10.5 =$ ▢
   a. 110.25
   b. 95.25
   c. 211.25

28. $0.75 \times 1.5 =$ ▢
   a. 2.015
   b. 7.555
   c. 1.125

29. $3.4 \times 0.92 =$ ▢
   a. 4.098
   b. 3.128
   c. 34.92

30. $6.7 \times 8.1 =$ ▢
   a. 45.72
   b. 27.52
   c. 54.27

Multiplying Two Decimals

Key Ideas

The number of digits to the right of the decimal point in a product equals the sum of the digits to the right of the decimal points in the factors.

Ms. Lawson earned $11.76 per hour. Her company gave her a 4% raise. How much more does she earn per hour?

What is 4% of $11.76? To find out, change 4% to a decimal and multiply.

How do you multiply 0.04 × 11.76? Suppose we change the decimals to fractions:

$$0.04 = \frac{4}{100} \qquad 11.76 = \frac{1176}{100}$$

$$0.04 \times 11.76 = \frac{4}{100} \times \frac{1176}{100} = \frac{4704}{10000}$$

To divide 4,704 by 10,000, move the decimal point four places to the left.

$$\frac{4704}{10000} \qquad 4.704$$

0.4704

Ms. Lawson will earn about $0.47 more per hour.

What multiplication was done to calculate 0.04 × 11.76?

4 × 1,176

What division was done to calculate 0.04 × 11.76?

4,704 ÷ 10,000

To multiply two decimals, multiply as though there were no decimal points. Then place the decimal point in the answer as many places to the left as the decimal points are to the left in the two factors. The examples on the next page will make this easier to understand.

ⓔTextbook This lesson is available in the *eTextbook*.

- 56.4 × 3.21 = ?

$$\begin{array}{r} 3.21 \\ \times\ 56.4 \\ \hline 1284 \\ 1926\ \\ 1605\quad \\ \hline 181.044 \end{array}$$

3.21 ⟵——— The decimal point is two places to the left.
× 56.4 ⟵——— The decimal point is one place to the left.
181.044 ⟵——— 2 + 1 = 3 Put the decimal point three places to the left in the answer.

The answer is 181.044.

Check to see that the answer makes sense. It should be more than 50 × 3 and less than 60 × 4. Is 181.044 between 150 and 240? It is, so the answer makes sense.

- 3.4 × 2.5 = ?

$$\begin{array}{r} 2.5 \\ \times\ 3.4 \\ \hline 100 \\ 75\ \\ \hline 8.50 \end{array}$$

2.5 ⟵——— one place
× 3.4 ⟵——— one place
8.50 ⟵——— 1 + 1, or two places

The answer is 8.50, or simply 8.5.

Check to see that the answer makes sense. It should be more than 3 × 2 and less than 4 × 3. Is 8.5 between 6 and 12? It is, so the answer makes sense.

Multiply. Check to see that your answers make sense.

1.
$$\begin{array}{r} 5 \\ \times\ 4 \\ \hline \end{array}$$

2.
$$\begin{array}{r} 50 \\ \times\ 40 \\ \hline \end{array}$$

3.
$$\begin{array}{r} 0.05 \\ \times\ 0.04 \\ \hline \end{array}$$

4.
$$\begin{array}{r} 0.5 \\ \times\ 0.4 \\ \hline \end{array}$$

5.
$$\begin{array}{r} 0.5 \\ \times\ 4 \\ \hline \end{array}$$

6.
$$\begin{array}{r} 5 \\ \times\ 0.4 \\ \hline \end{array}$$

7.
$$\begin{array}{r} 9 \\ \times\ 3 \\ \hline \end{array}$$

8.
$$\begin{array}{r} 900 \\ \times\ 300 \\ \hline \end{array}$$

9.
$$\begin{array}{r} 0.09 \\ \times\ 0.3 \\ \hline \end{array}$$

⑩   7
   × 8
   ▢

⑪   700
   × 800
   ▢

⑫   0.007
   × 0.008
   ▢

⑬   0.000007
   ×   0.08
   ▢

⑭   9
   × 7
   ▢

⑮   9000
   × 70
   ▢

⑯   0.0009
   ×   0.7
   ▢

⑰   0.09
   × 7
   ▢

⑱   0.09
   × 70
   ▢

⑲   0.09
   × 700
   ▢

⑳   1.23
   × 2.44
   ▢

㉑   12.3
   × 0.244
   ▢

㉒   12.3
   × 24.4
   ▢

㉓   123
   × 2.44
   ▢

㉔   1.23
   × 24.4
   ▢

Solve the following problems.

㉕ The recycling center pays $0.29 a pound for aluminum. Dan has collected 75.6 pounds of aluminum cans. How much money will he earn?

㉖ Kelly bought 1 pound of apples for $1.29. How much would 3.5 pounds of apples cost?

Answer this journal after playing the Make 25 Game.

Writing + Math Journal
Suppose you rolled 6, 5, 5, and 0. What number would you make? Explain your answer.

ⓔ Textbook This lesson is available in the *eTextbook*.

Game

Decimal Multiplication and Strategies Practice

Make 25 Game

Players: Two or more

Materials: *Number Cubes* (two 0–5 and two 5–10)

Object: To get the product closest to 25

Math Focus: Multiplication of decimals

HOW TO PLAY

1. Take turns rolling all four *Number Cubes*. If you roll a 10, roll that cube again.

2. Use each number once to make two two-digit numbers whose product is close to 25. You may make decimals. Do not use a pencil or paper when making these numbers.

3. The player with the product closest to 25 wins the round. Use a pencil and paper to check the products only if necessary.

SAMPLE GAME

Johnny rolled:

| 0 | 1 | 5 | 7 |

Louisa rolled:

| 1 | 5 | 5 | 2 |

Johnny made this problem:
5.1 × 7.0

Louisa made this problem:
5.1 × 5.2

Johnny and Louisa know that 5.1 × 7.0 is about 35 and that 5.1 × 5.2 is slightly more than 25. So, they know that Louisa is the winner of the round. If the products had been closer, Johnny and Louisa could have checked them using paper and a pencil.

Percent and Fraction Benchmarks

Key Ideas

A percent is a special fraction with a denominator of 100.

The word *per* is often used with ratios. For example,

A. They cost $3 *per* box.

B. On the average, there are 12 bad eggs *per* 1,000.

The ratios being used here are

A. $\frac{3}{1}$

B. $\frac{12}{1,000}$

Ratios with 100 in the denominator are useful in many ways. A special word is sometimes used for such ratios. The word is *percent*.

Instead of saying *7 per 100,* we sometimes say *7 percent.* (*Cent* means "hundred" or "hundredth.") Percent also has a special symbol. Like 100, it has two zeros in it. The symbol for percent is %.

Because 7% means $\frac{7}{100}$, if you want to use 7% in a calculation, you can use the fraction $\frac{7}{100}$ or the decimal 0.07.

To change a percent to a decimal, move the decimal point two places to the left. If there is no decimal point, insert one to the right of the ones place.

Example: Change 7% to a decimal.

$$7\% \longrightarrow 0.7. \longrightarrow .07 \text{ (or 0.07)}$$

So 7% = 0.07.

To change a decimal to a percent, move the decimal point two places to the right.

Example: Change 0.06 to a percent.

$$0.06 \longrightarrow 0.06. \longrightarrow 6\%$$

ⓔTextbook This lesson is available in the *eTextbook*.

Change each percent to a decimal or each decimal to a percent.

① 12%   ② 200%   ③ 1%   ④ 12.7%

⑤ 0.517   ⑥ 0.002   ⑦ 0.065   ⑧ 10

When you want to find a percentage of something, you can use the equivalent decimal or fraction. The one you use depends on the problem you are solving.

Say, for example, that the sales tax where you live is 7%. If you buy a calculator for $5, you would have to pay a tax equal to 7% of $5.

The expression 7% means 7 per hundred. For each 100¢ ($1) you will be charged 7¢ in tax. Or, for $5, you will be charged 5 × 7¢, or 35¢.

You could do this calculation several other ways.

For example,

A. $7\% = \frac{7}{100}$

$5 = 500¢

$500 \times \frac{7}{100} = \frac{3,500}{100} = 35$

The tax is 35¢.

B. $7\% = 0.07$

$5 \times 0.07 = 0.35$

The tax is $0.35.

You know that $0.35 = 35¢, so the answers are the same.

Calculate.

⑨ 5% sales tax on $6

⑩ 6% sales tax on $5

⑪ 7% sales tax on $12

⑫ 5% of 120

⑬ 25% of 120

⑭ 50% of 120

⑮ 100% of 120

⑯ 12% of 20

⑰ 15% of 20

⑱ 15% of 40

⑲ $0.72 = \frac{\boxed{}}{100} = \boxed{}\%$

⑳ $0.04 = \frac{\boxed{}}{100} = \boxed{}\%$

Percents can also be calculated on a calculator.

If you buy a calculator with a price tag of $14.98 and there is a 6% sales tax, how much will you pay? Many calculators are programmed to solve this problem easily.

Follow these steps.

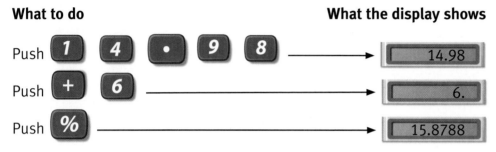

What to do	What the display shows
Push **1** **4** **·** **9** **8** →	14.98
Push **+** **6** →	6.
Push **%** →	15.8788

Because a penny has the least value of any U.S. coin, money amounts, such as 15.8788, are usually rounded to a whole cent. So, the total cost is $15.88.

Solve the following problems.

㉑ You are buying a football with a price tag of $19.98. If sales tax is 6%, how much will you have to pay altogether? Round your answer up to the next cent.

㉒ You could also answer the problem without using a calculator or paper and pencil.
   a. Is $19.98 about $20?
   b. If you pay $0.06 tax for each dollar, what is the tax on $20?
   c. What is this tax added to $19.98?

㉓ Kim is buying a book that costs $8.95. If sales tax is 6%, how much will she have to pay altogether? Round up your answer to the next cent.
   a. Is $8.95 about $9?
   b. If you pay $0.06 tax for each dollar, what is the tax on $9?
   c. What is this tax added to $8.95?

ⓔ Textbook This lesson is available in the *eTextbook.*

When eating in a restaurant, it is customary to leave a tip of about 15% of the total bill if you received good service. People usually estimate this amount and often round the total bill to the nearest dollar or half-dollar.

Suppose the bill is $24.16. What is 15% of $24.16?

We can think that 10% of $24.16 is about $2.50.

Then 15% is $2.50 plus $1.25 (half of $2.50).

So, the total tip should be about $3.75.

If we add $24.16 and $3.75, the total is about $28.00. So, we would pay $28.00, which includes $24.16 for the meal and the remainder for the tip. Of course, if the service is very good, we can leave a larger tip.

Solve.

24 For each of these amounts, estimate the amount of a 15% tip and the total bill, including the tip. Two problems have been done for you.

Amount (Dollars)	Estimated Tip (Dollars)	Amount Including Tip (Dollars)
36.50	5.50	42.00
18.75	3.00	21.75
30.00	☐	☐
16.41	☐	☐
23.31	☐	☐
25.00	☐	☐
20.00	☐	☐
10.00	☐	☐

Computing Percent Discounts

Key Ideas

A discount can be computed by multiplying the price by the percentage of the discount.

A newspaper advertisement says that hats are on sale at a 20% discount off the original price. What is the sale price of a hat with an original price of $8.75?

Percents are often subtracted from numbers instead of added. For example, a store that offers a 20% discount will subtract 20% of the price. Your calculator is programmed to subtract a percent.

What to do   **What the display shows**

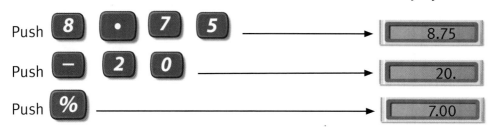

The discount price is $7. Sometimes you will have to round your answer to the appropriate cent, as when you added percents.

You can approximate answers in different ways. For example, to take 20% of $8.75, you might think of $8.75 as slightly less than $9. Because you save $0.20 on each dollar, you would save $1.80 (9 × $0.20) on $9 and slightly less than that on $8.75.

Or you might calculate the answer precisely.

$20\% = 0.20 = \frac{1}{5}$

$\frac{1}{5}$ of 8.75 = 1.75

$8.75 − $1.75 = $7.00

Compute the discounted price.

1. $20 with 15% off

2. $48 with 25% off

3. $50 with 35% off

4. $18 with 10% off

5. $67 with 30% off

6. $12 with 5% off

ⓔ Textbook This lesson is available in the *eTextbook*.

Solve.

7 Calculate the sale price of these items at the Bargain Store.

Item	Regular Price	Sale Reduction	Sale Price
oven	$569.95	$50 off	
bicycle	$79.99	$20 off	
binoculars	$39.99	50% off	
suitcase	$80.00	40% off	
alarm clock	$8.99	20% off	
suit	$89.00	20% off	
shirt	$9.99	20% off	
jeans	$15.99	25% off	
swimming suit	$19.99	25% off	
gloves	$7.99	25% off	
hat	$12.00	25% off	
coat	$65.99	25% off	

Use the advertisements below to answer the questions.

8. At which store do Mr. Crunchy candy bars cost the least?

9. At which store do Red Seal fire extinguishers cost the least?

10. At which store do Warm Wooly gloves cost the least?

11. At which store do Smooth-Rite notebooks cost the least?

12. At which store do Speed-O bicycles cost the least?

13. At which store would it cost less altogether to buy one pair of Warm Wooly gloves and one Red Seal fire extinguisher?

14. At which store would it cost less altogether to buy a box of Mr. Crunchy candy bars and two Smooth-Rite notebooks?

e Textbook This lesson is available in the *eTextbook.*

Game

Percent and Strategies Practice

Tips Game

Players: Two or more

Materials: *Number Cubes* (two 0–5 and two 5–10)

Object: To make the most money on tips

Math Focus: Calculating percents, adding amounts of money, place value, and mathematical reasoning

HOW TO PLAY

1. Each player is waiting on customers in a restaurant and will get five tips. One tip will be 10%; three tips will be 15%; and one tip will be 20%. (A person who waits on tables in a restaurant is usually given a tip by the customer. The tip is a percent of the customer's bill.)

2. Roll all four **Number Cubes**. Determine a customer's bill by using the numbers rolled to make an amount in dollars and cents. A 10 can be used anywhere but must be regrouped if it is not in the place for tens of dollars. For example, a roll of 10, 9, 5, and 5 could be $109.55 (10, 9, 5, 5); $100.55 (9, 10, 5, 5); or $96.05 (9, 5, 10, 5).

3. Decide which tip you will get from this customer. Then calculate the tip. Keep a record of your tips.

4. After five rounds, add your tips. The player with the most money wins.

SAMPLE ROUND

	Round 1	Round 2	Round 3
Ty rolled:	8, 3, 7, 3	1, 5, 5, 6	1, 6, 4, 10
Ty made:	$87.33	$65.51	$106.41
Ty chose:	15%	15%	20%
Ty's tip:	$13.10	$9.83	$21.28
Jo rolled:	3, 5, 0, 10	8, 5, 8, 4	3, 9, 6, 2
Jo made:	$105.30	$88.54	$96.32
Jo chose:	20%	15%	15%
Jo's tip:	$21.06	$13.28	$14.45

e Games This game is available in *eGames.*

Computing Interest

Key Ideas

Percents are used in many situations involving money.

Solve the following problems. Try to approximate the answers in advance.

1 The Bargain Center is advertising a sale in which every item in the store is on sale for 30% off the regular price. The store is located in a community where the sales tax is 6%. How much will you have to pay for a television that is regularly priced at $400?

2 In Problem 1, does it make a difference whether you subtract the 30% first and then add the 6%, or add the 6% first and then subtract the 30%? Try to explain your answer to other members of your group. Solve the problem both ways and compare your answers.

3 How much would you pay, including tax, for each of these items at the Bargain Center during the sale? The regular price is given.

a. jeans, $19.99

b. shirt, $11.99

c. sweatshirt, $9.00

d. wallet, $8.50

e. necklace, $12.00

f. scissors, $6.35

g. upholstery fabric, $6.99 per yard

h. fleece blanket, $19.99

e Textbook This lesson is available in the *eTextbook.*

Solve the following problems.

④ A bank pays its customers 6% interest per year. Suppose you put $250 in the bank.

  a. How much interest would you earn in 1 year?

  b. How much money would you have in the bank at the end of one year (if you did not withdraw any money)? After 2 years?

  c. **Extended Response** Why is the answer to b not computed as $265 plus $15?

  d. How much would you have after 3 years?

  e. How much would you have after 4 years?

  f. How much would you have after 5 years?

⑤ Mrs. Nguyen is borrowing $500 from a bank for one year. The bank is charging her 12% interest per year.

  a. How much total interest will she be charged?

  b. How much will she have to pay back altogether?

⑥ In which of the following instances would you earn more money: depositing $500 in the bank at 5% interest or depositing $490 at 8% interest?

⑦ The Campbells borrowed $8,800 from the bank to fix their house, and they will not make a payment for a year. The bank charges 9% interest on home loans. How much will the Campbells owe at the end of 1 year?

⑧ A bank pays 7% interest per year. Suppose you deposited $625 in the bank.

  a. How much interest would you earn in 1 year?

  b. How much money would you have in the bank at the end of 1 year if you did not withdraw any money?

  c. How much would you have after 2 years?

  d. After 3 years?

  e. After 4 years?

  f. After 5 years?

Exploring 💡 Problem Solving

When scientists and treasure hunters search for shipwrecks underwater, they use *sonar,* which is like radar. As the sonar device is towed behind the ship, it sends out a beam of sound waves. The beam spreads until it bounces off a solid object, such as a sunken ship or the ocean floor. The higher the device is above the ocean floor, the more the beam can spread.

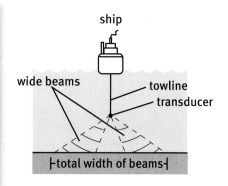

Imagine you are using sonar to help you search for the wreckage of a famous vessel from the American Civil War. You are traveling at 2.4 meters per second. As you travel, your sonar beam moves with you, scanning a rectangular path across the ocean floor. Your sonar beam scans an area of 432 square meters each second.

You plan to lower the sonar device so the width of the beam at the ocean floor is reduced by 10%. How much area can your sonar cover each second with the new beam width?

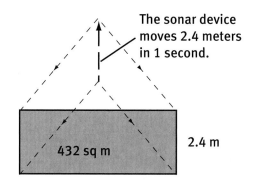

The sonar device moves 2.4 meters in 1 second.

432 sq m

2.4 m

Kai solved the problem this way:

I Made a Plan and Wrote Equations.

1. Find the old width of the beam.	Old width = 432 sq m ÷ 2.4 m
2. Find the new width of the beam.	New width = 90% of old width
3. Find the new area covered each second.	New area = new width × 2.4 m

ℯ Textbook This lesson is available in the *eTextbook.*

Think about Kai's strategy. Answer the following questions.

①   Why does Kai find the width of the beam before it is reduced?

②   Is Kai's first equation correct? Explain.

③   Do you agree that the new width is 90% of the old width? Explain.

④   Will Kai's strategy work? Why or why not?

⑤   Would you use Kai's strategy?

Jordan solved the problem another way:

I used Proportional Reasoning and Made a Diagram.

If I take away $\frac{1}{10}$ of the width,

I am taking away $\frac{1}{10}$ of the area.

Think about Jordan's strategy. Answer the following questions.

⑥   Why is Jordan thinking about taking away $\frac{1}{10}$ of the width?

⑦   Do you agree with Jordan's reasoning? Why or why not?

⑧   How can Jordan finish solving the problem?

⑨   Solve the problem. Use any strategy you think will work.

⑩   What strategy did you use? Why?

Cumulative Review

Angles and Sides of a Triangle Lesson 9.3

Solve.

If a triangle has one side with a length of 12 meters and another side with a length of 7 meters, can the third side be

1 3 meters?

2 5 meters?

3 5.1 meters?

4 18 meters?

5 19 meters?

Surface Area and Volume Lessons 10.12–10.13

Solve.

6 A box has a width of 3 feet, height of 7 feet, and a length of 9 feet. What is the volume of the box?

7 A cube has a side length of 4 inches. What is the surface area of the cube?

A cube has a side with an area of 36 square feet.

8 What is the surface area of the cube?

9 What is the volume of the cube?

10 A box has sides of 3 inches, 8 inches, and 6 inches. What is the surface area of the box?

Dividing by a Two-Digit or Three-Digit Number Lessons 8.8–8.10

Solve.

11 At a recent baseball game, the amount of money received from all tickets sold was $612,942. If the average price of a ticket sold for that game was $22, how many fans attended the game?

12 A school fund-raiser collected $4,114. If 242 people gave a donation, what was the average amount of each donation?

Divide.

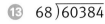

⑬ $68\overline{)60384}$ ⑭ $325\overline{)22425}$ ⑮ $365\overline{)276670}$

....

Adding and Subtracting Mixed Numbers **Lessons 7.3–7.4**

Solve.

⑯ Kang's math book is $1\frac{5}{8}$ inches thick, his science book is $1\frac{1}{4}$ inches thick, and his spelling book is $\frac{15}{16}$ of an inch thick. What is the total width of all 3 books?

⑰ Niran walked $1\frac{1}{5}$ miles to school. At lunch hour, he walked $\frac{2}{3}$ of a mile. After school, Niran walked home. How far did he walk that day?

Add or subtract.

⑱
$$\begin{array}{r} 5\frac{1}{4} \\ -\ 3\frac{2}{5} \\ \hline \end{array}$$

⑲
$$\begin{array}{r} 4\frac{1}{2} \\ +\ 2\frac{5}{7} \\ \hline \end{array}$$

⑳
$$\begin{array}{r} 3\frac{1}{8} \\ -\ \frac{5}{6} \\ \hline \end{array}$$

....

Ratios and Rates **Lesson 8.4**

Solve.

Koko reads about 30 pages in an hour.

㉑ About how many pages does she read in 40 minutes?

㉒ About how many pages does she read in $2\frac{1}{2}$ hours?

㉓ Koko is currently reading a book that is 176 pages long. She is on page 59. About how long will it take her to finish the book?

Olivia averages 64 miles per hour while driving on the highway.

㉔ Can she make a 150-mile trip in $2\frac{1}{2}$ hours?

㉕ About how far could she drive in $3\frac{3}{4}$ hours?

Percents Greater than 100%

Key Ideas

Percents can be greater than 100%.

We know that *percent* means "per hundred." Therefore, if you have 100% of something, you have all of that thing. People who talk about being "110% patriotic" or "1,000% certain" are talking mathematical nonsense. They do this to add emphasis, but it actually does not make sense.

However, percents greater than 100 can have meaning. If the national debt today is $1\frac{1}{2}$ times what it was five years ago, it would be correct to say that it is now 150% of what it was then. Or, if a puppy's weight is twice as much as it was five months ago, you could appropriately describe it as 200% of its previous weight.

For example, Raul bought a football trading card for $10. Two years later, a pricing guide stated that the card was worth $20. Its value increased by 100%, and its new value is 200% of the original value. After another year, a pricing guide said the card was worth $25. Its value is now 250% of the original value, and its value has increased by 150%.

One way to see this is

$\frac{5}{10} = \frac{1}{2}$ or 50%.

We can add 50% to 100% to find that the total percentage increase from the original price is 150%.

Another way:

Find the difference of the new amount from the old amount.
25 − 10 = 15

Divide the difference by the original amount.
15 ÷ 10 = 1.5

Multiply by 100. 1.5 × 100 = 150

Therefore, the answer is 150%.

ROWDIES

All Stars

e Textbook This lesson is available in the *eTextbook*.

Solve the following problems.

1 Mark purchased an old coin for $3.00. Three years later, he sold the coin for $9.00. Which of the following statements are true? Explain your answers.

  a. The value of the coin increased by $6.00.

  b. The value of the coin increased by 200%.

  c. The value of the coin is now 300% of its original value.

2 Sara purchased an old coin for $9.00. Three years later, the coin had declined in value and was worth $3.00. Which of the following statements are true? Explain your answers.

  a. The value of the coin decreased by $6.00.

  b. The coin lost $\frac{2}{3}$ of its value.

  c. The coin lost about 66.67% of its value.

3 Ten years ago the cost of riding the bus was $0.50. Since then the price has gone up 150%. How much does it cost to ride the bus now?

4 Ten years ago the price of a box of crayons was about $1.25. Today the price of that same box of crayons is about $3.00.

  a. What is the price difference?

  b. What is the percent increase?

  c. **Extended Response** Explain how you found your answer to Problem 4b.

5 **Extended Response** Mark purchased a sports card for $2.00. Later, it declined in value. "That card lost 200% of its value," Mark said. Is that possible? Why or why not?

6 Last year Sara charged $5.00 per hour for mowing lawns. This year there is a shortage of students willing to mow lawns, so she is able to charge $12.00 per hour.

  a. How much more per hour is Sara charging this year?

  b. What is the percent increase?

  c. **Extended Response** Is it fair to charge more because fewer people are willing to do the work?

Probability and Percent

Key Ideas

Probabilities can be expressed as fractions, percents, or decimals.

- If you want to write the fraction $\frac{1}{4}$ as a percent, you can first change it to a decimal (0.25) and then to a percent (25%).

  $$\frac{1}{4} = 25\%$$

- Another way to see this is to ask how many *per hundred* $\frac{1}{4}$ would give you. Take $\frac{1}{4}$ of 100, which is 25. So $\frac{1}{4} = 25\%$.

Sometimes fractions do not have a precise decimal equivalent.

If you try this for $\frac{1}{3}$, you divide 100 by 3 and get 33.333.... We could agree to stop at some place and say, for example, that $\frac{1}{3}$ is about 33%, or about 33.3%, or about 33.33%.

Another way you might try to handle this problem is to divide 100 by 3 and write a remainder of 1.

$$
\begin{array}{r}
33 \\
3\overline{)100} \quad \text{R1} \\
\underline{9} \\
10 \\
\underline{9} \\
1
\end{array}
$$

But people do not write 33 R1%. So, what does the remainder of 1 mean? After the last division by 3, you had 1 left over. You might divide the 1 by 3 if you continued.

What is another way to write 1 divided by 3?

Instead of writing "remainder 1," you may write "$\frac{1}{3}$" in the answer.

$$
\begin{array}{r}
33 \\
3\overline{)100} \quad \text{R1} \longrightarrow \quad \frac{1}{3} = 33\frac{1}{3}\%
\end{array}
$$

e **Textbook** This lesson is available in the *eTextbook.*

For example, write $\frac{4}{9}$ as a percent.

$$
\begin{array}{r}
44 \\
9\overline{)400} \text{ R4} \\
\underline{36} \\
40 \\
\underline{36} \\
4
\end{array}
$$
The remainder is 4.

So, $\frac{4}{9} = 44\frac{4}{9}\%$.

Write each of the following fractions as a percent. If necessary, use a fraction in the percent (for example, $33\frac{1}{3}\%$).

1 $\frac{1}{3} = $  %

2 $\frac{2}{3} = $ ▨ %

3 $\frac{1}{4} = $ ▨ %

4 $\frac{2}{4} = $ ▨ %

5 $\frac{2}{5} = $ ▨ %

6 $\frac{3}{5} = $ ▨ %

Probability refers to the likeliness of an event occurring.

Suppose you roll a 0–5 *Number Cube* many times.

7 About what fraction of the time would you expect the cube to land with 0 showing?

8 What percent is that?

Working with a partner, roll a 0–5 *Number Cube* 100 times and count how many times it lands with 0 showing.

9 What percent of the time did the cube land with 0 showing?

Collect all the results for your class.

10 What percent of the time did the ***Number Cubes*** land with 0 showing for the entire class?

Suppose you roll a 0–5 *Number Cube* and a 5–10 *Number Cube.*

⑪ What are the possible sums that could result?

⑫ Do you have 11 possible sums?

⑬ **Extended Response** What percent of the time would you expect the sum to be 10? Explain your answer.

Work with a partner. Roll a 0–5 and a 5–10 *Number Cube* 100 times and count how many times the resulting sum is 10.

⑭ What fraction of the time was the sum 10?

⑮ What percent of the time was the sum 10?

Study the results for your class.

⑯ What fraction of the time was the sum 10?

⑰ What percent of the time was the sum 10?

⑱ Why do you suppose the sum of 10 occurs so often?

⑲ What percent of the time do you think the sum of 5 occurs?

⑳ What percent of the time do you think the sum of 15 occurs?

㉑ Show the total number of times each sum occurred, and calculate the percents. You might want to use a calculator. The total of all percents should be 100.

Use the following information to answer the problems.

Number Cubes display the following numbers:

0–5 cube:  0, 1, 2, 3, 4, 5

5–10 cube: 5, 6, 7, 8, 9, 10

22 List all the possible ways you can get each sum from 5 to 15. (Hint: There are 36 ways altogether.)

There is only one way to get the sum of 5, and there are 36 sums in all. So, we would expect to get a sum of 5 about $\frac{1}{36}$ of the time. As a percent, $\frac{1}{36}$ is 2.8%; therefore, we could say that a sum of 5 occurs about 2.8% of the times the cubes are rolled.

23 Determine what fraction of the time each sum should occur. Change these fractions to approximate percents, and compare them with the percents you got when you actually rolled the two cubes.

> **Writing + Math** ▷ **Journal**
>
> Look at your results for Problems 16 and 17 on page 548 and explain your answers.

Simplifying Decimal Division

Key Ideas

Multiplying or dividing the numerator and denominator of a fraction by the same number keeps the value the same and can make computing easier.

Remember that we can think of a fraction as the result of a division problem.

Example: $\frac{1}{3}$ means $1 \div 3$. $\frac{7}{5}$ means $7 \div 5$.

- If you have a division problem, such as $755 \div 300$, you can change it to an easier problem by dividing the numerator and denominator by the same number.

$$755 \div 300 \longrightarrow \frac{755}{300} = \frac{(755 \div 100)}{(300 \div 100)}$$
$$= \frac{7.55}{3} \longrightarrow 7.55 \div 3$$

Of course, you do not have to write every step. You can simply move the decimal points to divide as follows:

$$300\overline{)755} \longrightarrow 3\underbrace{00}\overline{)7\underbrace{55}} \longrightarrow 3\overline{)7.55}$$

- Consider this problem. $75 \div 0.3$

Can you think of a way to make this division problem easier to solve?

To change a division problem, such as $75 \div 0.3$, you can multiply the divisor and dividend by the same multiple of 10. This allows you to rewrite the problem so that you are dividing by a whole number.

$$75 \div 0.3 \longrightarrow \frac{75}{0.3} = \frac{(75 \times 10)}{(0.3 \times 10)} = \frac{750}{3} \longrightarrow 750 \div 3$$

Of course, you do not have to write every step. Also, you can simply move the decimal points to multiply.

$$0.3\overline{)75} \longrightarrow \frac{0.3}{75.0} \longrightarrow \frac{3}{750}$$

e Textbook This lesson is available in the *eTextbook*.

- In some instances, you may want to approximate whole numbers by multiplying or dividing by powers of 10.

For example,

$783\overline{)95642}$ Round the divisor: $800\overline{)95642}$

$$800\overline{)95642} \longrightarrow \frac{95{,}642}{800} = \frac{(95{,}642 \div 100)}{(800 \div 100)} = \frac{956.42}{8} \longrightarrow 8\overline{)956.42}$$

Change each of the following to an equivalent division problem with a whole-number divisor. Do not do the division.

1. $0.3\overline{)51.6}$

2. $516 \div 82$

3. $0.03\overline{)4.08}$

4. $0.03\overline{)4.8}$

5. $4.8 \div 0.3$

6. $2{,}694 \div 587$

Select the appropriate approximation from the choices provided.

7. $9.4\overline{)0.94}$
   - a. 1
   - b. 0.1
   - c. 10

8. $64.27 \div 2.5 = $ ▢
   - a. 25.7
   - b. 2.57
   - c. 257

9. $0.49\overline{)66.5}$
   - a. 1.3
   - b. 0.13
   - c. 130

10. $835 \div 3.7 = $ ▢
    - a. 20.8
    - b. 208
    - c. 2.08

11. $0.65\overline{)401.693}$
    - a. 61.799
    - b. 617.99
    - c. 6,179.9

12. $51.283 \div 3.7 = $ ▢
    - a. 12.82
    - b. 1.282
    - c. 128.2

Approximate the following problems by simplifying each divisor to one digit.

13. $400\overline{)2650}$

14. $2.5\overline{)36.5}$

15. $185.26 \div 64 = $ ▢

16. $1.75 \div 70 = $ ▢

Dividing Two Decimals

Key Ideas

Dividing numbers with decimals is similar to dividing whole numbers, but the decimal point must be set correctly.

Raphael and Sue wanted to help Ms. Burns tile her dining room floor.

"Each tile is a square that is 0.3 meter on each side," said Ms. Burns. "The room is 4.8 meters across. How many tiles do I need to make one row across the room?"

"We have to divide 4.8 meters by 0.3 meter," said Raphael. Then he wrote:

$0.3 \overline{)4.8}$

"But we don't know how to divide by a decimal," said Sue.

Raphael had an idea. "Maybe we can change the decimal to a different unit to make the problem easier."

"Okay," said Sue. "We know that 0.3 meter is 3 decimeters, and 4.8 meters is 48 decimeters."

"Now we just have to divide 48 by 3," said Raphael.

$3 \overline{)48}$

"That's easy," said Sue. "The answer is 16. So Ms. Burns needs 16 tiles for a row across the room."

Look.

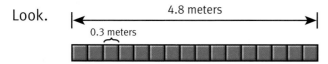

How many 0.3-meter tiles will fit across the 4.8-meter room?

Sixteen tiles will fit.

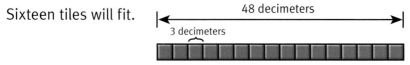

How many 3-decimeter tiles will fit across the 48-decimeter room?

Sixteen tiles will fit.

Why does 4.8 ÷ 0.3 result in the same answer as 48 ÷ 3?

If 4.8 and 0.3 are multiplied by 10, the result is 48 and 3.

ⓔ **Textbook** This lesson is available in the *eTextbook*.

To make a division exercise easier, you can multiply or divide the divisor and the dividend by the same amount. This allows you to rewrite the exercise so you are dividing by a whole number.

For example,

$0.9 \overline{)3.6}$ ⟶ Multiply both numbers by 10.

$0.9 \overline{)3.6}$ ⟶ $9 \overline{)36}$ ⟶ $9 \overline{)36}^{\,4}$

$0.05 \overline{)45}$ ⟶ Multiply both numbers by 100.

$0.05 \overline{)45.00}$ ⟶ $5 \overline{)4500}$ ⟶ $5 \overline{)4500}^{\,900}$

$0.007 \overline{)0.42}$ ⟶ Multiply both numbers by 1,000.

$0.007 \overline{)0.420}$ ⟶ $7 \overline{)420}$ ⟶ $7 \overline{)420}^{\,60}$

$600 \overline{)546}$ ⟶ Divide both numbers by 100.

$600 \overline{)546}$ ⟶ $6 \overline{)5.46}$ ⟶ $6 \overline{)5.46}^{\,0.91}$

Divide.

1. $0.7 \overline{)3.5}$

2. $0.07 \overline{)0.35}$

3. $7 \overline{)0.35}$

4. $0.42 \div 0.6 = $

5. $0.72 \div 0.8 = $

6. $0.8 \overline{)0.064}$

7. $0.5 \overline{)4.0}$

8. $4 \div 0.5 = $

9. $0.006 \overline{)3}$

10. $0.03 \overline{)0.06}$

11. $0.06 \overline{)0.36}$

12. $6.00 \div 0.03 = $

13. $0.03 \overline{)6}$

14. $16 \div 0.0004 = $

15. $0.7 \overline{)0.49}$

16. $800 \overline{)4000}$

17. $800 \overline{)400}$

18. $800 \overline{)40}$

19. $800 \overline{)4}$

20. $4,000 \div 80 = $

21. $8 \overline{)4000}$

22. $0.8 \overline{)4000}$

23. $0.08 \overline{)4000}$

24. $3,500 \div 5 = $

25. $0.5 \overline{)3500}$

26. $3,500 \div 50 = $

27. $50 \overline{)350}$

28. $35 \div 50 = $

29. $50 \overline{)3.5}$

30. $3.5 \div 0.005 = $

31. $0.9 \overline{)6.3}$

32. $0.063 \div 0.09 = $

August, 1973

Iron Shell under the Sea

After lying on the bottom of the sea for more than a century, the iron-covered walls of America's first metal warship deflected a beam of sound waves. Decades of searching ended when scientists confirmed that the reflected sonar was indeed coming from the upside-down wreckage of the famous Civil War vessel, the *Monitor*.

During the Civil War, the Union hurried the *Monitor* into action to prevent another ironclad, the *Merrimac*, from destroying the Union's entire fleet of wooden ships.

Cannon shells bounced off the *Monitor* and the *Merrimac* as the two ironclads fought to a stalemate in the 1862 battle that changed the history of naval warfare.

[from *National Geographic Magazine*, Jan. 1974]

Less than ten months later, a storm did what the *Merrimac* could not—it sank the "invincible" *Monitor*.

The discoverers of the *Monitor* had narrowed the search to a rectangle of ocean floor 25.7 kilometers long and 9.7 kilometers wide. Trying to find an object only 172 feet long and $41\frac{1}{2}$ feet wide in that much ocean was no easy task. The mission was made even more challenging by the discovery of more than twenty other shipwrecks in the same area.

This sonar image of the *Monitor* was recorded more than twenty-five years after her discovery. (Monitor Collection, NOAA)

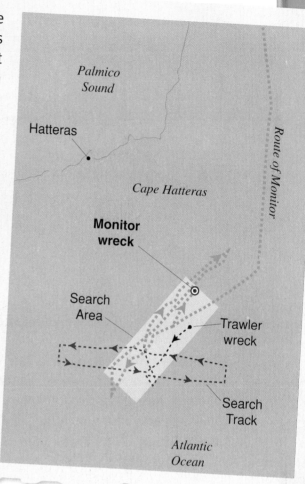

Answer the following questions. Use the information provided on both pages.

1 Suppose you covered 5% of the entire search area each day. What is the probability you would find the *Monitor* on the first day?

2 What is the probability you would find the *Monitor* within the first 2 days?

3 Suppose you could search 20 square kilometers each day, and you began on August 1. About what would your chances be of finding the *Monitor* by August 10?

4 Suppose your sonar beam was 0.2 kilometers wide at the seafloor, and you traveled in a straight line at 12 kilometers per hour. How many square kilometers would you scan in 12 hours?

Exploring Problem Solving

Imagine you are the chief scientist on a mission to find the wreckage of a historic ship. You have narrowed the search area to a square 3.6 kilometers wide. Your sonar beam will sweep a path 0.2 meters wide. You will search very slowly, at a speed of 1 kilometer per hour, for 8 hours each day until you find the ship.

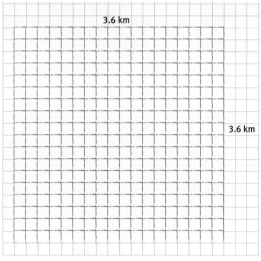

Work in groups to discuss and solve the following problems.

5. What is the width of each small square in the search grid above?

6. How many of the small squares will your sonar scan in 1 hour?

7. On graph paper, draw your own search grid and show the course you would take to cover the entire grid. You may start in any part of the grid, but you should not travel over a section more than once.

8. What is the probability you will find the ship within the first 4 days of searching?

9. Compare your answer to Problem 8 with other groups. Does the probability depend on what course you take?

10. Create your own search problem and exchange it with another group.

e Textbook This lesson is available in the *eTextbook.*

Cumulative Review

Percent and Fraction Benchmarks Lesson 11.3
Solve.

1. 50% of 16 = ▮

2. 25% of 16 = ▮

3. 75% of 8 = ▮

4. $\frac{1}{2}$ of 66 = ▮

5. $\frac{1}{4}$ of 88 = ▮

6. 25% of 80 = ▮

7. $12\frac{1}{2}$% of 80 = ▮

8. $\frac{1}{2}$ of 200 = ▮

9. $\frac{1}{4}$ of 400 = ▮

10. $\frac{3}{4}$ of 200 = ▮

Fractions of Fractions Lesson 6.2
Solve.

11. $\frac{2}{3}$ of 6 is ▮

12. $\frac{1}{2} \times \frac{1}{3} =$ ▮

13. $\frac{1}{3} \times \frac{1}{4} =$ ▮

14. $\frac{3}{4}$ of $\frac{5}{8} =$ ▮

15. $\frac{1}{5} \times \frac{4}{7} =$ ▮

16. $\frac{2}{5} \times \frac{2}{9} =$ ▮

Replace the ▮ to make each of the following statements true.

17. $\frac{1}{2} \times$ ▮ $= \frac{1}{8}$

18. $\frac{3}{5} \times$ ▮ $= \frac{12}{35}$

19. $\frac{3}{4}$ of ▮ $= \frac{6}{20}$

20. $\frac{7}{8} \times$ ▮ $= \frac{35}{72}$

Probability and Fractions **Lesson 6.9**

Solve.

A bag contains 3 red, 5 blue, and 4 white marbles.

21. What is the probability of pulling out a red marble?

22. What is the probability of pulling out a blue or white marble?

23. If a red marble is pulled out and not replaced, what is the probability of pulling out a blue marble next?

24. One red, one white, and one blue marble are pulled out and not replaced. What is the probability of pulling out another red one next?

25. How many blue marbles must be added to the original bag so that the probability of pulling out a blue marble is $\frac{1}{2}$?

· ·

Adding and Subtracting Decimals **Lesson 3.4**

Solve.

Hakeem and Carla were each buying school supplies. Hakeem wanted a notebook for $6.95, a package of pencils for $1.59, and a ruler for $0.79. Carla wanted a knapsack for $19.99, a package of pens for $2.59, and a compass for $1.49.

26. Hakeem had a $10 bill. Was that enough money to buy his supplies?

27. Carla had a $10 bill and three $5 bills. Was that enough money to buy her supplies?

28. Did each of them receive change after their purchase? If so, who received more change and how much more?

29. Jonah bought lunch at school. His pizza was $1.75, his salad was $1.29, and his drink was $0.85. How much change did Jonah receive if he gave the cashier a $5 bill?

30. Can Jonah then buy ice cream for $0.99? If so, how much money will he have left? If not, how much more will he need?

In this chapter you explored rational numbers and percent applications.

You learned how to multiply and divide decimals.
You learned how to compute percents as discounts and interest and how to use them to demonstrate probability.

Solve by selecting the appropriate answer from the box.

20.40	0.24	25.36	28.864

1 6.34 × 4 = ▢

2 3.52 × 8.2 = ▢

3 6% sales tax on $4 = ▢

4 $24 with 15% off = ▢

Solve the following problems.

5 Explain how something can be greater than 100%, and include an example in your explanation.

6 What is the probability of landing on a prime number when rolling a 5–10 **Number Cube**? Write the probability as a fraction and as a percent.

7 Explain how to simplify the division problem below, and then compute the quotient.

1,185 ÷ 600 = ▢

8 Suppose a bank pays its customers 7% interest annually on all savings accounts. How much interest would a customer earn on an account containing $275 after 1 year? After 2 years? After 3 years?

9 0.056 ÷ 7 = ▢

10 0.0056 ÷ 0.007 = ▢

Lesson 11.1 **Without** using a pencil and paper or a calculator, decide which is correct. In each case, only one answer is correct.

① $7.3 \times 3.2 =$ ▢   **②** $5.25 \times 2.85 =$ ▢   **③** $10.5 \times 20.5 =$ ▢

   a. 20.16   **a.** 14.9625   **a.** 215.25

   b. 23.36   **b.** 9.5165   **b.** 195.25

   c. 33.26   **c.** 18.6155   **c.** 311.25

Lesson 11.2 ## Multiply.

④ $\begin{array}{r} 7 \\ \times\, 0.8 \\ \hline \end{array}$ ▢

⑤ $\begin{array}{r} 2.50 \\ \times\, 3.60 \\ \hline \end{array}$ ▢

⑥ $\begin{array}{r} 0.35 \\ \times\, 0.64 \\ \hline \end{array}$ ▢

⑦ $\begin{array}{r} 0.468 \\ \times\, 0.9 \\ \hline \end{array}$ ▢

Solve.

⑧ Abby's aunt wanted to bake two pies, one cherry and one peach. Abby went to the store and picked out 1.4 pounds of cherries, which cost $1.49 per pound, and 1.2 pounds of peaches, on sale for $1.09 per pound. What was the total cost of the fruit?

Lesson 11.3 ## Calculate.

⑨ 5% sales tax on $9   **⑩** 6% sales tax on $20   **⑪** 7% sales tax on $17

⑫ 15% of 120   **⑬** 35% of 120   **⑭** 50% of 1,200

⑮ $0.88 = \dfrac{▢}{100} = ▢\,\%$ **⑯** $0.17 = \dfrac{▢}{100} = ▢\,\%$ **⑰** $0.52 = \dfrac{▢}{100} = ▢\,\%$

Lesson 11.4 ## Solve.

The Bike Outlet has bikes on sale for 20% off. The local sales tax is 5%. Maddie wants to buy a bike that normally costs $350.

⑱ What is the sale price of the bike?

⑲ What is the total cost of the bike, including tax?

⑳ If the sale changed to 30% off, what would be the sale price of the bike?

Lesson 11.5

Solve.

21 Felix is saving for a down payment on a house. He has $4,200 and needs a total of $5,000. If Felix puts the money into a bank account earning 7% interest per year, will he have enough money for the down payment in 2 years? If not, how much more does he need?

Lesson 11.6

Solve.

22 Luigi paid $510 for an antique lamp. A dealer offered him $1,275 for the lamp. What percent of Luigi's original cost was the dealer's offer?

23 Last year, Hank hit a total of 12 home runs. If this year's total is 175% of last year's total, how many home runs has Hank hit this year?

Lesson 11.7

Write each answer as a fraction and as a percent.

A standard die is numbered 1–6. If the die is rolled once, what is the probability that

24 the number rolled is even?

25 the number rolled is divisible by 3?

26 the number rolled is smaller than 2?

If a bag contains 13 red, 7 blue, and 5 white marbles, what is the probability of

27 selecting a red marble?

28 not selecting a white marble?

Lesson 11.9

Solve.

29 Jeremiah has $8.40 to spend on juice for his party. If juice costs 40¢ per can, how many cans can he buy?

30 Antwan has a goal to run 100 miles. If he runs 2.5 miles each day, how many days will it take Antwan to reach 100 miles?

Practice Test

CHAPTER 11

Decide which decimal number in each pair is greater.

1. 0.5×2.7 ▨ 1×3

2. 6×2 ▨ 6.4×1.5

3. 2.3×5.4 ▨ 2×5

4. 7×4 ▨ 6.8×3.5

Change each percent to a decimal.

5. 21%

6. 4.3%

Change each decimal to a percent.

7. 0.745

8. 0.014

Solve.

9. $35 with 10% off

10. $84 with 25% off

11. $49 with 15% off

12. $28 with 5% off

Divide.

13. $2.6\overline{)7.8}$

14. $0.4\overline{)0.64}$

15. $0.9\overline{)0.0036}$

ⓔ **Textbook** This lesson is available in the *eTextbook*.

Choose the correct answer.

16. Which answer has the decimal point in the correct place for 12.3×1.25?

Ⓐ 15.375
Ⓑ 1.5375
Ⓒ 153.75
Ⓓ 1,537.5

17. Carrie wants to buy a new tennis racquet. She finds one for $38, now on sale for 20% off. How much will Carrie save?

Ⓐ $6.70
Ⓑ $7.06
Ⓒ $7.60
Ⓓ $30

18. Mrs. Riley puts $750 in the bank. She earns 3% interest each year. How much interest will Mrs. Riley earn after one year?

Ⓐ $2.25
Ⓑ $22.50
Ⓒ $25.20
Ⓓ $225

19. Jane rolls a 5–10 **Number Cube** one time. What is the probability of her rolling an even number?

Ⓐ $\frac{1}{6}$
Ⓑ $\frac{3}{6}$
Ⓒ $\frac{4}{6}$
Ⓓ $\frac{5}{6}$

20. Mr. Mandra bought 1 notebook for $2.19. How much would 18 notebooks cost?

Ⓐ $3.42
Ⓑ $34.42
Ⓒ $39.04
Ⓓ $39.42

21. Which percent is equivalent to 0.259?

Ⓐ 0.259%
Ⓑ 2.59%
Ⓒ 25.9%
Ⓓ 259%

22. What is $\frac{3}{4}$ of 32?

Ⓐ 8
Ⓑ 16
Ⓒ 24
Ⓓ 28

23. Change the following to an equivalent division problem with a whole number divisor.

$$2.64 \div 3.4$$

Ⓐ $0.264 \div 0.34$
Ⓑ $26.4 \div 34$
Ⓒ $26.4 \div 3.4$
Ⓓ $264 \div 34$

24. What is $0.96 \div 0.8$?

Ⓐ 12
Ⓑ 120
Ⓒ 1.2
Ⓓ 0.12

25. Cleo bought lunch for $17.79. There is a 7% sales tax. How much will she have to pay altogether?

Ⓐ $10.94
Ⓑ $1.94
Ⓒ $19.04
Ⓓ $9.04

Choose the correct answer.

26. Cardone's Home Store buys a picture frame for $50. They then mark up the frame an additional 120% for retail sale. What will be the ticket price of the frame?

Ⓐ $70 Ⓑ $110
Ⓒ $120 Ⓓ $170

27. Carolyn works at the ballpark hot dog stand 3 days a week for $10 a game. How much will Carolyn make in 6 weeks?

Ⓐ $60 Ⓑ $18
Ⓒ $150 Ⓓ $180

28. Kevin has saved $53. He wants to buy a pair of sneakers that cost $67.50. How much more money does he need?

Ⓐ $14.50 Ⓑ $4.50
Ⓒ $45 Ⓓ $1.45

29. Carly put 6 marbles into a bag. If 3 are purple, 1 is yellow, and 2 are green, what is the probability that Carly will pull a purple marble out of the bag?

Ⓐ $\frac{1}{4}$ Ⓑ $\frac{1}{2}$
Ⓒ $\frac{3}{4}$ Ⓓ $\frac{2}{3}$

30. A triangle has side lengths of 5 inches and 3 inches. Which could be the length of the third side?

Ⓐ 1 in. Ⓑ 6 in.
Ⓒ 8 in. Ⓓ 10 in.

Ⓔ **Textbook** This lesson is available in the *eTextbook*.

Solve.

31. Before going to the register, Tiana added up everything she was buying. The total was $27.96. The sales tax in Tiana's state is 6%.

    a. Assuming that Tiana's calculations are correct, how much will the tax on her items be?

    b. What will be the total cost of Tiana's purchases with tax?

32. Jamie and her friends are playing a game in which they roll a ***Number Cube*** labeled 1–6 to move spaces on a game board.

    a. What is the probability that Darla will roll a 3 on her turn? Give your answer as a percent. Round to the nearest whole number.

    b. Darla landed on a space that allows her to roll the ***Number Cube*** two times and move the number of spaces equal to the sum of the two numbers she rolled. What are all the possible sums that Darla could roll?

    c. List all the possible ways you can get each sum.

	1	2	3	4	5	6
1						
2						
3						
4						
5						
6						

    d. What is the probability of Darla moving 6 spaces?

Measurement and Graphing

In This Chapter You Will Learn

- different ways to estimate measurements.
- how to convert measures.
- how to create, use, and interpret different kinds of graphs.

Problem Solving

On December 5, 1914, the *Endurance* and its crew, led by Ernest Shackleton, set sail from South Georgia Island. On January 18, 1915, the ship became trapped in the ice and could no longer be steered. The *Endurance* drifted for months at the mercy of giant slabs of frozen seawater. About how far did the *Endurance* drift?

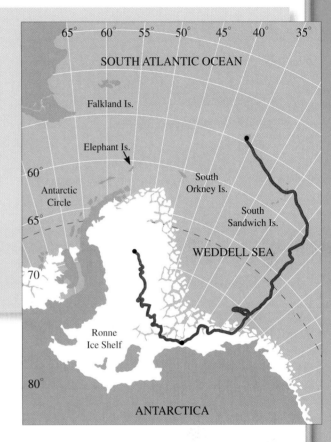

Answer the following questions.

1. About what fraction of the distance from the equator to the South Pole is Elephant Island?

2. The circumference of Earth is about 25,000 miles. About how many miles is it from the equator to the South Pole?

3. About how many miles would you travel if you went directly north from latitude 70° S to latitude 60° S?

4. How could you use the information from Problems 2 and 3 to estimate the scale of the map?

5. How far from where it began to drift in the ice did the *Endurance* sink?

Estimating Length

Key Ideas

Measures can be estimated using parts of your body.

One of the easiest body parts to use is your hand span.

Stretch out your hand on a ruler. Keep your thumb (or little finger) on the end. Note how many centimeters your hand can stretch. (It is probably between 15 and 20 centimeters.) If you want to measure something, you can count the number of times your hand span covers it. Multiply that number by the number of centimeters your hand span stretches. (Since you are growing, check your hand span from time to time to see if it changes.)

Example: Use the hand span to measure the width of the window.

This hand span is 20 centimeters. It takes 6 hand spans to cover the width of the window.

So, the width of the window is about $6 \times 20 = 120$ centimeters.

A smaller, but still useful, measure is the distance between the tip of your thumb and the knuckle. It is probably between two and three centimeters.

If you stretch out your arms and have someone measure the length from fingertip to fingertip, you will know your arm span. You can use this measure for longer distances, such as a window in a classroom.

e Textbook This lesson is available in the *eTextbook*.

Read the directions below and carefully record each piece of data in your responses.

1. Write down the measurements of your hand span, the distance between the tip of your thumb and your knuckle, your arm span, the length of your foot, and the distance from your fingertip to your elbow. You may need help from a classmate to determine some of these measurements.

2. Estimate various measurements, such as the length of a box, the length of a pencil, the length of the room, and the length of a table.

3. Measure these items with parts of your body, such as your foot or the distance between your elbow and your fingertip.

4. Check the estimates and the measurements by using a ruler, meterstick, or tape measure.

5. **Extended Response** Explain how you decided which body part to use for making your estimates. Do you think you could use any of these methods to measure any object? Explain.

 **Journal**

What have you learned about estimating measurements? When do you think you could use this knowledge?

Estimating Angles and Distances

Key Ideas

You can use the height of your fist to estimate the measures of angles and the length of your paces to estimate distance.

Hold your arm out straight in front of you and make a fist. The angle between the bottom of your fist, your eye, and the top of your fist is about 10°.

You can test this. Look at something at eye level that is not too close (at least five meters away).

Make a fist. Hold your arm out straight so that it appears to be resting on the distant object. Note the location of the top of your fist.

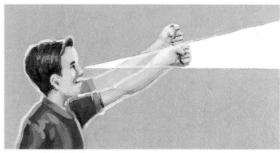

Then move your arm up slightly so that the bottom of your fist appears to be where the top was before.

Continue in this way until the top of your fist is directly above you. If this takes about 9 moves, your fist makes 10° angles because 9 moves add up to a 90° angle.

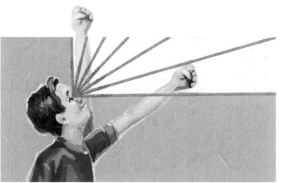

To help you estimate angles better, you can also use half a fist.

The measure from the bottom of your fist halfway to the top is about 5°. (*Halfway* is between your middle finger and ring finger.)

e Textbook This lesson is available in the *eTextbook*.

Work alone or in small groups to answer the following questions.

1 Find out how long your pace (distance between footsteps) is in meters. Use a meterstick or tape measure to find out how long ten of your paces are. Then divide to find the length of one pace.

2 Try to change your pace so that it is either 1 meter or 0.5 meter. If you learn how to take steps that are 1 meter or 0.5 meter each, it will be easier to pace off distances. Here is a way to change your pace: Measure out a 10-meter distance. Try to cover that distance in 10 or 20 paces.

3 Estimate the height of the front wall of your classroom (or of another room in the school). Use fists, paces, and a drawing to make your estimate.

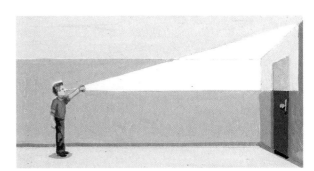

 a. Calculate your "eye level" in meters by measuring the distance from the floor to your eye. Record the result.

 b. Pace off 5 or 10 meters from the wall using your 1 meter or 0.5 meter paces. (For example, 10 paces at 0.5 meter each would equal 5 meters.)

 c. Use the fist method to estimate the angle from your (horizontal) eye level to the top of the wall.

 d. Create a scale drawing of your triangle on paper to find the height of the wall. Measure the height of the triangle in your drawing. What is your estimate for the height of the wall? (Do not forget to add your "eye level.")

4 See how close your estimate in Problem 3 was. Measure the height of the wall with a meterstick or tape measure. You may have to work with a classmate to find this measurement. Compare this measurement to your estimate.

5 Use the pace, fist, and drawing method to estimate heights of other tall objects. Compare your estimates with a classmate's estimates. When it is possible, find out the actual measured height and compare it with your estimate.

 **Journal**

When would you want to estimate a measure rather than find the actual measurement?

Applying Customary Measures

Key Ideas

Knowledge of fractions is useful when dealing with the customary system of measurement.

In the customary system, food and liquids are often measured based on the capacity of the container holding them. For instance, a gallon of milk is the amount of milk that fills up a container with a capacity of one gallon, and a teaspoon of sugar is the amount of sugar that fills up a teaspoon (a container with the capacity of a teaspoon). The relationships among the customary units of volume, such as teaspoons (tsp), tablespoons (tbsp), ounces (fl oz), cups (C), pints (pt), quarts (qt), and gallons (gal), are given below.

Customary Measures of Volume

3 teaspoons = 1 tablespoon	2 cups = 1 pint
2 tablespoons = 1 fluid ounce	2 pints = 1 quart
8 fluid ounces = 1 cup	4 quarts = 1 gallon

1 Using the information given above, copy and complete the table below.

Unit	Gallon(s) (gal)	Quart(s) (qt)	Pint(s) (pt)	Cup(s) (C)	Fluid Ounce(s) (fl oz)	Tablespoon(s) (tbsp)	Teaspoon(s) (tsp)
1 Tablespoon (tbsp)	▢	▢	▢	▢	▢	1	3
1 Fluid Ounce (fl oz)	▢	▢	▢	▢	1	▢	▢
1 Cup (C)	▢	▢	▢	1	▢	▢	▢
1 Pint (pt)	▢	▢	1	▢	▢	▢	▢
1 Quart (qt)	▢	1	▢	▢	▢	▢	▢
1 Gallon (gal)	1	▢	▢	▢	▢	▢	▢

Textbook This lesson is available in the *eTextbook*.

Solve the following problems.

2 Evan is going to make barbecued crab sandwiches. He has a recipe for 6 servings, but he wants to make only 2 servings. How much of each ingredient should he use?

Ingredients for 6 Servings

3 tablespoons butter or margarine

$\frac{1}{2}$ cup finely chopped celery

$\frac{1}{4}$ cup finely chopped onion

1 teaspoon instant chicken bouillon

$\frac{1}{2}$ cup tomato sauce

2 teaspoons Worcestershire sauce

2 teaspoons soy sauce

3 whole cloves

$\frac{3}{8}$ teaspoon salt

a pinch of pepper

$6\frac{3}{4}$ ounces crab meat

1 teaspoon parsley flakes

6 sandwich rolls

3 Kaya is planning to make cookies. Her recipe for Swedish pastry bonbons will make 60 cookies. How much of each ingredient does she need to make only 30 cookies?

Ingredients for 60 Cookies

1 cup butter

$\frac{2}{3}$ cup powdered sugar, sifted

1 cup pecans, finely chopped

1 teaspoon vanilla

2 cups flour, sifted

4 **Extended Response** Suppose you were adjusting a recipe, such as one of those above, and you had measuring cups for $\frac{1}{4}$ cup, $\frac{1}{3}$ cup, $\frac{1}{2}$ cup, and 1 cup. Explain what you would do if you needed to measure $\frac{1}{6}$ cup.

5 **Extended Response** If you only had 1 teaspoon, $\frac{1}{2}$ teaspoon, and $\frac{1}{4}$ teaspoon measuring spoons, how would you measure $\frac{1}{3}$ teaspoon?

6 Parker is going to make seven-minute icing. He wants to make only half the usual recipe. The recipe calls for 2 egg whites, $1\frac{1}{2}$ cups sugar, 5 tablespoons water, and $\frac{1}{4}$ teaspoon cream of tartar. The recipe says to cook the mixture over boiling water while beating it with a wire beater for seven minutes. Then add 1 teaspoon vanilla.

a. How much of each ingredient should Parker use to make half as much icing?

b. How long should he cook it?

Customary Measures of Weight

1 pound (lb) = 16 ounces (oz)

1 ton = 2,000 pounds

Use the information above to answer the following questions.

Jeri, Marshall, Ellen, and Cody shared the job of collecting cans after the sporting events at their school for a fund-raising activity. During the first 8 weeks, Jeri collected the cans twice, Marshall once, Ellen 3 times, and Cody twice. Mr. Finelli, the recycling plant owner, paid them 32¢ per pound for the cans. They earned $48 altogether for the 8 weeks.

7 What fraction of the time did Jeri collect cans? Marshall? Ellen? Cody?

8 What fraction of the time did Marshall and Ellen collect cans together?

9 What fraction of the money should each person get?

10 What fraction of the money should Jeri and Cody get altogether?

11 **a.** How much money should each person get?

  b. Based on your answer to question 9, why might some of the kids think the way they share the money is unfair?

12 How many pounds of cans did they collect altogether?

13 On average, about how many pounds did they collect per week?

14 If it takes 2 cans to make an ounce of aluminum, how many cans did Ellen probably collect?

15 Cody says that if they load the cans on his uncle's recycling truck, his uncle will pay them 55¢ per pound. How much more money would they make if they sold the cans to Cody's uncle rather than to Mr. Finelli?

Answer the following questions. Remember, the symbol ′ stands for feet, and the symbol ″ stands for inches.

The local cleaner charges $3.00 per square foot to clean a rug.

16 The Denizens have a rectangular rug that is $9\frac{1}{2}'$ long and $4\frac{3}{4}'$ wide. How much will the cleaners charge the Denizens to clean their rug?

17 The Denizens have another rectangular rug that is $6\frac{1}{4}'$ long and $4\frac{1}{2}'$ wide. How much should it cost to clean the rug?

18 How much would a rug that is 10′ 6″ by 6′ 8″ cost to clean?

19 **Extended Response** The clerk at the cleaners measured a circular rug, which had a diameter of 11′. About how much should it cost to clean the rug? Explain how you got your answer.

20 Suppose you wanted to give each of the 11 people on your camping trip an 8-ounce bag of trail mix. How many pounds of trail mix would you need?

21 Max needs $2\frac{1}{2}$ feet of material for each of the 12 costumes he is making for the school play. How many yards of material will Max need altogether?

22 **Extended Response** Tracy is making three 54–inch long shelves. If boards come in 8-foot lengths, how many boards does she need? Explain your answer.

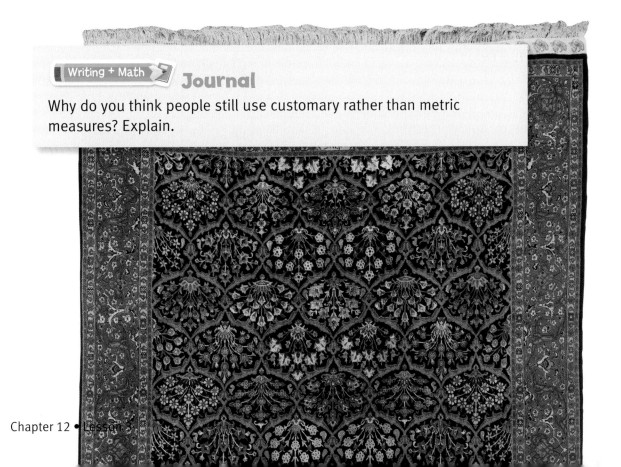

Writing + Math **Journal**

Why do you think people still use customary rather than metric measures? Explain.

Converting Measures

Key Ideas

It is useful to be able to communicate with others who use a different measurement system.

Most countries outside of the United States use the metric system. When we have measurements in one system, we can make rough estimates of what the measurements are in another system by using appropriate conversion factors.

For example, suppose Don was thinking about ordering a bookcase from a Web site and was not sure if it would fit in one spot of his room. If the space he had available was 3 feet 2 inches and the bookcase measured 75 centimeters, he could approximate the available space.

First, $3'2'' = 38''$ (inches).

Next, an inch is about $2\frac{1}{2}$ centimeters.

$38''$ is about $2\frac{1}{2} \times 38 = 95$ centimeters, so the bookcase should fit.

Don could have recognized that 75 centimeters is about $\frac{3}{4}$ of a meter. If he remembered that a yard ($3'$) is 0.9 meters, it would have been clear that the bookcase should fit.

This table lists some factors that we can use to estimate the metric equivalent for customary measurements.

Customary Unit	Approximate Metric Equivalent
Length	
1 inch	2.5 centimeters
1 foot	30 centimeters
1 yard	0.9 meters
1 mile	1.6 kilometers
Weight	
1 ounce	30 grams
1 pound	0.4 kilogram
Capacity	
1 fluid ounce	30 milliliters
1 gallon	4 liters

eTextbook This lesson is available in the *eTextbook*.

Use the table to estimate equivalents for the following measurements.

Metric Unit	Approximate Customary Equivalent
Length	
1 centimeter	0.4 inch
1 meter	40 inches
1 kilometer	0.6 miles
Mass	
1 kilogram	2.2 pounds
Capacity	
1 liter	1 quart

1 When you go hiking for the day, you should drink about 2 quarts of water. Will you have enough water if you take 2 full canteens, each of which holds 1 liter?

2 If you walk 3 miles per hour, about how many kilometers per hour will you walk? At that rate, how long would it take to walk 5 kilometers?

3 Anatoli says that the price of gas in Italy is about 65¢ per liter. If your gas tank holds about 15 gallons, how much would it cost to fill up there?

4 Jason would like to explain American football to his German friend Marcus. About how long is the 100-yard field in meters?

5 Marcus says that in his country, football is the most popular sport, but what they call football is what Americans call soccer. He says a World Cup football field can be as large as 110 meters by 75 meters. About what are the dimensions in yards?

6 The train from Munich to Paris travels 827 kilometers. About how many miles is that?

7 Marcus says his waist is 75 centimeters, and the inseam on his pants is 80 centimeters long. In inches, what size jeans should Jason send Marcus for his birthday (waist and inseam)?

8 Katie's pen pal, Hellé, lives in Norway. They both love snowboarding. Hellé wants to send Katie a new snowboard, but first they should make sure it is the right size for her weight. If Katie weighs 85 pounds, what should she tell Hellé her weight is in kilograms?

Measuring Time

Key Ideas

Fractions are a key part of time estimation and measurement.

Time is often reported by using fractions. If we measured time with a system based on 10, we would probably use decimals.

The fractions most often used with time are $\frac{1}{4}$, $\frac{1}{2}$, and $\frac{3}{4}$ of an hour.

For each quantity of hours, give the number of minutes.

1 $\frac{1}{4}$ hour

2 $\frac{3}{4}$ hour

3 $1\frac{1}{2}$ hours

4 $2\frac{1}{4}$ hours

5 $\frac{1}{3}$ hour

6 $\frac{1}{5}$ hour

Answer the following questions.

7 About how long would it take you to walk 10 miles if you could walk 1 mile in 20 minutes? In 18 minutes?

8 How long would it take for Michael to do 5 loads of laundry if each load takes 20 minutes to wash and 45 minutes to dry (assuming you can wash the next load while the previous one is being dried)?

9 If you read 8 articles in 1 hour, what was the average amount of time it took you to read each article?

10 Ricardo spent $3\frac{3}{4}$ hours writing a science report. How many minutes did he spend writing?

11 Heidi said she would meet Al at the corner of Fifth and Main in $2\frac{1}{2}$ hours. The time was 2:15 P.M. when Heidi said this. What time were they supposed to meet?

eTextbook This lesson is available in the *eTextbook*.

What time will it be

12 $3\frac{1}{2}$ hours after 7:15 P.M.?

13 $4\frac{1}{2}$ hours after 6:00 P.M.?

14 $6\frac{1}{4}$ hours after 4:30 A.M.?

15 10 hours after 1:45 A.M.?

16 12 hours after 1:45 P.M.?

17 1 hour after 11:45 P.M.?

18 $12\frac{1}{6}$ hours after 11:45 P.M.?

19 $12\frac{1}{5}$ hours after 1:45 A.M.?

Answer the following questions.

20 You would like to see a movie that starts at 2:25 P.M. and is 116 minutes long. What time would the movie be over?

21 The circus starts at 2:30 P.M. and ends $2\frac{1}{4}$ hours later. What time will it be over?

22 A train leaves New York at 12:45 P.M., and it arrives in Westbury $\frac{3}{4}$ hour later. What time does it get there?

23 Pedro runs for $1\frac{1}{2}$ hours each day. If he starts running at 3:30 P.M., what time will it be when he finishes?

24 Kate rode her bicycle for $\frac{1}{2}$ hour and then swam for $1\frac{3}{4}$ hours. If she started her bike ride at 9:15 A.M., what time did she finish doing both activities?

25 School begins at 8:15 A.M. If it takes $\frac{1}{4}$ hour to walk to school, what is the latest time you could leave home and still arrive at school on time?

26 If it takes 25 seconds for your video game to load and you play it once a day, how long do you wait for it per year (assuming 365 days)?

27 What time will it be $6\frac{3}{4}$ hours after 7:30 A.M.?

Some people (and some countries) use a 24-hour system, in which times can be written or said as 16:30 (or simply 1630). However, we usually start over when we pass 12:00 noon.

Answer the following questions.

28 What time would it be 6 hours before 5:30 A.M.?

29 What time would it be $2\frac{1}{4}$ hours before 10:00 A.M.?

30 How many hours are between 12:30 P.M. and 2:45 P.M.?

31 How many hours are between 10:30 A.M. and 2:45 P.M.?

32 How many hours are between 6:15 A.M. and 2:45 P.M.?

33 James K. Polk School is in session from 8:15 A.M. to 3:00 P.M. How many hours long is the school day?

34 A movie is playing at 2:00 P.M., 5:00 P.M., 8:00 P.M., and 11:15 P.M. The theater always allows at least $\frac{1}{4}$ hour between showings for cleaning. What is the greatest possible length of the movie?

35 Jennifer's grandparents are coming for a visit. Her family needs to allow $\frac{1}{2}$ hour to drive to the train station and $\frac{1}{4}$ hour to park and walk to the station. The train arrives at 12:15 P.M. What is the latest time Jennifer's family should leave for the train station?

36 Mrs. Lopez wants to serve a turkey dinner at 6:00 P.M. She also knows that she wants to take the turkey out of the oven $\frac{1}{2}$ hour before dinner. The turkey needs to cook for $4\frac{1}{4}$ hours. At what time should she start cooking the turkey?

e Textbook This lesson is available in the *eTextbook.*

Solve the following problems.

37 Marco wants to study his spelling words for at least $\frac{3}{4}$ hour before he watches any television. He studied from 3:45 P.M. to 4:15 P.M. Has he studied for $\frac{3}{4}$ hour yet?

38 Each of the 2 acts in the school play will take $\frac{3}{4}$ hour. The intermission will be $\frac{1}{4}$ hour long. If the play begins at 7:00 P.M., about what time will it end?

39 Tom began working on his book report at 6:45 P.M. He took a $\frac{1}{4}$-hour break at 8:00 P.M. He finished his report at 10:00 P.M. For how many hours did Tom work on his book report?

40 Jennifer takes 15 to 20 minutes to make an invitation. If she needs to make 20 invitations, about how long will it take her?

41 **Extended Response** Horst timed himself counting from 1 to 100. His stopwatch read 39.7 seconds. At that rate, about how long would it take him to count to 15,000? Why might your estimate be off?

42 It is 2:30 A.M. in London and 9:30 P.M. the previous day in Josiane's home town. Her mother is traveling to London on business, and her plane is scheduled to land at 7:45 A.M. in London. If it takes $2\frac{1}{2}$ hours to get through customs, get to her hotel and check in, and she promises to call Josiane as soon as she gets to her hotel room, at what time should Josiane expect her call?

Writing + Math **Journal**

Can you think of any reasons why the hour is divided into 60 minutes rather than some other number of minutes? Explain your reasoning.

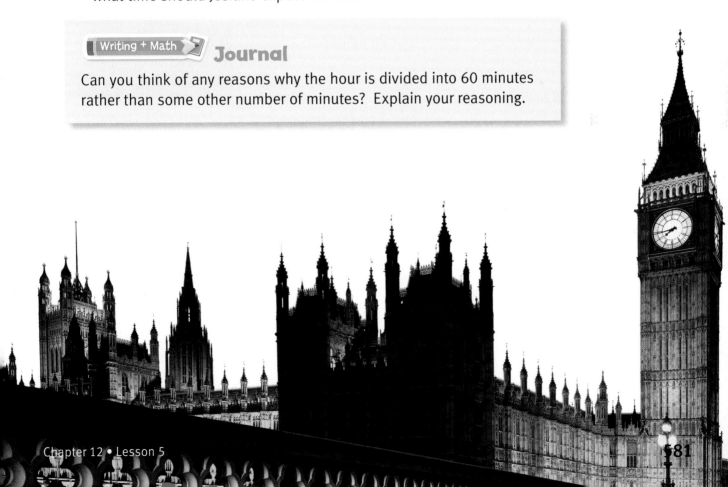

Key Ideas

Angle measurement and telling time with an analog clock are related.

A full circle is 360°, and there are 60 minutes in 1 hour. When the minute hand of a clock makes one complete circle around the clock, how far does the hour hand move? The answer is 30° because 360 ÷ 12 = 30. You can use this fact to help you find how many degrees the minute hand moves around the clock in different amounts of time.

If the minute hand moves 360° in 1 hour and 6° in 1 minute, how many degrees does it move in

1   5 minutes?

2   $\frac{1}{2}$ hour?

3   $\frac{3}{4}$ hour?

4   $\frac{1}{3}$ hour?

5   55 minutes?

6   59 minutes?

7   61 minutes?

8   2 hours?

9   $1\frac{1}{2}$ hours?

10   $1\frac{3}{4}$ hours?

11   $\frac{1}{4}$ hour?

12   45 minutes?

Answer the following questions.

13   If you divide a circle into 3 equally-sized sectors, what is the measure of each angle?

14   If you divide a circle into 9 equally-sized sectors, how many degrees would each sector have? Draw such a circle.

15   If a pie had equally-sized slices that were 30° each, how many slices would there be in the whole pie?

e Textbook This lesson is available in the *eTextbook*.

Answer the following questions.

16 Andrew was assigned to cut a cake at the picnic, but he was told that the older children should get pieces that were twice as big as those the younger children got. If there were 4 older children and 2 younger ones, answer the following:

    a. How many pieces should there be?

    b. How many degrees should the smaller pieces have?

    c. How many degrees should the larger pieces have?

    d. **Extended Response** Explain how you got your answers.

17 **Extended Response** Ethan said he ate $\frac{1}{2}$ of a cake on Tuesday, $\frac{1}{3}$ of the cake on Wednesday, and $\frac{1}{4}$ of the cake on Thursday. Is this possible? Explain.

18 Alameda looked at a circle graph of the yearly finances of her favorite charity. There was a section of 18° for operating expenses, and the rest of the money was used to care for orphaned children.

Charity's Children Budget

☐ operating expenses
■ child care

    a. What percent of the charity's total finances went toward operating expenses?

    b. What fraction of the total operating cost is that?

    c. If the charity raised $20,000 that year, how much of that money went toward caring for the orphans?

    d. If the charity raised $10,000 that year, how much of the money went toward caring for the orphans?

Writing + Math **Journal**

Explain in your own words how telling time relates to fractions.

The explorers of the Shackleton expedition knew they had been carried so far north by the ice flows that no one would find them. So they drifted, marched, sailed, and rowed, desperately trying to make their way back to solid land and civilization. When they traveled over frozen terrain, the explorers had to pull their boats behind them. In the summer months, they journeyed at night when the snow was less slushy.

These excerpts from Shackleton's diary describe part of a 7-day westward march. During this period, did the expedition travel faster or slower than $\frac{1}{3}$ mile per hour when they were on the move? Assume the stop for lunch was 1 hour.

> **Dec. 26.**
>
> At 9:30 P.M. we were off again. We did a good march of $1\frac{1}{2}$ miles before we halted for "lunch" at 1 A.M., and then on for another mile, when at 5 A.M. we camped by a little sloping berg. Nine P.M., the 27th, saw us on the march again. The first 200 yards took us about 5 hours to cross...We managed to get another $\frac{3}{4}$ of a mile before lunch and a further mile...before we camped at 5 A.M.

Clara solved the problem this way:

I decided to Make a Table.

I thought a table would help me organize the information I had, so I could find the time and distance the crew traveled.

Date	Time Interval	Hours on the Move	Miles Traveled
Dec. 26, 27	9:30 P.M.–1 A.M.	$3\frac{1}{2}$	$1\frac{1}{2}$
Dec. 27	(lunch) 1 A.M.–2 A.M.	0	0
Dec. 27	▢	▢	▢

Think about Clara's strategy. Answer the following questions.

1. What do you think Clara will write in the row next to Dec. 27?

2. How does the table help in solving the problem?

3. When Clara completes her table, what can she do next to continue to solve the problem?

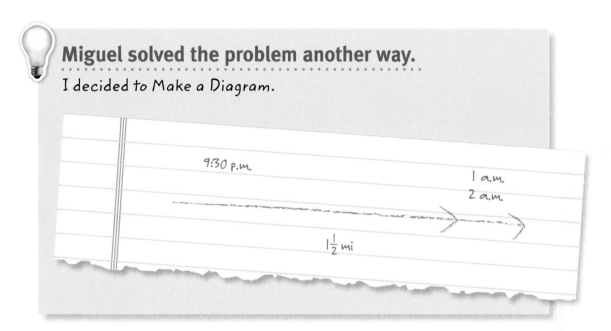

Miguel solved the problem another way.

I decided to Make a Diagram.

9:30 p.m.

1 a.m.
2 a.m.

$1\frac{1}{2}$ mi

Think about Miguel's strategy. Answer the following questions.

4. What do you think Miguel will write next?

5. How is Miguel's strategy like Clara's? How is it different?

6. Do you think Miguel's strategy will work? Explain.

7. Solve the problem. Use any strategy you think will work.

8. What strategy did you use? Why?

Cumulative Review

Comparing Fractions Lesson 6.7

Write $>$, $<$, or $=$.

1. $\frac{1}{6}$ ▢ $\frac{1}{4}$

2. $\frac{5}{6}$ ▢ $\frac{2}{4}$

3. $\frac{1}{2}$ ▢ $\frac{6}{12}$

4. $\frac{3}{4}$ ▢ $\frac{1}{2}$

5. $\frac{5}{12}$ ▢ $\frac{1}{2}$

6. $\frac{2}{4}$ ▢ $\frac{3}{4}$

7. $\frac{1}{3}$ ▢ $\frac{2}{6}$

8. $\frac{4}{8}$ ▢ $\frac{2}{3}$

Adding Fractions Greater than 1 Lesson 7.3

Add. Write your answers as mixed numbers, fractions, or whole numbers.

9. $\frac{1}{3} + 1\frac{2}{3} = n$

10. $4\frac{1}{5} + 2\frac{3}{10} = n$

11. $\frac{5}{4} + 7\frac{1}{4} = n$

12. $2\frac{1}{2} + 7\frac{5}{8} = n$

13. $2 + 1\frac{3}{7} = n$

14. $\frac{4}{5} + 3\frac{4}{5} = n$

15. $2\frac{2}{3} + 3\frac{1}{6} = n$

16. $7\frac{4}{9} + \frac{16}{9} = n$

Rounding Decimals Lesson 3.10

Round each of the following numbers to the nearest hundredth.

17. 4.7380389

18. 0.007

19. 4.735

Round each of the following numbers to the nearest thousandth.

20. 1.23456

21. 1.2345

22. 1.234499999

Space Figures Lesson 10.10

Picture a triangular prism.

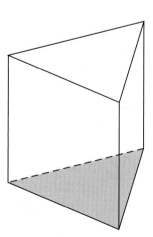

23. How many faces does the triangular prism have?

24. How many sides are there in these polygons?

25. How many edges does the triangular prism have?

26. How many corners do these polygons have?

27. How many vertices does the triangular prism have?

ⓔ Textbook This lesson is available in the *eTextbook*.

Multiplying Decimals by Whole Numbers Lesson 3.9
Multiply.

28 $617 \times 2.5 = $ ▢

29 $451 \times 82.3 = $ ▢

30 $256 \times 1.2 = $ ▢

31 $673 \times 5.6 = $ ▢

Solve.

32 Jerod needs 1 bag of fertilizer to fertilize 10 square meters of his garden. The length of the garden is 12 meters and the width is 6.5 meters. How many bags of fertilizer should he buy?

33 Bart is the manager of a baseball team. His team needs 13 new shirts. Each shirt costs $7.29. Bart has $75.

a. Does he have enough money?

b. If not, how much more money does Bart need?

Applying Math Lesson 3.5
Solve.

34 Mr. Quincy paid $2.10 for 7 onions. How much did each onion cost?

35 Antonio bought 9 glass beads for 72¢. How much should 10 glass beads cost?

36 The grocery store sells 2 cans of cat food for 48¢. How much would 1 can of cat food cost?

37 Greg drove for 8 hours. He traveled about 45 miles each hour. About how many miles did he drive?

38 Chrissy has 37 balloons. If she divides the balloons equally among 5 friends,

a. how many balloons should she give each friend?

b. will there be any balloons left over? If so, how many?

Pictographs and Data Collection

Key Ideas

Sometimes graphing data makes the information easier to understand; however, sometimes it can also be misleading. It is important to know how information in a graph or table was collected.

Juan wanted to find out how many books New City residents read per month. He conducted a survey, asking people about how many books they check out of their local library each month. He spent two afternoons at the library, asking the same question of people as they left. Juan's results are shown in the table below.

Number of People	1	8	12	14	20	25	51	35	24	4	3	2	1
Number of Books Checked Out per Month	15	13	10	9	8	7	6	5	4	3	2	1	0

Answer the following questions using the table above.

1. How fairly do Juan's results portray the reading habits of the people who live in New City? Explain your answer.

2. Did Juan's survey reach only people who use the library often?

e Textbook This lesson is available in the *eTextbook*.

As part of his report, Juan made the pictograph below to display the results of his survey.

Books Checked Out Per Month

0–2	3–5	6–8	9–12	12–15	10 People

Number of Books

Answer the following questions using the pictograph above.

3 **Extended Response** Study Juan's pictograph. Write questions that can be answered using the information in the graph.

4 Which method, the table or the pictograph, shows Juan's survey results in a way that makes it easier to see how many books his group says they check out?

5 What is the advantage of the table?

6 What is the advantage of the pictograph?

7 **Extended Response** If you wanted to show that your community needs a larger library, what kind of information would you collect?

Juan's little sister Marisa conducted a survey of all the children who visited the library. She asked them if they had their own library cards. She made two graphs of her data, as shown below.

Library Card Ownership

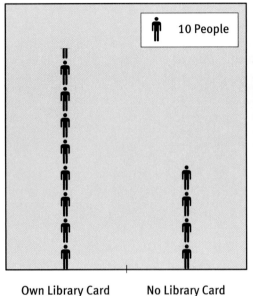

| Own Library Card | No Library Card |

Library Card Ownership

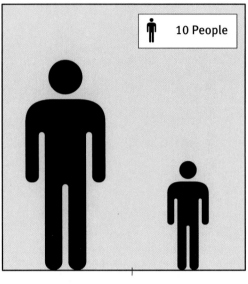

| Own Library Card | No Library Card |

Extended Response **Answer** the following questions using the graphs.

8. Do you find one of these graphs to be misleading? Why?

Suppose Juan also wanted to find out about how many books each of the library patrons checked out in the last year.

9. How could Juan estimate this without asking the question?

10. How could you tell if Juan used estimation?

11. How could Juan keep track of the responses to this question?

e Textbook This lesson is available in the *eTextbook*.

Juan's friend Lyla suggested that he make a stem-and-leaf plot. She said it would be easier for people to compare the number of books they checked out to the number of books other patrons checked out.

Suppose the first 20 people checked out the following numbers of books in the past year:

17, 82, 33, 21, 38, 11, 71, 78, 44, 99, 67, 45, 16, 58, 115, 111, 80, 1, 63, 62

Instead of writing a long list, you could set up a stem-and-leaf plot as follows:

0 | 1	(representing 1)
1 | 7, 1, 6	(representing 17, 11, and 16)
2 | 1	(representing 21)
3 | 3, 8	(representing 33 and 38)
4 | 4, 5	(representing 44 and 45)
5 | 8	(representing 58)
6 | 7, 3, 2	(representing 67, 63, and 62)
7 | 1, 8	(representing 71 and 78)
8 | 2, 0	(representing 82 and 80)
9 | 9	(representing 99)
10|	
11| 5, 1	(representing 115 and 111)

The first column contains the tens or hundreds digits (the stems), and the second column contains the ones digit for each entry (the leaves).

12 How many people from this group of 20 say they check out an average of 12 or more books per month? 3–5 books per month?

13 What is the median number of books this group of 20 checked out?

14 **Extended Response** Do you think the data from these 20 people corresponds to the data in the pictograph? Why or why not?

15 Suppose Lyla's class had the following grades on a test:

85, 25, 67, 99, 76, 74, 92, 88, 53, 71, 77, 83, 75, 60, 71

Make a stem-and-leaf plot of their grades.

Writing + Math **Journal**

Describe a situation in which you might want to use a stem-and-leaf plot. Explain why you think it would be an appropriate choice.

Making Circle Graphs

Key Ideas

There are different ways to display data in a graph. Choosing the most appropriate way for your purposes may require some thought.

Al, Janet, and Kim were running for fifth-grade president. Fritz decided to ask all 60 fifth graders who they wanted for president. Here are the first 10 responses:

Janet, Al, Al, Janet, Kim, Al, Janet, Kim, Kim, Al

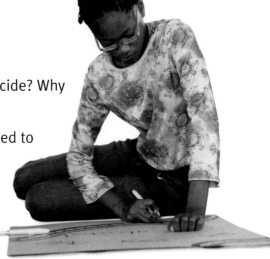

1 Who do you think is going to win?

2 Do you think you have enough information to decide? Why or why not?

Fritz is analyzing the data he has collected. He decided to just write the initial of each candidate instead of the whole name. Using that procedure, he repeated the first 10 and continued. He wrote the initials in groups of 10 to make it easier to tell if he had all 60 votes.

Here is what he wrote:

JAAJKAJKKA JJJAKKJAJA AJJAJJJJAJ JJAJAKAJJJ
KJJAJJAKJJ JKAAJJJAJJ

As you can see, it is not easy to tell who got the most votes. So, Fritz made a tally chart and a bar graph, as shown below.

3 Now can you decide which person received the most votes? If so, who did?

e Textbook This lesson is available in the *eTextbook*.

4 Is it easy to see whether that person received a majority of the votes? (Hint: Think about what *majority* means—more than half.)

Fritz decided to make a circle graph to display his data. Since he knew there were 60 votes and that there are 360° in a circle, he decided to let 6° stand for each vote.

5 Why did he do that?

Here is his circle graph:

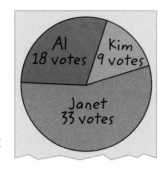

6 **Extended Response** Does this make it easier to quickly determine who received the most votes and whether that person has more than half, or 50%, of the votes? Explain why or why not.

7 **Extended Response** If there had been only 45 votes, how many degrees of the circle graph would have been needed to represent each vote? How did you get that number?

For each of the following numbers of votes, determine about how many degrees would be needed to represent each vote in a circle graph. Give your answers to the nearest tenth of a degree.

8 20

9 30

10 18

11 100

12 23

13 50

14 46

15 69

16 21

17 Using the following data, make a tally chart, a bar graph, and a circle graph: AABACCABAC CABACAACBB BACCACBACC ABCCAABABC.

    a. How many degrees did you allow for each piece of information?

    b. How many degrees did you use to show all the As?

    c. How many degrees did you use to show the Bs?

    d. How many degrees did you use to show the Cs?

    e. What is the total of those three numbers?

    f. Are more than half of the letters the same (A, B, or C)? If so, which?

18 Collect some data, such as how many siblings each classmate has. Show the information in a tally chart, a bar graph, and a circle graph.

Creating and Using Graphs

Key Ideas

There are situations in which one type of graph may show information better than another. A properly labeled graph can often communicate data effectively.

Mrs. Bonilla's fifth-grade class took a poll to see how many members of the class were born in each month. They made the following bar graph to display their results.

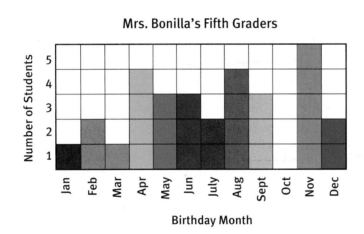

Mrs. Bonilla's Fifth Graders

(Number of Students vs. Birthday Month)

Chrysanthemum
November

Daisy
April

Use the bar graph above to answer the following questions.

1. How many of the students were born in January?

2. In which month were the most students born? How many students were born in that month?

3. In which month were the fewest students born? How many students were born in that month?

4. How many students are in Ms. Bonilla's class?

5. In how many different months were four students born?

6. In how many different months were three students born?

7. In how many different months were two students born?

8. In how many different months was just one student born?

The class also decided to make a circle graph to display the information about their birthdays.

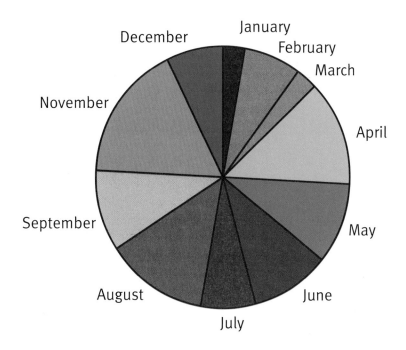

Mrs. Bonilla's Fifth Graders'
Birthday Months

Use the circle graph above to help you answer the following questions.

9 Does the circle graph seem to be correct? Explain your answer.

10 Can you tell from the circle graph how many people were born in each month?

11 Can you tell from the circle graph about what fraction of the people were born in November? Was it more than $\frac{1}{4}$ of the students?

12 **Extended Response** Were more than half of the students born in the first six months of the year or in the last six months of the year? Is this easier to tell from the bar graph or from the circle graph? Explain your answers.

On a bar graph, the lengths of the bars represent numbers, and the bars compare different items or objects. For example, with the graph on the previous page, you can use the bars to determine which month has the most birthdays for that class.

There are different ways to make a bar graph. The first step in making a bar graph is to collect data. Once you have your information and organize it, you have to find the best way to display it on the graph. A good bar graph has a title that explains what the data measures, along with appropriately labeled *x*- and *y*-axes.

Answer the following questions. Think about the activity you did in class.

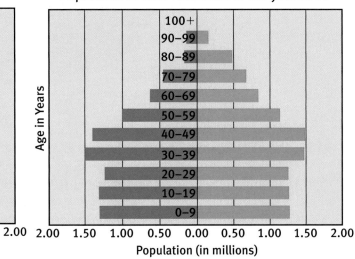

⓭ What were the largest age groups of males and females in New York in 2000?

⓮ In 2000, how many people were more than 99 years old?

⓯ **Extended Response** Which of the two graphs above is labeled better? Explain.

⓰ **Extended Response** Write some questions you could answer using the bar graph on the right.

e Textbook This lesson is available in the *eTextbook*.

Answer the following questions.

17. Jill jogs 5 miles to the park and 5 miles back every day.

   a. How many miles does Jill jog to and from the park each day?

   b. How far does she jog to and from the park in 1 week (7 days)?

   c. How far does Jill jog in 4 weeks?

18. Make a bar graph showing how far Jill jogs to and from the park in 4 weeks (0–28 days). Be sure to leave enough room so you can fit all the miles she will have jogged in 4 weeks (28 days).

19. **Extended Response** Suppose you were taking a survey about your classmates' favorite type of music. What type of graph would you use to display your survey results? Why?

20. **Extended Response** If your school was raising money for band camp and wanted to chart the progress of the fund-raising over time, what type of graph would you recommend? Why?

Making Line Graphs

Key Ideas

Line graphs display data effectively because they show trends more clearly than tables and are easy to create. These graphs are particularly useful for showing data that change over time.

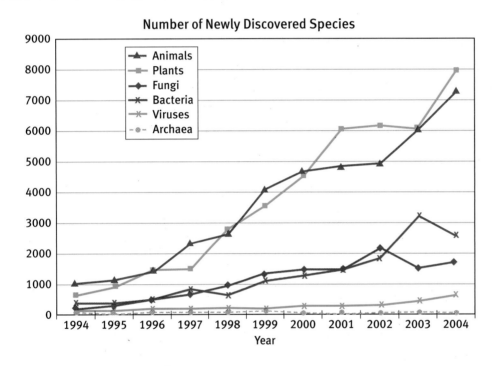

Number of Newly Discovered Species

Use the line graph above to answer Problems 1–10.

1 About how many new species of fungi were discovered in 2003?

2 Are there generally more discoveries of viruses or archaea (a kind of microorganism)?

3 In 2001, which category of species had the most newly discovered varieties?

4 About how many new species of that type were discovered that year?

5 Did this category have the most newly discovered species for every year in the graph?

6 In what year displayed in the graph were the most new species of fungi discovered?

e Textbook This lesson is available in the *eTextbook*.

7 **Extended Response** Are there more plant species than animal species? Explain.

8 **Extended Response** Were there more than 1,100 new species discovered in 1994? How do you know?

9 According to the graph, is the discovery rate of new animal species increasing, decreasing or staying the same?

10 **Extended Response** According to the graph, is the number of known bacteria species increasing, decreasing, or staying the same? How do you know?

11 The following table compares the changes in the pulse rates of two runners after they stopped exercising. Using data in the following table, make one line graph of the pulse rates of the two runners with the two lines on the same graph. Make sure to label your graph properly.

Pulse Rates after Finishing Exercise

Minutes after Stopping Exercise	0	1	2	3	4	5
Runner 1	148	122	107	96	89	85
Runner 2	142	95	80	75	74	73

Use your line graph to answer the following questions.

12 Which runner's pulse changed the most?

13 When did the two runners have the biggest difference between their pulse rates?

14 Which runner's pulse rate decreased more quickly?

Writing + Math **Journal**

Which runner would you guess to be more physically fit? Explain your reasoning.

Interpreting Graphs

Key Ideas

A graph is only useful if you can interpret the information it displays. Interpreting a graph requires thinking about the kind of graph being shown and determining what information it is presenting.

In 2002, the income of the federal government was distributed approximately as shown in the circle graph below. The total income was about 1.85 trillion dollars, or about $1,850,000,000,000.

U.S. Budget Income in 2002

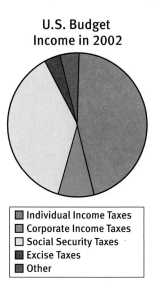

Individual Income Taxes
Corporate Income Taxes
Social Security Taxes
Excise Taxes
Other

Use the circle graph to answer the following questions.

1. What was the greatest source of income for the government? Was it more than half the total income?

2. What was the second greatest source of income? Together, did individual income taxes and social security taxes account for more than $\frac{3}{4}$ of the government's income?

3. What was the least source of income for the government included in this graph?

4. Was the least source of income less than $\frac{1}{4}$ of the total income?

5. Estimate the total amount of income provided by social security taxes, excise taxes, and corporate income taxes.

6. Were the two least sources of income greater than or less than $\frac{1}{4}$ of the total income?

7. Corporate income taxes contributed $148,044,000,000 to the federal government's income. Is this amount closer to $\frac{1}{4}$ or $\frac{1}{10}$ of the total income?

8. Individual income taxes and social security taxes combined are called *payroll taxes* because they are deducted from workers' paychecks. About what was the total payroll tax in 2002?

9. If there were about 287,940,000 people in the United States in 2002, about how much payroll tax was there for each person?

e Textbook This lesson is available in the *eTextbook.*

The graph below shows the per capita (or per person) income in 1999 for several states as well as the national average for the entire United States.

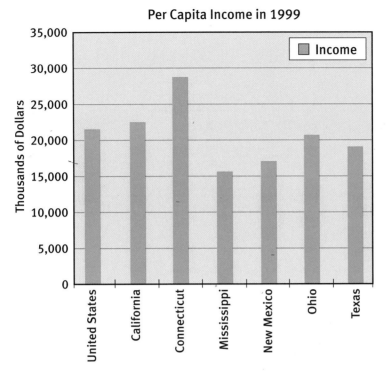

Per Capita Income in 1999

Use the bar graph above to answer the following questions.

10 Which state had the greatest per capita income?

11 Which state had the least per capita income?

12 What was the approximate difference in per capita income between the states with the greatest and least per capita income?

13 About what was the average per capita income for the United States?

14 Which of the states shown in the graph had per capita incomes below the national average?

15 Which of the states shown had per capita incomes greater than the national average?

16 **Extended Response** Mississippi's population is about $1\frac{1}{2}$ times the population of New Mexico. Which state has a higher total income for all residents? How can you tell?

 **Journal**

Compare and contrast the different graphs you have learned about. What are the advantages and disadvantages of each one?

Plotting the Impossible Rescue

Stranded on Elephant Island, the explorers realized their only hope of survival lay in a death-defying boat ride back to the island from which they had set sail more than a year earlier.

On April 24, 1916, Shackleton and five hand-picked crewmen boarded the *James Caird*, ready to face 50-foot waves and icy gales. To guide the craft to a tiny island across 800 miles of stormy Antarctic waters, the navigator, Frank Worsley, had only two instruments and some charts.

Only four times during the 17-day voyage did the sun peek through the clouds enough for Worsley to use this sextant to measure its angle in the sky.

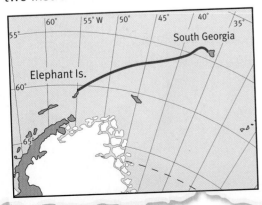

To determine longitude, Worsley used this chronometer, the last of the 24 accurate clocks with which the expedition had started.

e Textbook This lesson is available in the *eTextbook*.

As you know, longitude tells you how many degrees east or west of the prime meridian you are. You can find your longitude if you know the time difference between where you are and Greenwich, England. A navigator can use a chronometer to find that difference.

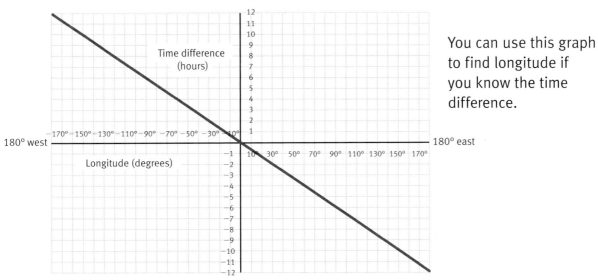

You can use this graph to find longitude if you know the time difference.

Think about and discuss the following questions.

1. Suppose you are at 30°W longitude. You know it is noon where you are because the sun is at its highest point in the sky. What time is it in Greenwich, England?

2. Suppose you are somewhere, and the sun is at its highest elevation. Your chronometer tells you it is 9 A.M. in Greenwich, England. What is your longitude?

3. How many hours does it take for Earth to turn 360°?

4. How many hours does it take for Earth to turn 15°?

5. How could you answer Problems 1 and 2 if you did not have the graph but you knew how Earth rotated?

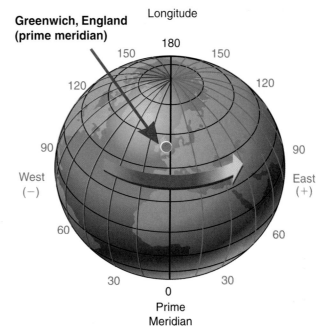

Imagine you are navigating the *James Caird* to South Georgia Island so the twenty-two crewmen waiting behind can be rescued. Two days have passed since you left Elephant Island. The skies have finally cleared. It is around noon. Despite the tossing waves, you take these readings with your sextant and chronometer.

Place	Latitude	Longitude
Elephant Island	61°S	55°W
South Georgia Island	54°S	38°W

Date	Computed Latitude	Time on Chronometer at Noon	Computed Longitude
April 26, 1915	$59\frac{3}{4}$°S	3:30 P.M.	▨

Work in groups to navigate your ship. Discuss and solve the following problems. Make a map like the one shown to help you.

6 What is your longitude?

7 How many miles from Elephant Island have you traveled? Remember what you learned about calculating distance from the Chapter Introduction.

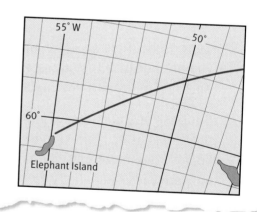

The next few days bring freezing winds and pounding waves. Everything is drenched—even your tables. Finally, on April 29, the weather allows another look at the sun. You take advantage of this opportunity to get more readings.

Solve the following problems. Look for strategies that will make your work easier.

8 What is your position now?

9 How should you change your course?

10 How many miles from Elephant Island have you traveled?

April 29, 1915

Computed Latitude	Time on Chronometer at Noon	Computed Longitude
$58\frac{2}{3}$°S	3:55 P.M.	▨

ⓔ **Textbook** This lesson is available in the *eTextbook*.

As you know, longitude tells you how many degrees east or west of the prime meridian you are. You can find your longitude if you know the time difference between where you are and Greenwich, England. A navigator can use a chronometer to find that difference.

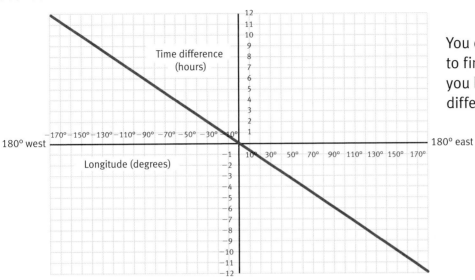

You can use this graph to find longitude if you know the time difference.

Think about and discuss the following questions.

1. Suppose you are at 30°W longitude. You know it is noon where you are because the sun is at its highest point in the sky. What time is it in Greenwich, England?

2. Suppose you are somewhere, and the sun is at its highest elevation. Your chronometer tells you it is 9 A.M. in Greenwich, England. What is your longitude?

3. How many hours does it take for Earth to turn 360°?

4. How many hours does it take for Earth to turn 15°?

5. How could you answer Problems 1 and 2 if you did not have the graph but you knew how Earth rotated?

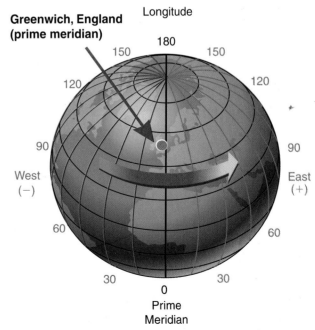

Exploring Problem Solving

Imagine you are navigating the *James Caird* to South Georgia Island so the twenty-two crewmen waiting behind can be rescued. Two days have passed since you left Elephant Island. The skies have finally cleared. It is around noon. Despite the tossing waves, you take these readings with your sextant and chronometer.

Place	Latitude	Longitude
Elephant Island	61°S	55°W
South Georgia Island	54°S	38°W

Date	Computed Latitude	Time on Chronometer at Noon	Computed Longitude
April 26, 1915	$59\frac{3}{4}$°S	3:30 P.M.	

Work in groups to navigate your ship. Discuss and solve the following problems. Make a map like the one shown to help you.

6 What is your longitude?

7 How many miles from Elephant Island have you traveled? Remember what you learned about calculating distance from the Chapter Introduction.

The next few days bring freezing winds and pounding waves. Everything is drenched—even your tables. Finally, on April 29, the weather allows another look at the sun. You take advantage of this opportunity to get more readings.

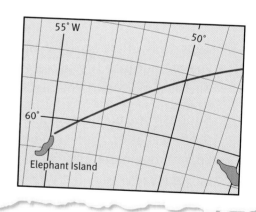

Solve the following problems. Look for strategies that will make your work easier.

8 What is your position now?

9 How should you change your course?

10 How many miles from Elephant Island have you traveled?

April 29, 1915

Computed Latitude	Time on Chronometer at Noon	Computed Longitude
$58\frac{2}{3}$°S	3:55 P.M.	

Cumulative Review

Subtracting Mixed Numbers Lesson 7.4

Solve the following subtraction exercises. Write your answers as mixed numbers, fractions, or whole numbers.

1. $n = 4\frac{4}{16} - 3\frac{1}{4}$

2. $3\frac{1}{16} + 1\frac{1}{4} = n$

3. $3\frac{5}{12} - 2\frac{1}{6} = n$

4. $\frac{1}{2} - \frac{1}{3} = n$

5. $n = 6\frac{2}{3} - 4\frac{1}{7}$

6. $4\frac{13}{16} - 3\frac{3}{4} = n$

Metric Units of Weight and Volume Lesson 3.7

Solve.

7. 3 mL = ☐ L

8. 500 mL = ☐ L

9. 0.025 L = ☐ mL

10. 63 mL = ☐ L

11. 0.725 L = ☐ mL

12. 5 L = ☐ mL

13. 2 g = ☐ kg

14. 805 g = ☐ kg

15. 40 g = ☐ kg

16. 0.005 kg = ☐ g

17. 0.3 kg = ☐ g

18. 620 g = ☐ kg

Applying Decimals Lesson 3.15

Solve these problems.

19. If 3 cans of soup cost $1.98, how much is 1 can of soup?

20. If 7 pencils cost $1.05, how much is that per pencil?

21. If 3 quarts of milk cost $1.74, how much is that per quart?

22. If 4 apples cost 92¢, how much is 1 apple?

23. Joni needs to buy 24 containers of yogurt for her classmates. She can buy 1 at 55¢, a 6-pack for $2.98, or she can buy a 12-pack for $5.80. What is the cheapest way to buy 24 containers? Why?

Estimating Quotients Lesson 8.10

For each division exercise below, several answers are given but only one is correct. Decide which is correct in each case.

24 $323 \div 19 = $ ▨

    Ⓐ 37

    Ⓑ 15

    Ⓒ 17

    Ⓓ 27

25 $6,776 \div 88 = $ ▨

    Ⓐ 77

    Ⓑ 107

    Ⓒ 78

    Ⓓ 84

26 $9,375 \div 125 = $ ▨

    Ⓐ 95

    Ⓑ 75

    Ⓒ 90

    Ⓓ 55

27 $27,830 \div 242 = $ ▨

    Ⓐ 90

    Ⓑ 110

    Ⓒ 85

    Ⓓ 115

Mean, Median, Mode and Range Lesson 8.2

Find the mean, median, mode, and range.

28 10, 11, 12, 14, 28

29 5, 5, 6, 9, 15

30 1, 2, 2, 3, 3, 3, 4, 4, 4, 4, 5, 5, 5, 6, 6, 7

31 There were 9 people who took a 40-word spelling test. Their scores were 39, 38, 30, 39, 26, 31, 35, 7, and 34.

    a. What was the average score?

    b. How many people had above-average scores?

    c. How many people had below-average scores?

32 How many people had average scores?

Key Ideas Review

In this chapter you explored measurements and graphing.

You learned how to apply and convert measurements.
You learned how to interpret and create various graphs.

Solve.

1 The recipe below serves 8 people. Peter wants to make only 2 servings. How should he modify the ingredients?

Irish Potato Cakes

2 cups butter   4 teaspoons baking powder
48 ounces white flour   24 cups potatoes, mashed
4 teaspoons salt

2 If a pizza is cut into 8 equal slices, what is the angle measure of each slice?

3 Johan bid on a concert ticket from an Internet auction Web site at 10:30 in the evening. The bidding ends 10 hours from then. At what time is the auction over?

Mr. Thurman's class has 24 students. Each student was asked what their favorite lunch menu item is at school. The students' responses are shown on the circle graph below.

Lunch Favorites

■ Pizza
■ Grilled Cheese Sandwich
▨ Spaghetti
■ Chicken Sandwich

4 Did more than 50% of the students select a specific lunch food as their favorite?

5 If 10 people selected pizza, what degree measurement should be shown on the circle graph?

Chapter Review

Lesson 12.3 **Solve.**

Sasha is making brownies for a picnic. A box of ready-to-mix brownies calls for 2 eggs, $\frac{1}{4}$ cup water, and $\frac{1}{2}$ cup oil.

1. If Sasha wants to make 3 boxes of brownies, how much of the above ingredients does she need?

2. Sasha later decides she wants to make $\frac{1}{2}$ a box of the same brownies. How much of the ingredients does she need?

3. Juan's car weighs about 5,000 pounds. How many tons does it weigh?

4. How many 10-ounce glasses can be poured from a gallon of water?

Lesson 12.4 **Solve.**

5. Jose says he is 64 inches tall. Carmen says she is 140 centimeters tall. Who is taller?

6. Emil wants to buy hamburger meat to make 20 quarter-pound burgers. About how many kilograms of meat would Emil need?

7. A marathon is about 26.2 miles. How many kilometers is that?

8. Cyrus says his shoes are 25 centimeters long. Does that make sense?

9. About how many 2-liter bottles of juice could you pour into a 1-gallon container?

Lesson 12.5 **Solve.**

10. Joanie's mother drops off Joanie and her 3 friends to see a movie that starts at 4:45 P.M. and is 127 minutes long. Her mother says she will be back at 7 P.M. sharp to pick them up. Will she be too early? Explain your answer.

11. Jess is training for a triathlon. He swims for 45 minutes, and then he bikes for $1\frac{1}{2}$ hours, and finally he runs for 30 minutes. If Jess begins his workout at 6:15 A.M., when will he finish?

Textbook This lesson is available in the *eTextbook*.

Lesson 12.6

Solve.

12 A pie is cut in half. One of the halves is then cut into 45° pieces. The other half is cut into 30° pieces. How many total pieces are there?

13 Suppose 3 adults and 2 children shared a pizza. If each adult had a 60° slice and each child had a 45° slice, how much pizza is left?

Lesson 12.7

Solve.

The results of Mr. Luker's class's writing tests are plotted on the stem-and-leaf plot below.

14 What were the highest, lowest, and median grades?

15 How many students scored better than 82?

16 How many students scored lower than 75?

Stem	Leaf
6	7, 5
7	8, 0, 4
8	7, 3, 5, 1
9	0, 5

Lesson 12.11

Use the graph to answer the following questions.

17 Which quarter had the most projects assigned?

18 Which quarter had the most English projects assigned?

19 Which quarter had the fewest math projects assigned?

20 How many more math projects were assigned in the 4th quarter than were assigned in the 2nd quarter?

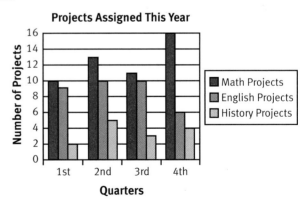

Answer the following questions.

1. How could you estimate the length of your desk?

2. How could you estimate the length of a hallway?

Complete the following conversions.

3. 15 teaspoons = ⬜ tablespoons

4. ⬜ gallons = 24 pints

5. ⬜ cups = 16 fluid ounces

6. 6 pounds = ⬜ ounces

7. About how many miles is 10 kilometers?

8. A bucket holds 15 quarts of water. About how many liters does the bucket hold?

Answer these questions.

9. What time is $5\frac{3}{4}$ hours after 1:30 P.M.?

10. How many seconds are in $\frac{1}{4}$ hour?

11. Julio jogged for 75 minutes. He started at 5:15 A.M. What time did he end?

12. How many degrees does the minute hand of a clock move in 23 minutes?

Tell how many degrees on a circle graph would be needed to represent the number of votes.

13. 13 of 26

14. 6 of 20

15. 11 of 50

Choose the correct answer.

16. About how many hand spans wide is a door?

  Ⓐ 1   Ⓑ 5

  Ⓒ 10   Ⓓ 25

17. Melinda's forearm is about 1 foot long. She measures the width of her bed and finds it is about 4 forearm lengths. About how many centimeters wide is her bed?

  Ⓐ 30   Ⓑ 50

  Ⓒ 80   Ⓓ 120

18. How many cups equal 2 gallons?

  Ⓐ 6   Ⓑ 16

  Ⓒ 24   Ⓓ 32

19. Paula needs to put 4 fluid ounces in her recipe. How many teaspoons does that equal?

  Ⓐ 24   Ⓑ 28

  Ⓒ 12   Ⓓ 8

20. About how many centimeters equal 1 inch?

  Ⓐ 1.5   Ⓑ 4

  Ⓒ 2.5   Ⓓ 3

21. About how many liters equal 3 quarts?

  Ⓐ 12   Ⓑ 6

  Ⓒ 3   Ⓓ $\frac{1}{3}$

22. Jeremy's camp group collected 127 pounds of recyclable tin cans. The recycling center paid them 45¢ a pound for the tin cans. How much money did Jeremy's camp group earn altogether?

  Ⓐ $57.15   Ⓑ $82

  Ⓒ $172   Ⓓ $571.50

23. The distance from Rome to Venice is 484 kilometers. About how many miles is that?

  Ⓐ 150   Ⓑ 300

  Ⓒ 600   Ⓓ 1,200

24. If you walk at the rate of 1 mile every 20 minutes, how long will it take you to walk 50 miles?

   Ⓐ 100 hours

   Ⓑ 50 hours 30 minutes

   Ⓒ 20 hours 20 minutes

   Ⓓ 16 hours 40 minutes

25. What time will it be $8\frac{1}{4}$ hours after 9:30 A.M.?

   Ⓐ 1:00 A.M.   Ⓑ 5:45 P.M.

   Ⓒ 7:15 P.M.   Ⓓ 8:30 P.M.

26. How many degrees does the minute hand move in 16 minutes?

   Ⓐ 16   Ⓑ 96

   Ⓒ 160   Ⓓ 235

27. Which can be the measure of an acute angle?

   Ⓐ 127°   Ⓑ 145°

   Ⓒ 90°   Ⓓ 70°

28. In the morning, the outdoor temperature was −3°F. The temperature rose 7°F during the day. At sunset, it dropped 5°F. What was the outdoor temperature at sunset?

   Ⓐ −3°F   Ⓑ −1°F

   Ⓒ 5°F   Ⓓ 12°F

29. Which fraction is equivalent to $\frac{15}{60}$?

   Ⓐ $\frac{1}{5}$ Ⓑ $\frac{1}{4}$

   Ⓒ $\frac{1}{3}$ Ⓓ $\frac{1}{2}$

30. Jackie's mother bought $2\frac{1}{4}$ pounds of sliced turkey and $3\frac{1}{3}$ pounds of salami. How many pounds of deli meat did Jackie's mother buy altogether?

   Ⓐ $5\frac{2}{7}$ Ⓑ $5\frac{7}{12}$

   Ⓒ $6\frac{2}{7}$ Ⓓ $6\frac{7}{12}$

31. What is 481.092 rounded to the nearest hundredth?

   Ⓐ 482   Ⓑ 481.1

   Ⓒ 481.09   Ⓓ 481

32. Which of the following is a composite number?

   Ⓐ 31   Ⓑ 33

   Ⓒ 37   Ⓓ 41

33. Yasser compared the average monthly temperatures recorded in London and New York. He made a line graph to show the data.

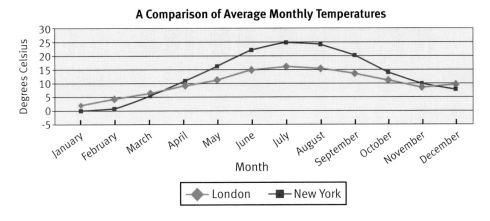

A Comparison of Average Monthly Temperatures

a. During which month was the difference in temperature between London and New York the greatest?

b. During which month was the difference in temperature between London and New York the least?

c. Yasser wants to display this data in a circle graph. Is it an appropriate graph for his data? Explain.

Real Math

Student Handbook

Problem-Solving Tips

If you need help solving a math problem, try this:

- Write the problem in your own words.
- Write what you are trying to find out.
- List the information you already know.
- List the information you need to find out.
- Discuss the problem with other people.
- Write possible ways you can find out what you need to know.
- Have you solved problems like this before? If so, how did you do it?
- Try to solve the problem.

After you think you have solved the problem, ask yourself:

- Does the answer make sense?
- Is there more than one answer?
- Is there a different way to solve the problem?
- Would a different way have been easier or better for some reason?
- What have you learned that will help you solve other problems?

Handwriting Models

Starting point, straight down

Starting point, around right, slanting left and straight across right

Starting point, around right, in at the middle, around right

Starting point, straight down, straight across right. Starting point, straight down, crossing line

Straight down, curve around right and up. Starting point, straight across right

Starting point, slanting left, around the bottom curving up around left and into the curve

Starting point, straight across right, slanting down left

Starting point, curving left, curving down and around right, slanting up right to starting point

Starting point, curving around left all the way, straight down

Starting point, straight down. Starting point, curving left all the way around to starting point

Number Line

Number lines show numbers in order.

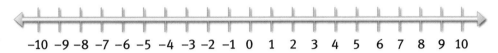

-10 -9 -8 -7 -6 -5 -4 -3 -2 -1 0 1 2 3 4 5 6 7 8 9 10

You can use a number line to

- count on.
- count back.
- skip count by 2s or 3s or any number.
- add.
- subtract.

Number Names

0	Zero			
1	One		1st	First
2	Two		2nd	Second
3	Three		3rd	Third
4	Four		4th	Fourth
5	Five		5th	Fifth
6	Six		6th	Sixth
7	Seven		7th	Seventh
8	Eight		8th	Eighth
9	Nine		9th	Ninth
10	Ten		10th	Tenth
11	Eleven	Ten and one	11th	Eleventh
12	Twelve	Ten and two	12th	Twelfth
13	Thirteen	Ten and three	13th	Thirteenth
14	Fourteen	Ten and four	14th	Fourteenth

15	Fifteen	Ten and five	15th	Fifteenth
16	Sixteen	Ten and six	16th	Sixteenth
17	Seventeen	Ten and seven	17th	Seventeenth
18	Eighteen	Ten and eight	18th	Eighteenth
19	Nineteen	Ten and nine	19th	Nineteenth
20	Twenty	Two tens	20th	Twentieth
30	Thirty	Three tens	30th	Thirtieth
40	Forty	Four tens	40th	Fortieth
50	Fifty	Five tens	50th	Fiftieth
60	Sixty	Six tens	60th	Sixtieth
70	Seventy	Seven tens	70th	Seventieth
80	Eighty	Eight tens	80th	Eightieth
90	Ninety	Nine tens	90th	Ninetieth
100	One hundred	Ten tens	100th	One hundredth

Place Value

A place-value table tells you how many hundreds, tens, and ones. Place value is important. Look what happens when the 5 is in the hundreds place or the ones place.

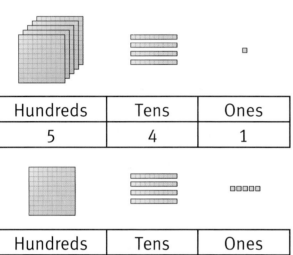

Hundreds	Tens	Ones
5	4	1

Hundreds	Tens	Ones
1	4	5

Big Numbers

Numbers go on forever. After trillions come quadrillions and then quintillions. A googol is written as 1 followed by 100 zeros. A googolplex is written as 1 followed by one googol zeros.

1	One	10,000,000	Ten million
10	Ten	100,000,000	One hundred million
100	One hundred	1,000,000,000	One billion
1,000	One thousand	10,000,000,000	Ten billion
10,000	Ten thousand	100,000,000,000	One hundred billion
100,000	One hundred thousand	1,000,000,000,000	One trillion
1,000,000	One million		

Addition Table

You can use the Addition Table to find basic addition and subtraction facts.

+	0	1	2	3	4	5	6	7	8	9	10
0	0	1	2	3	4	5	6	7	8	9	10
1	1	2	3	4	5	6	7	8	9	10	11
2	2	3	4	5	6	7	8	9	10	11	12
3	3	4	5	6	7	8	9	10	11	12	13
4	4	5	6	7	8	9	10	11	12	13	14
5	5	6	7	8	9	10	11	12	13	14	15
6	6	7	8	9	10	11	12	13	14	15	16
7	7	8	9	10	11	12	13	14	15	16	17
8	8	9	10	11	12	13	14	15	16	17	18
9	9	10	11	12	13	14	15	16	17	18	19
10	10	11	12	13	14	15	16	17	18	19	20

Addition and Subtraction Facts

Addition Fact Helpers

These strategies can help with many of the addition facts.

To add:	Think of:
0	No change
1	Counting on 1
2	Counting on 2
4	One less than adding 5
5	Finger sets—one more hand
6	One more than adding 5
9	One less than adding 10
10	Write 1 in the tens place

Subtraction Fact Helpers

These strategies can help with some of the subtraction facts. For other subtraction facts, think of the corresponding addition fact.

To subtract:	Think of:
0	No change
1	Counting back 1
5	Finger sets—taking away one hand
9	One more than subtracting 10
10	Subtracting 1 from the tens digit

Addition

One Way to Add

$$\begin{array}{r} 685 \\ + 267 \\ \hline \end{array}$$

  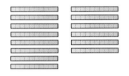

We start at the right because it is easier that way. Add ones.
5 + 7 = 12. 12 ones = 1 ten and 2 ones.

$$\begin{array}{r} 1 \\ 685 \\ + 267 \\ \hline 2 \end{array}$$

  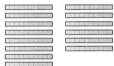

Add tens. 1 + 8 + 6 = 15. 15 tens = 1 hundred and 5 tens.

$$\begin{array}{r} 11 \\ 685 \\ + 267 \\ \hline 52 \end{array}$$

 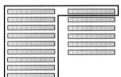

Add hundreds. 1 + 6 + 2 = 9.

$$\begin{array}{r} 11 \\ 685 \\ + 267 \\ \hline 952 \end{array}$$

  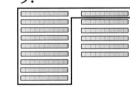

Handbook

Addition Laws

Commutative Law of Addition

The order of two numbers does not affect their sum. For example, the sum of $1 + 3$ is the same as the sum of $3 + 1$.

Associative Law of Addition

When adding three numbers, it does not matter whether the first pair or the last pair is added first.

$$5 + 4 + 3 = (5 + 4) + 3 = 5 + (4 + 3)$$

$$9 + 3 \qquad 5 + 7$$

Additive Identity

Adding a number to 0 gives that number.

$$6 + 0 = 6$$

Additive Inverse

Adding a positive number and a negative number with the same absolute value (distance from 0) gives 0.

$$4 + (-4) = 0.$$

Subtraction

One Way to Subtract

$$\begin{array}{r} 365 \\ -\ 178 \\ \hline \end{array}$$

Start at the right because it is easier.

There are not enough ones to subtract 8, so rename 6 tens as 5 tens and 10 ones.

$$\begin{array}{r} \overset{5\ 15}{3\cancel{6}\cancel{5}} \\ -\ 178 \\ \hline \end{array}$$

   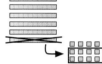

Subtract ones.

$$\begin{array}{r} \overset{5\ 15}{3\cancel{6}\cancel{5}} \\ -\ 178 \\ \hline 7 \end{array}$$

There are not enough tens to subtract 7, so rename 3 hundreds as 2 hundreds and 10 tens.
Subtract tens.

$$\begin{array}{r} \overset{2\ 15\,15}{\cancel{3}\cancel{6}\cancel{5}} \\ -\ 178 \\ \hline 87 \end{array}$$

 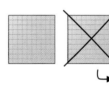 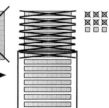

Subtract hundreds.

$$\begin{array}{r} \overset{2\ 15\,15}{\cancel{3}\cancel{6}\cancel{5}} \\ -\ 178 \\ \hline 187 \end{array}$$

Multiplication Table

You can use the Multiplication Table
to find basic facts.

×	0	1	2	3	4	5	6	7	8	9	10	11	12
0	0	0	0	0	0	0	0	0	0	0	0	0	0
1	0	1	2	3	4	5	6	7	8	9	10	11	12
2	0	2	4	6	8	10	12	14	16	18	20	22	24
3	0	3	6	9	12	15	18	21	24	27	30	33	36
4	0	4	8	12	16	20	24	28	32	36	40	44	48
5	0	5	10	15	20	25	30	35	40	45	50	55	60
6	0	6	12	18	24	30	36	42	48	54	60	66	72
7	0	7	14	21	28	35	42	49	56	63	70	77	84
8	0	8	16	24	32	40	48	56	64	72	80	88	96
9	0	9	18	27	36	45	54	63	72	81	90	99	108
10	0	10	20	30	40	50	60	70	80	90	100	110	120
11	0	11	22	33	44	55	66	77	88	99	110	121	132
12	0	12	24	36	48	60	72	84	96	108	120	132	144

Multiplication Facts

Fact Helper Strategies

To multiply by:

10 Write a "0" after the number.

 9 Subtract the number from 10 times the number.

 0 The answer is 0.

 1 The answer is the number.

 2 Add the number to itself.

 5 Multiply half the number by 10 if it is even. If the number is odd, multiply half of the next smaller number by 10 and add 5.

 4 Double the number, and then double that answer.

 3 Add the number to its double.

 8 Double 4 times the number, or subtract the number from 9 times the number.

 6 Double 3 times the number.

 7 If you've learned all the other facts and can remember that $7 \times 7 = 49$, you know all the multiples of 7.

Fact Families

Fact families show how multiplication and division are related.

$2 \times 3 = 6$	$6 \div 2 = 3$
$3 \times 2 = 6$	$6 \div 3 = 2$

Multiplication

Think of multiplication as finding many areas.

	100	100	100	10	10	10	10	6
10								
10								
10		$300 \times 50 = 15{,}000$			$40 \times 50 = 2{,}000$			
10								
10								
2		$300 \times 2 = 600$			$40 \times 2 = 80$			

$6 \times 2 = 12$

$6 \times 50 = 300$

Partial Products

Multiplying using partial products may help you keep track of place values. Starting with the rightmost column, multiply each position in the top number by the ones-column digit, then the tens-column digit, and so on. Then add the partial products to find the final product. You could start with any column, but it is easier if you start on the right.

$2 \times 6 = 12$

$2 \times 40 = 80$

$2 \times 300 = 600$

$50 \times 6 = 300$

$50 \times 40 = 2{,}000$

$50 \times 300 = 15{,}000$

Add partial products.

$$
\begin{array}{r}
346 \\
\times\ 52 \\
\hline
12 \\
80 \\
600 \\
300 \\
2000 \\
+\ 15000 \\
\hline
17992 \\
\end{array}
$$

A Shorter Way to Multiply

Beginning at the rightmost column, find the product. Write the ones digit of the product below the line in the ones column, and write the tens digit at the top of the tens column. Then repeat this process for each digit of the second factor.

$$\begin{array}{r} 346 \\ \times\ \ 52 \\ \hline \end{array}$$

Multiply 2 times the ones. $6 \times 2 = 12$
12 ones = 1 ten and 2 ones
Multiply 2 times 4 tens, and add the carried ten.
$(2 \times 4) + 1 = 9$

$$\begin{array}{r} 1 \\ 346 \\ \times\ \ 52 \\ \hline 2 \end{array} \qquad \begin{array}{r} 1 \\ 346 \\ \times\ \ 52 \\ \hline 92 \end{array}$$

Multiply 2 times 3 hundreds. $2 \times 3 = 6$

$$\begin{array}{r} 1 \\ 346 \\ \times\ \ 52 \\ \hline 692 \end{array}$$

Multiply 5 tens times 6 ones. $5 \times 6 = 30$
30 tens = 3 hundreds and 0 tens
Multiply 5 tens times 4 tens, and add the carried hundreds. $(5 \times 4) + 3 = 23$
23 = 2 thousands and 3 hundreds

$$\begin{array}{r} 3 \\ 346 \\ \times\ \ 52 \\ \hline 692 \\ 00 \end{array} \qquad \begin{array}{r} 2\ 3 \\ 346 \\ \times\ \ 52 \\ \hline 692 \\ 300 \end{array}$$

Multiply 5 tens times 3 hundreds, and add the carried thousands. $(5 \times 3) + 2 = 17$
17 thousands = 1 ten thousand and 7 thousands

$$\begin{array}{r} 2\ 3 \\ 346 \\ \times\ \ 52 \\ \hline 692 \\ 17300 \end{array}$$

Add partial products.

$$\begin{array}{r} 2\ 3 \\ 346 \\ \times\ \ 52 \\ \hline 692 \\ +\ 17300 \\ \hline 17992 \end{array}$$

Handbook

Division

One Way to Divide

$5\overline{)423}$

Five does not divide into 4, but it will divide into 42 eight times.

$$\begin{array}{r} 8 \\ 5\overline{)423} \\ 40 \end{array}$$

Subtract 40 from 42.

$$\begin{array}{r} 8 \\ 5\overline{)423} \\ -40 \\ \hline 2 \end{array}$$

Bring down the next digit, 3.

$$\begin{array}{r} 8 \\ 5\overline{)423} \\ -40 \\ \hline 23 \end{array}$$

Five divides into 23 four times.

$$\begin{array}{r} 84 \\ 5\overline{)423} \\ -40 \\ \hline 23 \\ 20 \end{array}$$

Subtract 20 from 23.

$$\begin{array}{r} 84 \\ 5\overline{)423} \\ -40 \\ \hline 23 \\ -20 \\ \hline 3 \end{array}$$

$423 \div 5 = 84$ R3

Divisibility Patterns

Divisibility by 2

An even number is a number divisible by 2. We can recognize even numbers because their last digit must also be divisible by 2 (the last digit must be 0, 2, 4, 6, or 8). For example, 78,950 has a 0 as its last digit; therefore, it's divisible by 2.

Divisibility by 3

A number is divisible by 3 if the sum of its digits is divisible by 3. The number 492,603 has a digit sum of 24. Twenty-four is divisible by 3; therefore, 492,603 is divisible by 3.

Divisibility by 5

We can recognize a number that is divisible by 5 because its last digit must be either a 0 or a 5. The number 47,825 has a 5 as its last digit; therefore, it's divisible by 5.

Divisibility by 11

A two-digit number is divisible by 11 if the two digits are equal to each other. Take 33, for example: 3 = 3, so 33 is divisible by 11. There are patterns for divisibility by 11 for numbers greater than 100. Can you find them?

Geometric Figures

Plane Figures

Circle A circle is composed of all points in a plane the same distance from the center.

Polygon A polygon is a closed figure with sides that are all line segments.

Angles Angles are measured based on the amount of turn they represent. A quarter turn is a right angle. Angles of less than a quarter turn are acute angles. Angles of more than a quarter turn but less than half a turn are obtuse angles.

Triangle A triangle is a polygon with three sides.

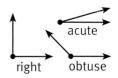

right   acute   obtuse

Polygons

Quadrilateral A polygon with four sides.

Rectangle A rectangle has four sides with opposite pairs of sides of equal length and four right angles.

Square A square is a quadrilateral with four equal sides and four right angles.

Rhombus A rhombus is a quadrilateral with four equal sides.

Trapezoid A trapezoid is a quadrilateral with two sides parallel.

Pentagon A pentagon is a polygon with five sides.

Hexagon A hexagon is a polygon with six sides.

pentagon

hexagon

Space Figures

Cube A cube is a space figure with six square faces.

Sphere A sphere is a space figure composed of all its points in space the same distance from its center.

Cone A cone is a space figure made by connecting every point on a circle or other plane figure to a point not on the figure.

Cylinder A cylinder is a space figure with two parallel bases (usually circles).

Polyhedron A polyhedron is a closed space figure whose faces are all polygons.

cube   sphere   cone   cylinder   polyhedron

Measurements

Decimal and Metric Prefixes

1000 = thousand = *kilo-*   0.10 = tenth = *deci-*
100 = hundred = *hecto-*   0.01 = hundredth = *centi-*
10 = ten = *deca-*   0.001 = thousandth = *milli-*

The basic units in the metric system are *meter*, *gram*, and *liter*.

Measuring Length

Metric	Equivalency
1 millimeter (mm)	1mm: -
1 centimeter (cm)	10 millimeters
1 decimeter (dm)	10 centimeters
1 meter (m)	100 centimeters
1 dekameter (dam)	10 meters
1 hectometer (hm)	100 meters
1 kilometer (km)	1,000 meters

Customary	Equivalency
1 inch (in.)	1 inch: ————
1 foot (ft)	12 inches
1 yard (yd)	3 feet
1 mile (mi)	5,280 feet 1,760 yards

Measuring Temperature

Celsius		Fahrenheit
0	Water Freezes	32
100	Water Boils	212

Handbook

Weight (Mass)

Metric	Equivalent
1 gram (g)	a dollar bill weighs about 1 gram
1 dekagram (dag)	10 grams
1 hectogram (hg)	100 grams
1 kilogram (kg)	1,000 grams
1 metric ton (t)	1,000 kilograms

Customary	Equivalent
1 ounce (oz)	11 pennies weigh about 1 ounce
1 pound (lb)	16 ounces
1 ton	2,000 pounds

Capacity

Metric	Equivalent
1 milliliter (mL)	an eyedropper holds about 1 milliliter
1 centiliter (cL)	0.01 liter
1 deciliter (dL)	0.1 liter
1 liter (L)	1,000 milliliters
1 dekaliter (daL)	10 liters
1 hectoliter (hL)	100 liters
1 kiloliter (kL)	1,000 liters

Customary	Equivalent
1 fluid ounce (fl oz)	approximately the volume of 1 ounce of water
1 cup (c)	8 fluid ounces
1 pint (pt)	2 cups
1 quart (qt)	2 pints
1 gallon (gal)	4 quarts

Time

Months of the Year

Month	Number of Days
January	31
February	28, except in leap year every four years when there are 29
March	31
April	30
May	31
June	30
July	31
August	31
September	30
October	31
November	30
December	31

Equivalents of Time

60 seconds	1 minute
60 minutes	1 hour
24 hours (the time it takes Earth to rotate)	1 day
7 days 168 hours	1 week
12 months $52\frac{1}{7}$ weeks 365.25 days (the time it takes Earth to revolve around the sun)	1 year

A.M. (ante meridiem; before midday) means between midnight and noon

P.M. (post meridiem; after midday) means between noon and midnight

Military or 24-Hour Time Equivalents

1:00	1 AM	7:00	7 AM	13:00	1 PM	19:00	7 PM
2:00	2 AM	8:00	8 AM	14:00	2 PM	20:00	8 PM
3:00	3 AM	9:00	9 AM	15:00	3 PM	21:00	9 PM
4:00	4 AM	10:00	10 AM	16:00	4 PM	22:00	10 PM
5:00	5 AM	11:00	11 AM	17:00	5 PM	23:00	11 PM
6:00	6 AM	12:00	12 Noon	18:00	6 PM	24:00	12 Midnight

A.D. or C.E. means the common era, after the year 0

B.C. or B.C.E. means before the common era, before the year 0

Frequency Tables

A frequency table shows tally marks and how often each kind of data occurs in a set of data.

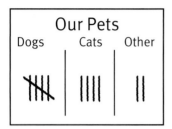

Tally Marks

Tally marks are used to keep count.

Tallies of Five

Tally marks represent 5 when four tallies are combined with one diagonal mark.

Graphs

Bar Graph

A bar graph is a graph with bars of lengths that represent amounts.

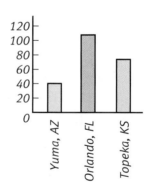

Circle Graph

A circle graph has sectors that represent different categories.

Line Graph

A line graph connects points to show change over time.

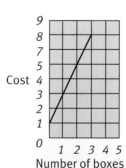

Fractions, Decimals, and Percentages

Fractions, decimals, and percentages are called *rational numbers* because they can be written as ratios. Whole numbers, counting numbers, integers, fractions, decimals, improper fractions, and mixed numbers are all examples of rational numbers.

Percentages are special ratios that compare a number to 100.

A ratio is the comparison of two quantities by division, such as a fraction.

Ratios are commonly used to relate one number to another. Ratios have no labels. There are three major representations of ratios: 3 out of 4, 3:4, and $\frac{3}{4}$. Probabilities are represented most often by ratios.

The ratio of blue to red dots can be written $\frac{2}{5}$.
The ratio of blue dots to the total number of dots is $\frac{2}{7}$.

A number line helps you think about rational numbers. You can see whole numbers, negative numbers, and fractions as belonging to the same system.

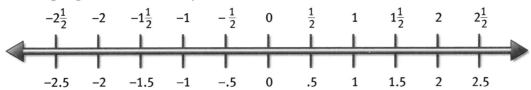

Benchmark for Fractions, Decimals, and Percentages

Fractions, decimals, and percentages can all represent the same rational number or part of a whole.

$1 = 1.0 = 100\%$

$\frac{3}{4} = 0.75 = 75\%$

$\frac{1}{2} = 0.5 = 50\%$

$\frac{1}{4} = 0.25 = 25\%$

$\frac{1}{8} = 0.125 = 12.5\%$

$\frac{3}{4}$ — *numerator* — *denominator*

Algebraic Functions

A function pairs a number (the input) with a second number (the output).
A function table lists the pairs of numbers.

If a girl is 3 years older than her brother, you can say:

Brother's age + 3 = Sister's age

No matter how old they are, the sister will always be three years older than her brother.

in	out
1	4
2	5
3	6
4	7
5	8

A **function machine** shows the input, output, and rule for a function. A **function rule** tells how the input of a function is related to the output of a function.

Composite functions involve more than one step in the function rule.

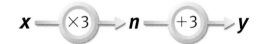

$$x \longrightarrow \boxed{\times 3} \longrightarrow n \longrightarrow \boxed{+3} \longrightarrow y$$

Linear functions create a straight line when graphed.

An **equation** is a mathematical statement showing that one quantity or expression is equal to another quantity or expression. These are the sentences of mathematical language.

Math Symbols

+	Plus Add	$7 + 3 = 10$
−	Minus Subtract	$10 - 3 = 7$
× or * on the computer	Times Multiply	$3 \times 2 = 6$
÷, ‾, or / on the computer	Divided by	$6 \div 2 = 3$
=	Is equal to	$4 + 2 = 6$
¢	Cents	39¢
$	Dollars	$1.00
°F	Degrees Fahrenheit	100°F
°C	Degrees Celsius	25°C
>	Greater than	$47 > 39$
<	Less than	$2 + 6 < 10$
4^3 ← exponent ↑ base	Exponents are used as a shorthand notation to show repeated multiplication.	$4^3 = 4 \times 4 \times 4 = 64$
∠	Angle	∠ABC
△	Triangle	△JKL
≅	Is congruent to	∠ABC ≅ ∠DEF
∽	Is similar to	△JKL ∽ △ABC

Glossary

A

absolute value *n.* the distance of a number from 0

acute angle \ə kūt'\ *n.* an angle which measures between 0° and 90°

These are acute angles:

addend \ad' end\ *n.* any number or quantity that is to be added to another; for example:

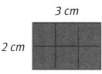

$$35 \text{ —— addend}$$
$$+\ 48 \text{ —— addend}$$
$$83 \text{ —— sum}$$

$$7 + 8 = 15 \text{ —sum}$$
$$\text{addend}$$
$$\text{addend}$$

algorithm \al' gə rith' əm\ *n.* a procedure for carrying out an operation, such as adding numbers or doing long division

approximate \ə prok' sə māt'\ *v.* to come near or close. \ə prok' sə mit\ *adj.* nearly correct or exact

approximation \ə prok' sə mā' shən\ *n.* something that is nearly correct, as an estimated amount

area \âr' ē ə\ *n.* the measure of the interior, or inside, of a figure; the area of this rectangle is 6 square centimeters:

3 cm

2 cm

Associative Law *n.* a law stating that the sum or product of three or more quantities will be the same no matter which way they are grouped: (7 + 3) + 8 = 7 + (3 + 8)

average \av' rij\ *n.* the typical or usual amount, which is found by dividing the sum of two or more quantities by the number of quantities

axis \ak' sis\ *n.* a reference line on a graph

B

balance \bal' əns\ *n.* the amount of money remaining in an account

base \bās\ *n.* a number that is raised to a given power

benchmark \bench märk\ *n.* something that serves as a standard or reference by which something else can be measured or compared

C

capacity \kə pas' i tē\ *n.* the maximum volume a container can hold

Celsius \sel' sē əs\ *n.* (sometimes called *centigrade*) the temperature scale on which the freezing point of water is 0 degrees and the boiling point is 100 degrees under standard atmospheric pressure

center of rotation *n.* the point in a plane figure with rotational symmetry about which it may be rotated less than a full turn to obtain a figure that looks the same.

centi– \sen' ti\ *prefix* a hundredth of a part

centimeter \sen' tə mē'\ tər\ *n.* a unit of length equal to one-hundredth of a meter; The prefix *centi*- means "one hundred."

centisecond \sen' ti sek' ənd\ *adj.* a hundredth ($\frac{1}{100}$) of a second

chord \kôrd\ *n.* a (straight) line segment that joins two points on a circle

circle \sûr' kəl\ *n.* a continuous, closed curved line, every point of which is equally distant from a given point called the center

circle graph *n.* a graph in the form of a circle that is used to compare parts of a whole; also commonly known as a *pie chart*

circumference \sər kum' fər əns\ *n.* the perimeter of a circle

clipped range \klipt 'rānj \ *n.* the range found after omitting the least and greatest values

clockwise \klok' wīz\ *adv., adj.* the direction in which the hands of a clock move

Commutative Law *n.* a law stating that the sum or product of two or more quantities will be the same regardless of their order: $7 + 3 = 3 + 7$

composite \kəm poz' it\ *adj.* made of various parts or elements

composite function *n.* a function with two or more operations

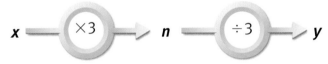

composite number *n.* a whole number with more than two factors; that is, factors other than itself and 1

concave \kon kāv'\ *adj.* shape of a figure in which there exists a line segment between two points of the figure that goes outside the figure

congruent \kən grü' ənt\ *adj.* figures that are the same size and same shape; that is, they fit perfectly when placed on top of one another

constant \kon' stənt\ *n.* something that does not change

convex \kon veks'\ *adj.* the shape of a figure in which every line segment between two points of the figure remains entirely inside the figure

convex polyhedron *n.* a polyhedron that contains any line segment connecting two points on the surface

coordinates \kō ôr' də nits\ *n.* a pair of numbers that gives the location of a point on a graph; also called an ordered pair of numbers. In the figure shown, for example, the coordinates of point A are (2, 3). The *x*–coordinate is 2 and the *y*–coordinate is 3.

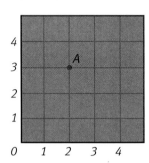

corresponding \kor' ə spon ding\ *adj.* matching or identical; having a similar function, position, or form

counterclockwise \koun' tər klok' wīz\ *adv., adj.* the direction opposite to the movement of a clock's hands

customary system *n.* a system of measurement used in the United States that uses units such as inches, teaspoons, pounds, and the Fahrenheit scale for measuring length, capacity, weight, and temperature

cylinder \sil' ən dər\ *n.* a solid geometric figure bounded by two equal, parallel circles and a curved surface that is formed by a straight line moving parallel to itself with its ends always on the circumferences of the circles

D

data \dā' tə, dat' ə\ *pl. n.* information from which conclusions can be drawn; facts and figures

decimal equivalent *n.* decimals that name the same amount as a fraction or a percentage

decimal point *n.* a dot used in separating the ones digit from the tenths digit

Glossary

degree \di grē'\ *n.* a unit of measurement for angles

deltahedron \del tə hē' drən\ *n.* a polyhedron whose faces are all equilateral triangles

denominator \di nom' ə nā' tər\ *n.* a number below the line in a fraction that indicates the number of equal parts into which the whole is divided

deposit \di poz' it\ *v.* to put in a bank or other safe place for safekeeping. *n.* something put in a place for safekeeping

diameter \dī am' i tər\ *n.* a straight line passing through the center of a circle or sphere, from one side to the other

difference \dif' rəns\ *n.* remainder left after subtracting one quantity from another
For example:

$$43 \text{ — minuend}$$
$$-16 \text{ — subtrahend}$$
$$27 \text{ — difference}$$

$$10 - 7 = 3 \text{ —difference}$$
subtrahend
minuend

digit \dij' it\ *n.* any of the ten Arabic numerals from 0 through 9

discount \dis' kount\ *n.* a deduction of a specified amount or percentage

Distributive Law *n.* a law stating that the product of multiplication is the same when the operation is performed on a whole set as when it is performed on the individual members of the set: $4 \times (2 + 5) = (4 \times 2) + (4 \times 5)$

dividend \div' i dend\ *n.* the number that is to be divided; for example:

$$6 \div 3 = 2 \text{ — quotient}$$
divisor
dividend

$$\begin{array}{r} 43 \\ 8\overline{)347} \\ -32 \\ \hline 27 \\ -24 \\ \hline 3 \end{array}$$

divisor — 8)347 — quotient / dividend

divisible \di viz' ə bəl\ *adj.* capable of being divided without a remainder

divisor \di vī' zər\ *n.* the number the dividend is to be divided by

doubles \dub' əls\ *n.* numbers that are the sums of numbers added to themselves, such as $12 + 12 = 12 \times 2 = 24$

E

edge \ej\ *n.* a line or place where an object or area begins or ends; extreme or outermost border; a line segment where two faces meet or a planar area begins or ends

equation \i kwā' zhən\ *n.* a mathematical statement showing that one quantity or expression is equal to another quantity or expression

equilateral triangle *n.* a triangle having all sides equal in length

equivalent fractions \i kwiv' ə lənt\ *n.* fractions that name the same rational number

estimate \n., es' tə mit; v., es' tə māt'\ n. a judgment or opinion, as of the value, quality, extent, size, or cost of something. v. to form a judgment or opinion (based on available information) about the extent or size of something; calculate

even number n. a number that can be divided exactly by two

exponent \ek spō' nənt\ n. a numeral or symbol placed at the upper right side of another numeral or symbol to indicate the number of times it is to be multiplied by itself

F

face \fās\ n. a plane figure that serves as one side of a space figure

factor \fak' tər\ n. numbers you multiply to get a product; for example:
3 (multiplier) × 5 (multiplicand) = 15 (product)

fraction \frak' shən\ n. a quantity expressing the division of one number by a second number, written as two numerals separated by a line

function \fungk' shən\ n. a relationship that pairs every element of one set with an element of a second set; for example, a relationship that pairs any number with another number

function machine n. a machine (sometimes imaginary) that does the same thing to every number that is put into it

G

graph \graf\ n. a diagram showing the relationship between two or more sets of data

greatest common factor n. the greatest factor shared by two or more numbers

grid \grid\ n. a pattern of intersecting lines that divides a map or table into small squares

H

heptagon \hep' tə gon'\ n. a plane figure having seven sides and seven angles

hexagon \hek' sə gon'\ n. a plane figure having six sides and six angles

hundredth \hun' dridth\ n. one of a hundred equal parts; $\frac{1}{100}$

hypotenuse \hī pot' ə nūs'\ n. the side of a right triangle opposite the right angle

hypothesize \hī poth' ə sīz'\ v. to form an idea based on some experience or information often used as the basis for an experiment

I

identity function n. a function that always gives back the same number that is put in

improper fraction n. a fraction whose numerator is greater than, or equal to, its denominator

inequality \in' i kwol' i tē\ n. mathematical statement showing that two numbers are not equal or that one number is greater than or less than another number

inference \in' fər əns\ n. a conclusion drawn from something that was known or hinted at

integer \in' ti jər\ n. any positive or negative whole number or zero

intersecting lines n. lines that cross each other

Glossary

inverse operation *n.* an operation that undoes the results of another operation; examples are multiplication and division; addition and subtraction

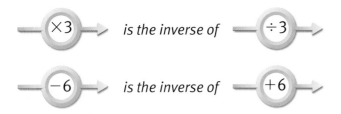

×3   *is the inverse of*   ÷3

−6   *is the inverse of*   +6

isosceles triangle *n.* a triangle with two equal sides

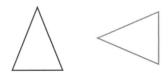

iterated \it′ ə rāt id\ *v.* something that has been done or said again and again

K

kilo– \kē′ lo; kil′ ō\ *prefix* one thousand

kilometer \ki lom′ i tər, kil′ ə mē′ tər\ *n.* a unit of length in the metric system equal to 1,000 meters

L

least common multiple *n.* the smallest multiple of two or more numbers

line of symmetry *n.* a line on which a figure can be folded so that one side of the figure overlaps exactly with the other

line segment *n.* a part of a line with two endpoints

linear equation *n.* an algebraic equation that creates a straight line when graphed

linear function *n.* a function that creates a straight line when graphed

M

map scale *n.* the ratio between the distances on a map and the corresponding actual distances

mean \mēn\ *n.* another name for *average*

median \mē′ dē ən\ *n.* the middle number in an ordered set of numbers, or the mean of the two middle values if there is no one middle number

metric system *n.* a decimal system of measurement that uses the meter as the fundamental unit of length

minuend \min′ ū end′\ *n.* the number from which another is to be subtracted

mixed number *n.* a number consisting of a whole number and a fraction

mode \mōd\ *n.* the most frequent value in a set of data

multiple \mul′ tə pəl\ *n.* any number that is the product of that number and any whole number

multiplicand \mul tə pli kand′\ *n.* a number multiplied by another number, the multiplier

For example:

$$
\begin{array}{r}
5 \\
\times\ 3 \\
\hline
15
\end{array}
$$

5 —— multiplicand
× 3 —— multiplier
15 —— product

$3 \times 5 = 15$ —product
multiplicand
multiplier

Glossary

multiplier \mul′ tə plī ər\ *n.* a factor of a product

multiply \mul′ tə plī′\ *v.* to add a number to itself a certain number of times (4 + 4 + 4 = 3 × 4 = 12)

N

negative \neg′ ə tiv\ *n.* less than zero

net \net\ *n.* a plane figure that can be folded to create a space figure

notation \nō tā′ shən\ *n.* a system of signs or symbols used to represent values, quantities, or other facts or information

number line *n.* a line of infinite extent whose points correspond to the real numbers according to their distance in a positive or negative direction from a point arbitrarily taken as zero

numerator \nü′ mə rā′ tər\ *n.* the number above the line in a fraction

O

obtuse angle *n.* an angle that is greater than 90°

These are obtuse angles:

octagon \ok′ tə gon′\ *n.* a polygon having eight sides and eight angles

odd number *n.* a number leaving a remainder of 1 when divided by 2

ordered pair *n.* two numbers written so that one is considered before the other; coordinates

of points are written as ordered pairs, with the *x*–coordinate written first, and then the *y*–coordinate—an example is (3, 4)

outcome \out′ kum\ *n.* a result or consequence

P

parallel \par′ ə lel′\ *adj.* going in the same direction and always being the same distance apart at every point, so as never to meet

parallel lines *n.* lines that are the same distance apart and that go in the same direction and never meet

parallelogram \par′ ə lel′ ə gram′\ *n.* a plane figure with four sides whose opposite sides are parallel and equal in length

parentheses \pə ren′ thə sēz\ *n.* curved marks ( ) used to enclose symbols or numbers to indicate which expression to evaluate first

partial product *n.* the product that comes from multiplying the multiplicand by one of the digits of the multiplier: for example:

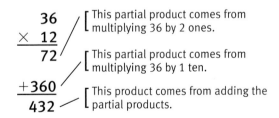

pattern \pat′ ərn\ *n.* an element that is characterized by repetition

pentagon \pen′ tə gon′\ *n.* a polygon with five sides and five angles

percent, percentage \pər sent′\ *n.* a special fraction with a denominator of 100

Glossary

perimeter \pə rim′ i tər\ *n.* the distance around the boundary of a closed plane figure

perpendicular \pər′ pən di′ kyə lər\ *adj.* lines that intersect at right angles

pictograph \pik′ tə graf\ *n.* a type of bar graph that uses pictures or symbols to display specific amounts of data

place value *n.* the value of a digit within a number

plane \plān\ *n.* a flat surface wholly containing every line connecting any two points on it

plane figure *n.* a figure having only height and width

polygon \pä′ lē gän′\ *n.* a closed plane figure with three or more line segments as sides

polyhedron \pä′ lē hē′ drən\ *n.* a closed space figure with polygons for faces

power \pou′ ər\ *n.* the number of times a given number or expression is multiplied by itself

prime number *n.* a whole number that has only two factors—the number itself and 1

prism \priz′ əm\ *n.* a solid having two congruent and parallel faces, and whose other faces are parallelograms

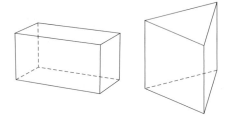

probability \prob′ ə bil′ i tē\ *n.* how likely it is for something to happen

probability experiments *n.* Sometimes called *trials*, these models help us predict what will probably happen over many, many tries.

product \prod′ əkt\ *n.* the result of multiplying two or more numbers (factors)

profit \prof′ it\ *n.* the amount remaining after all the costs of a business have been paid

proportional \prə pôr′ shə nəl\ *adj.* having the same or a constant ratio

pyramid \pir′ ə mid′\ *n.* a solid figure having a polygon for a base and triangular sides intersecting at a point

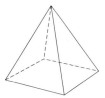 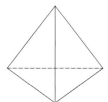

Pythagorean Theorem *n.* named for the Greek mathematician Pythagoras. For any right triangle, the square of the length of the hypotenuse is equal to the sum of the squares of the lengths of the other two sides. It is written as $a^2 + b^2 = c^2$, where c is the length of the hypotenuse and a and b are the lengths of the other sides.

Q

quadrant \kwod′ rənt\ *n.* any of the four parts into which a plane is divided by perpendicular coordinate axes

quadrilateral \kwod′ rə lat′ ər əl\ *n.* a polygon with four sides and four angles

quotient \kwō′ shənt\ *n.* the answer to a division problem

R

radius \rā' dē əs\ *n.* a line segment going from the center to the outside of a circle or sphere

range \rānj\ *n.* the difference between the least and greatest values in a set of numbers

rate \rāt\ *n.* a ratio written with units in which the second number is usually 1, as in *20 miles per hour*

ratio \rā' shō, shē ō\ *n.* the comparison of two numbers by division

rational number *n.* a number that can be expressed as a quotient of two integers or as an integer; for example, $\frac{3}{4}$, 5

ray \rā\ *n.* a set of points that has one endpoint and extends forever in one direction

rectangle \rek' tang' gəl\ *n.* a parallelogram having four right angles

reflection \ri flek' shən\ *n.* a change in the location of a figure when it is flipped over a line

regroup \rē grüp\ *v.* to rename a number to make adding and subtracting easier

$$\begin{array}{r} \overset{1\ \ 15}{\cancel{2}\cancel{5}} \\ -\ 17 \\ \hline 8 \end{array}$$

[To subtract in the ones column, 2 tens and 5 is regrouped as 1 ten and 15.

regular polygon *n.* a convex polygon in which all sides have the same length and all angles are equal

relation signs *n.* the three basic relation signs are > (greater than), < (less than), and = (equal to)

remainder \ri mān' dər\ *n.* the number that is left over after dividing; for example, when you divide 25 by 4, the quotient is 6 with a remainder of 1

$$\begin{array}{r} 6\ \ \text{R1} \\ 4\overline{)25} \\ -\ 24 \\ \hline 1 \end{array}$$

right angle *n.* an angle forming a 90° angle

right triangle *n.* a triangle with a right angle

rotation \rō tā' shən\ *n.* a change in the location of a figure when it is turned in a circle around a point

rotational symmetry *n.* a property of a figure in which a rotation of the figure by a certain amount of degrees about the center point or axis (less than 360°) results in the same figure; If a rotation of 360° is the smallest such rotation, the figure is said to have no rotational symmetry.

rounding \round' ing\ *v.* changing a number to another number that is easier to work with and that is close enough for the purpose

S

scale \skāl\ *n.* the ratio between the distances on a scale drawing and the corresponding actual distances

scalene triangle \skā-lēn'\ *n.* a triangle with three unequal sides

Glossary

sector \sek'tər\ *n.* a plane figure bounded by two radii of a circle and an intercepted arc

similar \sim' ə lər\ *adj.* figures that have the same shape, but that differ in size

sphere \sfîr\ *n.* a round three-dimensional figure having all the points at an equal distance from the center

square \skwâr\ *n.* a plane figure having four sides of equal length and four right angles

standard form *n.* a number written with one digit for each place value

stem-and-leaf plot *n.* a data display that shows groups of data arranged by place value where the *leaf* is the number in the smallest place value and the *stem* includes the numbers in the larger place values

straight angle *n.* an angle measuring 180 degrees

subtrahend \sub' trə hend\ *n.* the number that is to be subtracted from another

sum \sum\ *n.* a result obtained from addition

surface area *n.* the surface area of a polyhedron is the sum of the areas of its faces

symmetrical figure *n.* a figure that can be divided in half so that each half is a mirror image of the other

symmetry \sim' i trē\ *n.* an arrangement of parts that are alike on either side of a central line

T

tenth \tenth\ *n.* one of ten equal parts

translation \tranz la' shən\ *n.* a change in the location of a figure in which it slides without being turned

trapezoid \trap' ə zoid'\ *n.* a figure having four sides with only two sides parallel

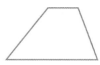

triangle \trī' ang gəl'\ *n.* a plane figure with three sides and three angles

U

unit cost *n.* the cost of one out of a number of equally priced goods or services

upper and lower bounds *n.* numbers that an answer must be less than or greater than

V

vertex \ver' teks\ *n.* 1. the point where two or more rays meet. 2. the point of intersection of two sides of a polygon. 3. the point of intersection of three or more edges of a space figure

volume \vol' ūm\ *n.* the amount of space occupied by an object

W

withdrawal \with drô' əl\ *n.* the act of taking away or removing

whole number *n.* a number that tells how many complete things there are

Z

zero \zîr' ō\ *n.* the number that leaves any number unchanged when it is added to it

Index

A

Absolute value, 174–175
Absolute zero, 80, 182
Acute angles, 402–405, 406–409
Acute triangles, 490–491
Addition
    Associative Law of Addition, 20–21
    Commutative Law of Addition, 20–21
    Decimals, 104–105, 106–107, 138–139
    Fractions, 258–261, 278–279, 282–283
    Generalized Commutative Law of Addition, 20–21
    Identity Element for Addition, 20–21
    Integers, 174–175
    Measurements, 56–57, 284–286, 306–307
    Mixed numbers, 302–303, 306–307, 316–319, 320–321
    Money, 97–99, 107, 138–139
    Multidigit, 22–25, 30–31
Algebra, 16–19, 20–21, 62–63, 98, 111, 155, 160–161, 166–167, 168–169, 170–173, 198–199, 200–201, 202–205, 206–207, 208–209, 212–213, 222–225, 226–227, 228–229, 247, 475
    Composite functions, 200–201, 214–217, 218–219, 220–221, 226–227
    Function machines, 160–161, 166–167, 168–169, 198–199, 212–213
    Function rules, 160–161, 166–167, 168–169, 170–173, 198–199, 200–201, 222–225
    Functions, standard notation, 222–225, 226–227
    Graphing functions, 206–207, 208–209
    Inverse functions, 212–213, 214–217, 220–221
    Inverse of a composite function, 214–217, 220–221
    Linear equations, 228–229
    Ordered pairs, 198–199
    Standard notation for composite functions, 226–227
    Standard notation for functions, 222–225, 226–227
    Variables, 16–18
A.M., 579–581
Analyzing data, 588–591, 592–593, 594–597
Angles, 402–405, 406–409, 410–413, 414–415, 570–571, 582
    Acute, 402–405, 406–409

Clocks, 582
    Degrees, 406–409, 414–415
    Estimating, 570–571
    Labeling, 403–405, 414–415
    Measuring, 406–409, 410–413, 414–415
    Obtuse, 402–405, 406–409
    Protractors, 406–409, 414–415
    Right, 402–405, 406–409
    Straight angles, 402–405, 406–409
Angles and clocks, 582
***Anything But 10* Game**, 277
Approximation, 30–31, 60–61, 126–127
    Decimal products, 524–525
    Decimal quotients, 551
    Quotients, 354–356, 358–359, 362–363, 368–369, 370–371, 373–375
Area, 54, 114–115, 423, 430–433, 465, 468–469, 470–473, 474–475, 476–477, 478–479, 508–509, 523, 540–541, 554–556
    Circles, 474–475
    Irregular figures, 476–477
    Parallelograms, 468–469
    Right triangles, 470–473
    Surface area, 502–505
    Triangles, 470–473
Arm span, 569
Art Curriculum Connections, 55
Associative Law of Addition, 20–21
Associative Law of Multiplication, 20–21
Averages, 336–339, 344–345, 372–375, 376–379, 381–383, 384–385
    Interpreting, 344–345
    Population density, 384–385
Axis of symmetry, 495

B

Bar graphs, 6–7, 355, 377, 592, 594–597
Base (exponents), 72–73
Base (triangles), 470–473
Batting averages, 372–375
Break the Problem into Smaller Parts, 309

C

Calculators, 72–73, 78, 154–155, 156–157, 166–167, 168–169, 170–173, 314–315, 316–319, 352, 358, 384–385, 419, 466–467, 524–525, 532, 534
    Constant function, 156–157

Capacity, 110–111, 572–573, 576–577
    Cups, 572–573
    Fluid ounces, 572–573, 576–577
    Gallons, 572–573, 576–577
    Hectoliters, 110–111
    Kiloliters, 110–111
    Liters, 110–111, 112–113, 576–577
    Milliliters, 110–111, 576–577
    Pints, 572–573
    Quarts, 572–573
    Tablespoons, 572–573
    Teaspoons, 572–573
Celsius scale, 80–81, 182, 220–221
Center of rotation, 486–487
Centigrade scale, 80–81
Centigrams, 110–111
Centiliters, 110–111
Centimeters, 4, 6, 110–111, 112–113, 376–379, 568–569, 576–577
Cents sign (¢), 96–99
Centuries, 77–79
Chapter Review, 40–41, 88–89, 146–147, 186–187, 236–237, 290–291, 328–329, 394–395, 458–459, 516–517, 560–561, 608–609
Charts, 35–36, 121, 505
Choosing appropriate units of metric measures, 112–113
Chords, 466–467
Circle graphs, 243, 583, 592–593
Circles, 466–467, 474–475
    Chords, 466–467
    Circumference, 466–467
    Diameter, 466–467, 474–475
    Pi (π), 467, 474–475
    Radius, 466–467, 474–475
    Sectors, 474–475
Circumference, 466–467
Closed plane figures, 446–449, 450–451
Combinations (probability), 264–265, 272–273
Combining shapes, 465, 468–469, 476–477
Common denominators, 268–271, 278–279, 280–281
Common factors, 257, 260
Commutative Law of Addition, 20–21
Commutative Law of Multiplication, 20–21
Comparing
    Data, 376–377
    Decimals, 96, 101, 102–103, 253, 319, 525
    Fractions, 253, 262–263, 268–271, 319
    Ratios, 346–349

Index

Index

Index

Index

Photo Credits

iii (br)©Richard Hutchings/PhotoEdit, Inc.; iv (br) ©PhotoDisc/Getty Images, Inc.; ix ©Adamsmith/Getty Images, Inc.; v ©BrandXPictures/Getty Images, Inc.; vi ©Park Street/PhotoEdit,Inc.; vii ©JupiterImages; viii ©Royalty-Free/CORBIS; x ©Jim Cummins/CORBIS; xi ©Royalty-Free/CORBIS; xii ©PhotoDisc/Getty Images, Inc.; xiii ©Royalty-Free/CORBIS; xiv, 4 ©Matt Meadows; 10 (br) ©Royalty-Free/CORBIS; 11 ©Matt Meadows; 16 ©Richard Hutchings/PhotoEdit, Inc.; 17 ©C Squared Studios/Getty Images, Inc.; 2 ©Michael Newman/PhotoEdit, Inc.; 21 ©C Squared Studios/Getty Images, Inc.; 22, 26 ©Matt Meadows; 28 ©Hisham F. Ibrahim/Getty Images, Inc.; 30 ©PhotoDisc/Getty Images, Inc.; 32 ©CORBIS; 46 ©Duomo/CORBIS; 48 ©Matt Meadows; 49 ©Robert W. Ginn/PhotoEdit, Inc.; 51 (b) ©Massimo Listri/CORBIS; 51 (c) ©CORBIS; 52 ©Jon Feingersh/CORBIS; 56 ©BrandX/Getty Images, Inc.; 56, 57 ©BrandX/Getty Images, Inc.; 58 ©LWA-Dann Tardif/CORBIS; 59 ©Paul Barton/CORBIS; 62 ©Roy Morsch/CORBIS; 66 ©Matt Meadows; 67 ©Stone+/Getty Images, Inc.; 69 ©Richard Lewisohn/Digital Vision/Getty Images, Inc.; 70 ©Matt Meadows; 72 ©Comstock, Inc.; 73 (br)©Matt Meadows; 74 ©Jim Cummins/Getty Images, Inc.; 75 ©Jupiter Images; 76 ©PhotoDisc/Getty Images, Inc.; 77 ©JupiterImages; 78 ©PhotoDisc/Getty Images, Inc.; 79 ©PhotoDisc/Getty Images, Inc.; 80 (tr) ©David Young-Wolff/ PhotoEdit, Inc.; 81 (t)(b)©PhotoDisc/Getty Images, Inc.; 83 ©Trinette Reed/CORBIS; 94 ©Galen Rowell/CORBIS; 95 (c) (br) ©Royalty-Free/CORBIS; 95 (bl) ©Yann Arthus-Bertrand/CORBIS; 96 ©Matt Meadows, (b) ©SRA File; 97 ©PhotoDisc/ Getty Images, Inc.; 98 (tr) ©Thinkstock/Getty Images, Inc., (b) ©Royalty-Free/CORBIS; 103 ©Matt Meadows; 104 ©Frank Siteman/PhotoEdit, Inc.; 105 ©PhotoDisc/Getty Images, Inc.; 107 ©BrandXPictures/PunchStock; 109 ©Ed Bock/CORBIS; 111 ©Matt Meadows; 112 ©BrandXPictures/Getty Images, Inc.; 113 ©Getty Images, Inc.; 118 ©PhotoDisc/Getty Images, Inc.; 120 ©Digital Vision/Getty Images, Inc.; 123 ©PhotoDisc/Getty Images, Inc.; 124 (tr)©PhotoDisc/Getty Images, Inc., ©CORBIS; 125 ©Patrik Giardino/CORBIS; 127 ©Brand X Pictures/Getty Images, Inc.; 129, 130 ©Royalty-Free/CORBIS; 131 ©PhotoDisc/Getty Images, Inc.; 133, 134 ©Brand X/Getty Images, Inc.; 137 ©CORBIS SYGMA; 138 ©AFP/Getty Images, Inc.; 139 ©PhotoDisc/Getty Images, Inc.; 140 (tr) ©David Muench/CORBIS, (cl)Reprinted with permission from Sofaer et al., SCIENCE 206:283(1979).; 141 (tr) (c) (cr) Reprinted with permission from Sofaer et al., SCIENCE 206:283(1979).; 142 (tl) (tr)(cl) (cr) Reprinted with permission from Sofaer et al., SCIENCE 206:283(1979).; 152–153 ©Digital Vision/PunchStock; 153 (tr) (bl) ©Brand X Pictures/PunchStock; 154 ©Stone/Getty Images, Inc.; 155, 157, 158 ©PhotoDisc/Getty Images, Inc.; 160 ©Stuart Westmoreland/CORBIS; 161 ©The Image Bank/Getty Images, Inc.; 167 ©Matt Meadows; 171 ©Staffan Widstrand/CORBIS; 172, 173 ©Jeff Hunter/Getty Images, Inc.; 175 ©Park Street/ PhotoEdit, Inc.;177 ©PhotoDisc/Getty Images, Inc.; 178 ©Matt Meadows; 180 ©Brand X Pictures; 192 ©AFP/Getty Images, Inc.; 195 ©Dennis McDonald/PhotoEdit, Inc.; 196 (b) ©Royalty-Free/CORBIS; 196 (tr) ©Alan Schein Photography/ CORBIS; 197 ©Michael & Patricia Fogden/CORBIS; 199 (cr) ©Comstock Images/Getty Images, Inc.; 200 ©PhotoDisc/Getty Images, Inc.; 206 ©Royalty-Free/CORBIS; 207 ©Ronnie Kaufman/CORBIS; 213 ©Burke/Triolo Productions/PhotoDisc/ Getty Images, Inc.; 216 (br) ©Jules Frazier/Getty Images, Inc., ©John W. Banagan/Getty Images, Inc.; 217 ©Pankaj & Insy Shah/Getty Images, Inc.; 219 (c) ©C Squared Studios/PhotoDisc/Getty Images, Inc.; 219 ©Doug Menuez/PhotoDisc/Getty Images, Inc.; 220 ©JupiterImages; 226 Getty Images, Inc.; 227 ©David Young-Wolff/PhotoEdit, Inc.; 227 ©PhotoEdit; 229 ©Adam Gault/Digital Vision/Getty Images, Inc.; 242 ©Royalty-Free/CORBIS; 244 (tr) ©BrandXPictures, (c) (cr) (br) ©Matt Meadows; 245 (b) ©Getty Images, Inc., (br) ©PhotoDisc/Getty Images, Inc.; 246 (tc) ©Matt Meadows, (bc) ©PhotoDisc/ Getty Images, Inc.; 247 ©Royalty-Free/CORBIS; 248 ©Matt Meadows; 249 PhotoDisc/Getty Images, Inc.; 250 ©Matt Meadows; 250, 251, 252 (b) ©PhotoDisc/Getty Images, Inc., (br) ©CORBIS; 254, 258 ©Matt Meadows; 259 ©Royalty-Free/CORBIS; 261 (bc), 263 ©PhotoDisc/Getty Images, Inc. 268 ©Charlie Samuels/CORBIS; 271 ©Bryan F. Peterson/ CORBIS; 274 (c) ©Matt Meadows, (br) ©PhotoDisc/Getty Images, Inc., 276 ©Matt Meadows; 279 ©PhotoDisc/Getty Images, Inc.; 281 ©Matt Meadows; 282, 284 (cl) (br), 285 (tr) ©PhotoDisc/Getty Images, Inc., (cr) ©BrandXPictures/ Royalty Free CORBIS; 296 ©North Wind/North Wind Picture Archives; 298 ©Matt Meadows; 299 ©Jim Cummins/CORBIS; 299 ©Matt Meadows; 300 (cr) ©PhotoDisc/Getty Images, Inc.; 301 ©Catherine Wessel/CORBIS; 303 ©Adamsmith/Getty Images, Inc.; 305 ©PhotoLink/Getty Images, Inc.; 307 ©PhotoDisc/Getty Images, Inc.; 308 ©Angelo Hornak/CORBIS; 313 ©PhotoDisc/Getty Images, Inc.; 316 ©Jutta Klee/CORBIS; 320 ©Ronnie Kaufman/CORBIS; 321 ©Scenics of America/ PhotoLink/Getty Images, Inc.; 322 (c) (bl) ©Reuters/CORBIS, (br) ©AFP/Getty Images, Inc.; 334 ©North Wind/North Wind Picture Archives; 336 (b) ©Bettmann/CORBIS; 337 ©Jim Cummins/CORBIS; 338 ©PhotoDisc/Getty Images, Inc.; 340 ©Comstock; 341 ©Kaminesky/CORBIS; 344 ©Jim Cummins/CORBIS; 345–347 ©PhotoDisc/Getty Images, Inc.; 348 ©BrandXPictures/Getty Images, Inc.; 349 ©Frans Lemmens/zefa/CORBIS; 350 ©Royalty-Free/CORBIS; 351 ©Ed Wargin/ CORBIS; 353 ©PhotoDisc/Getty Images, Inc.; 354 ©Owaki-Kulla/CORBIS; 355 ©Alamy; 356 ©Pablo Corral V/CORBIS; 358 ©PhotoDisc/Getty Images, Inc.; 359 ©RF/CORBIS; 361 ©Mike Powell/Getty Images, Inc.; 363 ©Royalty-Free/CORBIS; 368 ©Neal & Molly Jansen/SuperStock; 369 ©Alan Schein/zefa/CORBIS; 370 (tr) ©Kim Eriksen/zefa/CORBIS; 371–372 ©PhotoDisc/Getty Images, Inc.; 373 ©PhotoDisc/Getty Images, Inc.; 374–376 ©PhotoDisc/Getty Images, Inc.; 377 ©Mark Anderson/Rubberball Productions/Getty Images, Inc.; 379 ©Matt Meadows; 380–381 ©Royalty-Free/CORBIS; 382 ©Mitchell Funk/Getty Images, Inc.; 384–385 (b) ©Bryan Allen/CORBIS; 386 ©DK Limited/CORBIS; 387 (tl) ©Brand X Pictures, (tc) (tr) ©PhotoDisc/Getty Images, Inc.; 388, 389 ©Clements Library; 400 ©Buddy Mays/CORBIS; 404 (t) ©Salvatore Vasapolli/AnimalsAnimals/Earth Scenes; 405 ©AnimalsAnimals/Earth Scenes; 406–407 ©Adam Woolfitt/

Photo Credits